THE ROMAN INSCRIPTIONS OF BRITAIN II, Fasc. 8

R.G. Collingwood and R.P. Wright

THE ROMAN INSCRIPTIONS OF BRITAIN

Volume II
Instrumentum Domesticum

(Personal Belongings and the like)

Fascicule 8

Graffiti on Coarse Pottery cut before and after firing; stamp on Coarse Pottery.
Addenda and Corrigenda to Fascicules 1–8

(*RIB* 2502–2505)

Edited by S.S. FRERE and R.S.O. TOMLIN

with contributions by M.W.C. HASSALL

Published for the Administrators of the Haverfield Bequest
by Alan Sutton Publishing Limited
1995

First published in the United Kingdom in 1995 by
Alan Sutton Publishing Ltd · Phoenix Mill · Far Thrupp · Stroud · Glos.

British Library Cataloguing in Publication Data

A catalogue record for this book is available from the British Library.

ISBN 0 7509 0916 1

Typesetting and origination by
Alan Sutton Publishing Limited.
Printed in Great Britain by
WBC, Bridgend, Mid Glamorgan.

CONTENTS

PREFACE

The eighth and last fascicule of *RIB* ii contains graffiti cut on coarse pottery before (2502) and after (2503) firing, and also lists Addenda (2504) and Corrigenda (2505) to previous fascicules. It will be followed by a volume containing the combined Epigraphic Indexes for *RIB* ii.

Like its predecessors this fascicule has been compiled by S.S. Frere from the archive collected by R.P. Wright and from other records of finds made down to the end of 1986. Critical assistance, especially on readings and expansions, has been given by Dr. R.S.O. Tomlin. The Administrators are grateful to Mr. M.W.C. Hassall and Dr. Tomlin for providing drawings of graffiti published by them in the annual epigraphic reports in *Britannia*, the entries from which have formed the essential basis for much of the present publication.

The Editors wish to thank the Trustees of the British Museum, the Society of Antiquaries of London and the Roman Society for permission to reproduce illustrations. They are grateful also to the following individuals and institutions for similar permission and for providing information, photographs and drawings: P.T. Bidwell, Robin Birley, G.C. Boon, Professor K. Branigan, Richard Brewer, Dr. P.C. Buckland, I. Caruana, Miriam Daniels, Lady (Aileen) Fox, C.J. Going, Nicholas Griffiths, Dr. A.R. Hands, Dr. Brenda Heywood, D.B. Kelly, L.V. Marley, Dr. Valerie Maxfield, Dr. Martin Millett, Tim Padley, Nicholas Palmer, Dr. W.J. Rodwell, A.G. Rook, Dr. D.J. Tomalin, Dr. G.A. Webster, Miss Marion Wilson, P.J. Woods; and the Ashmolean Museum, Oxford, the Bowes Museum, the Carlisle Archaeological Unit, English Heritage, the National Museum of Wales, R.C.H.M. (England), the Vindolanda Trust and the Warwickshire Museum. Frances Mawer and Michael Still are thanked for submitting some *corrigenda*.

Miss Sarah Frere and Miss Liz Wild are thanked for their careful work on the typescripts.

A.K. Bowman

LIST OF PLATES

(at end)

ABBREVIATIONS

This list contains only items not already listed in *RIB* i pp. xix–xxii and in the lists of Abbreviations in *RIB* ii, fascicules 1–7, which should be consulted for the remainder.

ICUR	*Inscriptiones Christianae urbis Romae*
T. Leics. AS	*Transactions of the Leicestershire Architectural and Archaeological Society*

BIBLIOGRAPHY

This list contains only items not already listed in the Bibliographies of *RIB* i (pp. xxiii–xxxi) and *RIB* ii fascicules 1–7, which should be consulted for the remainder.

Going, *The Mansio . . . The Roman Pottery*	C.J. Going, *The Mansio and other Sites in the South-eastern Sector of Caesaromagus: The Roman Pottery* (1987)

RIB 2502. GRAFFITI ON COARSE POTTERY CUT BEFORE FIRING

Graffiti cut before firing were evidently inscribed at the potter's workshop (compare *RIB* 2493 and 2496). This chapter contains one (perhaps two) dedications (No. 1 and compare No. 9), one statement of ownership (No. 2), one aphorism (perhaps in verse: No. 3) and two graffiti giving the names of vessels (Nos. 4 and 5). Three or perhaps four others are inscribed with alphabets, recalling some of the inscribed tiles (*RIB* 2491.135–45), and perhaps like them to be taken as indicating instruction in literacy carried on at the work-place (compare *CIL* xiii 10016.12). There are also two possible dates (Nos. 33, 44). The majority, however, as expected, record the potter's name either alone or followed by *fecit* (Nos. 30, 31, 32, 43 cf. 4): some of these are unfortunately acephalous (Nos. 28–48). Of names unaccompanied by a verb, six (Nos. 18, 23, 27, 33, 38, 61) are in the nominative case; eight names are in the genitive (Nos. 10, 13, 15, 16, 22, 24, 25, 34). Attention is drawn to No. 14, a graffito in Neo-Punic script, presumably written by a legionary of North African origin. Finally there are nine numerals (Nos. 54–62), one of which (No. 62) specifically records a surprisingly high total of vessels manufactured (although by no means approaching the production-numbers recorded at La Graufesenque).

(a) Dedication

2502.1 York (*Eboracum*). Part of a buff jar (½), found before 1873. Yorkshire Museum. Drawn by R.P.W., 1946.

CIL vii 1337.61. *EE* ix p. 673. Watkin, *Arch. J.* xxxviii (1881), 297 (with defective reading). G. Home, *Roman York* (1924), pl. facing p. 102. RCHM, *York* i (1962), 134 fig. 87.32.

graffito on the wall: ṂẸṚ|QVR|IO
Mercurio
'To Mercury'

For an example of this spelling see *ILS* 3190; and for a similar dedication, *CIL* xiii 10016.1.

2502.1

For another possible dedication see *RIB* 2502.9.

(b) Ownership

2502.2. London (*Londinium*). Neck of a buff jug (½), found in 1932 during tunnelling at a depth of 30 feet (9.1 m) below King William Street. Museum of London. Reproduced from Dunning.

JRS xxiii (1933), 215 No. 13 with fig. 20. Dunning, *Antiq. J.* xxi (1932), 438 with fig.

graffito: GAI SVM | PIICVLIARIS
Gai sum peculiaris
'I am the property of Gaius'

Lagona is to be understood.

For the formula compare *RIB* 2420.48, 2503.352 and compare 2441.9.

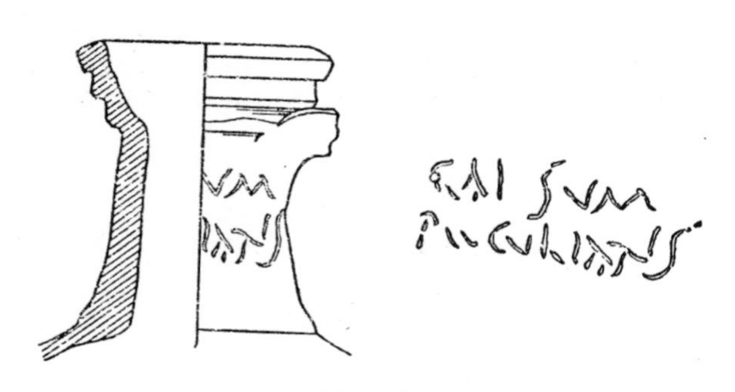

2502.2

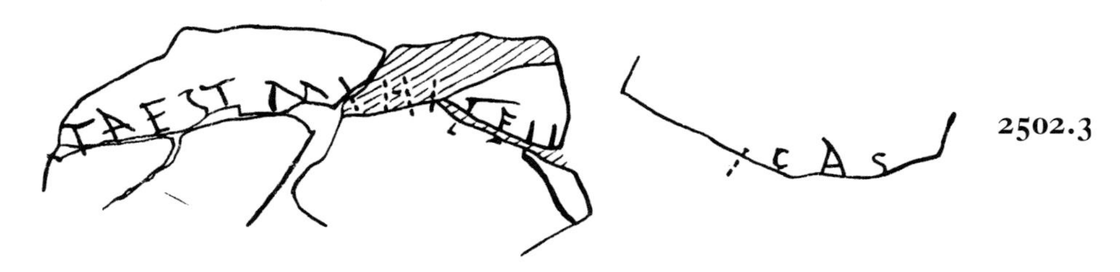

2502.3

(c) Aphorism

2502.3. Elmswell, Humberside [Yorkshire]. Fragments of a grey hemispherical flanged bowl (½) of Crambeck type 5a, found in 1955 on a chalk-and-cobble pavement on Bramble Hill. In private possession. Drawn by R.P.W., 1956.

JRS xlvi (1956), 151 No. 38a.

graffito around the inside at flange-level:
(a) [. . .]ẠTAESTMI . . FELỊ[. . .]
[. . .]ata est mi[hi] feli[x . . .] or *feli[citer]*

Perhaps part of a hexameter

(b) detached portion, [. . .]ṾCAS[. . .]

(d) Names of Vessels (*RIB* 2502.4–5)

2502.4. Godmanchester, Cambridgeshire [Huntingdonshire]. Fragment from the neck of a buff storage jar (½), found in 1965 during excavations at the *mansio*. Museum of Archaeology and Anthropology, Cambridge. Drawn by S.S.F. from rubbings and squeezes by R.P.W., 1971.

Britannia ii (1971), 296 No. 50.

cursive graffito: FΛXỊΛTIS[. . .] | LΛGONΛM[. . .]

As text, and perhaps *faxiatis [amici] | lagonam [amplam]*, 'May you produce, (?) my friends (?) a large storage-jar', R.P.W.

Instead of ΛX, R and EI (or H) could also be read. If some allowance is made for differences in script and drawing, this could be a text similar to *RIB* 2502.46; that is, '[name] made this jar'. R.P.W.'s 'variant spelling' **faxiatis* is dubious, and his tentative restoration too much of a guess. R.S.O.T.

2502.4

2502.5 Droitwich (*Salinae*), Hereford and Worcester [Worcestershire]. Part of a bowl (½) in Severn Valley ware, found in 1978 in a pit containing fourth-century pottery during excavations at the salt-working site at Old Bowling Green, Rickett's Lane. Hereford and Worcester Archaeology Unit. Drawn by M.W.C.H.

Britannia xv (1984), 343 No. 29.

graffito on the wall: [. . .]VΛS CIILLΛ[. . .]

Vascella, 'vessel' (i.e. brine-pan ?), M.W.C.H., who suggests that *vascella* is an alternative to *vascellum*, for which see *CIL* vi 3428 (= ILS 8112), an inscription of A.D. 214, where the word refers to a cinerary urn. It is a diminutive of *vas*, the more common form being *vasculum*. For further commentary see *Britannia* loc. cit., 354 note 45.

Another possibility is *vas cella[rium]*, 'store-room jar'; compare *Digest* 32, 93, 4, *vasa vinaria . . . quae in cella defixa sunt*, R.S.O.T.

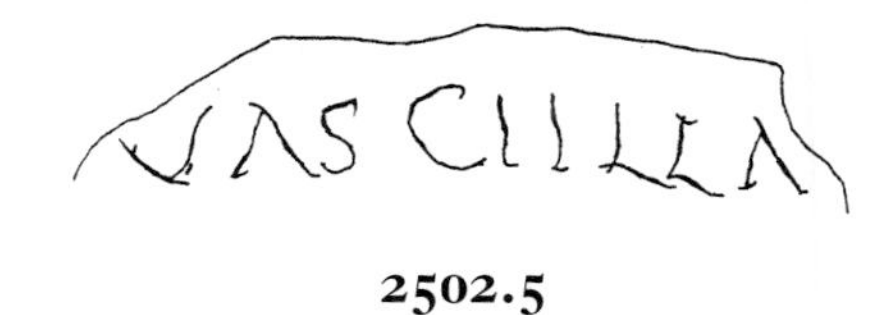

2502.5

(e) Alphabets (*RIB* 2502.6–8)

2502.6. York (*Eboracum*). Part of a (?) lid in buff ware (½), found in 1900 on the site of the North-eastern Railway office at a depth of *c.* 20 feet. Yorkshire Museum. Drawn by R.P.W., 1943.

G. Home, *Roman York* (1924), pl. facing p. 102. RCHM, *York* i (1962), 134 fig. 87.34.

graffito on the underside: ABCDIKṢṾX̣

2502.6

2502.7. Richborough (*Rutupiae*), Kent. Base of a vessel in hard buff ware ($\frac{1}{2}$). In store at Dover Castle. Drawn by R.P.W.

graffito around the base: ABCDḲNG̣HQ̣RSNO

R.G.C. and R.P.W. read K as F, which is possible. The second N is probably a mistake for TV.

2502.7

2502.8. Wall (*Letocetum*), Staffordshire. Part of a large vessel ($\frac{1}{2}$), with plain rim and cylindrical neck, found in 1975 unstratified during excavations at the *mansio*. Wall Museum. Drawn by M.W.C.H.

Britannia xx (1989), 342 No. 58.

graffito on the flat upper surface of the rim: leaf-stop(?) ΛBC[. . .]

Q(?), M.W.C.H. Leaf-stop, R.S.O.T.

The rim was long enough to accommodate the whole alphabet and a space, this interval being marked by a leaf-stop or similar.

2502.8

(f) Names, presumably of potters (*RIB* 2502.9–27)

2502.9. Corbridge (? *Coria*), Northumberland. Fragment of a large grey urn ($\frac{1}{2}$) carrying figures applied in relief, found in 1910 during excavations. Corbridge Museum. Drawn by R.P.W., 1940.

EE ix 1353. Haverfield, *Arch. Ael.*[3] vii (1911), 202 (repr., 60) with pl. VII. Spain, *PSAN*[3] ix (1920), 154. Richmond, *Arch. Ael.*[4] xxi (1943), 192 with pl. X G. Leach, *Arch. Ael.*[4] xl (1962), 36 No. 5 with pl. VI.4. J.M.C. Toynbee, *Art in Britain under the Romans* (1964), 402.

two graffiti, (a) on an *appliqué* rectangle supporting an (?) anvil: ALLIITIO

(b) on the side, below an *appliqué* standing figure: ALLIITIO

AƧƧIITIO, *EE* with misgivings.

The nomen *Alletius* is borne by three Vigiles at Rome in A.D. 205 (*CIL* vi 1056 column 4, 68, 69, 81); and compare TLL s.v. *Aletius*. *Alletio* if nominative is otherwise unattested but would be the name of the potter. However, as Leach suggests (ibid., 37–8), it may be the name of the deity (in the dative case) to whom the anvil is 'dedicated'. No god *Alletius* is known, but Leach associates this and related fragments with a Celtic smith-god; this is more convincing than Richmond's identification (loc. cit.) of them with the cult of Jupiter Dolichenus.

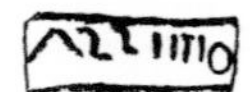

2502.9

2502.10. Caersws, Powys [Montgomeryshire]. Part of a dish ($\frac{1}{2}$) in sandy reduced fabric with orange surface, found in 1985–6 during excavations in the *vicus* of the fort. Clwyd-Powys Archaeological Trust. Drawn by M.W.C.H.

Britannia xx (1989), 343 No. 64.

graffito beneath the base: Λ̣ṆCARII or ṂỊCARII

Ancarius is a rare but attested nomen: see Solin and Salomies, *Repertorium*. Following the graffito are possible traces of two further letters, perhaps O and I. Below this are what may be traces of a second graffito in much smaller characters.

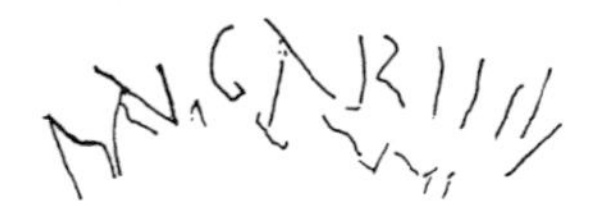

2502.10

2502.11. Winchester (*Venta Belgarum*), Hampshire. Part of a small jar ($\frac{1}{1}$) in grey fabric, found in 1970 in a residual context at Wolvesey Palace. Winchester Museum. Drawn by M.W.C.H.

Britannia xx (1989), 337 No. 34.

graffito on the shoulder: Perhaps IXI

Compare *RIB* 2501.280 with note. Perhaps a mark of identification, X between parallel lines, R.S.O.T.

2502.11

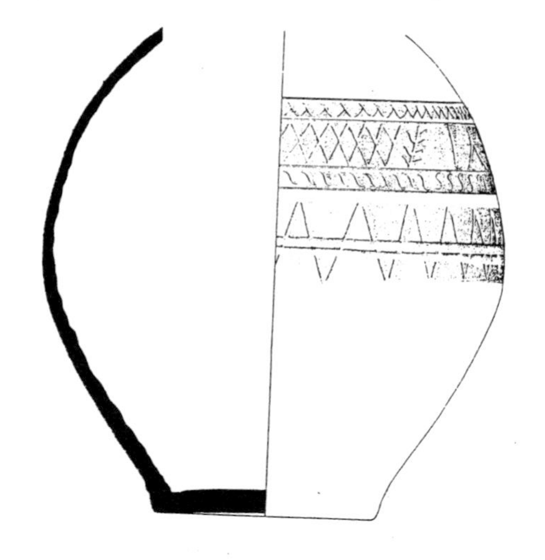

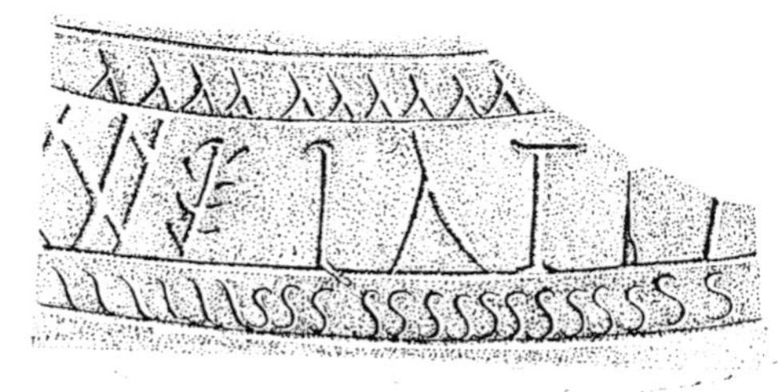

2502.12

2502.12. Doncaster (*Danum*), South Yorkshire. Large gritty grey-ware jar (½ and ¼), found in 1978 in a pit dug in the north rampart of the fort in the second century or later. Doncaster Museum. Drawing by courtesy of Dr. P.C. Buckland.

Britannia xi (1980), 415 No. 59.

graffito on the shoulder: [. . .] stop (?) LATIṆ[. . .]
Probably *Latin[us]*

2502.13 Cirencester (*Corinium*), Gloucestershire. Sherd from a vessel with spout (½) in orange fabric, found in 1974 in the filling of a slot for a timber building of the military phase during excavations at Admiral's Walk. Corinium Museum. Reproduced from Wacher and McWhirr.

Britannia viii (1977), 440 No. 75. Hassall in J. Wacher and A. McWhirr, *Early Roman Occupation at Cirencester* (1982), 203 No. 2 with fig. 66.2.

2502.13

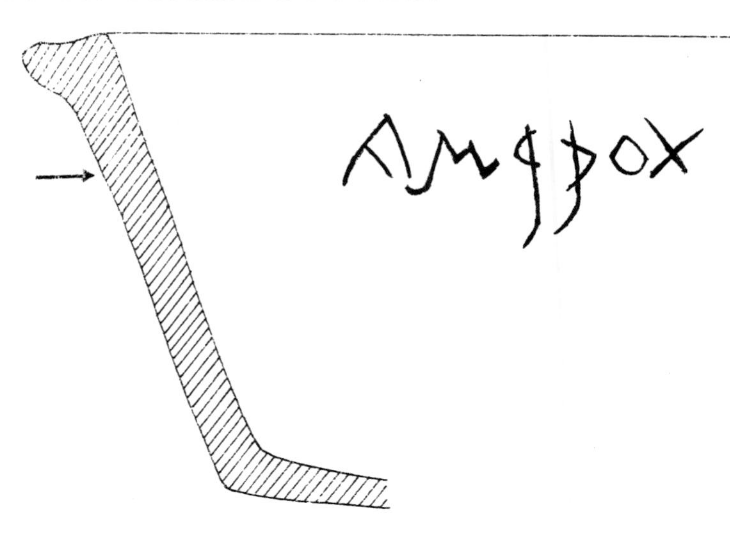

2502.14

graffito on the shoulder: LIVỊỊ[. . .]*retrograde*, LIVII
Livii Livii
'(Product) of Livius'

2502.14. Holt, Clwyd [Denbighshire]. Part of a flanged dish (½) in coarse red ware, found in 1907–15 during excavations at the legionary works depot. National Museum, Cardiff. Drawn by G.C. Boon.

JRS xlvi (1956), 151 No. 41. W.F. Grimes, *Holt* (1930), 133 No. 26. Guillaume, *Illus. Lond. News*, 12 August, 1939 (erroneously describing it as a tile); idem *Iraq* vii (1940), 67 with pl. V. Thacker and Wright, *Iraq* xvii (1955), 90–1. Guillaume, *Iraq* xvii (1955), 92. Swan, *J. Roman Pottery Studies* v (1992), 4.

graffito in neo-Punic script: M'QRYN'
Macrinu(s)

AMQPOX, Grimes. M^C^QR TYN, Guillaume, *Iraq* vii (1940), 67.

'The second and seventh letters, here transcribed as rough and smooth breathing respectively, represent the vowels, in this case of a Latin word', Thacker and Wright. We follow their reading and interpretation; the writer was presumably a legionary of the Twentieth, of African origin (ibid.)

'Cut after firing', R.P.W., *JRS*. Examination, however, by Vivien Swan (loc. cit.), kindly confirmed by G.C. Boon and Richard Brewer (1994), shows that it was cut *ante cocturam*. Macrinus was presumably employed as a potter.

2502.15. Colchester (*Camulodunum*), Essex. Fragment from a globular storage jar (½) in buff fabric with a cream slip, found in 1972 with second- to fourth-century material. Colchester Museum. Drawn by M.W.C.H.

Britannia viii (1977), 438 No. 65.

graffito inverted in relation to the base:
[. . .]MΛRINI
Marini
'(Product) of Marinus'

[. . .]MRINI, *M(a)rini*, M.W.C.H., *Britannia*. As text, R.S.O.T.

2502.15

2502.16. Ibid. Fragment from a globular storage jar (½) in buff fabric with a cream slip, found in 1976 in a second- to third-century context north of the road leading to the Balkerne Gate. Colchester Museum. Drawn by M.W.C.H.

Britannia viii (1977), 438 No. 61.

graffito on the body, inverted in relation to the base:
MARTI | [. . .]CIVI
Perhaps *Marti [Las]civi*
'(Product) of Martius Lascivus'

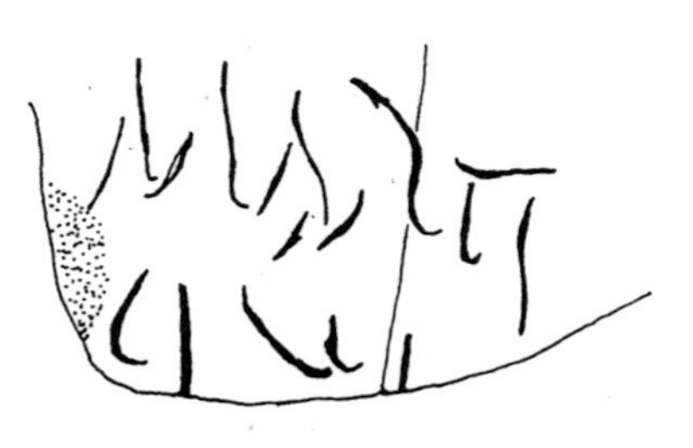

2502.16

2502.17. York (*Eboracum*). Part of a buff jar (½), found in 1870–77 during excavations for the Railway. Yorkshire Museum. Drawn by R.P.W., 1943.

Watkin, *Arch. J.* xxxviii (1881), 297. G. Home, *Roman York* (1924), pl. facing p. 102. RCHM, *York* i (1962), 134 fig. 87.30.

graffito on the rim: MERC[. . .]
Merc[urii] or *Merc[urialis]*
'(Product) of Mercurius *or* Mercurialis'

2502.17

2502.18. Cliffe, Kent. Fragment from the lower part of a black cooking pot (¼), found in 1966 unstratified on the beach at Cliffe Marshes. Present whereabouts unknown. Drawn by S.S.F. from rubbings by R.P.W., 1966.

JRS lvii (1967), 210 No. 50.

graffito: MIIṬRIΛ
Metria

The name is very rare: Schulze (591, addendum 297) cites only *Mél. d'arch. et d'histoire* 1898, 469 No. 39 (Lambaesis), *Metria Catulina* daughter of *M. Metrius Catulinus*.

2502.18

2502.19. Wroxeter (*Viroconium*), Shropshire. Fragment of a storage jar found in 1912–14 during excavations. Wroxeter Museum. Drawn by R.P.W., 1958.

two graffiti: (a) A
(b) in smaller script, PỌ[. . .] | .[. . .]

2502.19

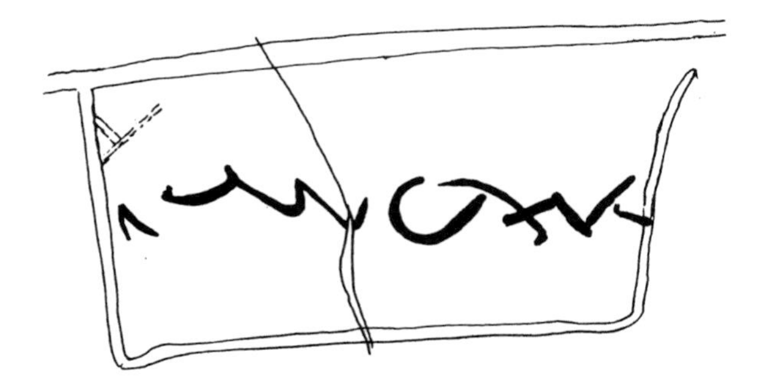

2502.20

2502.20. Sutton Courtenay, Oxfordshire [Berkshire]. Grey jar ($\frac{1}{4}$), height 140 mm, diameter at the mouth 152 mm, found in 1965 on a Roman site. There is lattice decoration around the shoulder interrupted by three panels, one of them almost completely lost. Ashmolean Museum, Oxford. Drawn by S.S.F. from rubbings by R.P.W., 1965.

JRS lvi (1966), 224 No. 56.

three cursive graffitti: (a) PVECAM (?)
(b) [. . .]. .
(c) [. . .]VENV (?)

(a) RICOMI, R.P.W., *JRS*. RAXOMI, R.P.W., *RIB* archive.

(c) ONNA, R.P.W.

If we assume that both lattice and graffiti were incised from left to right, it is clear that *both* were incised with the pot inverted, the lattice first. R.P.W. read the inscription the other way up, and in any case some of his letter-forms are hardly possible. The cursive is so free that any reading is conjectural. R.S.O.T.

2502.21. Wroxeter (*Viroconium*), Shropshire. Part of a large red bead-rim storage jar ($\frac{1}{2}$), found in 1913 during excavations. Rowley's House Museum, Shrewsbury. Drawn by R.P.W., 1947.

J.P. Bushe-Fox, *Wroxeter 1913*, 22 with pl. XI.1.

graffito on the shoulder: SEṬMAPEM[. . .]

A second E may have been inserted by another hand after S. There is uninscribed surface to the left of S, precluding a reading *[. . .]s et Mapem[. . .]*.

2502.21

2502.22. Caerleon (*Isca*), Gwent [Monmouthshire]. Part of a Black-burnished dish ($\frac{1}{2}$) of third-century date (Gillam type 329), found in 1962 in a third-century drain at the parade-ground. Caerleon Museum. Rubbing by R.P.W., 1962. Drawn by G.C. Boon.

JRS liii (1963), 167 No. 56. Boon in G.C. Boon (ed.) *Cambrian Monographs & Collections* i (1978), 21 No. 21 with fig. 6.21.

cursive graffito beneath the base: SIIVIIRIΛNI
Severiani
'(Product) of Severianus'

2502.22

2502.23. Dorchester (*Durnovaria*), Dorset. Two conjoining sherds ($\frac{1}{2}$), preserving almost one-third of the neck of a large narrow-necked Black-burnished jar with everted frilled lip, found in 1984 during excavations in The Greyhound Yard. Dorchester Museum. Drawn by R.S.O.T. See also PL. IA.

2502.23

Britannia xx (1989), 336 No. 26. Tomlin in P.J. Woodward et al., *Excavations at Greyhound Yard, Dorchester, 1981–4* (1993), 284 No. 14.

graffito: [. . .]ACITVSPRIMVS .[. . .]
[T]acitus Primus .[. . .]

The space after *Primus* coincides with a handle, and the text may have begun with the exaggerated descender (probably I or H) to the right. The exaggerated S might mark the end of the text. Since *Tacitus* and *Primus* are both cognomina, they must name two persons, and it is likely the text was originally a list of about six personal names.

2502.24. Mucking, Essex. Fragment of a grey lid-seated jar (½), found in 1968 in a ditch close to Kiln III. Department of the Environment. Drawn by S.S.F. from a rubbing by W.J. Rodwell.

Britannia ii (1971), 296 No. 43.

graffito deeply cut below the rim: VERI[. . .]
Perhaps *Veri*
'(Product) of Verus'

2502.24

2502.25. South Shields (*Arbeia*), Tyne and Wear [Durham]. Part of a jug (½), found in 1883 during excavations. Museum of Antiquities, Newcastle upon Tyne. Drawn by R.P.W., 1940.

Bruce, *Arch. Ael.*² x (1885), 252 with fig.

cursive graffito on the shoulder:
[. . .]VICTORIS[. . .]
Victoris
'(Product) of Victor'

This item is identical with *RIB* 2493.77, which should now be deleted.

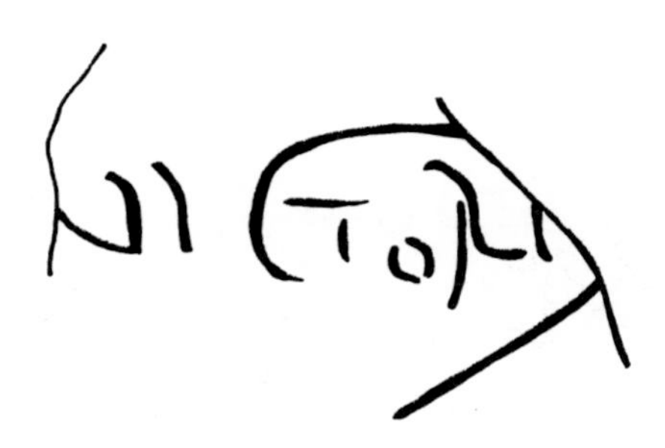

2502.25

2502.26. Rushden, Northamptonshire. Shoulder and rim (½) of a small colour-coated beaker with an orange slip over a white fabric, found in 1971 in an Antonine context while excavating pottery kilns. Northamptonshire County Council. Drawn by P.J. Woods.

Britannia iii (1972), 359 No. 39.

graffito on the shoulder: VITALIS[. . .]
Vitalis
'(Product) of Vitalis'

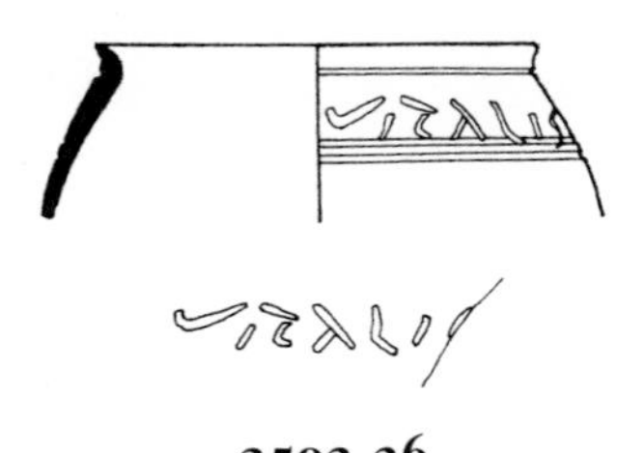

2502.26

2502.27. Wilderspool, Cheshire. Sherd (½) in soft red ware, curved like an imbrex (but hardly thick enough) and having part of a circular perforation above the right-hand end of the inscription. Found in or before 1906 when it was presented to Warrington Museum. Drawn by R.P.W., 1952.

graffito: [. . .]VITALVS·VI[. . .]
probably *Vitalus Vi[. . .]*

Vitalus is probably a variant of *Vitalis*: compare Kajanto, *Cognomina*, 274.

2502.27

(g) Acephalous or Uninterpreted
(*RIB* 2502.28–53)

2502.28. Mancetter (*Manduessedum*), Warwickshire. Neck of a grey jar (½), found in 1969 in the stokehole of a late third- to fourth-century pottery kiln. Birmingham City Museum. Not illustrated.

Britannia viii (1977), 445 No. 105.

graffito on the inner side of the neck:
[. . .]ALI AR[. . .]
Perhaps *[. . .]aliar[is]*.

2502.29. Chichester (*Noviomagus*), West Sussex. Part of the base (¼) of a Black-burnished dish, found in 1973 during excavations in Chapel Street. Chichester Museum. Drawn by R.S.O.T. from a photograph. See also PL. IIA.

Britannia vii (1976), 391 No. 62. A. Down, *Chichester Excavations* iii (1978), 275 No. 2 with pl. XIX.

burnished letters on the unburnished underside of the base:
[. . .]ẠVIM[. . .] | [. . .]VDITI[. . .] | [. . .]ṚN[. . .]

[. . .].ṆILḶ.[. . .] | [. . .]N(*or* V)DITI.[. . .] | [. . .]P̣.Ṭ[. . .], R.S.O.T. (from a photograph). As text, M.W.C.H.

2502.29

2502.30. Saltersford, Little Ponton, Lincolnshire. Part of a grey (formerly handled) storage jar (½), found probably in 1898. Grantham Museum. Drawn by R.P.W., 1947.

JRS xxxviii (1948), 104 No. 27. Hawkes and Richmond, *Arch. J.* ciii (1947), 17.

graffito on the shoulder, inverted, probably cut before firing:
[. . .]DICCVSFIICIT
[. . .]diccus fecit
'. . .diccus made (this)'

This may be a name otherwise unattested, but compare *Veldicca* (*RIB* 358), itself unique; Oswald, *Index* s.v. *Diccius* (?); and *BJ* 57 (1876), 67, *Diccius*.

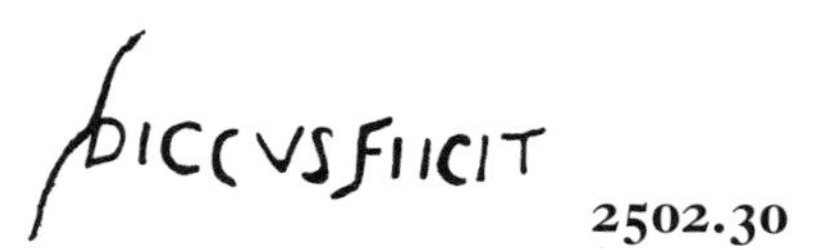

2502.30

2502.31. Stonegate, East Sussex. Base of a cup in dark fabric 'with some sort of slip', diameter *c.* 51 mm, found in or before 1915 on the site of a Roman bloomery 1.8 km north of Ticehurst Road railway station. Now lost. Reprinted from Haverfield.

Haverfield, *Sussex AC* lviii (1916), 195 No. 1. Winbolt, *VCH* Sussex iii (1935), 31 No. 6.

graffito on the base: [. . .]ECIT
[. . .f]ecit
'. . . made (this)'

2502.32. Irchester, Northamptonshire. Three fragments of a buff storage jar (½), found in 1962 in road-works south of the walled town. Northampton Museum. Drawn by S.S.F. from rubbings and a squeeze by R.P.W., 1966.

JRS lvii (1967), 209 No. 47 with pl. XX.3.

cursive graffito:
[. . .]FIICI[. . .] | [. . .]RI | [. . .]NTIṚIO | [. . .]RICO FILIVS | [IN]FIIRAS FIICII▲
[. . .]feci[. . .] | [. . .]ri | [. . .]ntirio | [. . .] rico | filius | [in]feras feci⟨i⟩

This is presumably a potter's memorandum, perhaps of the contents of the kiln.

A patronymic might have been expected after FILIVS, but R.P.W. noted that there is a greater space between ll. 3 and 4 than between ll. 4 and 5, and that *-ico* can terminate a Celtic name; he suggested, therefore, that the last two lines were an addition by the son of the potter: 'I, . . .ico, his son, made the lower ones'.

2502.32

2502.33. (?) Colchester (*Camulodunum*), Essex. Part of a buff storage jar (½), found probably at Colchester and given in 1926 to Colchester Museum. Drawn by R.P.W., 1943.

JRS xxxiv (1944), 91 No. 26.

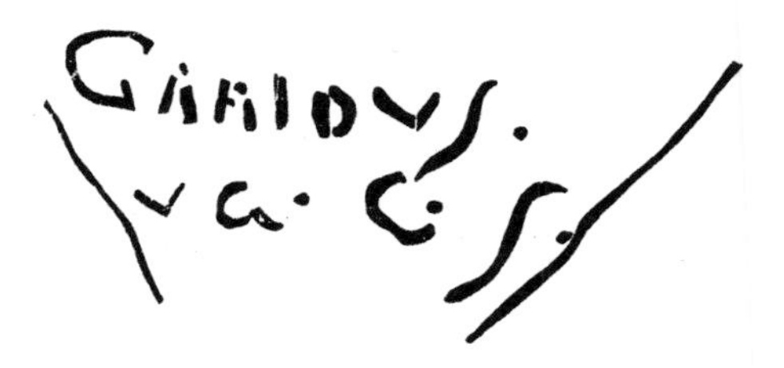

2502.33

graffito on the shoulder:
[. . .]GA̧ŖIDVS· | [. . .]VG·C·S·[. . .]

1.2 probably *[. . .A]ug*. This would suggest an imperial consular date, *[. . .A]ug(usto) c[o](n)s(ule)* [ordinal numeral].

2502.34. Corbridge (? *Coria*), Northumberland. Part of a buff storage jar (½), found in 1947 unstratified in an excavation-dump. Corbridge Museum. Drawn by R.P.W., 1947.

JRS xxxviii (1948), 104 No. 28.

cursive graffito on the wall: [. . .]IDORI

[. . .]IDARI, *JRS*. As text, R.P.W., 1955.

The genitive of a Greek theophoric name, for example *Artemidorus*.

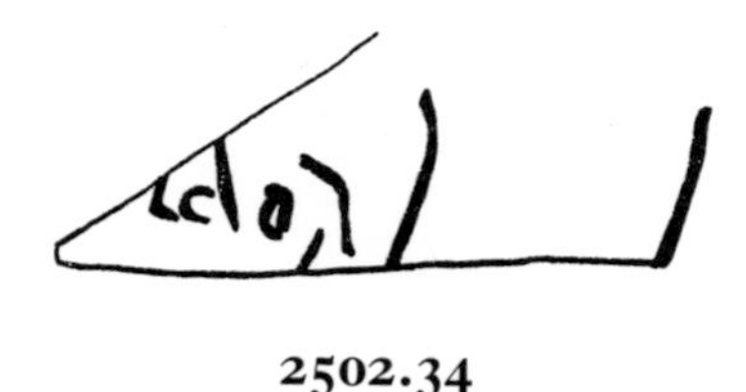

2502.34

2502.35. Caistor St. Edmund (*Venta Icenorum*), Norfolk. Upper part of a grey-ware vessel (½) of indeterminate shape, height 70 mm, maximum diameter 127 mm, to the sides of which four grotesque heads have been applied, of which two are extant and the position of a third survives. Above was a slightly projecting flange sloping inwards and upwards at about 45° and broken at the top, of which about two-fifths survives. Norwich Museum. Drawn by R.P.W., 1951.

Britannia ii (1971), 300 No. 68. Atkinson, *JRS* xxii (1932), 45 with pl. XII a–c.

graffito on the flange: [. . .]IFOSVRRVIILL[. . .]

EGO SVRR(exi) VIIII [Kal . . .], Atkinson, tentatively, loc. cit.

[. . .]IFOSVRRVIḶḶI[. . .], R.P.W., *Britannia*. As text, R.P.W., *RIB* archive.

Possibly an alphabet misunderstood by the potter, i.e. [. . . I]IFGHIKLMN[. . .], R.S.O.T.

2502.35

2502.36. Corbridge (? *Coria*), Northumberland. Part of a large jug (½), found before 1914. Corbridge Museum. Drawn by R.P.W., 1940.

graffito on the wall: [. . .]. | [. . .]ỊOṬ[. . .]

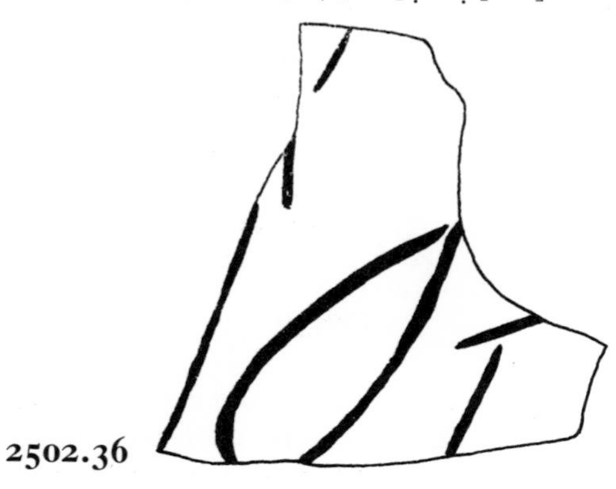

2502.36

2502.37. Caerleon (*Isca*), Gwent [Monmouthshire]. Two conjoining fragments of a buff storage jar (¾), found in 1957 unstratified *c.* 145 m west of the north-west angle of the fortress. Now lost. Drawn by G.C. Boon from rubbings and a squeeze by R.P.W., 1957.

JRS xlviii (1958), 154 No. 38.

cursive graffito: . . .[. . .] | MIṆIAPI[. . .]

[. . .]ANVLṚṾ | [. . .]ỌṆ ỊV, R.P.W., reading it inverted.

Since the sherds are now lost we cannot check whether they do indeed belong to a 'buff storage jar' and not a Dressel 20 (?) amphora bearing part of the potter's signature. However, the letters as drawn do not really support R.P.W.'s reading, and hesitantly we read then inverted, taking the first stroke of N to have been overlooked. The hand would be comparable to that of stilus-tablets of *c.* A.D. 75–125.

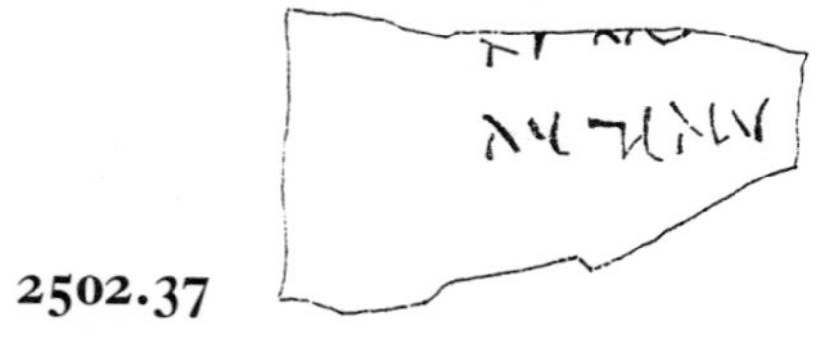

2502.37

2502.38. Heronbridge, Cheshire. Part of a red dish with bead and small flange (½), found in 1930. Grosvenor Museum, Chester. Drawn by S.S.F. from a rubbing by W.J. Williams..

graffito below the rim on the inside:
[. . .]ṆINVṢ[. . .]

2502.38

2502.39. Colchester (*Camulodunum*), Essex. Fragment (½) from the base of a vessel in hard reduced fabric, with a bevel at the junction with the wall and with internal burnishing, found in 1973 in floor make-up for a building erected after A.D. 61. Colchester Museum. Drawn by M.W.C.H.

Britannia viii (1977), 438 No. 67.

graffito below the base: [. . .]ONΛΛI

2502.39

2502.40. Eccles, Kent. Part of a grey jar (½), found in 1963 during excavations at the Roman villa. Maidstone Museum. Drawn by S.S.F. from rubbings by R.P.W., 1964.

JRS liv (1964), 185 No. 47 b.

graffito on the shoulder, probably cut before firing: [. . .]PAB.[. . .]

2502.40

2502.41. Beckford, Gloucestershire. Fragment of a buff storage jar (½), found in 1953 in a second- to third-century corndrier in Elmont Coppice on the site of a Romanized native settlement on the lower slopes of Bredon Hill. In private possession. Drawn by R.P.W., 1953.

JRS xliv (1954), 110 No. 45. Moray-Williams, *TBGAS* lxxiii (1954), 230.

undeciphered cursive graffito

2502.41

R.P.W. (*JRS*) reads [. . .]P̣ANΛ I | [. . .]IΛ II, which is unacceptable, not least because the repeated letter is almost certainly R not Λ. Nevertheless, compare *pana communis* on a samian (Dr. 37) sherd from Passau (*Rom.-Germ. Korresbl.* vii (1914), 58 Abb. 28; *Germania Romana* v (1924), Taf. XXXIX.4).

2502.42. York (*Eboracum*). Sherd (½) in buff fabric with a black slip, found in 1979 during excavations in Coppergate. Yorkshire Museum. Drawn by R.S.O.T., 1980.

Britannia xii (1981), 394 No. 105 with fig. 29.

cursive graffito:
[. . .]Q̣VEIBIḶẠTE[. . .] | [. . .]ẸMEN·ṢIḶ.[. . .]

'Not enough is preserved for decipherment', *Britannia*.

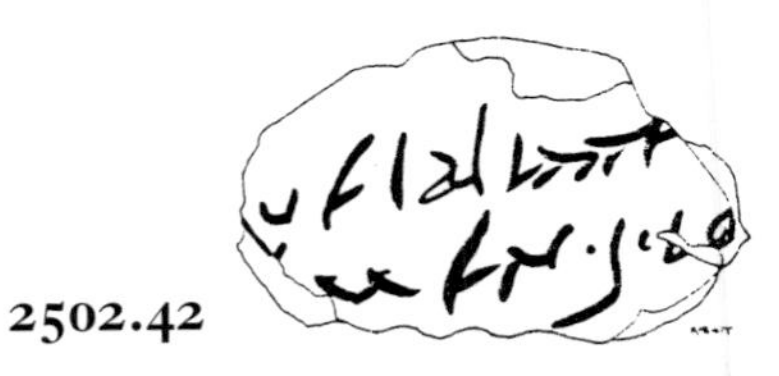

2502.42

2502.43. Camelon (? *Colania*), Central Region [Stirlingshire]. Part of an 'incense-cup' (½) in red ware with a serrated flange, diameter once *c.* 130 mm, found before 1936. National Museums of Scotland, Queen Street, Edinburgh. Drawn by S.S.F. from a photograph by J.G. Callender.

graffito, inverted: [. . .]Ṣ FIICIT
[. . .]s fecit
'. . . made (this)'

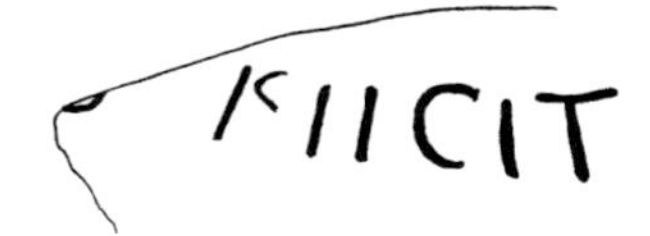

2502.43

2502.44. Rockbourne, Hampshire. Sherd of New Forest ware (½), found in 1964 at the bottom of a timber-lined well south-west of Room XXXII at the West Park Roman villa. Hampshire Museum Service. Drawn by S.S.F. from rubbings by R.P.W., 1964.

2502.44

JRS lv (1965), 228 No. 52.

graffito: [. . .]ṢPERΛṂ[. . .] | [. . .]ỌETΛN[. . .]
[. . .]s per am[. . .] or *[. . . pro]speram [. . .]* | *[. . .]o et An[. . .]*

l.2. may be a consular date (e.g. for A.D. 295), but there are many other possibilities.

2502.45. Wiggonholt, West Sussex. Two fragments, not conjoining, from a colour-coated beaker (½), in buff fabric with a black coating, found in 1964 and 1967 respectively during excavations near the Roman bath-house. Worthing Museum. Drawn by S.S.F. from rubbings by R.P.W., 1965, 1967.

JRS lv (1965), 228 No. 53; lviii (1968), 214 No. 77. Evans, *Suss. AC* cxii (1974), 127 No. 12 with fig. 9.12.

two graffiti: (a) [. . .]SVṂ[. . .]
(b) [. . .]ṚVΛ

SVΛ̣ and SVṆ are less satisfactory, R.P.W.

The graffiti are sealed by the black colour-coating.

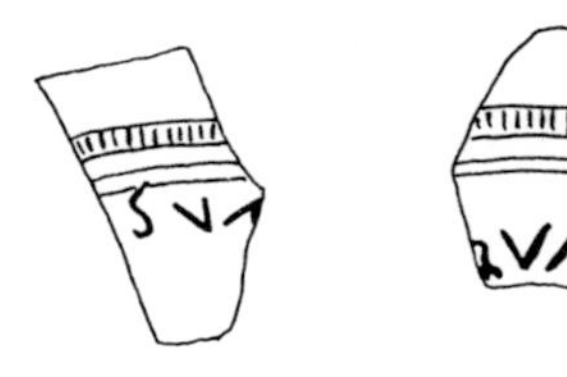

2502.45

2502.46. Heronbridge, Cheshire. Two fragments of a buff storage vessel (½), found in 1948 during excavations. Grosvenor Museum, Chester. Drawn by R.P.W., 1958.

JRS xlviii (1958), 155 No. 44.

two graffiti on the shoulder: (a) in cursive script:
[. . .]THIṚISCIS | [. . .]ṚT FIROṢ
(b) in capitals: OỊ[. . .] | SṾ[. . .]

As text, R.P.W.

(a) Perhaps a potter's signature, as in *RIB* 2502.4 (q.v. with note), a name ending in *-iscus*; H here is not convincing. l.2 looks like [LΛGON]ΛM FECIT, irregularly incised or misunderstood. R.S.O.T.

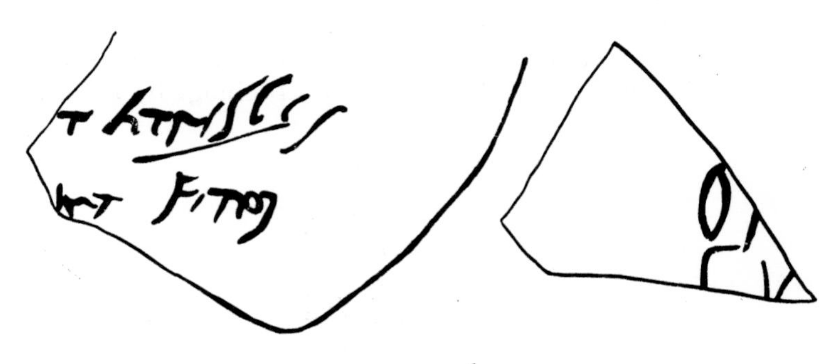

2502.46

2502.47. Thenford, Northamptonshire. Sherd from a small grey-ware jar (¾), found in 1971 unstratified at the site of the Roman villa. Present whereabouts unrecorded. Drawn by S.S.F. from rubbings by M.W.C.H.

Britannia iii (1972), 360 No. 40.

cursive graffito on the shoulder: [. . .]ṾPIG̣[. . .]

2502.47

2502.48. York (*Eboracum*). Part of a shallow Black-burnished flanged dish (½) with lattice decoration, found in 1971 outside the west end of the Minster, to the north-west of the *principia*. York Minster. Drawn by S.S.F. from rubbings by R.P.W., 1974.

Britannia vi (1975), 290 No. 35.

two graffiti, (a) in flowing capitals on the outside:
[. . .]VRNΛ[. . .]
(b) on the inside: Q[. . .]

Possibilities for (a) include *[Sat]urna, [Sat]urna[lis]* and *[Noct]urna*.

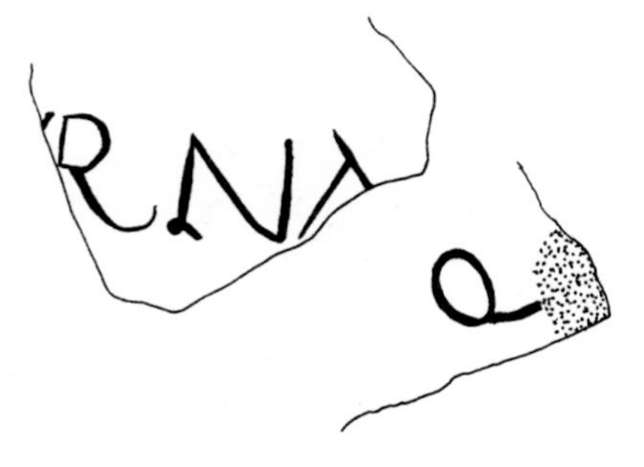

2502.48

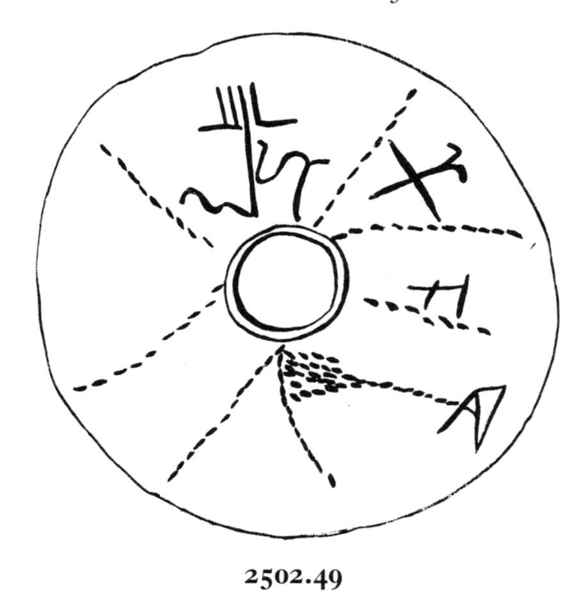

2502.49

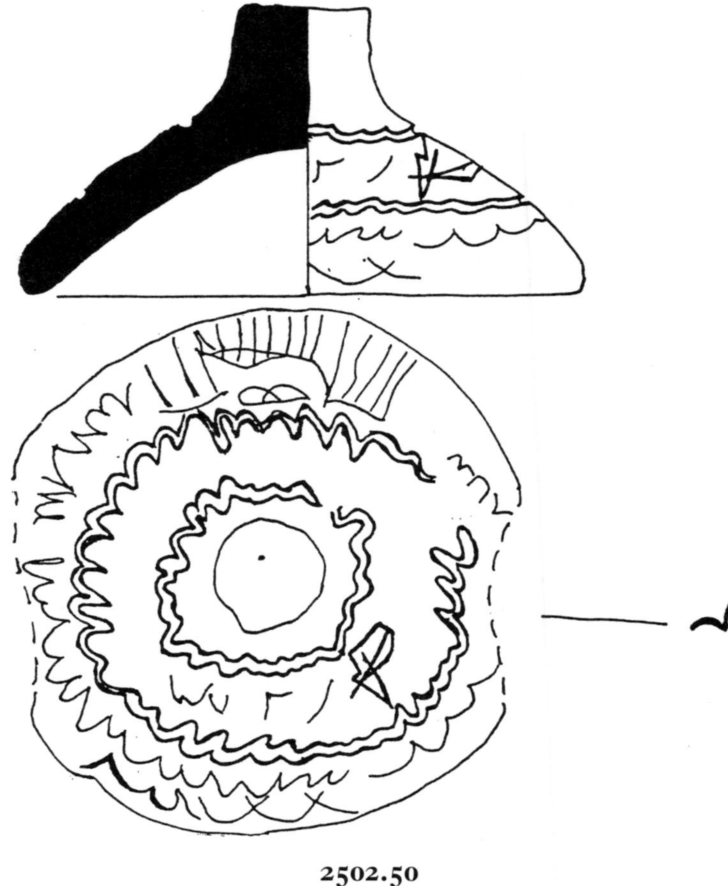

2502.50

2502.49. Bitterne (*Clausentum*), Hampshire. Nearly circular buff lid for a storage jar (½), with flat lower face and a knob broken from the top, diameter 140 mm, thickness 10 mm, probably found in 1901. God's House Tower Museum, Southampton. Drawn by R.P.W., 1965.

JRS lvi (1966), 224 No. 57.

graffito on the upper face: before firing the surface was divided by dotted lines into eight uneven sectors; four of them carry what seem to be magical symbols (*charakteres*).

(a) reversed S, trident and horizontally placed S;
(b) X; (c) F; (d) A, R.P.W., *JRS*.

W. Dale attended excavations at Bitterne in 1901 and before his death in 1925 gave the object to Winchester Museum. It was later transferred to Southampton. *JRS* loc. cit., note 64.

'The letters seem to be intentional rather than decorative symbols, but no explanation has been found', R.P.W., *JRS*. For comparable *charakteres* see J.G. Gager, *Curse Tablets and Binding Spells from the Ancient World* (1992), 56 fig. 7, 66 fig. 8, 181 fig. 20.

2502.50. Malton (*Derventio*), North Yorkshire. Lid in black calcite-gritted ware (1/1), probably of fourth-century date, diameter 75 mm, height 40 mm, found in 1970 in the *vicus* south of the fort. Malton Museum. Sketch by R.P.W., 1970. Drawing by courtesy of Brenda Heywood.

Britannia ii (1971), 303 No. 91. Tomlin in B. Heywood, Malton report (forthcoming), No. 5.

(a) Upper surface: before firing the potter scored two zig-zag circles using a broad point. Outside the first, using a sharper point, he added a figure resembling a capital B on its side, possibly intended as a symbol for '1000' with suprascript bar (compare *RIB* 1263, 2093, 2155 etc.). This is enclosed on three sides by parallel vertical lines with a suprascript bar; each side of these a spidery zig-zag completes an outer circle, with a further length of zig-zag outside this opposite the vertical strokes. Between the two broad-stroke zig-zag circles are *c*. 5 squiggles resembling letters but making no sense.
(b) On the underside: a two-stroke letter like a modern cursive V, incised twice.

(a) between the broad-stroke zig-zag circles, in cursive letters MMANNAA; outside the circles, 5 digits; and below B, placed horizontally, 9 digits and 3 digits; and beyond this round the lid letters giving variations of MANV but without adding a name. Below this the potter added similar variations on MANV for half the circumference, R.P.W.

To read MANV involves reading the letters anti-clockwise from left to right, in the reverse sequence to that in which they were incised. The marks are better regarded as a decorative scribble. R.S.O.T.

(b) Λ, R.P.W. This interpretation is excluded by the sequence of strokes.

2502.51. St Albans (*Verulamium*), Hertfordshire. Base sherd of a shallow bowl in very hard buff ware (½). Found in 1954 unstratified in a rubbish-pit 10 yards south of the outer circuit of the theatre. Verulamium Museum. Drawn by R.S.O.T., 1994. See also PL. IB.

JRS xlv (1955), 149 No. 29.

Cursive graffito within the bowl:

[. . .]CAS
[. . .]. . RIDAS
[. . .]barred S S1–2ASE 1–2ONA[. . .]
[. . .]ALLARICAS
5 [. . .] CONTICVE[. . .]
[. . .] INT . . [. . .]

[. . .]IAS[. . .] | [. . .]. DEBIS[. . .] | [. . .]SIS ARSVRI QVI[. . .] | [. . .] AVDEBIS [. . .] | [. . .]S QVOS IVRE [. . .] | [. . .]S(C)RIBO[. . .], R.P.W. *JRS*. As text, R.S.O.T.

The cursive is fluent and practised, but too little survives to resolve the various ambiguities of letter-form. It also looks as if ll. 5 and 6 (and possibly the end of 3) are by a second hand. The graffito superficially resembles the notes made before firing of samian potters and their output (see R. Marichal, *Les graffites de La Graufesenque* (1988)), but there are no personal names or numerals here; however, the ends of ll. 1, 2 and 4 look like accusative plurals (with numerals now lost?) as if from totals. The barred S looks like a symbol, perhaps *sextarios*. If the third(?) letter of l.5 is indeed N peculiarly made in three unjoined strokes, *conticue[re]* can be read; this would suggest the popular Vergilian tag (*Aen.* ii 1) also found in *RIB* 2491.148; but in l. 6 it is difficult to read *inte[ntique]*.

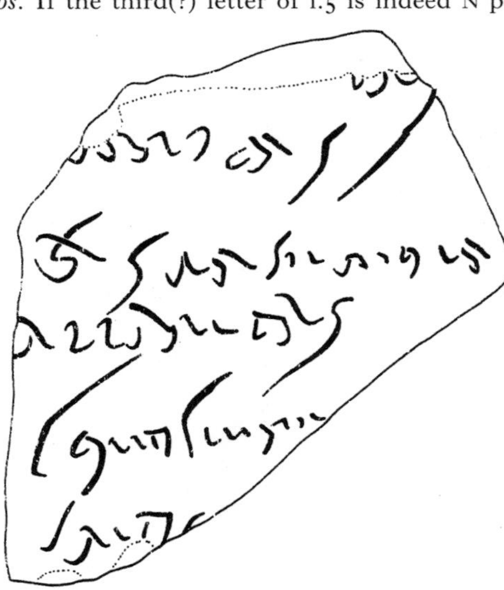

2502.51

2502.52. Brompton on Swale, North Yorkshire. Part of a bowl in coarse grey fabric (½), found during excavations in 1975. Yorkshire Museum, York. Drawn by R.S.O.T., 1977.

Britannia ix (1978), 481 No. 70.

undeciphered 3-line cursive graffito

The numerals in l.1 apparently include a note of weight, PVIII, *p(ondo (librae) octo*, and in l.2 MANV ('from the hand of') suggests that it is a potter's tally, perhaps the weight and number of pots in a firing, followed by his signature. R.S.O.T.

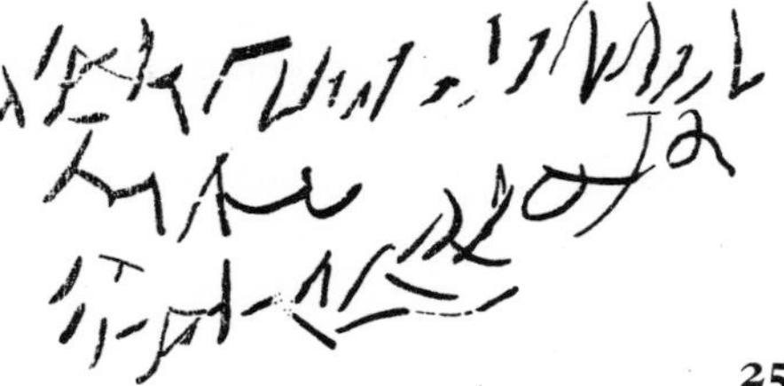

2502.52

2502.53. Dexthorpe near Ulceby, Lincolnshire. Two conjoining sherds of a large jar in coarse grey ware with black surface (⅔), found in 1926 during excavation of a Romano-British settlement. Lincoln Museum. Drawn by R.G.C., 1926.

illegible graffito

There are two incised zig-zag lines and, at a different alignment, at least one line of cursive letters too irregular and damaged for decipherment.

For the site, which lies *c.* 18 km east of Horncastle, see *JRS* xiv (1924), 224 and Tatham, *Lincolnshire Notes and Queries* xiii (1914–15), 34–7, 193–203; xv (1918–19), 33–47; xvi (1921), 181–5, 234–9; xvii (1923), 113–22.

R.G.C., *RIB* archive, 1927, suggested LIINTVS MRIBIS MVANI as a possible reading.

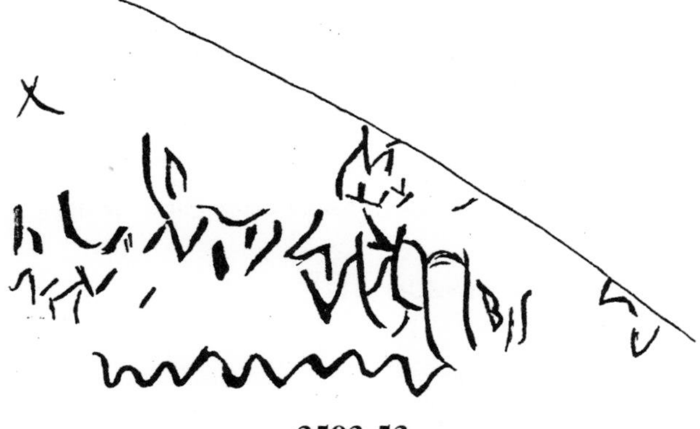

2502.53

(h) Numerals (*RIB* 2502.54–62)

2502.54. Densworth, West Sussex. Grey urn ($\frac{1}{2}$), height 254 mm, diameter at the mouth 197 mm, found in 1857 in a burial cist. Worthing Museum. Drawn by R.P.W., 1952.

graffito below the lip: III with cross-stroke
'Three'

Compare *RIB* 2503.77.

2502.54

2502.55. Chelmsford (*Caesaromagus*), Essex. Fragment ($\frac{1}{2}$) in coarse shell-tempered fabric, found in 1971 on Site K in a first-century context. Chelmsford Museum. Drawn by M.W.C.H.

Britannia xix (1988), 500 No. 59.

graffito below the rim: $\overline{\text{IIII}}$
'Four'

2502.55

2502.56. Ibid. Fragment ($\frac{1}{2}$), found in 1970 during excavations at Site D. Chelmsford Museum. Drawn by M.W.C.H.

Britannia xix (1988), 500 No. 60.

graffito: $\overline{\text{IIII}}$
'Four'

2502.56

2502.57. Ibid. Part of a ledge-rimmed jar ($\frac{1}{2}$) in shell-tempered ware, found in 1972–3 during excavations at Nos. 59–63 Moulsham Street. Chelmsford Museum. Reproduced from Going.

C.J. Going, *The Mansio . . .: the Roman Pottery* (1987), 102 with fig. 49.1.

graffito on the shoulder: $\overline{\text{IIII}}$[. . .]
Probably 'Four'

2502.57

2502.58. Ibid. Part of a ledge-rimmed jar ($\frac{1}{2}$) in shell-tempered ware, found in 1972–3 during excavations at Orchard Street Hall. Chelmsford Museum. Reproduced from Going.

C.J. Going, *The Mansio . . .: the Roman Pottery* (1987), 102 with fig. 49.2.

graffito on the shoulder: $\overline{\text{IIII}}$
'Four'

2502.58

2502.59. Ibid. Part of a ledge-rimmed jar ($\frac{1}{2}$) in shell-tempered ware, found in 1977–8 during excavations at No. 30 Orchard Street. Chelmsford Museum. Reproduced from Going.

C.J. Going, *The Mansio . . .: the Roman Pottery* (1987), 102 with fig. 49.3.

graffito on the shoulder: $\overline{\text{IIII}}$[. . .]
Probably 'Four'

2502.59

2502.60. Ibid. Part of a ledge-rimmed jar ($\frac{1}{2}$) in shell-tempered ware, found in 1972–3 during excavations at Nos. 59–63 Moulsham Street. Chelmsford Museum. Reproduced from Going.

C.J. Going, *The Mansio . . .: the Roman Pottery* (1987), 102 with fig. 49.4.

graffito on the shoulder: $\overline{\text{IIII}}$
'Four'

2502.60

2502.61. Maiden Castle, Dorset. Part of a New Forest beaker ($\frac{1}{4}$), found in 1934–7 in a late fourth-century deposit. Dorchester Museum. Reproduced from Wheeler.

R.E.M. Wheeler, *Maiden Castle* (1943), 250 No. 49 with fig. 80.49.

two graffiti on the lower part of the wall: (a) XXX
(b) [. . .]EI
(c) graffito cut after firing on the base: ✳ (owner's mark)

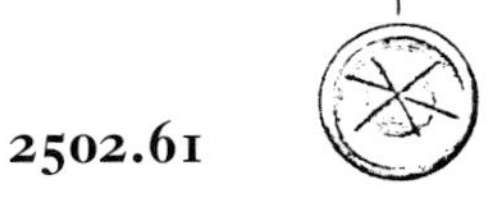

2502.61

2502.62. (?) Kent. Narrow-necked flask (½ and ⅟) in dark brown fabric, height 140 mm, diameter 114 mm, acquired by the Gravesend Historical Society *c.* 1905 from a local collector. No provenance recorded. Gravesend Museum. Drawn by R.P.W., 1959.

JRS lii (1962), 199 No. 53.

graffito below the medial girth-bands:
Φϵ MΛNVV|CH͡ΛRMIDΛNΛX
'505 (items) by (his) hand, Charmidanax'

Charmidanax seems to be unmatched, but *Charmides* is a well known Greek name and *-anax* a frequent termination, R.P.W.

This is a potter's tally. The numeral is in Greek script. R.P.W.

2502.62

RIB 2503. GRAFFITI ON COARSE POTTERY CUT AFTER FIRING

The graffiti in this chapter are arranged in the following categories:

(a)	Nos. 1–5.	Indications of Contents
(b)	Nos. 6–33.	Weight or Capacity
(c)	Nos. 34–95.	Numerals
(d)	Nos. 96–109.	Exhortations, Slogans and Aphorisms
(e)	Nos. 110–115.	Descriptions of vessels
(f)	Nos. 116–120.	Military graffiti
(g)	Nos. 121–136.	Religious dedications
(h)	Nos. 137–161.	Funerary graffiti
(i)	Nos. 162–168.	Alphabets
(j)	Nos. 169–466.	Personal Names
(k)	Nos. 467–619.	Acephalous and uninterpreted graffiti
(l)	Nos. 620–621.	Falsa.

Most are illustrated at 1:2, but in a few instances, where clarity or size dictated, scales of 1:1 or 1:4 have been employed.

Graffiti cut after firing on coarse pottery form a numerous group, second only to the graffiti on samian ware (*RIB* 2501), which are almost a third more numerous. Unlike the latter, however, few can be dated on the information available, except where the recorded fabric or the stratification provide a clue. As on the samian, some owners were content, or only able, to inscribe an epigraphic mark rather than a name. A simple X occurs most frequently, but sometimes more elaborate marks are found such as the 'palm-branch' on No. 252 or the crossed parallel lines on No. 386. Unless accompanied by other letters, such marks are excluded from *RIB* save where X may be a numeral.

When we remember the far greater ubiquity of coarse-pottery vessels over samian on sites of all types, the relative infrequency of coarse-pottery graffiti compared with those on samian requires discussion. The main types of vessel catalogued in this chapter can be tabulated as follows:

Beakers in colour-coated ware:	30	(4.85%)
Beakers in polished coarse ware:	38	(6.15%)
Jugs:	58	(9.38%)
Dishes and bowls:	139	(22.49%)
Jars:	250	(40.45%)

Beakers of both kinds may be classed as table-ware, and they achieved their widest circulation in the period following the demise of the samian industry, when they formed the normal drinking vessels of those insufficiently wealthy to drink from silver, pewter or perhaps glass. Most jugs also may be considered as table-ware, and together these categories comprise a fifth of the graffiti. Considerations similar to those discussed for samian ware in the Introduction to *RIB* 2501 will doubtless have influenced their owners to inscribe their names on these vessels.

Coarse-ware jars, bowls and dishes yield 63% of the graffiti in this chapter. These vessels (together with the jugs) were in general locally produced, and would have been much cheaper to buy than samian, not only because of their more utilitarian character but also because of much lower transport costs. Save perhaps in large households of slaves, they would have been used more often in the kitchen or store-cupboard than on the table at communal meals. Theft would be correspondingly less easy and less attractive. We may also suppose that slaves and kitchen-servants, less educated than their masters, would be less prone to cut literate graffiti.

By no means all jars, bowls and dishes, however, should be regarded as kitchen utensils, as some of the categories of use described below make plain. A few graffiti in this chapter (Nos. 1–5) record the contents of vessels: commodities mentioned include honey, peas, wine and also perhaps coriander seeds and gold coins. A larger group (Nos. 6–33) record weights, normally using the formula *t(esta) p(ondo)*. . . or just *p(ondo)*. Three of these graffiti give two sets of numerals, indicating the weight of the empty vessel and also when full. The latter figures never fall below 20 *librae* (No. 3, 24 *librae* = 7859 gm; No. 22, 43½ *librae* = 14244 gm; No. 28, 20 (or more) *librae* = 6049+ gm), and we may reasonably assume that the graffiti which record only one weight, all of which show much lower figures, give the weight of the vessel when empty. This would, indeed, be the more useful record, for the weight of contents of whatever kind could easily then be obtained by subtracting this given figure from the result of a new weighing. It is interesting that this type of graffito is not confined to storage jars, but is found also on jugs. Another graffito (No. 33) indicates an exceptionally large capacity for a storage jar, if measured in *modii*.

Nos. 34–95 display plain numerals; there is an almost unbroken sequence between 1 and 21 and then a gap to 30. The significance of these numerals is not immediately apparent. Many are too low to be interpreted as notes of weight or capacity. Some are cut on the rim, to be visible when the vessel was upright; perhaps they relate in some way to ownership, or to position in a store or on shelves, if indeed they are not batch-numbers cut after firing but while still at the pottery. Others are inscribed beneath the base.

Nos. 96–109 comprise a variety of exhortations, slogans and aphorisms. Three (Nos. 103, 108, 109) are concerned with drinking; another (No. 104) is in verse, apparently part of a pentameter. No. 107 displays the well-known formula, SPQR, though scarcely in any context of government.

Nos. 110–115 usefully name the vessels on which they appear, adding to the names already noted in previous fascicules (*RIB* 2414.30, 31; 2417.31; 2491.149; 2492.7; 2493.16, 29; 2496.3; 2497.4; 2501.18, 307; 2502.5, 48). A few graffiti (Nos. 116–120) give military information, naming centuries, a cohort, a tribune and a gladiator (who was possibly attached to *legio xxx Ulpia Victrix*). Another group (Nos. 121–136) consists of religious dedications. Although several of these are on very ordinary pots, even perhaps unprepossessing in appearance, it was presumably the contents – gifts of food or drink – which were the real objects of dedication. Two seem to be offered to Epona, a Celtic goddess whose cult is otherwise rare in Britain (see note to No. 123); No. 131 names Toutatis, of whom the same is true; and another rare cult, of Isis, is attested on No. 127. No. 125 may be connected with the Imperial Cult. Finally, there are five Christian Chi-Rho monograms, three of them in the later form of that design.

Twenty-five graffiti (Nos. 137–161) were cut on vessels containing or associated with burials. Nineteen carry names, of which most are doubtless those of the deceased;[1] among them eight are certainly men and five are women. Where the case is explicit, the nominative is used five times for masculine names and the genitive thrice. Two of the female names are in the nominative and three in the genitive. Although this is not, of course, a statistically valid sample, it is interesting to note that these figures, such as they are, run counter to the general tendency in graffiti for masculine names to favour the genitive and female names the nominative (see the Introduction to *RIB* 2501 and Table I there together with TABLE I in this chapter). Perhaps the reason is that names on cinerary urns were rarely cut by the person named.

Nos. 162–168 comprise a small group of alphabets (compare *RIB* 2491.135–145). Three of these were apparently cut on whole vessels, sometimes in a confused or incomplete sequence, and four were inscribed on sherds apparently in a secondary usage after breakage. Although the alphabet possessed a mystical significance in the practice of astrology as a paradigm of the ordered universe (see P. Merlat, *Répertoire des inscriptions et monuments figurés . . . de Jupiter Dolichenus* (1951), 102–3, compare Lang, *Archaeologiai Értesitö*[3] vii–ix (1946–8), 157–68) and could be used in divination (Ammianus Marcellinus xxix.1, 28–32), it is probable that the majority

[1] For a probable exception see No. 138.

of the crudely executed examples in this chapter merely formed part of the apparatus for imparting basic literacy.

By far the largest group (Nos. 169–466) comprise personal names (presumably of owners), to which most of the Acephalous group (Nos. 467–619) should be added. The result is a large sample of 450 graffiti, which provides a statistical basis for comparison with the categories distinguished among the samian graffiti. It is interesting to note (TABLE I) that masculine cognomina again appear more frequently in the genitive case than in the nominative (12.62% against 11.16%), although now in the proportion of 6.3:5.9 rather than 2:1 on samian; and that feminine cognomina again show the reverse, with 5.99% in the nominative against only 1.78% in the genitive (a proportion of 3:1 rather than the 8:1 found on samian). The less pronounced differences between the sexes here is probably of less significance than the confirmation that the differences in usage are real.

TABLE II sets out the typology of the names recorded: it should be compared with *RIB* 2501, Table II. There are only two instead of twelve examples of the full *tria nomina* of Roman citizens, and only eleven instead of eighteen examples thought to be *tria nomina* in abbreviation; but when viewed as percentages of the respective combined totals, the proportions are not greatly dissimilar (3.38% for samian and 2.10% for coarse pottery). There is only one example of a Praenomen and Nomen with no cognomen (No. 148); if genuine, it may record an imperial freedman or auxiliary veteran, and unlike samian examples of this combination it dates to the late second century or later. The combination of Nomen and Cognomen, which also in all probability denotes a holder of Roman citizenship, occurs twelve times, in much the same proportion as on samian (1.94% as against 3.1% on samian).

By far the greatest number of coarse-pottery graffiti (252 on TABLE III) display a single name written out in unabbreviated (or once unabbreviated) form. These far outnumber abbreviated names, the various forms of which are also set out in TABLE III, which should be compared with the corresponding Table of Names on samian (*RIB* 2501, Table III). The percentages are very similar.

	SAMIAN	COARSE POTTERY
Name in full	28.26	40.71
Omission of final letter	2.06	1.13
Omission of two final letters	0.8	0.97
Omission of three final letters	0.69	0.65
Abbreviation to two letters	0.8	1.78
Abbreviation to three letters	7.89	6.78
Abbreviation to four letters	1.72	1.29

The clearest instance of abbreviation is the pair of bowls from Pakenham (Nos. 446 and 447), which both belonged to the same woman, who inscribed her name indifferently as *Vetula* in full and as *Vetu. . . .* Many abbreviations of three letters or less, whether the initials of *tria nomina* or ambiguous abbreviations such as *Mar. . .*, *Cun. . .*, or *Dom. . .* (which have several possibilities of expansion), can only have been intelligible within a limited domestic circle.

Although a few of the single names are formally nomina and may indicate Roman citizens who lacked or for some reason here did not use a cognomen, the majority can be taken to be the personal names or 'cognomina' of *peregrini* who lacked Roman citizenship (see the Introduction to *RIB* 2501, Fascicule 7, pp. 2–3). Five of them, *Aelius* (one), *Aurelius* (one), *Claudius* (two ?), *Flavius* (one ?) and *Iulius/a* (seven ?), are common imperial nomina (see TABLE II). Purely native names are over twice as common (31 to 14) as on samian (masculine: Nos. 138, 157, 176, 180–83, 236–39, 277, 312, 336, 337, 355, 411, 439, 444, 457; feminine: 141, 160, 177, 203, 230, 234, 243, 244, 335, 441, 464) and this (together with the increased proportion of names in the nominative case) may suggest a slightly larger component of less Romanized persons among those who inscribed coarse pottery (5.02% against 1.6%). Nevertheless, the presence of five graffiti in cursive script and no less than eleven in Greek, attests also a more sophisticated element – a conclusion supported by twenty-six graffiti which are thought to name holders of Roman citizenship.

Only one certain example of peregrine filiation occurs (No. 111), with three other possible instances (Nos. 341, 426 and 614).

Five graffiti are in cursive script and three others carry cursive letter-forms amongst their capitals (TABLE IV). Unlike the samian cursives, all are on vessels of second-century or later date, except perhaps Nos. 375 and 525 which are not dated. Five come from towns (Caistor St Edmund, Cirencester, St Albans and Wroxeter), one from a villa (Gadebridge Park) and one from a fort (Housesteads).

All the other graffiti are in capitals more or less roughly cut, save only Nos. 287 and 362 which may be described as 'elegant'. There are twenty-one examples of ligatures; these illustrate the influence of monumental inscriptions on the spread of writing. The same influence can be seen in the use of interpunct (TABLE IV), a form of punctuation which in written documents was becoming obsolete by the early second century (see Introduction to *RIB* 2501). While casual damage misunderstood as interpunct cannot be ruled out in some examples in the list (e.g. Nos. 102, 292, 352, 454, 529 and compare No. 444), and in others the small size of the surviving sherds has left only a single stop surviving, several excellent examples are certain (e.g. Nos. 156, 261, 393). Dating, where available, is in general later than for the samian examples. Only one of the graffiti (No. 261) belongs to the first century (it is pre-Flavian). Seven examples are not dated, but Nos. 352 and 374 are Antonine, Nos. 454 and 529 are probably late second-century, and Nos. 102, 108 and 339 belong to the third century or later. There are three examples of leaf-stops, another form of punctuation taken over from monumental inscriptions (see the Introduction to *RIB* 2501, p. 4); No. 116 can be assigned to the second century to judge by the centurion's name, and No. 398 to the late third century; No. 292 is not dated.

TABLES V and VI show the variations in form of the letters A and E respectively, for comparison with *RIB* 2501, Tables VI and VII. For A by far the most common form is the open Λ, 38.97% of all examples of this letter, compared with 54.39% on the samian Table. The carelessly written variant λ, resembling a cursive form, is represented by 14.70% here and 10.40% on the samian Table. ⩘ is less frequent on the coarse pottery than in the samian graffiti (12.50% compared with 17.59%), whereas the reverse is true of A (23.90% on coarse pottery, but only 15.31% on samian). The form ⩘ comprises only 8.09% of the coarse pottery, but 12.7% on the samian. The coarse pottery also shows three examples of the form ⩘, not found on the samian; it may be merely a variant of the last, but on all three examples is carefully cut. The differing forms of the letter probably have little significance, for on Nos. 101, 104, 111, 196, 243, 368, 372 and 480 more than one form is found in the same graffito.

The letter E appears in two forms, E and II; unlike on the samian the former slightly outnumbers the latter (55.41% and 44.59% respectively, compared with 46 and 52% on samian). On Nos. 243 and 254 both forms occur in the same graffito.

Graffiti rarely provide evidence that an individual owned more than one vessel, and never show ownership of more than two. Eight such graffiti were noted among the samian, but here there are only two (Nos. 313–314 and Nos. 446–447). Successive ownership on the other hand is more commonly attested: eleven (or perhaps nineteen) examples were noted among the samian and here there were twenty-two. Nos. 107, 157, 193, 277, 281, 350, 380, 433 and perhaps 502, 505 and 541 record two names, probably successive, and Nos. 581 and 583 appear to record three. Nos. 257, 278, 301, 354, 400, 411, 416, 460 and 464 carry one name and a mark of ownership (usually X but occasionally another letter, A, M or V); these graffiti presumably indicate successive owners, one literate and one not; but No. 460 may be an exception, where both name and mark appear to be a single inscription.

Although the precise location of a graffito on its vessel is often, as with the samian graffiti, imprecisely recorded in our sources, the information available makes clear that differences exist between the two classes of pottery, as indeed is to be expected from the differences in shape. Whereas samian vessels are mainly open forms such as dishes, bowls and plates, coarse-ware vessels are mainly enclosed forms such as beakers, jugs and jars. Although exact figures are difficult to arrive at, given the variety of locations listed in our sources (such as 'below the rim' or 'on the neck') it is clear that the great majority of coarse-pottery graffiti occur on the outside surface of the vessel, on the shoulder or neck (about 199 = 32.2%) or lower down on the wall (about 197 = 31.9%), and were inscribed to be read with the vessel upright. Forty-four are cut on the top of the rim and nine inside it; thirteen more are inscribed on the upper surface of the base of a dish or bowl as if intended to be visible on a shelf with the inside facing the front, but a further twenty-five dishes and bowls are marked on the underside of the base (with one, No. 252, marked in both places); so there was evidently no compelling fashion. Of the ninety-six vessels inscribed beneath the base, sixty-one are jars or beakers, which may therefore have been stored inverted.

It is interesting to note that as on the samian vessels it was easier to inscribe the far side of the base than the nearer side (43 examples to 12). But the graffiti on the shoulders and walls of coarse-ware vessels were nearly all inscribed with the vessel on its side with the base at the bottom. Only nine graffiti (Nos. 135, 180, 185, 187, 232, 300, 495, 545, 578) are described as inverted in relation to the base, and were probably inscribed with the vessel standing on its rim; all are bowls or dishes save 300 (a jar) and 578 (a jug).

TABLE VII lists the sites where five or more coarse-ware graffiti have been found, the number of samian graffiti from each site being added in brackets. When compared with the corresponding table for samian (*RIB* 2501, Table VIII), it shows far fewer military sites qualifiying for inclusion (12 as against 31), whereas the number of Towns and Villas is increased. To a certain though unquantifiable extent this may represent a chronological difference, because the use of samian ceased a century and a half before that of coarse pottery, the number of occupied forts tended to decrease with time, and the *floruit* of villas lay in the third and fourth centuries. Among the military sites in TABLE VII eight out of twelve have yielded more samian graffiti than coarse pottery examples; at Chester, Corbridge, Usk and York the proportion is as much as *c.* 4:1 and at Caerleon and Housesteads about 3:2, while at the rest the numbers are more nearly equal. Although in past excavations samian sherds have often been accorded greater interest than those of coarse pottery, and graffiti on them have been more readily recognised, these figures reinforce the view put forward in the Introduction to *RIB* 2501 that it was the greater value of samian vessels and their frequent use at communal tables which encouraged owners to mark their property.

Out of fifteen towns only London (with a coarse-pottery to samian ratio of 32:93), Cirencester (5:13), Leicester (8:13), Silchester (18:25) and Southwark (6:10) resemble the military sites in the respective proportions of their graffiti. At the remaining ten towns in TABLE VII coarse-pottery graffiti outnumber the samian, as they do also at the three villas listed. The differential is most marked[2] at Canterbury, Colchester and St Albans, where it is about 2:1. This contrast between the respective proportions at these two sets of towns is hard to explain. Even if we deduct the beakers and jugs (as representing table-wares) from the figures for the second group of towns (Canterbury 9, Colchester 14, St Albans 17), this still leaves Canterbury with seven more coarse-pottery graffiti than samian, and Colchester with six more; only at St Albans is the expected ratio (now 9:16) recovered. It would be a mistake, however, to suppose that these comparatively small anomalies imply a serious divergence in social behaviour. The supply of samian was not universally uniform, but we lack the statistics to assess whether sites with more coarse-pottery graffiti than samian were simply those where less samian was in use. Possibly all that is indicated is the plentiful availability of local wares from the large-scale potteries in the vicinities of these towns (which may have reduced dependence upon imported samian), and perhaps also the success of basic education among their populations.

In Britain 178 places have yielded graffiti cut after firing on coarse pottery, twenty-seven more than have produced graffiti on samian. For a combined distribution-map see *RIB* 2501, fig. 2. The thirty most prolific are listed in TABLE VII. Of the remainder, thirty-nine are military sites, thirteen are towns or large settlements (many of which had a military origin, irrelevant to the date of the graffiti, however), thirty-one are villas and fifty-eight are minor settlements, rural sites or cemeteries. The individual graffiti may be discovered from the Index of Sites at the end of this Fascicule.

In summary, the figures show that whereas almost half the sites yielding samian graffiti (72 out of 151) were military, in the present chapter 120 out of 178 sites are civilian, and of these 58 out of 178 fall in the category of minor settlements, rural sites or cemeteries. The figures illustrate the spread of basic literacy among the civilian population of the province.

[2] The exceptional proportion of 8:1 at Alcester may be discounted since it is caused almost entirely by numerals, while Dorchester is anomalous in yielding no samian graffiti at all.

RIB 2503: TABLE I

Case-Endings of Personal Names

NOMINATIVE (MASCULINE) Names ending in *-is* are omitted as being of uncertain case, as also are names which are the subject of a verb expressed or understood				GENITIVE (MASCULINE)				NOMINATIVE (FEMININE)		GENITIVE (FEMININE)
32	253 (?)	340	438	112	282	367	466(?)	140	382	147
102	256	343	439	120(?)	283(?)	371	485	141	386	160
107	263(?)	345(?)	461	139	286	372	486	177(?)	408(?)	199
117	271	347	471	150	287	379	487	178(?)	412	210
119	272	351	489	155	295	380(?)	505(?)	186	414	219
145	285	353(?)	525(?)	171	299	383	515	190(?)	441	234(?)
148	288	355	530(?)	172(?)	300	389	517	203	444	244
157	294	364	531	189(?)	306	390	518(?)	209	446	362
159	304	366	533	191	307(?)	415(?)	520(?)	230	460	400(?)
174	305	368	537	194	309	419	524(?)	240	463	440
197	310	369	551	195	312	423	536	243	464(?)	595(?)
200	311	375	556(?)	196	315	434	546	250	469	
211	320	378	564	206	316	435	547	284	493	
220(?)	325	398	581(?)	207	317	436	548	289	506(?)	
222	326	411	583(?)	231	318	443	552	296	516	
224	327	418(?)	601(?)	236	319	449	554	335	527	
226(?)	336	420	608	242	338	451	584	341	545	
			613	259	349	453	607	342	572	
				260(?)	358	456	615	376(?)		
				277	363	457	616a			
TOTAL		69				80			37	11
PERCENTAGE:		11.15				12.92			5.98	1.78

RIB 2503: TABLE II

Classification of Personal Names

TRIA NOMINA	INITIALS ONLY OF TRIA NOMINA	PRAENOMEN ONLY UNLESS USED AS COGNOMEN	PRAENOMEN AND NOMEN	NOMEN ONLY UNLESS USED AS COGNOMEN	
379	245 DMR	306 Lucius	148(?)	174 Aelius	318 Marius(?)
418(?)	270(?) GIS	307(?) Luci[us]		200 Avitius [. . .?]	150 Maurusius
	302 LVA	601 [L]uciu[s](?)		148 M. Aurelius	340 Maurucius
	313(?) MAP	315 Marcus		207 Baebius	351 Montius
	314(?) MAP	316 Marcus		229 Clau[dius]	151 Namelia(?)
	329(?) MAS			107 Cl[audius?]	32 Nicerius
	385 PPD			241 Deme[trius . . .?]	383 Postumius
	392(?) PVN			265 Flav[ius . . .?]	421 Tamm[onius . . .?]
	428 TPD			147 Iulia	449 Vicarius
	430(?) TRO			289 Iul(i)a(?)	456 [V]incentius
	431 TVA			290 Iul[ius . . .?]	465 Ursic[ius?]
				291 Iul[ius . . .?]	485 [. . .] attius(?)
				292 Iul(ius)	489 [. . .] . . brius
				293 Iuli[us . . .?]	533 [. . .] . lius
				294 Iuliu[s . . .?]	
				296 Iunia	
				297 Iun(ius)	
				298 Iun(ius)	
				304 [L]olliu[s . . .?]	
				309 Maecius	
TOTAL					
2	11	5	1	34	
PERCENTAGE					
0.32	1.78	0.81	0.16	5.49	

RIB 2503 TABLE II (continued)

NOMEN AND COGNOMEN	COGNOMEN ONLY												
	MASCULINE							PROBABLY MASCULINE			FEMININE		
107(?)	32(?)	202	255	299	347(?)	390	451	142	247	392	140	296	464(?)
116	101	205	256	300	349	393	453	143	248	394	141	334	469
149	102	206	258	305(?)	351(?)	395	455	146	257	397	147	335	493
195	117(?)	207(?)	259	306	352	396(?)	456	158	264	399	151(?)	341	516
231	119	211(?)	260	307(?)	353	398	457	176	265	402	160	342	527(?)
295	138	212	262	308	354(?)	411	458	180(?)	290	403	177	362	545(?)
374(?)	145	214	263(?)	309(?)	355	415	459	181(?)	291	409	178	376	572(?)
426(?)	150	216	266	310	358	416	466	182(?)	293	410	186	382	
452(?)	155	220	267(?)	312	360	417	517	183(?)	297	413	187(?)	386	
461	157	222	268	315	363	419	518(?)	184	298	421	190	400	
530(?)	159	223	269	316	364	420	520(?)	185	322	424	199	404(?)	
531(?)	170	224	271	317	365(?)	423	536(?)	188	323	430(?)	203	405(?)	
	171	226	272	318(?)	366	433	537(?)	201	324	437	209	408(?)	
	172(?)	228	274	320	367	434	551(?)	204	328	442	210	412	
	173	232	275(?)	325	368	435(?)	581	217	330	462	219	414	
	174(?)	236(?)	276	326	369	436	596(?)	218	333		230	432(?)	
	189(?)	237	277	336(?)	371	438	601(?)	221	344		234	440	
	191	238	280	337	372	439	613(?)	225	348		240	441	
	193	239	282	338	373	443	616a(?)	227	357		243	444	
	194	241(?)	283	340	375	445		229	370		244	446	
	196	242	286	343	378	448		233	377		250	447	
	197	249	287	345(?)	380(?)	449		235	388		284	460	
	198	252(?)	288	346	383	450		246	389		289	463	
TOTAL 12	157							61			53		
PERCENTAGE 1.94	25.36							9.87			8.58		

RIB 2503: TABLE III

Abbreviations

NAME IN FULL (or once in full)												NAME OMITTING THE FINAL LETTER	
32	157	203	231	271	305	338	368	408(?)	444	487(?)	552	142	CVPIT (i?)
102	159	205	232(?)	272	306	340	369	409	445	489	554	157	VASSV(s)
107	160	206	233	273	307	341	371	411	446	493(?)	556	176	AESVC(i?)
109	170	207	234	277	309	342	372	412	449	505	564	187	ANN(a?)
111	171	209	236	282	310	343	373(?)	414	450	506	572	193	[. . .]ITV(s)
112	172	210	240	283	311	345	375	415	451	515(?)	581(?)	214	BRVT(i?)
114	173(?)	211	241(?)	284	312	346(?)	376	416	453	516	583	549	[. . .]MINV(s)
116	174	212	242	285	315	347	378	417	456	517	584		
117	177	216	243	286	316	349	379	419	457	518	585(?)		
119	178(?)	218(?)	244	287	317	351	380(?)	420	460	520(?)	586(?)		
120	186	219	248(?)	288	318	353(?)	382	421(?)	461(?)	524	591		
139	189	220	249(?)	289	319	355	383	423	463	525	595(?)		
140	190	222	250	290(?)	320	358	386	433	464	527	596		
141	191	223	253	291(?)	321(?)	359(?)	387	434	469	533	599(?)		
145	194	224	255	293	325	360	389	435	470(?)	536(?)	601(?)		
147	195	225	256	394	326	362	390	436	471	537	607		
148	196	226	258	295	327	363	393	438	473	545	608		
150	197	227(?)	259	296	333	364	396	439	474	546	613		
151(?)	199	228	260	299	335	365	398	440	475	547	614(?)		
155	200	229(?)	262	300	336	366	400	441	485	548	615		
156	202(?)	230	267	304(?)	337	367	406	443	486	551	616a		
TOTAL						252						7	
PERCENTAGE						40.71						1.13	

RIB 2503: TABLE III (continued)
Abbreviations

NAME OMITTING THE LAST TWO LETTERS	NAME OMITTING THE LAST THREE LETTERS	ABBREVIATION TO TWO LETTERS	ABBREVIATION TO THREE LETTERS not thought to be initials of tria nomina		ABBREVIATION TO FOUR LETTERS
297 IVN(ii?)	198 AVENT(ini?)	(a) by first two	16 IVN	323 MAR	102 EGNA(?)
298 IVN(ii?)	243 DESIM(ena)	letters of name	143 CVR	330 MAT	269 GETL(?)
361 VAB(ri)(?)	292 IVL (ius?)		180 AMB	331 MAT	334 MATR
447 VETV(la)	303 LAT(ini?)	117(?) LO	181 AMB	332 MAT	377 PERE
458 VITAL(is)		204 BE	182 AMB	344 MER	394 QVIN
462 VITV(li?)		213 BR	183 AMB	348 MIN	447 VETV
		215 BV	185 ANI	352 NAT	452 VICT
		235 CV	217 CAN	370 PAT	462 VITV
		252 ER	237 CVN	388 PRI	
		275 IA	246 DOM	392(?) PVN	
			257 FAV	399 SAL	
			266 FOR	401 SAS	
		(b) by likely first	268 GER	402 SAT	
		letters of nomen	274 HIL	403 SAT	
		and cognomen	276 IAN	404 SAX	
			337 INI	413 SIIR(=SER)	
		107 TC	280 INT	424 TER	
		261 F·F	292 IVL	430 TRO	
		384 PP	297 IVN	361 VAB	
		427 TL	298 IVN	437 VAR	
			303 LAT	442 VIIN(=VEN)	
			322 MAR	538 MAN	
6	4	11	42		8
0.97	0.65	1.78	6.78		1.29

RIB 2503: TABLE IV

Unusual Forms of Graffiti

RETROGRADE GRAFFITI	CURSIVE GRAFFITI	GRAFFITI WITH SOME CURSIVE LETTER-FORMS	GREEK GRAFFITI	USE OF INTERPUNCT	LEAF STOPS	LIGATURES
60 IIV	101	190	93	24	116	16 $\widehat{\text{TP}}$
65 IIIV	219	414(?)	108	102	292	56 $\widehat{\text{IV}}$(?)
81 IIIVX	224	443	137	108	398	107 $\widehat{\text{AP}}$
	375		251	149		114 $\widehat{\text{NAV}}$
	525		255	156		115 $\widehat{\text{TI}}$(?)
			268	261		151(?) $\widehat{\text{ME}}$, $\widehat{\text{LI}}$
			364	272(?)		156 $\widehat{\text{VE}}$, $\widehat{\text{RI}}$
			378	292		164 $\widehat{\text{AN}}$
			501	339(?)		168 $\widehat{\text{XV}}$, $\widehat{\text{MN}}$
			537	352		192 $\widehat{\text{IO}}$(?)
			551	374(?)		196 $\widehat{\text{TI}}$
				393		210 $\widehat{\text{AE}}$
				454		266 $\widehat{\text{OR}}$
				529(?)		325 $\widehat{\text{NVS}}$
				571(?)		334 $\widehat{\text{MA}}$, $\widehat{\text{TR}}$
						346 $\widehat{\text{NE}}$
						362 $\widehat{\text{TR}}$
						391 $\widehat{\text{VA}}$(?)
						437 $\widehat{\text{VA}}$
						536 $\widehat{\text{NTI}}$
						539 $\widehat{\text{MA}}$
TOTAL						
3	5	3	11	15	3	21
PERCENTAGE						
0.48	0.81	0.48	1.78	2.43	0.48	3.40

RIB 2503: TABLE V
The Letter A: Variation in Form

Λ					⩚		A			λ		⩓	⋀	ᐱ
97	186	305	369	480	27	379	32	257	432	101	338	104	149	119
100	187	310	386	486	163(?)	402	98	271	446	102	353	110	285	140
101	188	311	399	490	164	404	103	273	463	104	371	111		555
104	190	313	401	502	175	433	112	278	464	127	391	145(?)		
109	195	315	405	516	177	441	125	309	475	150	396	157(?)		
111	198	316	406	520	179	449	128	320	478	171	398	168(?)		
113	206	317	407	529	193	466	138	322	479	184	412	192		
114	218	318	408	552	196	474	139	325	480	191	425	194		
115	222	323	411	572	217	485	156	334	481	203	438	197		
131	229	324	426	586	240	493	165	352	487	219	444	220		
141	236	326	436	592	241	506	167	361	488	231	445	221		
146	243	327	437	595	242	527	170	368	492	232	448	225		
147	256	328	439	598	250(?)	531	173	370	497	243	457	319		
152	263	329	440	599	333	539	176	373	503	267	482	321		
155	264	332	458	614	354	540	185	374	536	289	491	331		
160	265	335	459		357	563	196	382	538	303	535	372		
162	275	336	460		372	591	199	387	546	312	542	393		
166	279	339	467				201	421	551	314	545	400		
169	284	340	469				202	422	581	330	558	471		
174	292	341	472				205	423	587	337	568	507(?)		
175	296	363	473				209	429	600			561(?)		
180	301	365	476				210	431				617		
183	302	368	477											
TOTAL	106				34		65			40		22	2	3
PERCENTAGE of A	38.97				12.50		23.90			14.70		8.09	0.75	1.10

RIB 2503: TABLE VI

The Letter E: Variation in Form

E				II			
32	199	333	456	3	224	377	596
102	204	336	507(?)	100	225	393	612
105	205	342	509(?)	101	226	407	618
107	206	344	511	104	233	409	
109	210	346	512	106	240	411	
111	219(?)	347	513	121	241	412	
114	227	371	523	123	242	413	
116	234	376	543	125	243	414	
119	243	380	576	129	250	433	
122	244	395	578	130	254	434	
124	249	397	579	147	269	436	
126	252	398	580	149	273	440	
156	253	406	589	153	309	441	
160	254	410	593	158	335	442	
162	256	418	594	168	343	444	
163	258	419	602	174	345	446	
166	259	424	606	195	355	447	
169	262	435	610	198	356	506	
176	271	439	611	207	358	510	
193	272	443		208	359	544	
197	292	445		223	365	561	
TOTAL		82			66		
PERCENTAGE of E		55.41			44.59		

RIB 2503: TABLE VII

PLACES YIELDING FIVE OF MORE GRAFFITI ON COARSE POTTERY
(with corresponding figures for samian shown in brackets)

MILITARY			TOWNS			VILLAS		
Brecon	5	(5)	*Alcester	16	(2)	Dicket Mead	6	(2)
Caerleon	16	(23)	*Canterbury	34	(17)	Eccles	9	(6)
Castleford	5	(8)	*Chelmsford	5	(1)	Gadebridge Park	7	(0)
Chester	6	(24)	*Cirencester	5	(13)			
Chesterholm	17	(16)	*Colchester	41	(18)			
Corbridge	14	(66)	Dorchester	10	(0)			
Housesteads	9	(14)	*Exeter	6	(5)			
Ribchester	5	(10)	*Gloucester	6	(4)			
Richborough	14	(9)	*Leicester	8	(13)			
Usk	6	(24)	London	32	(93)			
Wallsend	9	(7)	*St Albans	26	(16)			
York	8	(34)	*Silchester	18	(25)			
			Southwark	6	(10)			
			Wilderspool	8	(2)			
			*Winchester	7	(3)			
TOTAL	12			15			3	

*The eleven places marked with an asterisk were the sites of early forts, but few of the graffiti can be shown to date so early. London also had a military presence.

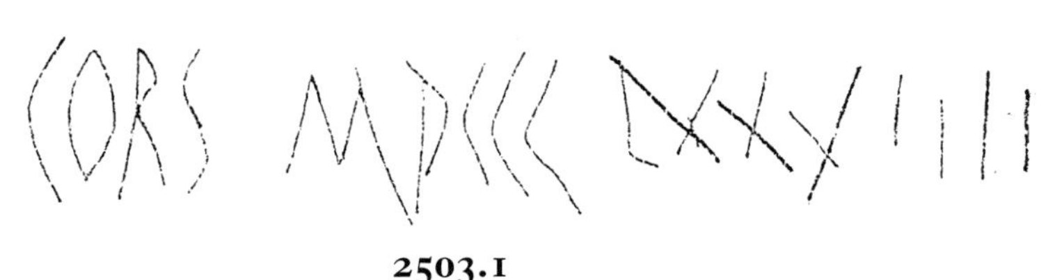

2503.1

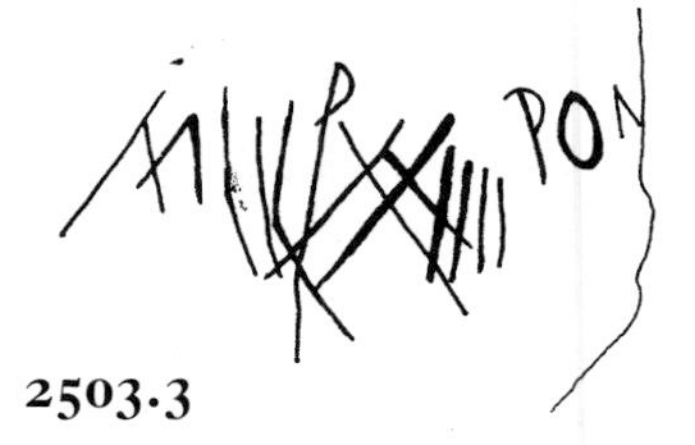

2503.3

(a) Indications of Contents (*RIB* 2503.1–5)

2503.1. Chesterholm (*Vindolanda*), Northumberland. Part of a narrow-necked black storage jar (½), found in 1986 in a context dated *c.* A.D. 90–95. Vindolanda Museum. Drawing: the Vindolanda Trust and R.S.O.T.

Britannia xix (1988), 503 No. 79. E., R., and A. Birley, *Vindolanda* ii (1993), 97 No. 2 with fig. 12.1.

graffito on the shoulder: CORS MDCCCLXX̣X̣IIII
perhaps *Cor(iandri) s(emina) MDCCCLXXXIIII*
'1,884 seeds of coriander'

C is probably the first letter, but a small sherd is missing just left of it, sufficient to carry 1–2 letters. The graffito is clearly a note of contents, something granular but large and valuable enough to be counted rather than weighed: perhaps coriander (*coriandrum*). R. Birley, loc. cit., suggests *cor(iandri) s(emina)*; compare Pliny *NH* xix 119, *semen coriandri*.

Coriander seeds are used for flavouring or seasoning a large variety of foods.

2503.2. Terling, Essex. Small pot (½), found in *c.* 1824, containing a hoard of 28 or 30 gold coins of the houses of Valentinian and Theodosius together with two gold rings. In private possession. Drawn by R.P.W. from rubbings by G.R. Strutt.

O'Neil, *Num. Chron.*[5] xiii (1933), 151 fig. 2, 152 fig. 3.

graffito on the wall: INTVXVIII

No such personal name is known, and it is tempting to see a reference to the contents, for example *in t(esta) [x]xviii* '28 (coins) in the jar'.

2503.2

2503.3. Southwark, south London. Sherd from a grey storage vessel (½), found in 1974 with first- and early second-century material in a pit during excavations at Nos. 1–7 St. Thomas Street. Museum of London. Drawn by S.S.F. from rubbings by M.W.C.H.

Britannia vi (1975), 288 No. 24. Dennis in J. Bird et al. (eds.), *Southwark Excavations 1972–74* ii (1978), 378 No. 11 with fig. 171.11.

two graffiti, (a) first hand: MIILPXXIIII
Mel p(ondo) xxiiii
'Honey, twenty-four (*librae*)'
(b) second hand: PON[. . .]
pon[do. . .]
'By weight . . .'

Dennis, loc. cit., states that 'the weight is far too great for the vessel, and it may be that the broken sherd was used to scratch tallies on'. This seems improbable in view of the fracture. Twenty-four *librae* of honey amounts to *c.* 8.4 litres or 14.8 pints, weighing 7859 gm (or 17 lb 5 oz).

2503.4. Wallsend (*Segedunum*), Tyne and Wear [Northumberland]. Fragment of a pink jug (½), found in 1975 during excavations at the fort. Wallsend Museum. Drawn by R.S.O.T., 1992.

Britannia vii (1976), 390 No. 56.

graffito: [. . .]ḶSVM
Perhaps *[mu]lsum*
'(Honey-)sweetened wine'

2503.4

2503.5. Great Chesterford, Essex. Part of a two-handled storage jar (¼), in white ware, height 451 mm, found in or before 1860. Museum of Archaeology and Anthropology, Cambridge. Drawn by R.P.W., 1951.

CIL vii 1332.5. Neville, *Arch. J.* xvii (1860), 126 with fig.

graffito between the handles: PISI M̄IIS
Pisi m(odii) ii s(emis)
'Two and a half *modii* of peas'

21.88 litres. The capacity of the vessel is *c.* 28 litres.

For peas in Roman military diet see R.W. Davies, *Service in the Roman Army* (1989), 199. Barred M for *modii* occurs in the Vindolanda tablets and on *RIB* 2492.7 and 2494.44.

2503.5

(b) Weight or Capacity (*RIB* 2503.6–33)

2503.6. London (*Londinium*). Sherd from a jar in sandy micaceous fabric with a black burnished exterior (½), found in 1974 unstratified during excavations at Billingsgate Buildings. Museum of London. Reproduced from Jones.

Britannia ix (1978), 480 No. 55. Hassall in D.M. Jones, *Excavations at Billingsgate Buildings . . . . 1974* (1980), 136 No. 712 with fig. 79.712.

graffito on the wall: PII=–
p(ondo) (librae) ii (unciae) iii
'Two (pounds) three (ounces) in weight'

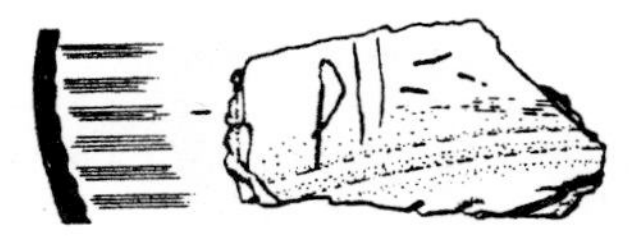

2503.6

2503.7. York (*Eboracum*). Buff jug (½ and ¼), of the mid second century, height 178 mm, found in 1951 while excavating an inhumation in the Roman cemetery at Trentholme Drive. Yorkshire Museum. Drawn by R.P.W., 1953, and the jug reproduced from R.C.H.M.

JRS xliii (1953), 131 No. 19. L.P. Wenham, *The Romano-British Cemetery at Trentholme Drive, York* (1968), 59 No. 1 with fig. 19.1. RCHM, *York* i (1962), 135 No. 153 with fig. 77.xiii.

graffito on the shoulder: PIĪI
p(ondo) iii
'By weight three (*librae*)'

Three *librae* is the equivalent of 982.3 gm. The jug when empty weighs 481.9 gm and when full of water 1247.38 gm.

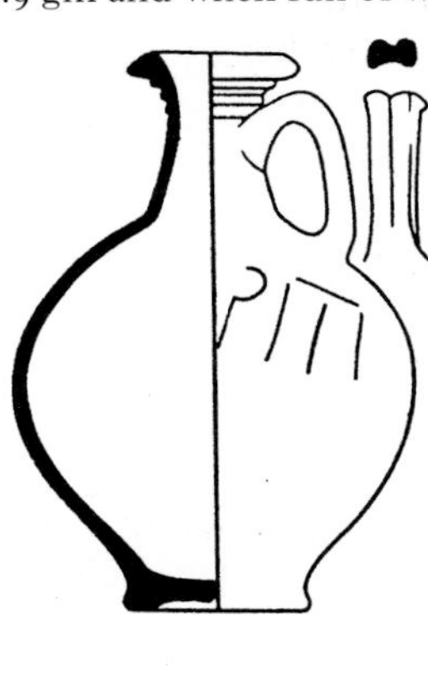

2503.7

2503.8. Richborough (*Rutupiae*), Kent. Fragment of a cream-coloured vessel (½), found before 1940. In store at Dover Castle. Drawn by S.S.F. from a tracing by R.G.C.

graffito: [. . .]IIISII | [. . .]OLPVII
(librae) [. . .]iii se(mis) | [. . .]ol(a) p(lena) vii
'. . . three and a half . . . jar when full seven (pounds)'

The graffito probably gives the empty and full weights of the vessel. Compare *RIB* 2503.11, 22 and 28.
7 *librae* are the equivalent of 2292.15 gm.

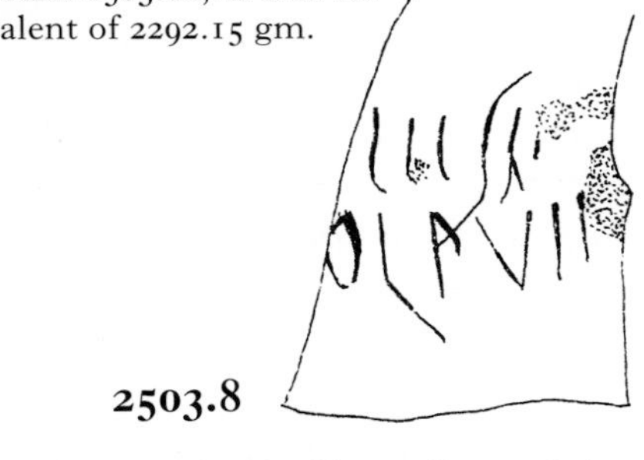

2503.8

2503.9. Springhead (*Vagniacis*), Kent. Part of the shoulder of a grey jar (½), found in 1959 during excavations in the Temple area. Gravesend Museum. Drawn by S.S.F. from a rubbing by R.P.W., 1961.

JRS li (1961), 197 No. 44.

graffito on the shoulder: P IIII
p(ondo) (librae) iiii
'By weight, four (pounds)'

2503.9

Four *librae* is the equivalent of 1309.8 gm.

2503.10. Silchester (*Calleva*), Hampshire. Part of a jar (½) found before 1916. Reading Museum. Reproduced from May.

T. May, *Silchester* (1916), 284 No. 23 with pl. LXXXV.23.

graffito on the shoulder: IIIIS
(librae) iiii s(emis)
'Four and a half (pounds)'

1473.5 gm.

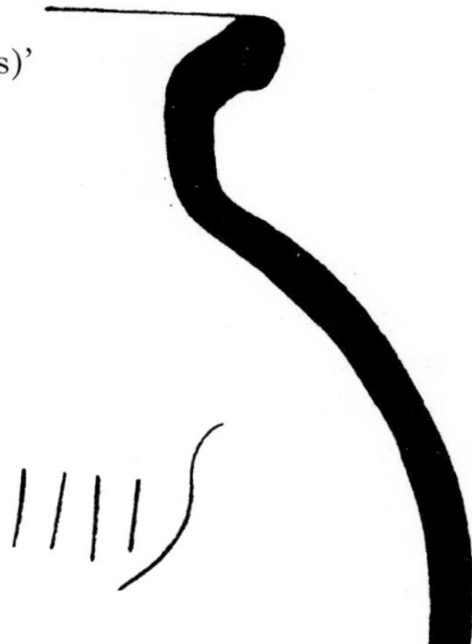

2503.10

2503.11. Birrens (*Blatobulgium*), Dumfries and Galloway [Dumfriesshire]. Part of a grey jar (½), found in 1895 during excavations at the fort. National Museums of Scotland, Queen Street, Edinburgh. Drawn by R.P.W.

Anderson, *PSAS* xxx (1895–6), 188 No. 26.

graffito on the shoulder: TPVPP

Presumably *t(esta) p(ondo) (librae) v p(lena) p(ondo)* [. . . ?]

'Vessel by weight five (pounds), weight full [*numerals lost*]'

'Jar . . . with a rude face or mark projecting under the lip', Anderson. 'Projecting lug', R.P.W. The vessel is not among those face-jars listed by Braithwaite, *Britannia* xv (1984), 99–131.

Compare *RIB* 2503.8, 22 and 28.

2503.11

2503.12. Droitwich (*Salinae*), Hereford and Worcester [Worcestershire]. Part of a Black-burnished cooking pot (½) of the third or fourth century, found unstratified in 1972. Present whereabouts not recorded. Drawn by M.W.C.H.

Britannia xxiii (1992), 319 No. 31.

graffito on the shoulder above the lattice decoration: VS

Presumably *(librae) v s(emis)*

'Five and a half (pounds)'

1801 gm.

2503.12

2502.13. Great Chesterford, Essex. Squat red-ware jug with two handles (½), height 190 mm, maximum diameter 179 mm, diameter at the mouth 76 mm, found in or before 1860. Museum of Archaeology and Anthropology, Cambridge. Reproduced from Neville.

CIL vii 1332.6. Neville, *Arch.J.* xvii (1860), 124 with fig.

graffito on the neck between the handles: VS

Presumably *(librae) v s(emis)*

'Five and a half (pounds)'

1801 gm.

The figure is probably the weight of the vessel when empty. 5½ *librae* is the equivalent of 1801 gm, a reasonable weight for an empty vessel (compare *RIB* 2503.11, 23, 27). If, however, the figure relates to *sextarii*, *(sextarii) v s(emis)* rather than *v s(extarii)* should be read. 5½ *sextarii* is the equivalent of 2.73 litres, whereas the capacity of the vessel seems to be only *c*. 2.2 litres.

As the vessel is apparently complete, it would have been useful to discover its true weight and capacity, in order to resolve these problems. The vessel carries the Museum Accession Number 1948.770, but unfortunately cannot now be found (information from Dr. Christopher Chippindale, 1 September, 1993).

2503.13

2503.14. Richborough (*Rutupiae*), Kent. Wide-mouthed grey jar (½), height 235 mm, diameter 241 mm, dated *c*. A.D. 40–80, found in 1928–31 during excavation of Area IX. In store at Dover Castle. Drawn by R.P.W., 1953.

J.P. Bushe-Fox, *Richborough* iv (1949), 260 No. 384 and 255 No. 9 with pl. LXXXVII.384.

graffito on the shoulder: TPVI

t(esta) p(ondo) (librae) vi

'Vessel by weight six (pounds)'

Six *librae* is the equivalent of 1964.7 gm. Compare *RIB* 2503.16.

2503.14

2503.15. London (*Londinium*). Handle of a storage jar ($\frac{1}{2}$), found in 1965 in a rubbish pit in Church Alley on the north side of Guildhall. Museum of London. Drawn by S.S.F. from a rubbing and squeeze by R.P.W., 1966.

JRS lvi (1966), 224 No. 53.

graffito on the handle: [. . .]MVI | [. . .]IIIIII
M(odii) vi|iiiii
'Six *modii*'

Six shallow strokes have been summed up in the figure cut later above them, R.P.W.

Six *modii* is the equivalent of 52.5 litres, which suggests that the handle may be that of an amphora.

Compare *RIB* 2494.39.

2503.15

2503.16. Lower Halling, Kent. Narrow-necked grey jar ($\frac{1}{4}$), height 315 mm, weight 2232.56 gm, containing a cremation; found in 1882 with other urns in a Roman cemetery while making a railway-line to the chalk-pit of the Formby Cement Works. Museum of Archaeology and Anthropology, Cambridge ex Cole Ambrose collection. Drawn by R.P.W., 1955.

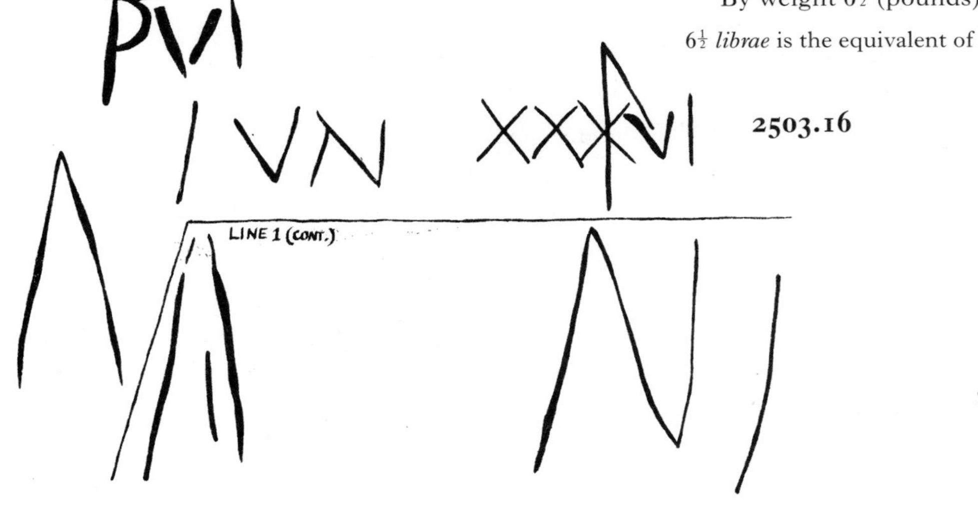

2503.16

On the wall, at least three graffiti: (a) TPVI
t(esta) p(ondo) (librae) vi
'vessel by weight six (pounds)'
(b) IVN XXXVI
perhaps *Iun(ius)* . . .
(c) Λ A NI|Λ

TPVI is deeply cut. Graffito (c) overlaps (b), but it is not certain which was cut first.

Six *librae* is the equivalent of 1964.7 gm (72 *unciae*), and is 9.8 *unciae* below the actual weight of the vessel (12%). From this we conclude that P is to be expanded *p(ondo)* and not *p(lena)* ('full').

2503.17. Silchester (*Calleva*), Hampshire. Large grey-black storage jar ($\frac{1}{2}$) with two bands of cross-hatching, height 565 mm, diameter 559 mm, diameter at the lip 241 mm, found in 1897. Drawn by R.P.W.

T. May, *Silchester* (1916), 167 with pl. LXIX B (without mention of the graffito).

graffito on the shoulder: VI=
'Six (*librae*), one *sextans* (or two *unciae*)'

2019.3 gm. This might represent the weight of the vessel when empty, for it is said to hold *c.* 10 gallons (45.5 litres), and the weight of 10 gallons of water is *c.* 45431 gm.

2503.18. Wroxeter (*Viroconium*), Shropshire. Three conjoining sherds ($\frac{1}{2}$), from the shoulder of a large grey-ware jar, found in 1983 in a Hadrianic context at the *macellum*. Wroxeter Museum. Not illustrated.

Britannia xv (1984), 345 No. 48.

cursive graffito: PVIS[. . .]
P(ondo) (librae) vi s(emis)
'By weight $6\frac{1}{2}$ (pounds)'

$6\frac{1}{2}$ *librae* is the equivalent of 2128.4 gm.

2503.17

2503.19. Colchester (*Camulodunum*), Essex. Grey narrow-necked jar ($\frac{1}{2}$), height 305 mm, diameter 240 mm, weight 2075 gm, found in 1870 in a grave. Colchester Museum, ex Joslin collection. Drawn by R.P.W., 1954.

CIL vii 1332.4. *EE* ix p. 673. T. May, *Cat.* (1930), 14 and 245 No. 2 with fig. 9.2.

graffito on the side: PVISS=

p(ondo) (librae) vi s(emis) ⟨*S*⟩ *ii(unciae)*

'By weight six and a half (pounds) . . . two (ounces)'

PLVISSI, *p(ondo) l(ibrae) vi s(emis) s(emimodius)*, 'thus giving a weight of $6\frac{1}{2}$ *librae* and a volume of $\frac{1}{2}$ a *modius*', May.

PVISS=, *p(ondo) vi s(emis) s(ubtracto) s(extante)*, '$6\frac{1}{2}$ pounds less one *sextans*' [i.e. 6 pounds, 4 ounces]', R.P.W.

= is the symbol for a *sextans* of two *unciae* and S= for a *bes* of eight unciae.

The actual weight of the vessel is 2075 gm (M.R. Davies to M.W.C.H., 1977). This is equivalent to 6 (Roman) pounds, 4 ounces [2074 gm], hence the expansion *s(ubtracto)* suggested by R.P.W. But such a formulation seems to be unparalleled, and it is difficult to see why it should have been preferred to PVI= =.

If the second S, which looks like an insertion, is otiose, the graffito will indicate 6 *librae* one *bes* (of 8 *unciae*), the equivalent of 2183 gm, which is only 5.2% over the real weight, an acceptable variation (see Introduction to *RIB* 2412).

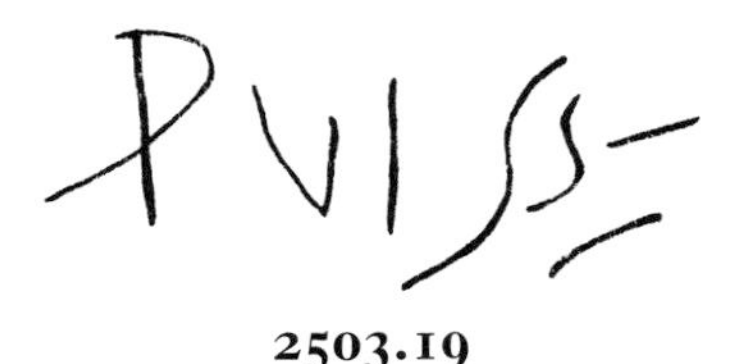

2503.19

2503.20. St. Albans (*Verulamium*), Hertfordshire. Fragment of a large grey jar ($\frac{1}{2}$), found in 1957 below Building XIV.3 in a deposit dated *c.* A.D. 130–145. Verulamium Museum. Rubbing by R.P.W., 1958. Drawn by M.G. Wilson.

JRS xlviii (1958), 155 No. 43. S.S. Frere, *Verulamium Excavations* iii (1984), 278 No. 7 with fig. 115.7.

graffito on the shoulder: T P VII

t(esta) p(ondo) (librae) vii

'Vessel by weight seven (pounds)'

Seven *librae* is the equivalent of 2292.15 gm.

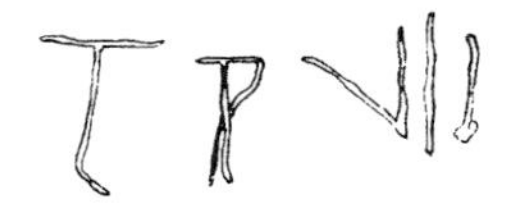

2503.20

2503.21. Number not used.

2503.22. Chesterholm (*Vindolanda*), Northumberland. Two conjoining sherds ($\frac{1}{2}$) from the shoulder of a dark grey jug found in 1973 and 1985 respectively in the bottom of a fort ditch which had been sealed by the middle of the second century. Vindolanda Museum. Drawn by S.S.F. from a rubbing by R.P.W. 1973 and a drawing from the Vindolanda Trust.

Britannia v (1974), 468 No. 47; xvii (1986), 454 Addendum (d). E., R., and A. Birley, *Vindolanda* ii (1993), 97.

graffito on the shoulder: [. . .]PVIIISPPXXXXIIIS

[t(esta)] p(ondo) (librae) viii s(emis) p(lena) p(ondo) xxxxiii s(emis)

'Vessel weighing $8\frac{1}{2}$ (pounds), (when) filled $43\frac{1}{2}$ (pounds)'

The weights are respectively 2783.3 and 14244 gm.

Compare *RIB* 2503.8, 11 and 28.

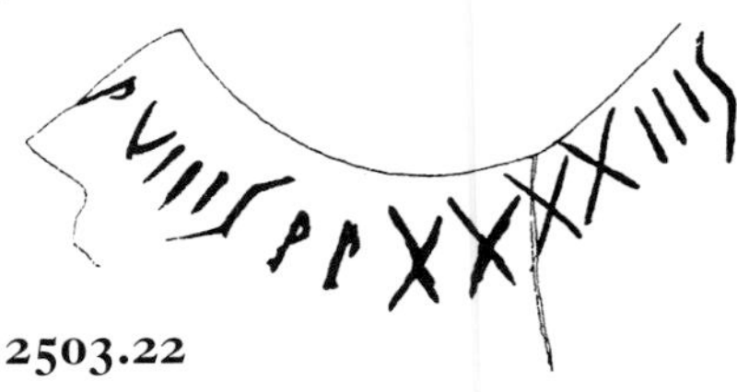

2503.22

2503.23. Richborough (*Rutupiae*), Kent. Graffito ($\frac{1}{2}$) found before 1956. In store at Dover Castle. Drawn by R.P.W.

graffito: LVIII

l(ibrae) viii

'Eight pounds'

2503.23

Eight *librae* is the equivalent of 2619.6 gm, perhaps the weight of the vessel when full.

'Fifty-eight' could also be understood, but seems less likely.

2503.24. (?) York (Eboracum). Part of a buff storage jar ($\frac{1}{2}$). Yorkshire Museum. Drawn by R.P.W., 1953.

graffito on the shoulder: [. . .]·VIIIIS–[. . .]

'Nine (*librae* and) a septunx (= seven *unciae*)'

The figures are the equivalent of 3138 gm, so perhaps indicate the weight of the vessel when full. Compare *RIB* 2503.8.

2503.24

2503.25. Cambridge (*Duroliponte*). Fragment (½) from a grey-ware storage jar with burnished surface except for a zone on the shoulder decorated with vertical combing, found in 1976 in a shaft used for an infant burial. Museum of Archaeology and Anthropology, Cambridge. Drawn by M.W.C.H.

Britannia x (1979), 347 No. 13.

graffito on the shoulder: P X
p(ondo) (librae) x
'weight ten (pounds)'

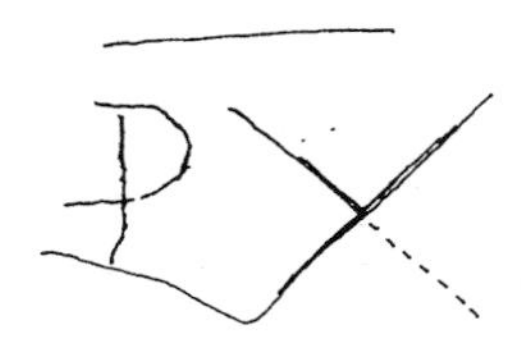

2503.25

2503.26. Leicester (*Ratae*). Fragment (½) from a jar of calcite-gritted ware datable *c.* A.D. 50–150, found in 1962 unstratified at St. Nicholas Circle. Leicester Museum. Drawn by M.W.C.H.

Britannia xx (1989), 340 No. 49.

graffito: PX[. . .] (?)
p(ondo) (librae) x[. . .]
'By weight ten (or more) pounds'

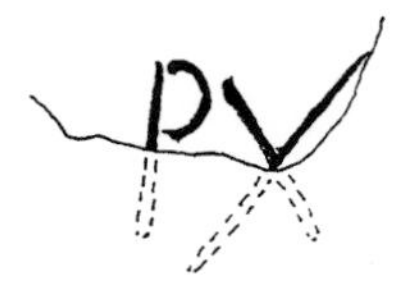

2503.26

2503.27. Colchester (*Camulodunum*), Essex. White two-handled jar used as a cinerary urn (½), height 305 mm, diameter 279 mm, present weight 2693.2 gm (which exceeds the original weight because of plaster repairs). Found before 1930. Colchester Museum. Drawn by R.P.W., 1943.

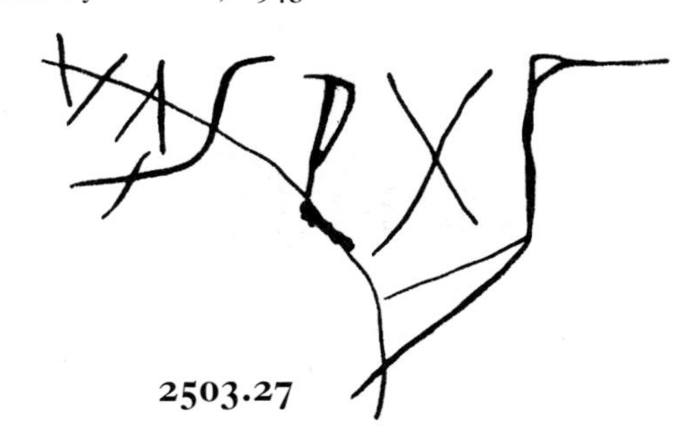

2503.27

T. May, *Cat.* (1930), 132 and 245 No. 1 with fig. 9.1.

graffito on the wall: VAS PXS[. . .]
vas p(ondo) (librae) x s(emis)
'The vessel by weight ten and a half (pounds)'

10½ *librae* is the equivalent of 3438.2 gm, so the graffito evidently indicated the weight of the vessel when full.

2503.28. Saunderton, Buckinghamshire. Part of a yellow jug (½), found in 1937 unstratified at the Roman villa. Aylesbury Museum. Drawn by R.P.W.

JRS xxix (1939), 229 No. 15 with fig. 21.1 (deficient). Ashcroft, *Records of Bucks* xiii (1939), 411 with fig. (deficient).

graffito on the wall: [. . .]ṬPX̣[. . .] | [. . .]P̣P̣XX̣[. . .]
t(esta) p(ondo) (librae) x [. . .] | [. . .] p(lena) p(ondo) xx [. . .]
'Vessel by weight ten (or more) (pounds), weight full twenty (or more) (pounds)'

Compare *CIL* xiii 10008.55; xv 4851.3. Compare also *RIB* 2503.8, 11 and 22.

2503.28

2503.29. Foulness Island, Essex. Fragment of a storage jar (½) in grey ware, found in 1976 in the filling of a ditch with late second- to mid third-century material at the former Little Shelford Farm. Present whereabouts not recorded. Drawn by M.W.C.H.

Britannia viii (1977), 438 No. 68.

graffito: PXI[. . .]
p(ondo) (librae) xi[. . .]
'Weight eleven (or more) (pounds)'

2503.29

2503.30. Silchester (*Calleva*), Hampshire. Fragment of a black jar in rough fabric (½), found before 1951. Reading Museum. Drawn by R.P.W., 1951.

graffito on the shoulder: XIIIIS
(librae) xiiii s(emis)
'Fourteen and a half (pounds)'

4748 gm.

The X is crossed by casual damage, R.P.W.

Despite the absence of *p(ondo)* the unit of measurement is assumed to be *librae*: see note to *RIB* 2503.31. But if *sextarii*, the contents would be the equivalent of 7.93 litres.

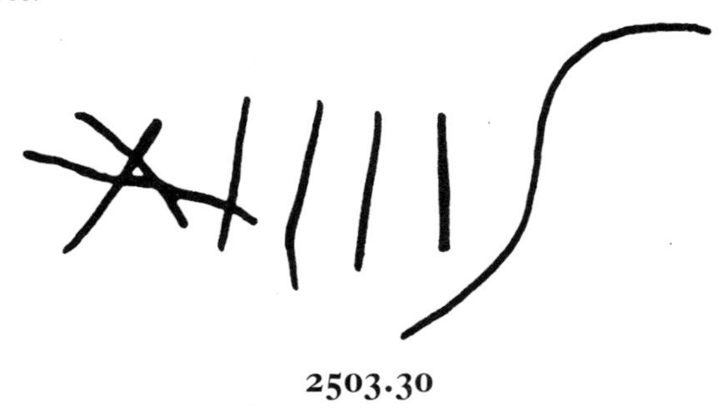

2503.30

2503.31. Southwark, south London. Fragment of a buff jug (½), found in 1974 with material of the first half of the second century in the filling of a streambed during excavations at Nos. 93–5 Borough High Street. Museum of London. Drawn by S.S.F. from rubbings by M.W.C.H.

Britannia vi (1975), 287 No. 20. J. Bird et al. (eds.), *Southwark Excavations 1972–74* ii (1978), 460 No. 19 with fig. 205.19.

graffito: [. . .]XVIS
(librae) xvi s(emis)
'Sixteen and a half (pounds)'

Probably complete.

The figure probably indicates the weight in *librae* (16½ *librae* = 5402.9 gm). Save in No. 30, this unit is attested or implied in all the other members of this group (Nos. 6–29), and the figure is a possible weight for a large empty jug (compare Nos. 25 and 29), or a small full one (compare No. 8). However, a jug being a container for liquids, the unit might possibly be the *sextarius*: 16½ *sextarii* are the equivalent of 8.79 litres, a figure closely approximating to the 8.4 litres calculated for *RIB* 2503.3, and is not an impossible capacity for a large jug: compare S.S. Frere, *Verulamium Excavations* i (1972), fig. 122 No. 809, which has a calculated capacity of *c.* 8.5 litres. 16½ *sextarii* amounted to one *modius* and half a *sextarius*; but the capacity may have been expressed in *sextarii* for simplicity.

2503.31

2503.32. Winchester (*Venta Belgarum*), Hampshire. Fragments (½) from the upper part of a large globular storage jar decorated with horizontal zones of burnishing and combed lattice-pattern, found in 1971 during the excavation of a late fourth-century workshop in Lower Brook Street. The vessel is stated to have an estimated capacity of 107.6 litres. Winchester Museum. Drawn by M.W.C.H.

Britannia viii (1977), 442 No. 88.

two graffiti on the shoulder: (a) Ạ
(b) NICẸRIVS M VIII
Nicerius m(odii) viii
'Nicerius: eight *modii*'

70 litres.

(a) Ṇ, *Britannia*. As text M.W.C.H., 1994.

(b) *Nicerius m(ensuravit) viii (urnas)*, M.W.C.H., *Britannia*. As text, S.S.F., R.S.O.T.

2503.32

An *urna* was the equivalent of 24 *sextarii* or 1½ *modii*, and eight *urnae* (192 *sextarii*) is the equivalent of 105 litres, close to the estimated capacity of the vessel. Nevertheless we prefer to read *m(odii)*, for the unit *urna* is not found elsewhere in *RIB*, whereas *modii* are common.

2503.33. Twyford, Hampshire. Fragment (½) from the wall of a grey storage jar of New Forest ware, found in 1958 during excavations at the Roman villa. Winchester Museum. Not illustrated.

Britannia viii (1977), 441 No. 84.

graffito on the wall: [. . .]MXVI
m(odii) xvi
'Sixteen *modii*'

16 *modii* is the equivalent of 140 litres. If the interpretation is correct this must have been a vessel of exceptional capacity. Even the largest Dressel 20 amphorae hold only *c.* 85 litres. However, a few exceptionally large storage jars are known, e.g. from Chelmsford (C.J. Going, *The Mansio . . .: the Roman Pottery* (1987), fig. 13 No. G 43.11, which can be calculated to hold *c.* 140 litres), Verulamium (S.S. Frere, *Verulamium Excavations* iii (1984), fig. 97 No. 2328 (*c.* 139 litres)) and Alice Holt (M.A.B. Lyne and R.S. Jefferies, *The Alice Holt/Farnham Roman Pottery Industry* (1979), 44 No. 4.45 (*c.* 123 litres))

(c) Numerals (*RIB* 2503.34–95)

2503.34. Alcester, Warwickshire. Part of a storage jar (¼), found in 1964–66 in a late fourth-century context during excavations in the extramural area. Warwickshire Museum. Drawing by courtesy of Nicholas Palmer.

S. Cracknell and C. Mahany (eds.), *Roman Alcester* i: *The Southern Extramural Area* (1994), fig. 57.5.

graffito inside the rim: I
'One'

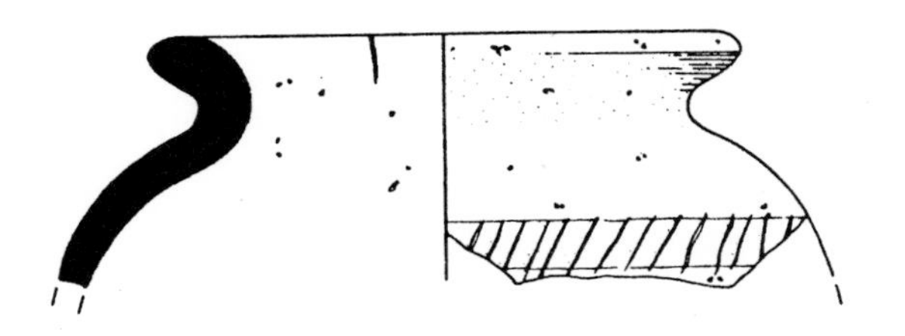

2503.34

2503.35. Ibid. Part of a storage jar (¼), found as *RIB* 2503.34. Drawing by courtesy of Nicholas Palmer.

S. Cracknell and C. Mahany, op.cit. fig. 57.8.

graffito on the rim: I
'One'

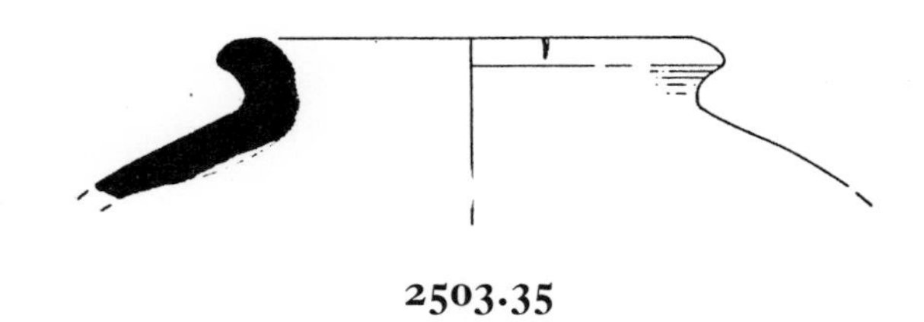

2503.35

2503.36. Ibid. Part of a storage jar (¼), found in 1964–66 during excavations in the extramural area. Warwickshire Museum. Drawing by courtesy of Nicholas Palmer.

S. Cracknell and C. Mahany, op. cit. fig. 58.32.

graffito on the rim: II
'Two'

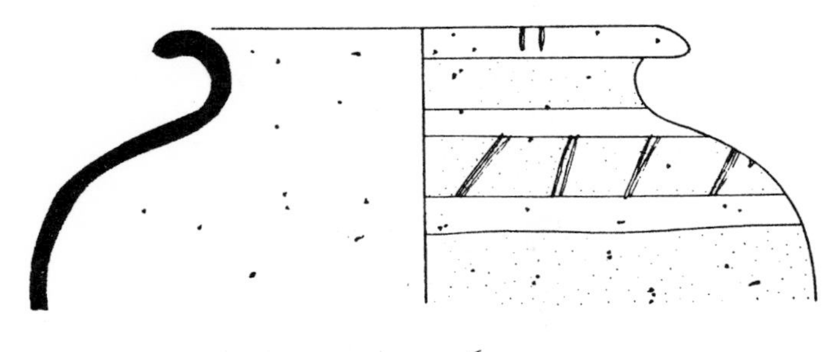

2503.36

2503.37. Ibid. Part of a large storage jar (¼) found as *RIB* 2503.36. Warwickshire Museum. Drawing by courtesy of Nicholas Palmer.

S. Cracknell and C. Mahany, op. cit., fig. 59.38.

graffito on the rim: II
'Two'

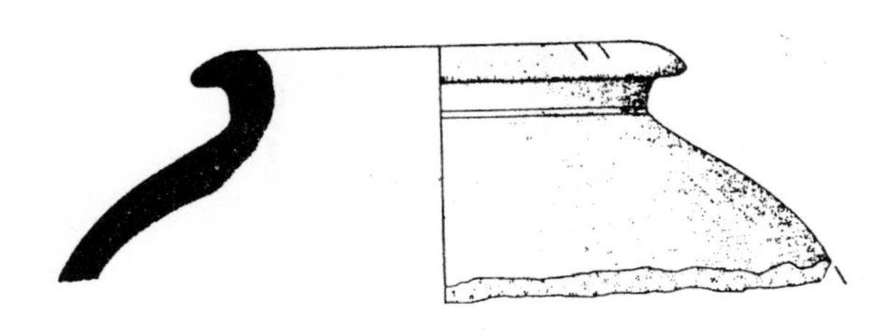

2503.37

2503.38. Canterbury (*Durovernum*), Kent. Fragment ($\frac{1}{2}$) from the upper part of a storage jar in grey grog-tempered fabric with a brown external surface burnished on the shoulder, found in 1980 in a late second- or third-century context at the Marlowe IV site. Canterbury Museum. Drawn by M.W.C.H.

Britannia xiii (1982), 415 No. 48.

graffito on the shoulder: II

2503.38

2503.39. Beckfoot (? *Bibra*), Cumbria [Cumberland]. Cinerary urn ($\frac{1}{4}$), found in 1908 in the cemetery south of the fort. Tullie House Museum, Carlisle. Drawn by Ian Caruana.

Britannia xix (1988), 495 No. 25.

graffito: II
'Two'

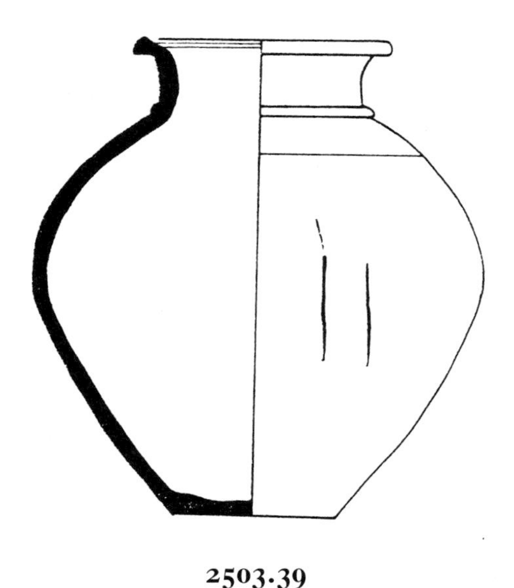

2503.39

2503.40. Alcester, Warwickshire. Part of a storage jar ($\frac{1}{4}$), found in 1964–66 in an early to mid fourth-century context during excavations in the extra-mural area. Warwickshire Museum. Drawing by courtesy of Nicholas Palmer.

S. Cracknell and C. Mahany (eds.), *Roman Alcester* i: *The Southern Extramural Area* (1994), fig. 57.4.

graffito inside the rim: $\overline{\text{II}}$
'Two'

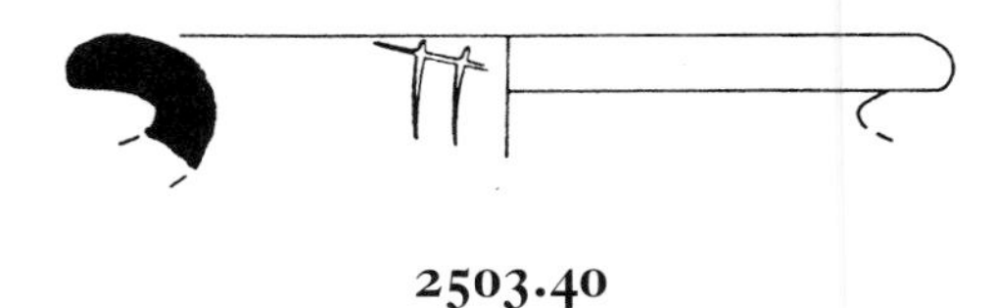

2503.40

2503.41. Dorchester (*Durnovaria*), Dorset. Complete flanged bowl ($\frac{1}{2}$), in Black-burnished ware, found in 1984 during excavations in Greyhound Yard. Dorchester Museum. Not illustrated.

Britannia xx (1989), 336 No. 22. P.J. Woodward et al., *Excavations at Greyhound Yard, Dorchester 1981–4* (1993), 284 No. 7.

graffito on the upper face of the base: III
'Three'

CII or LII could also be read.

2503.42. Castleford (*Lagentium*), West Yorkshire. Part of the rim ($\frac{1}{2}$) of a Black-burnished bowl, found in 1985. West Yorkshire Archaeological Service. Not illustrated.

Britannia xviii (1987), 377 No. 56.

graffito on the lip: III
'Three'

2503.43. Bierton, Buckinghamshire. Part of the rim ($\frac{1}{2}$) of a grey-ware jar, found in 1964 during contractors' work in the Vicarage garden, south-east of the site of the Roman villa. In private possession. Drawn by M.W.C.H.

Britannia xiv (1983), 343 No. 15.

graffito on the outer lip of the rim: III
'Three'

2503.43

2503.44. Canterbury (*Durovernum*), Kent. Part of a storage jar ($\frac{1}{2}$) in grog-tempered ware, found in 1980 at the Marlowe site, in the upper filling of an early Roman ditch dated *c.* A.D. 40–70. Canterbury Museum. Drawn by M.W.C.H.

Britannia xiii (1982), 415 No. 50.

graffito on the neck: III
'Three'

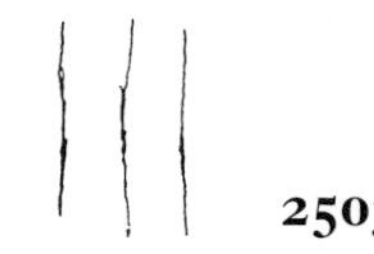

2503.44

2503.45. Ibid. Part of a Black-burnished dish ($\frac{1}{2}$), found in 1980 in a residual context at the Marlowe IV site. Canterbury Museum. Drawn by M.W.C.H.

Britannia xiii (1982), 415 No. 49.

graffito on the upper surface of the flat rim: III
'Three'

2503.45

2503.46. Colchester (*Camulodunum*), Essex. Beaker ($\frac{1}{2}$) of polished fine grey ware, found in 1927–29 at the 'Mithraeum' in Holly Trees Meadow (Insula 15). Colchester Museum. Reproduced from Hull.

M.R. Hull, *Roman Colchester* (1958), 144 No. 142 with fig. 71.142.

two graffiti, (a) on the rim: III
'Three'
(b) below the carination: +++

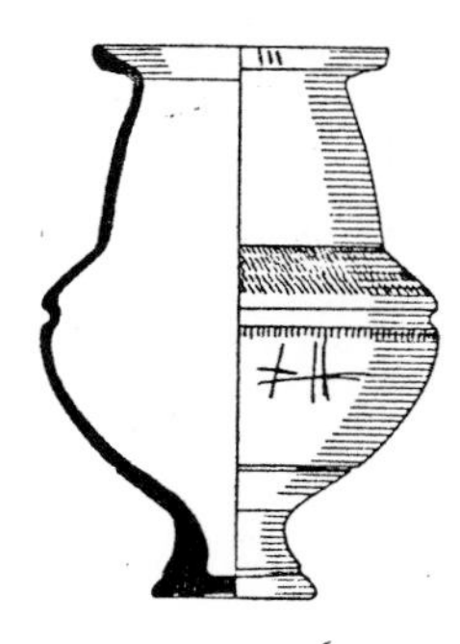

2503.46

2503.47. Alcester, Warwickshire. Part of a storage jar ($\frac{1}{4}$), found in 1964–66 in an early to mid fourth-century context during excavations in the extramural area. Warwickshire Museum. Drawing by courtesy of Nicholas Palmer.

S. Cracknell and C. Mahany (eds.), *Roman Alcester* i: *The Southern Extramural Area* (1994), fig. 57.7.

graffito on the rim: $\overline{\text{III}}$
'Three'

The third digit is shorter than the others.

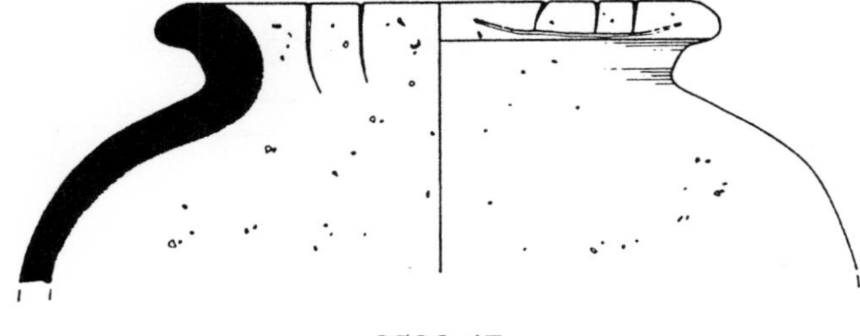

2503.47

2503.48. Ibid. Part of a storage jar, found as *RIB* 2503.47. Drawing by courtesy of Nicholas Palmer.

S. Cracknell and C. Mahany, op. cit., fig. 57.12.
graffito on the shoulder: $\underset{\cdots}{\overline{\text{III}}}$

Alternatively this could be E inscribed vertically or merely a square with a central vertical line.

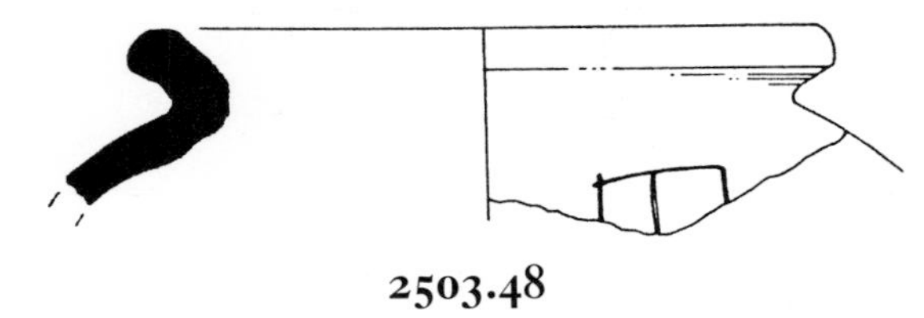

2503.48

2503.49. Ibid. Part of a grey storage jar ($\frac{1}{2}$), burnished on rim and shoulder, found in 1964–66 in an early to mid fourth-century context during excavations in the extramural area. Warwickshire Museum. Drawing by courtesy of Nicholas Palmer.

S. Cracknell and C. Mahany, op. cit., fig. 57.1.

graffito on the rim: $\overline{\underline{\text{III}}}$
'Three'

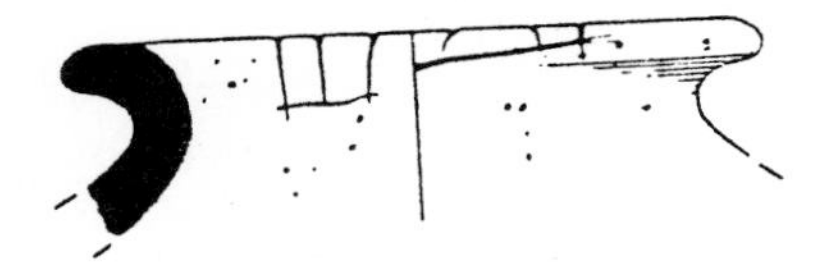

2503.49

2503.50. Uley, Gloucestershire. Large grey-ware storage jar ($\frac{1}{4}$), found in 1977–79 during excavation of a shrine on West Hill. British Museum. Reproduced from Woodward and Leach (copyright, English Heritage).

A. Woodward and P. Leach, *The Uley Shrines* (1993), 224 No. 73 with fig. 165.73.

graffito on the rim: III
'Three'

2503.50

2503.51. Wallsend (*Segedunum*), Tyne & Wear [Northumberland]. Part of the rim ($\frac{1}{2}$) of a grey-ware jar, found in 1975–84 in the courtyard surface of the *valetudinarium* of the fort. Wallsend Museum. Not illustrated.

Britannia xix (1988), 504 No. 90.

graffito on the rim: III
'Three'

2503.52. Latimer, Buckinghamshire. Base of a jar ($\frac{1}{2}$), found in 1964–71 during excavations at the Roman villa. Latimer Villa Museum. Reproduced from Branigan.

K. Branigan, *Latimer* (1971), 136 No. 434 with fig. 35.434.

graffito on the base: $\overline{\text{III}}$
'Three'

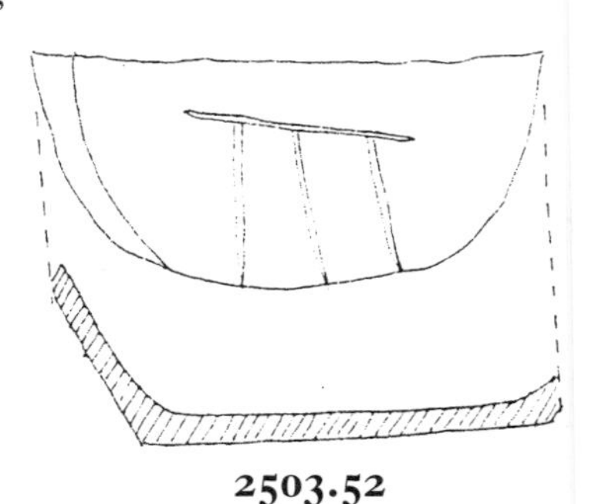

2503.52

For another example of III see No. 103, and for III with an oblique cross-stroke see *RIB* 2502.54, 2503.77.

2503.53. Latimer, Buckinghamshire. Rim of a reddish jar ($\frac{1}{2}$), found in 1968 in a fifth-century context at the Roman villa. Latimer Villa Museum. Reproduced from Branigan.

Britannia i (1970), 315 No. 52. K. Branigan, *Latimer* (1971), 136 No. 435 with fig. 35.435.

graffito on the inner face of the rim: IIII
'Four'

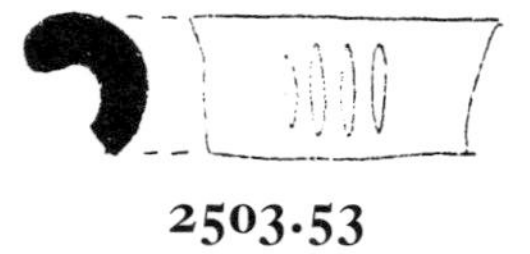

2503.53

2503.54. Malton (*Derventio*), North Yorkshire. Part of the base ($\frac{1}{2}$) of a creamy-buff jug, found in 1969 in build-up over Antonine levels in the *vicus* of the fort. Malton Museum. Drawn by R.S.O.T.

Britannia xix (1988), 504 No. 98.

graffito beneath the base: IV
'Four'

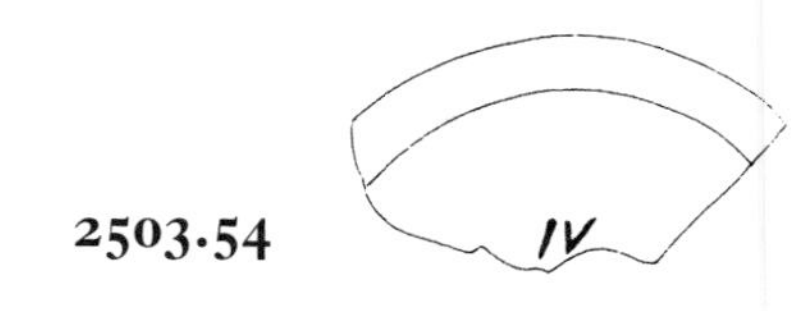

2503.54

2503.55. Wallsend (*Segedunum*), Tyne and Wear [Northumberland]. Part of the rim (½) of a Black-burnished 2 pot, found in 1975–84 unstratified. Wallsend Museum. Drawn by Miriam Daniels.

Britannia xix (1988), 504 No. 91.

graffito on the rim: [. . .?]IV
'Four'

Probably a complete numeral.

2503.55

2503.56. Canterbury (*Durovernum*), Kent. Part (½) of a storage jar in coarse grog-tempered fabric, found in 1980 in a late first-century pit at the Marlowe III site. Canterbury Museum. Drawn by M.W.C.H.

Britannia xiii (1982), 415 No. 40.

graffito on the neck: ÎV II *or* (*inverted*) ṆṾ

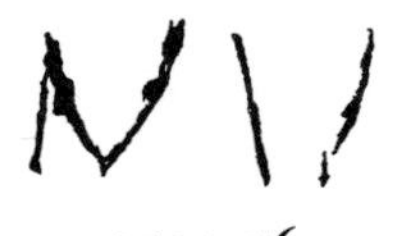

2503.56

2503.57. Alcester, Warwickshire. Part of a storage jar (¼), found in 1964–66 during excavations in the extramural area. Warwickshire Museum. Drawing by courtesy of Nicholas Palmer.

S. Cracknell and C. Mahany (eds.), *Roman Alcester* i: *The Southern Extramural Area* (1994), fig. 57.9.

graffito on the rim: VI
'Six'

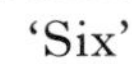

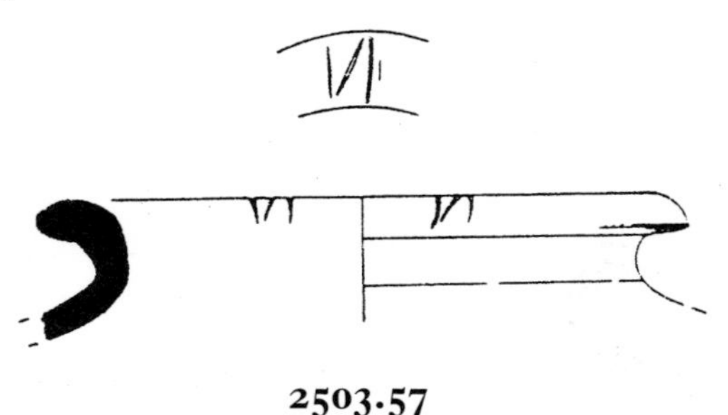

2503.57

2503.58. Braughing, Hertfordshire. Small jar (¼) in grey ware, found at an unrecorded date at the Roman cemetery at Fordstreet. Present whereabouts unrecorded. Reproduced from Partridge.

Partridge, *Herts. Arch.* v (1977), 102 No. 19 with fig. 42.19.

graffito on the inside of the rim: VI

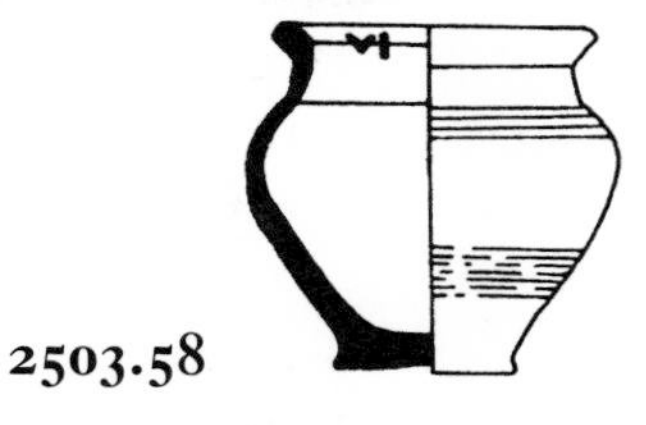

2503.58

For [. . .]. .VI IIII see No. 296.
For VI beside III (erased) see No. 323.

2503.59. Usk (*Burrium*), Gwent [Monmouthshire]. Crudely-modelled open lamp(?) (½), in badly-fired greenish fabric, found in 1970 unstratified during excavations at the pre-Flavian fortress. National Museum, Cardiff. Reproduced from Hassall.

Britannia viii (1977), 446 No. 110. Hassall in G.C. Boon and M. Hassall, *Usk* (1982), 58 No. 45 with fig. 5.45.

graffito beneath the base: VII
'Seven'

VIÇ, Hassall loc. cit. As text, M.W.C.H., 1994.

2503.59

2503.60. Lyne (? *Carbantoritum*) Borders Region [Peebleshire]. Graffito (½) found before 1956. National Museums of Scotland, Queen Street, Edinburgh. Drawn by R.P.W.

graffito: IIV
vii (retrograde)
'Seven'

2503.60

2503.61. Canterbury (*Durovernum*), Kent. Fragment (½) of fine grey ware, found in 1980 in the filling of a late fourth-century posthole at the Marlowe III site. Canterbury Museum. Drawn by M.W.C.H.

Britannia xiii (1982), 415 No. 41.

graffito: Ṿ I.[. . .] or Ẋ I.[. . .]

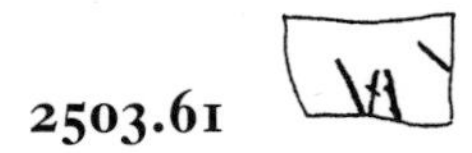

2503.61

2503.62. Silchester (*Calleva*), Hampshire. Part of a second-century black dish (½) with lattice decoration, found before 1900. Reading Museum. Drawn by R.P.W.

graffito on the rim: VII[. . .]
'Seven (or more)'

2503.62

2503.63. Wallsend (*Segedunum*), Tyne and Wear [Northumberland]. Part of the rim (½) of a Black-burnished 2 bowl, found in 1975–84 unstratified. Wallsend Museum. Drawing not available.

Britannia xix (1988), 504 No. 92.

graffito on the rim: IIX
'Eight'

2503.64 Wall (*Letocetum*), Staffordshire. Part of a storage jar (½), found before 1951. Wall Museum. Drawn by R.P.W., 1951.

graffito on the wall: IX VII
'Nine' 'Seven'

2503.64

2503.65. St. Albans (*Verulamium*), Hertfordshire. Part of the flattened everted rim of a large buff storage jar (scale uncertain), found before 1942. Verulamium Museum. Drawn by S.S.F. from a sketch by R.P.W., 1954.

graffito on the flattened rim: [. . .]IX IIIV
'Nine, eight (*retrograde*)'

2503.65

2503.66. Dicket Mead, Welwyn, Hertfordshire. Base in orange-buff ware with a grey core (⅓), found in 1969–70 in Building I during excavations at the Roman villa. Welwyn Archaeological Society. Reproduced from Rook.

Rook, *Herts. Arch.* ix (1983–6), 156 No. 8 with fig. 66.8.

graffito beneath the base: IX *or* XI
'Nine' *or* 'Eleven'

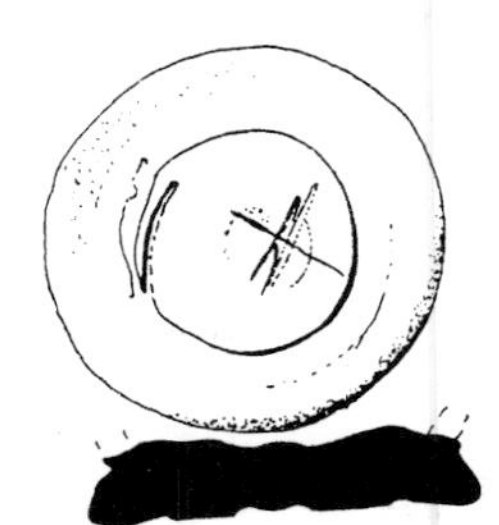

2503.66

For another example of IX or XI see No. 215.

2503.67. Wallsend (*Segedunum*), Tyne and Wear [Northumberland]. Fragment of a large reddish pot (½), found in 1975–84 unstratified. Wallsend Museum. Drawing not available.

Britannia xix (1988), 504 No. 93.

graffito on the wall: X
'Ten'

Perhaps only a mark of identification.

2503.68. Alcester, Warwickshire. Part of a storage jar (¼), found in 1964–66 during excavations in the extramural area. Warwickshire Museum. Drawing by courtesy of Nicholas Palmer.

S. Cracknell and C. Mahany (eds.), *Roman Alcester* i: *The Southern Extramural Area* (1994), fig. 58.30.

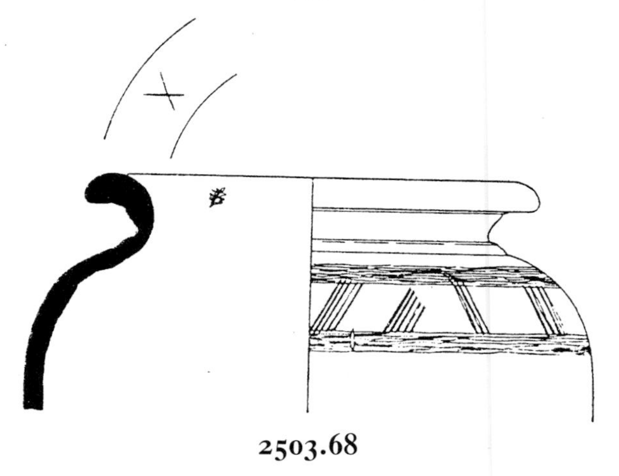

2503.68

two graffiti, (a) on the rim: X
'Ten'
(b) inside the rim: incised leaf-motif

(a) Perhaps only a mark of identification.

2503.69. Ibid. Part of a storage jar ($\frac{1}{2}$), found in a late fourth-century context during excavations in the extramural area. Warwickshire Museum. Drawing by courtesy of Nicholas Palmer.

S. Cracknell and C. Mahany, op. cit., fig. 57.13.

graffito on the wall: X̣ within a square (?).

This is probably an owner's mark rather than a numeral. There is no reason to suspect it of being a Christian symbol.

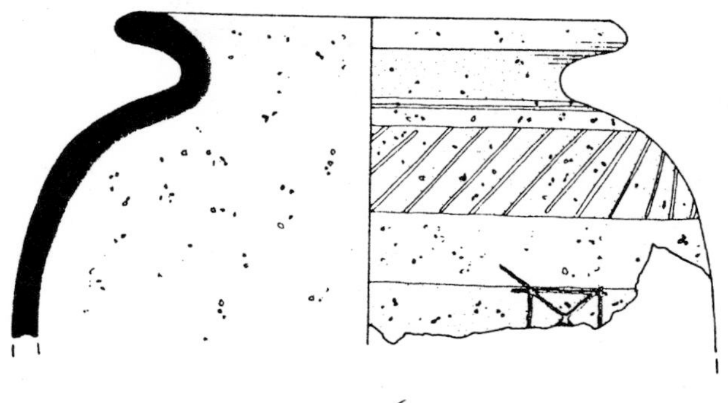

2503.69

2503.70. Skeleton Green, Hertfordshire. Sherd from a coarse-ware storage jar ($\frac{1}{2}$), found in 1972 on the pre- or early Roman land-surface beneath the first-century Roman settlement. Hertford Museum. Drawn by M.W.C.H.

Britannia x (1979), 350 No. 30.

graffito on the shoulder: X

Perhaps only a mark of identification.

2503.70

2503.71. Number not used.

2503.72. Chester (*Deva*). Part of a dark grey dish ($\frac{1}{2}$) with lattice decoration, found in 1935 during excavations in the Deanery Field. Grosvenor Museum. Drawn by R.P.W., 1970.

JRS xxvi (1936), 267 No. 9 c. Newstead and Droop, *Liv. Ann.* xxiii (1936), 35 No. 3.

graffito on the rim: XI
'Eleven'

2503.72 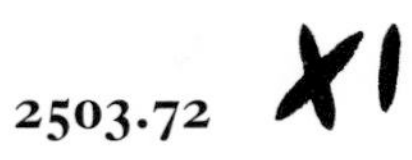

2503.73. Wallsend (*Segedumum*), Tyne and Wear [Northumberland]. Fragment of Black-burnished 2 ware ($\frac{1}{2}$), found in 1975–84 during excavations at the fort. Wallsend Museum. Drawn by Miriam Daniels.

graffito: XII
'Twelve'

2503.73 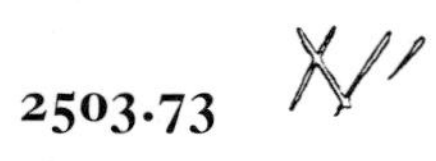

2503.74. Old Kilpatrick, Strathclyde [Dunbartonshire]. Sherd of coarse reddish ware ($\frac{1}{2}$), found in 1923–24 during excavations at the Antonine Wall fort. Hunterian Museum, Glasgow. Reproduced from Miller.

S.N. Miller, *The Roman Fort at Old Kilpatrick* (1928), 50 No. 7 with pl. XVII.7.

graffito below a groove on the wall: [. . .]X̣II

[. . .]VII could also be read. As text, R.P.W.

2503.74

2503.75. Latimer, Buckinghamshire. Part of a grey bowl ($\frac{1}{2}$), found in 1968 in a late fourth- or early fifth-century context during excavations at the Roman villa. Latimer Villa Museum. Reproduced from Branigan.

Britannia i (1970), 315 No. 53. K. Branigan, *Latimer* (1971), 136 No. 436 with fig. 35.436.

graffito on the wall: [. . .]X̣II
'Twelve (or more)'

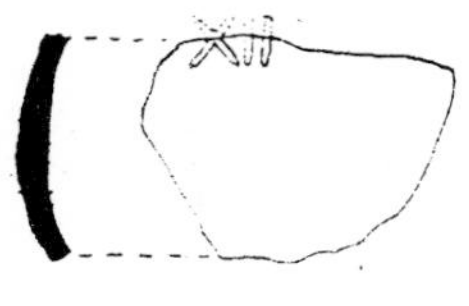

2503.75

2503.76. Wattisfield, Suffolk. Grey jar (½), found in 1935 during excavation of pottery kiln No. 7 at Foxledge Common. Ipswich Museum. Drawn by R.P.W.

JRS xlii (1952), 109 No. 38a. Moore, *P. Suffolk IA* xxii (1934–6), 187 with fig. 6.

graffito on the base: XIII
'Thirteen'

The last two digits are bent and have led to the graffito being read inverted as CCIX. R.P.W.

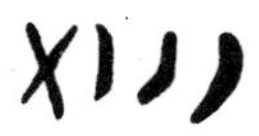

2503.76

2503.77. Ibid. Grey Jar (½), found in 1935 during excavation of pottery kiln No. 7 at Foxledge Common. Ipswich Museum. Drawn by R.P.W., 1951.

JRS xlii (1952), 109 No. 38 b. Moore, *P. Suffolk IA* xxli (1934–6), 187 with fig. 6.

two graffiti, (a) beneath the base: XIII
(b) at the bottom of the wall on the outer rim of the base: III (with cross-stroke) I

(a) Because of the curvature of the digits the graffito has been read inverted as CCCX, R.P.W.

(b) Compare *RIB* 2502.54.

2503.77

2503.78. London (*Londinium*). Sherd from a hand-made jar or storage vessel (½), found in 1974 during excavations at Billingsgate Buildings. Museum of London. Reproduced from Jones.

Britannia ix (1978), 480 No. 56. Hassall in D.M. Jones, *Excavations at Billingsgate Buildings . . . 1974* (1980), 136 No. 710 with fig. 79.710.

graffito on the wall: [. . .]Ḥ XIIII
'. . . fourteen'

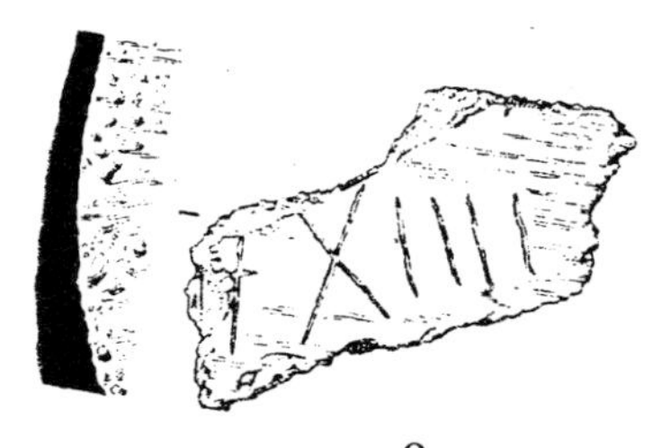

2503.78

2503.79. Leicester (*Ratae*). Part of a grey jar (scale uncertain), found in 1936–39 during the Jewry Wall excavations. Leicester Museum. Drawn by S.S.F. from a sketch by R.P.W., 1951.

graffito on the shoulder: [. . .]XIIII
'Fourteen (or more)'

2503.79

2503.80. Canterbury (*Durovernum*). Base of a small jar (½) in smooth grey ware, found in 1978 in a second-century context during excavations at No. 16 Watling Street. Canterbury Museum. Drawn by M.W.C.H.

Britannia xi (1980), 413 No. 51.

graffito below the base: X | V
Perhaps 'Fifteen'

2503.80

For examples of XVI see *RIB* 2503.475, 493.

2503.81. Mucking, Essex. Cordoned grey-ware jar (½), found in 1978 in a grave-pit dug for a stone coffin containing a gypsum burial in Cemetery IV. Mucking Excavation Committee. Drawn by M.W.C.H.

Britannia x (1979), 349 No. 22.

graffito on the shoulder: IIIVX
'Eighteen' cut retrograde

2503.81

2503.82. Wallsend (*Segedunum*), Tyne and Wear [Northumberland]. Part of the rim (½) of a Black-burnished 2 bowl, found in 1975–84 unstratified. Wallsend Museum. Drawn by Miriam Daniels.

Britannia xix (1988), 504 No. 94.

graffito on the rim: XX
'Twenty'

2503.82

2503.83. Silchester (*Calleva*), Hampshire. Small beaker in buff ware (½), height 70 mm, diameter 51 mm, found in or before 1909 without details of provenance. Reading Museum. Drawn by R.P.W., 1953.

JRS xliv (1954), 111 No. 50.

graffito on the shoulder: XX
'Twenty'

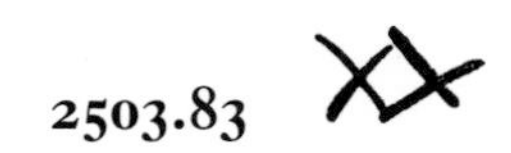
2503.83

2503.84. Beckfoot (? *Bibra*), Cumbria [Cumberland]. Cinerary urn (¼ and ½), found in 1973 in the cemetery south of the fort. Tullie House Museum, Carlisle. Drawn by Ian Caruana.

Britannia xix (1988), 495 No. 26.

graffito: XX
'Twenty'

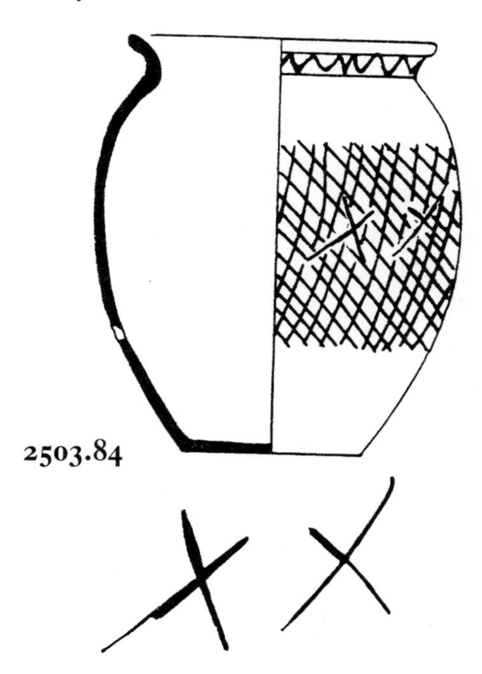
2503.84

2503.85. York (*Eboracum*). Part of the rim (½) of a large dark grey narrow-mouthed jar, found in 1971 immediately outside the west end of the Minster, to the north-west of the *principia*. York Minster. Drawn by S.S.F. from rubbings and a squeeze by R.P.W., 1974.

Britannia vi (1975), 290 No. 36.

graffiti by different hands on the rim: (a) +
(b) XX

2503.85

2503.86. Winchester (*Venta Belgarum*), Hampshire. Base of a small grey-ware beaker or jar (½) with pedestal foot, found in 1970 in a residual context at Cathedral Green. Winchester Museum. Drawn by M.W.C.H.

Britannia xx (1989), 338 No. 35.

graffito below the base: X͡X or (less probably) H

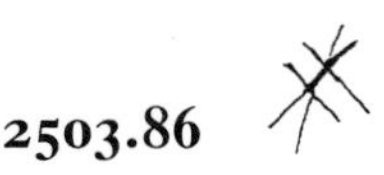
2503.86

2503.87. Ribchester (*Bremetennacum*), Lancashire. Sherds (½) from a jug in hard white fabric, found in 1977 in the top filling of a Hadrianic drainage channel during excavations in the *vicus*. Ribchester Museum. Traced by M.W.C.H. from a drawing by Paul Gibbons.

Britannia xii (1981), 388 No. 57.

two graffiti, (a) [. . .]XX[. . .]
(b) [. . .]C[. . .] *or* [. . .]O[. . .]

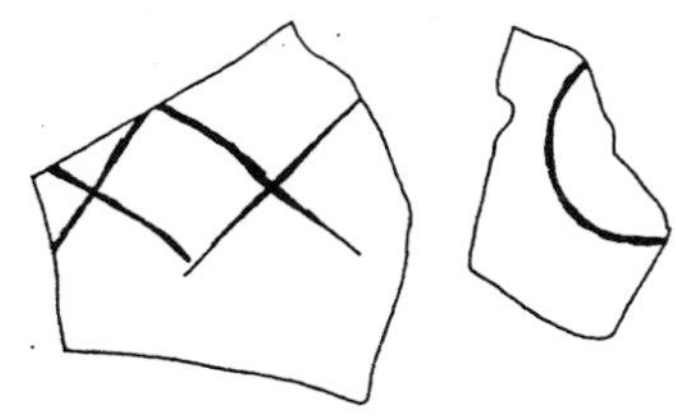
2503.87

2503.88. Ibid. Part of a Black-burnished 1 dish (½) with flat rim, found in 1977 in a Hadrianic or early Antonine context in the *vicus*. Ribchester Museum. Traced by M.W.C.H. from a drawing by Paul Gibbons.

Britannia xii (1981), 388 No. 58.

graffito: [. . .]X̣XI
'Twenty-one (or more)'

Alternatively *[M]Ạ XI(MI)* could be read, M.W.C.H., 1994.

2503.88

2503.89. Alcester, Warwickshire. Part of a storage jar ($\frac{1}{4}$), found in 1964–66 during excavations in the extramural area. Warwickshire Museum. Drawing by courtesy of Nicholas Palmer.

S. Cracknell and C. Mahany (eds.), *Roman Alcester* i: *The Southern Extramural Area* (1994), fig. 58.31.

graffito on the rim: XXX
'Thirty'

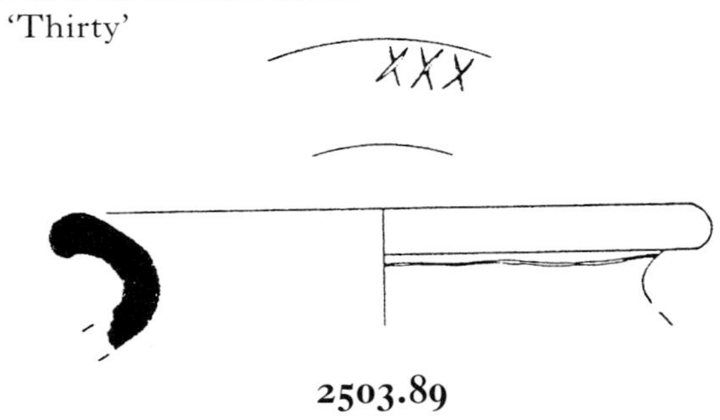

2503.89

2503.90. Canterbury (*Durovernum*), Kent. Part of a small grey-ware jar ($\frac{1}{2}$) with a zone of burnishing on the shoulder, found in 1978 in a late second- to late third-century context at No. 16 Watling Street. Canterbury Museum. Drawn by M.W.C.H.

Britannia xiii (1982), 414 No. 37.

graffito on the upper side of the everted rim:
XX X[. . .]

The letters are so spaced as to suggest that originally there were eight paired letters arranged symmetrically around the pot; if so perhaps ornamental rather than epigraphical.

2503.90

2503.91. Alcester, Warwickshire. Part of a storage jar ($\frac{1}{4}$), found in 1964–66 in a late fourth-century context during excavations in the extramural area. Warwickshire Museum. Drawing by courtesy of Nicholas Palmer.

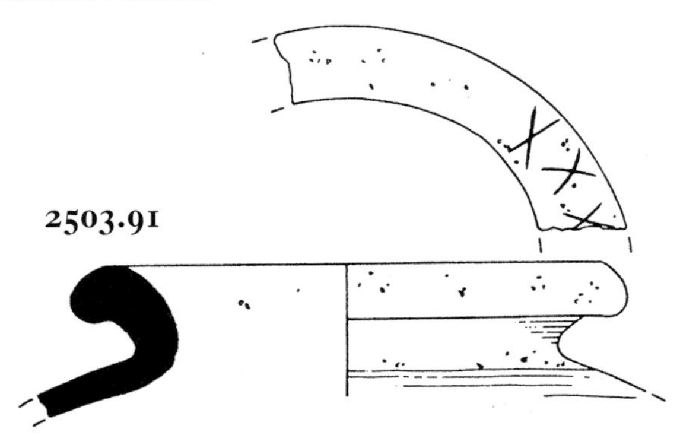

2503.91

S. Cracknell and C. Mahany (eds.), *Roman Alcester* i: *The Southern Extramural Area* (1994), fig. 57.6.

graffito on the rim: XXX[. . .]
'Thirty (or more)'

2503.92. Corbridge (? *Coria*), Northumberland. Part of a third-century grey jar ($\frac{1}{2}$), found before 1940. Corbridge Museum. Drawn by S.S.F. from a contact-drawing by R.P.W., 1940.

graffito on the rim: [. . .]XXX LXVIII[. . .]
'Thirty (?) Sixty-eight *or* sixty-nine'

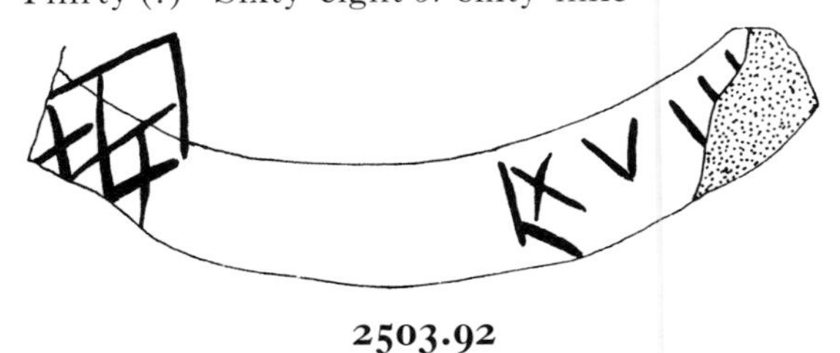

2503.92

2503.93. Silchester (*Calleva*), Hampshire. Buff butt-beaker of Claudian or earlier date ($\frac{1}{2}$), found in 1907 at the bottom of Pit 9 in Insula XXXV. Reading Museum. Drawn by G.C. Boon, 1963.

Hope, *Arch.* lxi (1908), 210 with fig. 7. T. May, *Silchester* (1916), 185 No. 3 with pl. LXXVI.3, without illustration of the graffito, and in error printing 'chi, theta alpha'. Boon, *Arch.* cii (1970), 34 note 6.

graffito on the base in Greek letters: ΧΦΑ

Possibly a numeral, '691'. Compare *RIB* 2502.62, 2503.1.

2503.93

2503.94. Skeleton Green, Hertfordshire. Part of a wide-mouthed urn ($\frac{1}{2}$), found in 1972 during excavation of a cemetery. Hertford Museum. Reproduced from Partridge.

Hassall in C. Partridge, *Skeleton Green* (1981), 273 No. 2 with fig. 108.2.

graffito inside the rim: illegible

Perhaps an attempt to reproduce random Roman numerals, M.W.C.H.

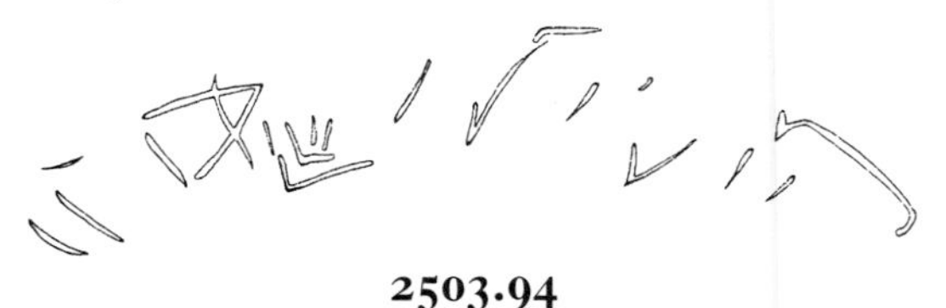

2503.94

2503.95. York (*Eboracum*). Grey jar (½ and ¼), found in 1861 with other pottery vessels and a glass bottle containing a cremation, all associated with the tombstone of Corellia Optata (*RIB* 684). Yorkshire Museum. Drawn by R.P.W., 1957, and the vessel reproduced from RCHM.

Handbook to the Antiquities . . . in the Museum of the Yorkshire Philosophical Society (ed. 8 by J. Kenrick and J. Raine, 1891), 119. RCHM, *York* i (1962), 96 with fig. 73.H142.

graffiti (inverted) on the wall:
NV IIIΛIII (V III *deleted*) | RL | XX. .IV.IIII . . |
VBXIĪĪ (*or* ITI) | X | ÇIXΛ
I AXXQꟼPXXBIS | XXṢ

The graffiti presumably refer to former contents, and the vessel was re-used in the burial, RCHM.

The transcript is very questionable. The graffito looks like a mixture of numerals and magical 'characters', R.S.O.T.

2503.95

(d) Exhortations, slogans and aphorisms
(*RIB* 2503.96–109)

2503.96. Wallsend (*Segedunum*), Tyne and Wear [Northumberland]. Two conjoining fragments (½) from a coarse grey-ware pot, found in 1983 in the filling of a drain south-east of the re-routed *via principalis* in the fort. Wallsend Museum. Drawing not available.

Britannia xv (1984), 348 No. 59.

graffito: ΛMΛ N

Compare *RIB* 2419.73, 2421.1, 2422.2 and 48 for *ama*, 'love (me?)'; but this seems rather unlikely here.

2503.97. Benwell (*Condercum*), Tyne and Wear [Northumberland]. Part of a buff pot (½), found in 1926 during excavations at the fort. Museum of Antiquities, Newcastle upon Tyne. Drawn by R.P.W., 1946.

Petch, *Arch. Ael.*[4] iv (1927), 185 with fig. 12.1. *PSAN*[4] iii (1927), 11.

graffito: [. . .]ΛVITΛB[. . .]
Perhaps *[Ars long]a vita b[revis]*, R.P.W.
'Art is long, life short'

For the proverb see Hippocrates, *Aphorismoi* 1; Seneca, *de brevitate vitae* 1.1.

2503.97

2503.98. Chedworth, Gloucestershire. Sherd from a vessel in red ware (½), found in 1946 with other Roman objects on the crest of a hill nearly 1 mile slightly west of south from the Roman villa. In 1948 on loan to the Corinium Museum, Cirencester. Drawn by R.P.W., 1947.

JRS xxxvii (1947), 182 No. 18 (wrongly giving the find spot as Ablington; xxxviii (1948), 104 No. 29.

graffito on the wall: VITA.[. . .]

The I intersects V but was cut separately. Perhaps [. . .] *vita[brevis . . .?]*, each word written at right-angles to the next; compare *RIB* 2503.97, R.P.W.

2503.98

2503.99. Neatham, Hampshire. Part of the base (½) of a grey-ware vessel, found in 1978–9 unstratified on a building site. The vessel can be attributed to the Alice Holt potteries and to a late third- to fourth-century date. In private possession. Drawn by Dr. M. Millett from a rubbing by M. Lyne.

Britannia xii (1981), 384 No. 37 with fig. 26.

graffito beneath the base: BO[. . .] | NORP
Perhaps for *bo|no r(ei) p(ublicae nato)*
'Born for the good of the state'

If interpreted correctly, the text may have been copied from a late Roman milestone, since it is a slogan that occurs not infrequently on them. M.W.C.H.

2503.99

2503.100. London (*Londinium*). Part of a grey dish (½), of Trajanic-Hadrianic date, found at an unrecorded date and site in London and rediscovered in 1969 among items stored in the Guildhall Museum. It carries two figures which are perhaps intended as a satire against gluttony and lust. On the left is part of the figure of a goose facing right, confronted by a dwarf-sized man in a knee-length tunic, whose nose has been elongated into a phallus; he holds what may be an egg in his right hand. Museum of London. Rubbings by R.P.W., 1970. Drawn by Nicholas Griffiths, 1993.

Britannia ii (1971), 299 No. 62. Turnbull, *Bulletin of the [London] Institute of Archaeology* xv (1978), 200–1 with fig. 1.

graffito on the wall: CAVII.[. . .]
Perhaps *Cave [malum]*
'Look out for trouble'

CAVII M[. . .], R.P.W.

For *cave malum* as a warning addressed to a thief or *cacator* see *CIL* iv 3782, 5438, 6253 and *RIB* 2501.21.

In the Celtic area the goose provides the means for gluttony (compare Pliny, *NH* x 52, 56). For instances of a man with a nose caricatured as a phallus see *CIL* iv 7248; M. della Corte, *Notizie degli Scavi* 1946, 90 Nos. 44, 45; J.P. Cèbe, *La Caricature et la parodie dans le monde romain . . .* (1966), 375; P. Castrén & H. Lilius, *Graffiti del Palatino* ii (1970), 128 No. 36, and Wheeler, *Arch.* lxxviii (1928), 188 with pl. XXXIII.4. The last, from a deposit at the Caerleon amphitheatre dated *c.* A.D. 130–160, depicts a crane or stork confronting a human figure with a nose in the form of a phallus, and holding a conical basket in his right hand.

Although pygmies fighting cranes are known in classical mythology (Homer, *Iliad* iii 7, Juvenal xiii 167), the goose is not so found. Turnbull (loc. cit.) suggests that the London and Caerleon graffiti represent some legend well-known at the time which has not survived in any other form.

R.P.W. noted the figure of a pig facing right between the goose and man, partly merged with both, but this appears to be mistaken (Turnbull). Nicholas Griffiths reports that R.P.W. had joined certain lines to create the pig, but that the surface is well-preserved, showing no lines at the appropriate points.

2503.100

2503.101. Ibid. Part of a black cordoned jar (½), found in 1949 unstratified in Eastcheap. Museum of London. Drawn by R.P.W., 1951.

JRS xli (1951), 144 No. 23.

cursive graffito on the shoulder:
CAVII MARTIAL[. . .]
apparently *cave Martial[em]*
'Beware of Martialis!'

The slogan is obscure. Perhaps *Gavii Martial[is]* is the true reading, or C was written for G: '(Property) of Gavius Martialis'. Both nomen and cognomen are common, R.S.O.T.

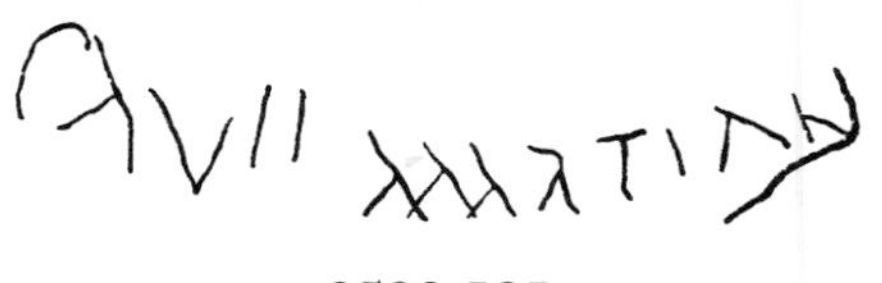

2503.101

2503.102. Chester (*Deva*). Cooking pot in Black-burnished ware (½), found in 1976 in the filling of a wall associated with late third-century material at No. 23 Castle Street. Grosvenor Museum. Drawn by M.W.C.H.

2503.102

2503.103

Britannia viii (1977), 436 No. 46.

graffito on the shoulder above lattice decoration:
DEXTER·FELICITER CONECLAMAN[. . .]ECNA
Dexter feliciter con(e)claman[t . . . et] Egna(tius)
'Good luck Dexter, . . . and Egnatius shout together'

2503.103. Ickleton, Cambridgeshire. Part of the everted rim and neck ($\frac{1}{2}$) of a grey jar, found in 1848 during excavations at the Roman villa. Museum of Archaeology and Anthropology, Cambridge. Drawn by R.P.W., 1951.

CIL vii 1335.7. Neville, *JBAA*[1] iv (1849), 364 with fig.; *Arch. J.* vi (1849), 16 with fig. Haverfield, *Roman Britain in 1914*, 33; *The Romanization of Roman Britain* (1915), 33 with photographs, fig. 8. Bös, *Kölner Jahrb.* iii (1958), 25 note 39.

two graffiti, (a) on the lip: III
'Three'
(b) in the hollow of the neck: [. . .]ICAMICIBIBVN[. . .]
[h]ic amici bibun[t]
'Friends drink here'

[ex ho]c amici bibunt, Neville. *[Ho]c amici bibunt*, Huebner, *CIL*. *[ex ha]c amici bibun[t]*, Haverfield. As text, Bös.

2503.104. St. Albans (*Verulamium*), Hertfordshire. Three conjoining sherds ($\frac{1}{3}$) from the reeded rim of a carinated bowl in buff ware, found in 1957 during excavation of Room 2A of Period II D in Insula XIV, in a deposit dated *c.* A.D. 150–155/60. Verulamium Museum. Drawn by M.G. Wilson.

JRS xlviii (1958), 154 No. 40. S.S. Frere, *Verulamium Excavations* i (1972), 364 No. 2 with fig. 140.2.

graffito on the reeded rim:
[. . .]LIASMVLTASOLIINDAVIDIIS
[. . .]lias multa sol(v)enda vides
'. . . you see many things that must be fulfilled (*or* paid, released)'

It would seem that the intended phrase was metrical, but this has been achieved only at the cost of orthography by suppressing the V in *solvenda* (as *solenda* is an impossible gerundive), R.P.W. The graffito has been unsuitably inscribed on the uneven surface of the reeded rim.

2503.104

2503.105. Aldborough (*Isurium*), North Yorkshire. Part of a tall 'slate-coloured' (possibly colour-coated) beaker ($\frac{1}{2}$), found before 1852. Now lost. Drawn by R.P.W. after Smith.

CIL vii 1338.22. H.E. Smith, *Reliquiae Isurianae* (1852), pl. XXXIII.

graffito below the lip: PONEL[. . .]

Mócsy, *Nomenclator*, cites *Ponelius* once as a nomen (in Gallia Cisalpina), but we have not found the reference (it is not in Schulze). A motto seems more likely, *pone l[iber]* or *l[ibens/ter]* 'serve freely', or *pone* with a reference to *Liber*, god of wine. There is no parallel in *CIL* xiii 10018.

2503.105

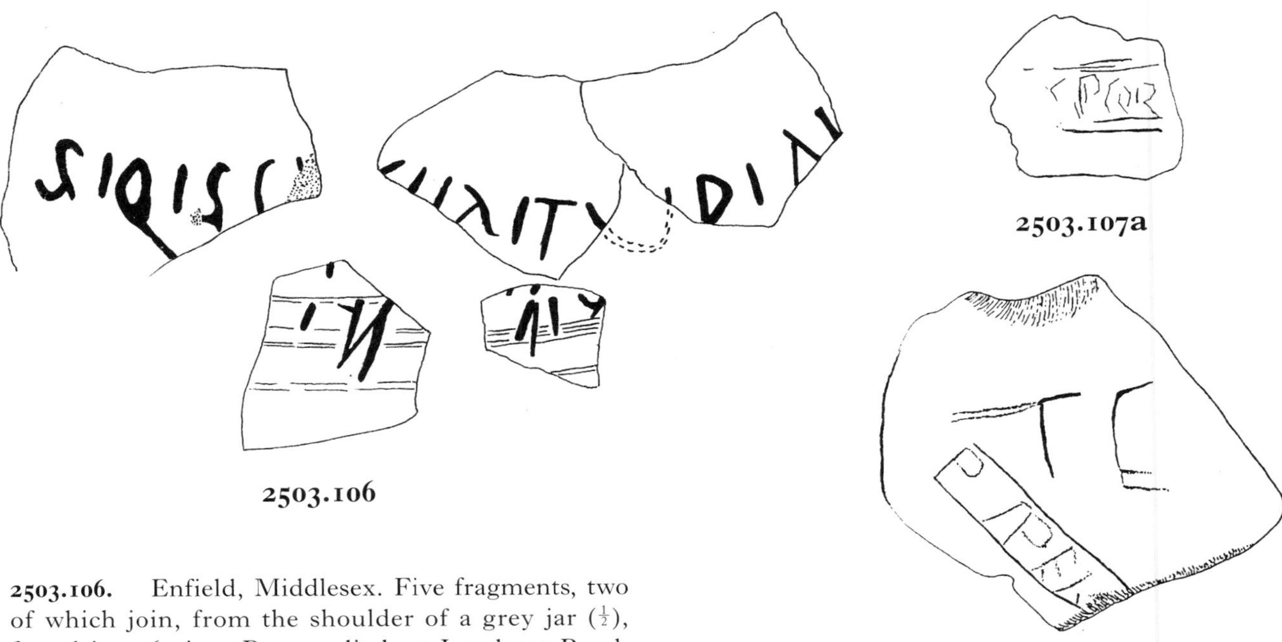

2503.106

2503.107a

2503.107b and c

2503.106. Enfield, Middlesex. Five fragments, two of which join, from the shoulder of a grey jar (½), found in 1965 in a Roman ditch at Landseer Road. Enfield Archaeological Society. Drawn by S.S.F. from rubbings by R.P.W., 1970.

Britannia i (1970), 314 No. 45.

graffito in two lines on the shoulder:
SIQISCṾ[. . .]ṾIIRITṾDIṆ[. . .] | [. . .]IИ[. . .]
IIṾ[. . .]

Perhaps *Si q(u)is cu[pit (?) se]veritudin[em]* . . .
'If anyone desires austerity . . .'

2503.107. Harlow, Essex. Fragment of grey ware (a, ½; b, c, ⅟), found in 1962 during excavations at the Romano-Celtic temple. Harlow Museum. Drawn by M.W.C.H. See also PL. VB for (b) and (c).

Britannia xv (1984), 343 No. 28.

Three graffiti, (a) on the outer face between parallel lines: ṢPQR

Presumably *S(enatus) P(opulus) q(ue) R(omanus)*
'The Senate and Roman People'

(b) on the inner face: TC

(c) on the inner face, very lightly incised within a more deeply cut frame, and at an angle to (b): P ΛPER

Presumably *P(ublicius ?) Aper*
'Publicius Aper'

(a) is best taken as a slogan. 'There seems no reason to regard it as a modern hoax or part of an alphabet as [. . .]OPQR[. . .],' M.W.C.H., *Britannia*.

(b) CL retrograde, conceivably for *Cl(audius)*, M.W.C.H., loc. cit.

(c) The reading is uncertain because of the faintness of the letters.

2503.108. South Shields (*Arbeia*), Tyne and Wear [Durham]. Fragment (½) from a grey-ware jar of late second- to early third-century date, found in 1985 unstratified during excavations. South Shields Museum. Drawing by courtesy of Paul Bidwell.

Britannia xvii (1986), 449 No. 77. N. Hodgson and P.T. Bidwell (forthcoming), No. 54.

graffito in Greek capitals: ΥΓΕ·ΠΙ̣[. . .]

Perhaps ὑγ(ιαιν)ε πι[ε]
'Be healthy: drink'

Note the form of the infinitive ὑγενιν for ὑγιαινειν (F.T. Gignac, *A Grammar of the Greek Papyri of the Roman and Byzantine Periods* i, 71) which would imply an imperative ὑγενε (for ὑγιαινε), corresponding to Latin *vale* or *valeas*. The form ὑγε would then be an extreme contraction or due to the accidental omission of -νε by homoioteleuton.

2503.108

2503.111

2503.109. St. Albans (*Verulamium*), Hertfordshire. Part of a colour-coated beaker (¾ and ½) in pale orange-brown fabric with a very dark grey-brown slip, decorated with barbotine scrolls. Found in 1956 in Insula XIII during excavations in the car park of the Museum. Verulamium Museum. Reproduced from Greep.

Britannia xii (1981), 386 No. 42. Greep, *Herts. Arch.* viii (1980–82), 207 No. 3 with figs. 1.3 and 2.3.

graffito below the rim:
[. . .]C̣IANVS BIBITE R[. . .]
[. . .]cianus bibite r[. . .]
'. . . drink . . .'

Possible names include *Lucianus, Marcianus* and *Senecianus*. The plural *bibite* suggests that there were at least two names, one of which began with R. Alternatively the invocation continued with (e.g.) *r[eplete me]*, 'fill me up'; compare *CIL* xiii 10018.155 a–f, *reple me*. M.W.C.H.

2503.109

(e) Descriptions of Vessels (*RIB* 2503.110–115)

2503.110. Godmanchester, Cambridgeshire [Huntingdonshire]. Part of a dish (½) in Black-burnished ware, found in 1975 at the site of the *mansio*. Present whereabouts not recorded. Drawn by M.W.C.H.

Britannia ix (1978), 478 No. 43.

graffito beneath the base: CVPPA
'Dish'

2503.110

A variant of the classical Latin *cupa*, 'tub' or 'vat'. In medieval Latin the meaning is 'cup': compare J.F. Niermeyer, *Mediae Latinitatis Lexicon Minus* (1976), s.v. *cuppa*.

2503.111. Ospringe, Kent. Buff one-handled jug (½), found in 1925 in Group CXVII in No. 2 Roman cemetery. British Museum. Drawn by R.P.W., 1957, corrected 1963.

W. Whiting, W. Hawley and T. May, *Ospringe* (1931), 44 No. 389 with pl. LII.389. G.C. Dunning, *Maison Dieu, Ospringe* (1958), 18. Schleiermacher, *Germania* xl (1962), 337, Abb.2.

graffito on the wall: DIVIXTVSMETTILAGONΛ
Divixtus Metti lagona(m)
'Divixtus (son of) Mettus (owns *or* gave this) jug'

DIVIXTV METTI IACONΛ, May, loc. cit. A crack has obscured the base of L and the graffito is faint and hard to read. As text Schleiermacher, R.P.W.

These Celtic names are well attested: see Holder s.v.

For the spelling *lagona* compare *RIB* 2502.4 and Bakker and Galsterer-Kröll, *Graffiti* (1975), 171 No. 563; for *lagunum* compare *RIB* 2492.7. In written sources the usual spelling is *lagoena*.

2503.112. York (*Eboracum*). Part of the rim of a colour-coated beaker (*c.* ½), found in 1973 at Bishophill. Yorkshire Museum. Drawn by S.S.F. from a sketch by R.P.W.

Britannia viii (1977), 446 No. 108.

graffito above rouletting and a row of white barbotine dots: [. . .]TINI OLA
[. . .]tini ol(l)a
'The jar of . . . tinus'

Olla, a jar or cooking-pot, is developed from an earlier form *aula* (see W. Hilgers, *Lateinische Gefässnamen* (1969), 112–16) and is sometimes spelled *ola* in inscriptions. See the Index to *CIL* vi, and compare *RIB* 2503.8, 113, 114, 156(?) and 568(?).

2503.112

2503.113. Corbridge (? *Coria*), Northumberland. Part of a late third-century black cooking pot (½), found unstratified sometime before 1936. Corbridge Museum. Drawn by R.P.W., 1948.

JRS xxxviii (1948), 104 No. 25.

graffito on the wall: OLΛ
 Presumably *ol(l)a*
 'cooking pot'

Compare No. 112 with note.

2503.113

2503.114. Dunstable (*Durocobrivae*), Bedfordshire. Major part of a colour-coated beaker (½), found in 1977 in a grave in the inhumation cemetery. Manshead Archaeological Society. Reproduced from *Britannia*.

Britannia xi (1980), 406 No. 7 with fig. 24.

graffito on the lower part of the wall:
OLLΛ DINDROEORORVMVEREGILLI | NVS DONΛVIT
 olla(m) d[e]ndrofororum Ve(r)(ulamiensium) Regillinus donavit
 'Regillinus presented the pot of the *dendrophori* of Verulamium'

'Reading VE(R) REGILLINVS, the suggestion of Professor J.J. Wilkes, rather than VEREGILLINVS. Neither *Veregillinus* nor *Regillinus* are attested as personal names, but the latter is a possible formation from the cognomen Regillus', M.W.C.H.

Dunstable is 12 miles north-west of Verulamium. For *dendrophori* in Britain and Germany see *Britannia* loc. cit.

2503.115. Brecon (? *Cicucium*), Powys [Brecknockshire]. Base of a grey jar (½), found in 1924–25 during excavations at the fort. National Museum, Cardiff. Drawn by R.P.W., 1960.

R.E.M. Wheeler, *Brecon* (1926), 248 with fig. 105.10.

graffito on the base: INVTILIS[. . .] | NΛ | cross
 Perhaps *inutilis [ur]na* with mark of ownership
 'useless vessel'

As text, Wheeler. The reading TI for what looks like a second mark of ownership is not convincing. Nor does there seem any point in marking a jar as 'useless'. R.S.O.T.

For *Vas*, see *RIB* 2503.27.

(f) Military Graffiti (*RIB* 2503.116–120)

2503.116. Caerleon (*Isca*), Gwent [Monmouthshire]. Part of a large storage jar (½) of Caerleon ware, found in 1928 unstratified in the School Field. National Museum, Cardiff. Drawn by R.P.W., 1952.

JRS xix (1929), 217 No. 11; lviii (1968), 214 Corrigendum c. Boon, *AC* cxv (1966), 48 fig. 1.2. and pp. 54–5.

graffito on the shoulder on a plain band between areas of combing:
[. . .]CITER leaf stop ⟩AEL RO|MVLI leaf stop
 [Genio feli]citer (centuriae) Ael(i) Romuli
 'Good fortune [to the Genius] of the century of Aelius Romulus'

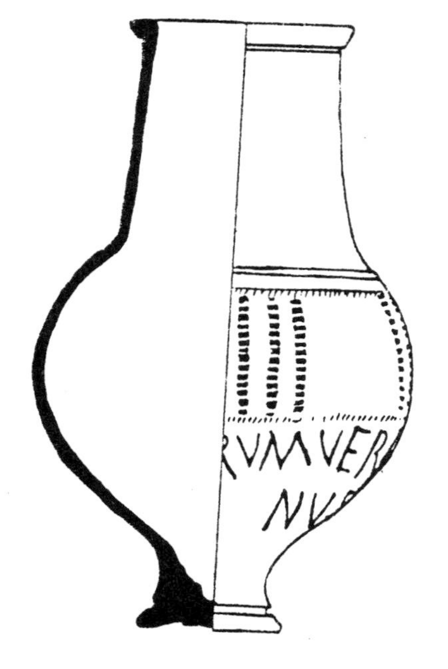

2503.114

2503.115

2503.116

2503.119

The restoration *Genio* was conjectured by both E. Birley and R.W. Davies independently: Boon, loc. cit., note 4. The second leaf stop defines the name of the centurion, which is complete.

2503.117. Caernarvon (*Segontium*), Gwynedd. Rim of a Black-burnished 1 bowl ($\frac{1}{2}$), found in 1977 in the *praetentura* of the fort in a Flavian-Trajanic context. Segontium Museum. Drawing not available.

Britannia xi (1980), 417 No. 64. Tomlin in P.J. Casey et al., *Excavations at Segontium (Caernarfon) Roman Fort, 1975–79* (1993), 232 No. 1.

graffito on the rim: ƆLOAṂṂOIVS
Perhaps *(centuria) Lo(ngini) Ammo(n)ius*
'Ammonius in the century of Longinus'

The L is separated from the first O by two vertical strokes incised *before* firing. It is possible that the writer of the graffito intended to incorporate them as II (=E); but in view of the rarity of names in *Leo-* compared to those in *Lo-*, the restoration of a name such as *Lo(ngini)* is preferred. R.S.O.T.

2503.118. Richborough (*Rutupiae*), Kent. Part of a jug ($\frac{1}{2}$), found in 1926–27 during excavation of Pit 32, associated with first- and second-century material. In store at Dover Castle. Drawn by R.P.W.

J.P. Bushe-Fox, *Richborough* iii (1932), 165.

graffito on the base: C I B
Perhaps *C(ohors) i B(aetasiorum)*

L T B, Bushe-Fox.

Cohors i Baetasiorum was the third-century garrison of the nearby fort at Reculver; compare *RIB* 2468.

2503.118

2503.119. Colchester (*Camulodunum*), Essex. The 'Colchester Vase', a colour-coated hunt-cup in red fabric, with additional gladiatorial figures in colour-coated barbotine ($\frac{1}{2}$ and $\frac{1}{4}$), height 216 mm, diameter at the mouth 159 mm, found in 1848 in a grave at West Lodge, associated with Antonine pottery. Colchester Museum ex Taylor collection. Graffiti drawn by R.P.W., 1943, and the design reproduced from Hull. See also PL. III.

CIL vii 1335.3. T. Wright, *Intellectual Observer* vii (1865), 463 with pl. T. May, *Cat* (1930), 293 with pl. XCII.14. *T. Essex AS*[1] xxv (1955), 16. R.J. Charleston, *Roman Pottery* (1955), pl. 65. J.M.C. Toynbee, *Art in Roman Britain* (1962), 190 No. 158 with pls. 176–7; *Art in Britain under the Romans* (1964), 411, 413, M.R. Hull, *The Roman Potters' Kilns of Colchester* (1963), 96 with fig. 51.3. R. Dunnett, *The Trinovantes* (1975), 130 with fig. 39.

graffiti associated with figures of (a) two *venatores* (huntsmen) and (b and c) two gladiators:

(a) SECVNDVS MARIO
'Secundus (and) Mario'

(b) MEMNON SΛC VIIII
Memnon sac (for *sec(utor)) viiii*
Perhaps 'Memnon the *secutor* (victor) nine (times)'

(c) VALENTINV LEGIONIS XXX
'Valentinu(s) of the Thirtieth Legion'

(b) SAL, for *Sal(vini)* or *Sal(villi)*, Hull, on whose drawing VIIII has been omitted. As text, R.G.C., R.P.W.

The scenes represent events in the arena.

(a) The first two figures are huntsmen (*venatores*), one of them brandishing a whip over a bear.

(b) The *secutor* or 'Samnite' was a light-armed gladiator who fought a *retiarius* armed with a net and trident. Toynbee, locc. citt., suggests that VIIII may represent the number of Memnon's victories.

(c) Valentius, a *retiarius* (net-thrower) has lost his net and dropped his trident; he raises a finger in token of defeat.

Legio XXX Ulpia Victrix was based at Xanten (*Vetera* II) in Lower Germany from A.D. 122.

The graffito, being cut after firing, cannot be taken as evidence that the vessel is of Rhenish manufacture, and it is generally accepted as a product of the Colchester kilns.

Toynbee (locc. citt.) notes that 'some legions may have had their own troupes of gladiators and *venatores*' (compare Tacitus, *Ann.* i 22; Suetonius, *Tiberius* 72.2) and that 'the names on this jar could be those of 'stars' attached to the Thirtieth Legion but famed throughout the northern provinces'. However, this vase is the only explicit evidence for that practice cited by G. Ville, *La Gladiature en Occident des origines à la mort de Domitien* (1981), 214.

The name *Mario* is Celtic (see Holder s.v.) and *Memnon* Greek (Solin, *Namenbuch*, 500–1).

2503.120. Wilderspool, Cheshire. Part of a storage jar (½), found in 1900. Warrington Museum. Drawn by R.P.W., 1952.

graffito on the shoulder: [. . .]RVITITRI.[. . .]
Perhaps *[Pat]ruiti trib[uni]*
'(Property) of the tribune Patruitus'

For the name *Patruitus* see *CIL* xiii 6095 and 10010.1513.

2503.120

(g) Religious Dedications (*RIB* 2503.121–136)

2503.121. Richborough (*Rutupiae*), Kent. Shoulder of a buff jug (½), found in 1931 unstratified within the south-west sector of the fort. In store at Dover Castle. Drawn by R.P.W., 1948.

JRS lv (1965), 227 No. 45. Wright in B.W. Cunliffe (ed.), *Richborough* v (1968), 183 No. 1 with fig.

graffito on the shoulder: DIIΛ[. . .]
Dea[e . . .]
'To the goddess . . .'

As there seems to be no personal name beginning with *Dea* . . ., this vessel will have been used for worship of a goddess whose identity would have been clear on the missing part of the text, R.P.W., *Richborough* v.

Alternatively, *Deṃ [. . .]* might be read. R.S.O.T.

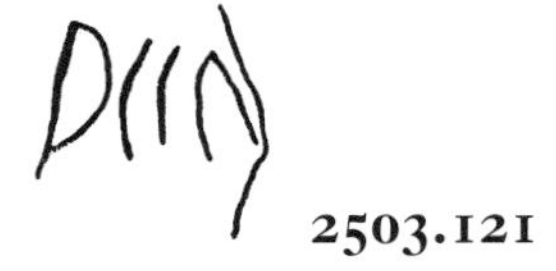

2503.121

2503.122. Brancaster (*Branodunum*), Norfolk. Fragment from the rim of a Lower Nene Valley ware jar (½), found in 1942 in the burial area on the east side of the fort. In private possession. Drawn by R.P.W., 1957.

JRS xlvii (1957), 234 No. 41.

2503.122

graffito below the rim: [. . .]ỌLICEṆ[. . .}

In the absence of a comparable personal name, *[Iovi D]olic(h)en[o]* seems likely. 'To Iupiter Dolichenus'

The final letter could be M, R.P.W. For the spelling compare *RIB* 1725.

2503.123. Alcester, Warwickshire. Complete buff jar (½ and ¼), found in 1965 during excavation of a Roman pit. Alcester Museum. Drawings by courtesy of Nicholas Palmer.

JRS lvi (1966), 224 No. 55. Birley *ANRW* ii.18 (1986), 46–7.

graffito on the shoulder: IIPON
Presumably *Epon(ae)*
'To Epona'

Dedications to the Celtic rider goddess Epona are frequent in northern Gaul, but uncommon in Britain: see *RIB* 1777, 2177 and perhaps 967; for a bronze figurine 'from Wiltshire' in the British Museum see Alcock, *Antiq. J.* xliii (1963), 119 with pl. XIX c, and for a fragmentary figure in stone from Colchester see *CSIR* 1.8, No. 14 (Hull, *T. Essex. AS*² xix (1930), 198–9 with pl.).

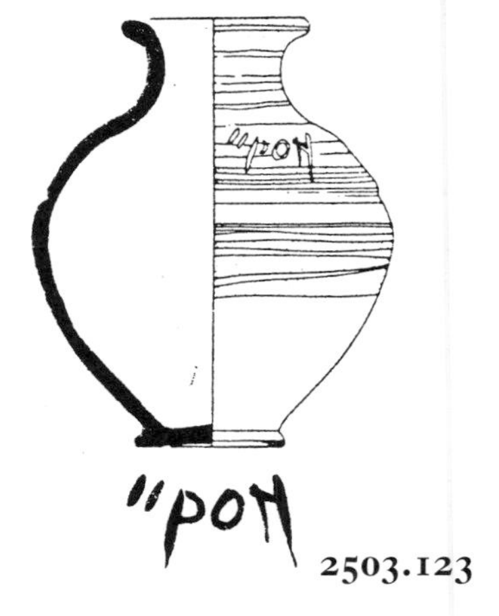

2503.123

2503.124. Chichester (*Noviomagus*), West Sussex. Part of a grey jar (½), found in 1935 unstratified on the site of Marks and Spencer, East Street. Chichester Museum. Drawn by R.P.W., 1952.

graffito on the shoulder: [. . .]EPOṂ[. . .

The last letter could be N with sloping lines, R.P.W. Perhaps therefore *Epon[ae]*; but compare *RIB* 2503.251.

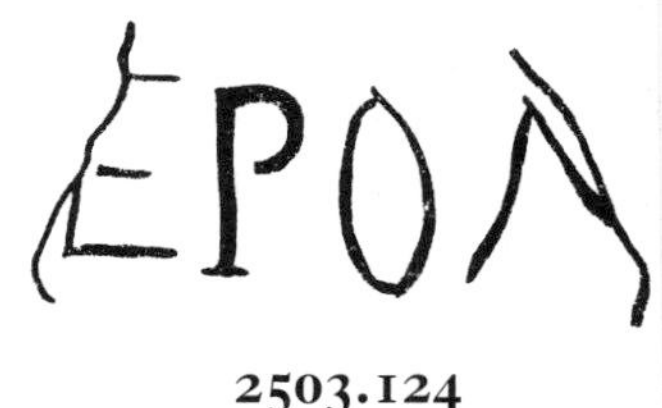

2503.124

2503.125. Colchester (*Camulodunum*), Essex. Part of the shoulder of a grey jar (½), now in two fragments; found in 1929 in Holly Trees Meadow (Insula 15). Colchester Museum. No. 125 (b) drawn by R.P.W., 1943. No drawing exists of (a).

JRS xxxiv (1944), 91 No. 29.

two portions of a graffito: (a) [. . .]MMA[. . .]
(b)[. . .]MARCIAVRIILI[. . .]

The lettering is very carefully cut, and if *Mammaea* is the correct restoration of (a) the best way of associating the two fragments seems to be:

[Iuliae Ma]mma[eae matri . . .] Marci Aureli [Severi Alexandri . . .]
'To *Julia Mammeae, mother of Marcus Aurelius Severus Alexander . . .*'

Compare *RIB* 2503.148.

2503.125

2503.126. Topsham, Devon. Part of the shoulder of a buff bowl (½), found in 1935. Exeter Museum. Drawn by R.P.W., 1953.

JRS xxvii (1937), 250 No. 20. Montague, *Devon Arch. Explor. Soc.* ii (1933–6), 200 (with 'fanciful interpretation' suggested by Winbolt).

graffito below the shoulder groove: IVNO VVE

IVN VVE, R.G.C., *JRS*. *Iunoni ut voverat E*, Winbolt. As text, R.P.W. The O is very dubious.

2503.126

2503.127. Southwark, south London. Jug (½) of late first-century type, found in 1912 in Tooley Street. Museum of London. Drawn by R.G.C.

2503.127

EE ix 1372. Collingwood, *JRS* xii (1922), 283 No. 13 with fig. 15. RCHM *Roman London* (1928), 43 with pl. 53; 177 No. 104 with fig. 90. R.E.M. Wheeler, *London in Roman Times* (1930), 25 with pl. v; 51. R. Merrifield, *Roman London* (1969), 141 with fig. 53. P. Marsden, *Roman London* (1980), 48 with pl. E. Birley, *ANRW* ii.18 (1986), 83 No. 11.

faint graffito on the shoulder:

LONDINI | ADFANVMISIDIS
Londini ad fanum Isidis
'At the temple of Isis, London'

l.1. LONDIN, F.H., *EE*. As text, R.G.C. 'after prolonged examination in various lights'.

This graffito was the first evidence for the cult of Isis in Britain; the temple is also mentioned on an altar, probably of third-century date, found in 1975 in Lower Thames Street, London (*Britannia* vii (1976), 378 No. 2), but the building is as yet undiscovered. Two gems also attest the cult; see M. Henig, *Corpus* (1974), No. 359 (Wroxeter) and 369 (Lockleys, Hertfordshire, = *RIB* 2423.1).

2503.128. Housesteads (*Vercovicium*), Northumberland. Rim of a Black-burnished dish (½), found before 1936. Housesteads Museum. Drawn by R.P.W., 1940.

graffito on the rim: [. . .]MARTI

Perhaps a dedication to Mars, since the only alternative appears to be the rare cognomen *Camars* of which one example is noted by Mócsy, *Nomenclator*, in Narbonensis.

2503.128

2503.129. Rocester, Staffordshire. Part of a Black-burnished jar (½) of mid to late second-century date, found in 1960 while digging a sewer-trench in Mill Lane. Derby Museum. Rubbings by R.P.W. Drawn by G.A. Webster.

JRS li (1961), 197 No. 42. Birley, *ANRW* ii.18 (1986), 31.

graffito on the shoulder: [. . .]MIIRCVRIO[. . .]
Mercurio
'To Mercury'

2503.129

For other vessels dedicated to Mercury, see *RIB* 2499.1, 2501.16 and 2503.130 (?).

2503.130. London (*Londinium*). Part of a grey 'fumed-ware' bowl ($\frac{1}{2}$), found in 1954 in a late first-century context during excavations for the Bank of England at Friday Street. Museum of London. Drawn by R.P.W., 1954.

JRS xlv (1955), 149 No. 31.

graffito below the rim: MIIRC[. . .]Λ

Perhaps a dedication to Mercury by a female, but if the space allows, *Merc[uri]a* seems more likely.

Compare *RIB* 2503.129 with note.

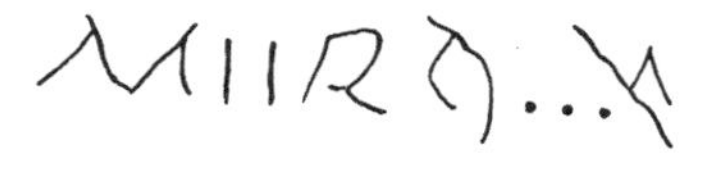

2503.130

2503.131. Kelvedon, Essex. Part of a grey-ware jar ($\frac{1}{2}$), found in 1977 with much Flavian pottery in a gas-main trench in St. Mary's Road. Present whereabouts not recorded. Drawn by M.W.C.H.

Britannia ix (1978), 478 No. 41.

graffito on the shoulder: TOVTΛTIS
Toutatis

For Mars Toutatis compare *RIB* 219 with note, *RIB* 1017, and perhaps *RIB* 2422. 36–40 and *Britannia* xxv (1994), 306 No. 38 (TOT rings).

2503.131

For another religious dedication, *olla(m) dendrofororum . . . donavit*, see *RIB* 2503.114.

2503.132. Ibid. Base ($\frac{1}{2}$) of a colour-coated bowl in Oxfordshire ware, found in the late 1950s and presented to Colchester Museum in 1960. Drawn by M.W.C.H.

Britannia xiv (1983), 343 No. 17.

graffito below the base: X͡P
Chi-Rho

A superfluous stroke partially bisects the Chi.

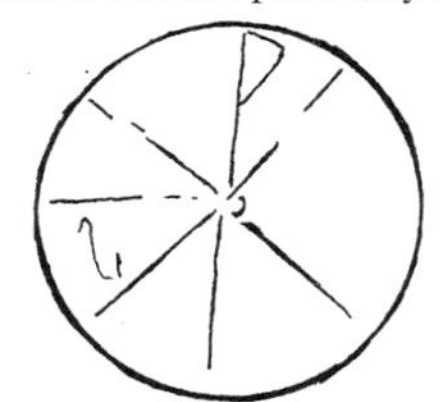

2503.132

2503.133. Colchester (*Camulodunum*), Essex. Part of a grey-ware storage jar ($\frac{1}{4}$ and $\frac{1}{2}$), found in 1950 in a fourth-century context during excavations in Colchester Castle Park. Colchester Museum. Reproduced from Drury.

Britannia xi (1980), 411 No. 33. M.R. Hull, *Roman Colchester* (1958), 186 No. 4 with fig. 95.4 (omitting the loop of Rho). Drury, *Britannia* xv (1984), 47 No. 10 with fig. 16.10.

graffito on the rim: X͡P
Chi-Rho

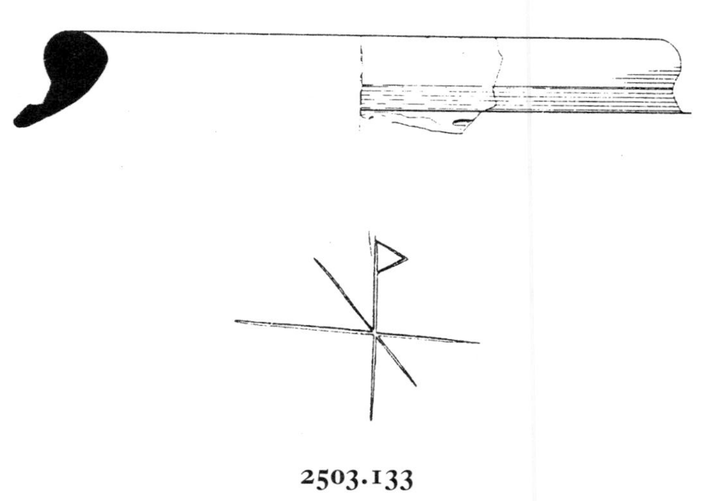

2503.133

2503.134. Exeter (*Isca Dumnoniorum*), Devon. Part of the shoulder of a black cooking-pot ($\frac{1}{2}$), found in 1946 during excavations at the South Street site near St. George's Church. Exeter Museum. Drawn by R.P.W., 1947. See also PL. VII A.

JRS xxxvii (1947), 182 No. 20. A. Fox, *Roman Exeter* (1952), 92 No. 1 with pl. X A.

graffito on the wall: X͡P
Chi-Rho

This is the later form of the Chi-Rho. See. C. Thomas *Christianity in Roman Britain to A.D. 500* (1981), 87–8 for the development of the symbol, and compare *RIB* 2420.61 (with note), 2501.435 and 2503.135–6.

2503.134

2503.135. Richborough (*Rutupiae*), Kent. Red colour-coated bowl (½), found in 1931 unstratified during excavations in the south-west part of the fort. In store at Dover Castle. Reproduced from Greene.

Britannia viii (1977), 442 No. 92. Greene, *Britannia* v (1974), 393–5 with fig. 6.

graffito on the lower part of the wall, inverted in relation to the bowl: X͡P
Chi-Rho

For this (later) form of Chi-Rho compare *RIB* 2503.134 with note.

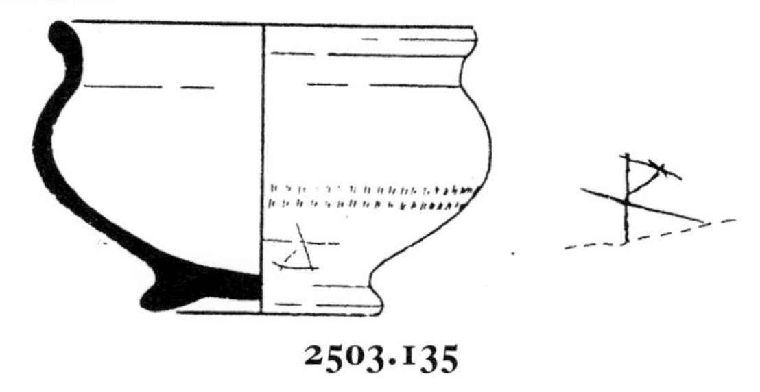

2503.135

2503.136. Gatcombe, Somerset. Sherd (½) from the rim of a red beaker, found in 1975 during excavation of Building 19. Bristol Museum. Reproduced from Branigan.

Britannia viii (1977), 444 No. 100. K. Branigan, *Gatcombe Roman Villa* (1977), 109 No. 370 with fig. 24.370.

graffito below the rim: X͡P
Chi-Rho

'With the loop of the Rho in three straight cuts incised on the second stroke of the Chi', R.P.W.

Compare *RIB* 2503.134 with note.

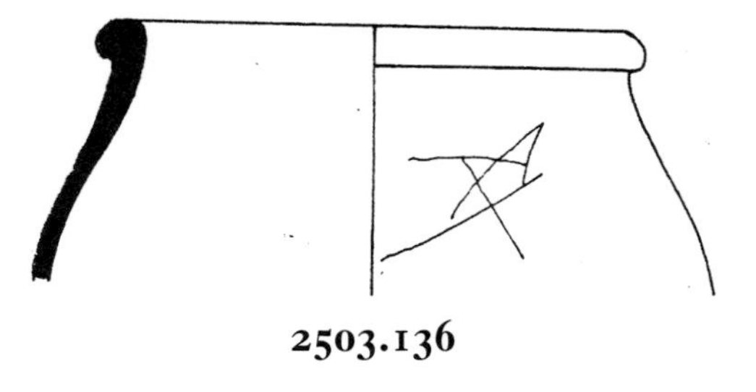

2503.136

(h) Funerary Graffiti (*RIB* 2503.137–161)

2503.137. Rougham, Suffolk. Small cinerary urn found in 1844 in the most south-westerly of the four tumuli on Eastlow Hill. Lost before 1873. Reprinted from Henslow.

Henslow, *P. Suffolk IA* iv (1874), 273 (ed. by Babington). Fox, *VCH* Suffolk i (1911), 315.

graffito in Greek letters: αεολ..λα

αεολ..λα perhaps for ἀεὶ ὄλωλα ['I have perished forever'], Henslow.

As the original was lost before 1873 Babington was unable to check the reading. It may be a personal name, now damaged; a slogan seems very unlikely. R.P.W., *RIB* archive.

2503.138. St. Albans (*Verulamium*), Hertfordshire. Grey pedestalled and cordoned tazza (½) in grog-tempered ware, found in 1967 in the female Burial 322 (dated to the Augustan period) during excavation of the pre-Roman cremation cemetery at King Harry Lane. Verulamium Museum. Drawn by S.S.F. from rubbings by R.P.W., 1968.

JRS lix (1969), 244 No. 63. *Britannia* xix (1988), 501 No. 62. I.M. Stead and V. Rigby, *Verulamium: The King Harry Lane Site* (1989), 202 No. 1 with fig. 55.1 and 354 No. 322 with fig. 155.322.

graffito on the underside of the base within the pedestal foot: ANDOC

Compare R.P. Mack, *Coinage of Ancient Britain* (1964), No. 200 for ANDOCO(. . .)

Since *Andoc* . . . or *Andoco* . . . is thought to be a male name, the vessel appears to have been re-used in the burial or was presented for the purpose. Compare Millet in M. Struck (ed.) *Römerzeitliche Gräber als Quellen zu Religion, Bevölkerungsstructur und Sozialgeschichte* (Archäologische Schriften . . ., Band 3, 1993), 266.

2503.138 ANDOC

2503.139. Castell Collen, Powys [Radnorshire]. Grey jar (½) with countersunk handles and decorated with a lattice pattern, found in 1909 near the waterworks north of Llandrindod Wells and east of the fort. It contained fragments of bone and may have been a cinerary urn. Llandrindod Wells Museum. Drawn by R.P.W., 1953.

JRS xliv (1954), 110 No. 47. Anon, *AC* cxi (1911), 120. Thomas, *AC* cxi (1911), 149 with pl. RCHM, *Radnor* (1913), No. 112 b.

graffito on the shoulder: ẠTTILḶI
Attilli
'(Property *or* Ashes) of Attillus'

This cognomen is cognate with *Atto* (etc.). The nomen *Attillius*, whose genitive could also be read, is much less likely.

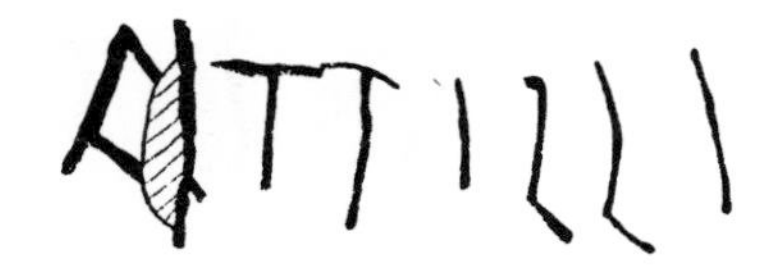

2503.139

2503.140. Chilham, Kent. Grey poppy-head beaker (½), found in 1962 associated with a cremation on Bagham Farm. In private possession. Drawn by S.S.F. from a rubbing by F. Jenkins.

JRS liii (1963), 166 No. 53.

graffito on the wall: CAMPANA
Compana

The cognomen is common; compare *RIB* 2491.148.

2503.140

2503.141. Guilden Morden, Cambridgeshire. Upper half of a flask (½), found *c.* 1880 'with many other urns in a clunch-pit at Great Morden'. Museum of Archaeology and Anthropology, Cambridge, ex Cole Ambrose collection. Drawn by R.P.W.

graffito on the shoulder: COBROVA
Cobrova

Compare *Cobrovius* (*CIL* xiii 4165) and *Cobrovillus* (xii 2356).

The clunch-pit had disturbed part of the Roman cemetery: see Lethbridge, *P. Camb. Antiq. Soc.* xxvii (1924), 49 ff.

2503.141

2503.142. Basingstoke, Hampshire. Parts of a grey cooking pot (½), height 140 mm, diameter of mouth 133 mm, diameter of base 70 mm, found *c.* 1912 among vessels in a Roman burial while digging foundations for the County Mental Hospital at Park Prewett Farm. Basingstoke Museum. Drawn by R.P.W., 1941.

JRS xxxii (1942), 118 No. 14.

graffito below the shoulder: CVPIT
Probably *Cupit(i)*
'(Property *or* Ashes) of Cupitus'

2503.142

2503.143. Wickford, Essex. Part of the base (½) of a grey-ware jar, found in 1978 in a pipe-line trench cut across a cemetery of the first and second centuries. Billericay Archaeological Society. Drawn by M.W.C.H.

Britannia x (1979), 349 No. 23.

graffito beneath the base: CVR

Compare *RIB* 321 and 2501.153.

2503.143

2503.144. Newbury, Berkshire. Sepulchral urn found in or before 1837 with *RIB* 2441.10. Now lost. Reprinted from Watkin.

EE iii 57; vii 843. Anon., *Gent. Mag.* (February 1827), 161–2. Watkin, *Arch. J.* xxxi (1874), 351.

graffito: DOM | SML and other letters
Perhaps *D(is) M(anibus)* | *SML* . . .

From the small size of the O it is taken to be a stop, Watkin.

2503.145. Ospringe, Kent. Globular grey jug with narrow flanged neck (½), found in 1925 in a burial. Ospringe Museum. Drawn by R.P.W., 1961.

W. Whiting, W. Hawley and T. May, *Ospringe* (1931), 69 No. 505 with pl. LII.505.

graffito on the wall: FLAVINVS
Flavinus

2503.145

2503.146. Brougham (*Brocavum*), Cumbria [Westmorland]. Fragment from the shoulder of a jar in dull red ware (½), found in 1966 unstratified in the Roman cemetery east of the fort. Department of the Environ-ment. Drawn by S.S.F. from rubbings by R.P.W., 1960.

JRS lvii (1967), 210 No. 48.

graffito on the shoulder: [. . .]ḤILA[. . .]
Probably *Hilarus* or a cognate name

Otherwise a name of Greek etymology in -*[p]hila*.

2503.146

2503.147. Welwyn, Hertfordshire. Two conjoining sherds from the top of a grey necked jar with cordon (½), found in 1908–10 on the north-east side of The Grange and north of St. Mary's churchyard, with other pottery in a pre-Roman cemetery. Hertfordshire Museum. Drawn by R.P.W., 1966.

Andrews, *The Antiquary* xlvii (1911), 58 with fig. 4 No. 92.

graffito on the lip: IVLIΛII
Iuliae
'(Property *or* Ashes) of Iulia'

IVIIΛII, Andrews. As text, R.P.W.

Perhaps the name of the deceased whose ashes were in the vessel.

2503·147

2503.148. Blackheath, near the east corner of Greenwich Park, south London. Large globular urn in fine red clay, found in 1710 with many other urns; it contained a cremation. Now lost. Reprinted from *CIL*.

CIL vii 1332.1. Taylor et al., *VCH* Kent iii (1932), 147. Gale in Leland, *Itinerary* (ed. T. Hearne, 1711) vi 103; ed. 3 (1769), 128.

graffito roughly incised under the rim:
MARCVS AVRELIVS IIII
'Marcus Aurelius, four'

Huebner, *CIL*, mistakenly relates this find to Newington, the find-spot of *CIL* vii 19 (*RIB* 2503.156).

Gale records the vessel's girth as 6 ft 3 in (1.9 m), *CIL* and *VCH* record it as 3 ft 3 in (0.99 m).

Compare *RIB* 2503.125. But unlike the latter (which is probably a dedication), the present graffito is in the nominative case and thus perhaps the name of the deceased, an auxiliary veteran of imperial freeman, if IIII represents a misinterpreted cognomen. However, the graffito may well be modern, prompted by a coin of Marcus Aurelius IMP.IIII (i.e. A.D. 166 or 167).

2503.149. Chichester (*Noviomagus*), West Sussex. Two conjoining fragments (½) from a narrow-mouthed vessel in reduced shell-tempered fabric, found in 1986 during excavation of a possible cremation pit at No. 73 North Street. Chichester Museum. Drawn by M.W.C.H.

Britannia xviii (1987), 372 No. 27.

graffito: [. . .]MAR·CALVIIỊ[. . .]
Perhaps *Mar(i) Calven[tiani]*
'(Property *or* Ashes) of Marius Calventianus'

2503·149

2503.150. St. Albans (*Verulamium*), Hertfordshire. Colour-coated indented buff-ware beaker (¼ and ½) in orange-buff fabric with darker surfaces, found in 1930–34 in a male inhumation dated *c.* A.D. 300 in a cemetery west of the Chester Gate overlying the Fosse earthwork. Verulamium Museum. Reproduced from Greep.

Wheeler, *Verulamium* (1936), 137 No. 4 with pl. CXV A. Greep, *Herts. Arch.* viii (1980–82), 207 No. 6 with figs. 1.6 and 2.6.

graffito on the neck: MΛVRVSI
Maurusi
'(Property *or* Ashes) of Maurusius'

Perhaps the name of the deceased.

For the name compare *CIL* xiii 11561. It is presumably developed from *Maurus* (see Kajanto, *Cognomina*, 206, but not cited by him).

2503·150

2503.151. Exeter (*Isca Dumnoniorum*), Devon. 'Small sepulchral unguent vase, or ampulla, of dark clay', found before about 1832 on the site of the Post Office Inn. Now lost. Drawn by R.S.O.T. from Shortt.

CIL vii 1338.17. W.T.P. Shortt, *Sylva antiqua Iscana* (no date, but *c.* 1832), 121 with pl. X.

graffito above the base: NAMELIE

A name *Namelia* is not attested. Shortt, pl. X, is inadequate, but the A is clearly wrong; the graffito looks more like AIM . . ., possibly *Aemilii*. R.S.O.T.

2503·151

2503.152. Skeleton Green, Hertfordshire. Grey-ware dish, broken but complete (½), found in 1972 during excavation of a third-century cremation-cemetery. Hertfordshire Museum. Reproduced from Partridge.

Britannia viii (1977), 442 No. 89. Hassall in C. Partridge, *Skeleton Green* (1981), 273 No. 1 with fig. 108.1.

two graffiti: (a) on the wall, illegible (not illustrated)
(b) on the base: ỌSVΛ FII | XX

(b) Perhaps *os(s)ua fe(re) XX*, 'about twenty bones,' the spelling *ossua* being frequent for *ossa* in inscriptions (compare Dessau, *ILS* Index xvi, 834), M.W.C.H.

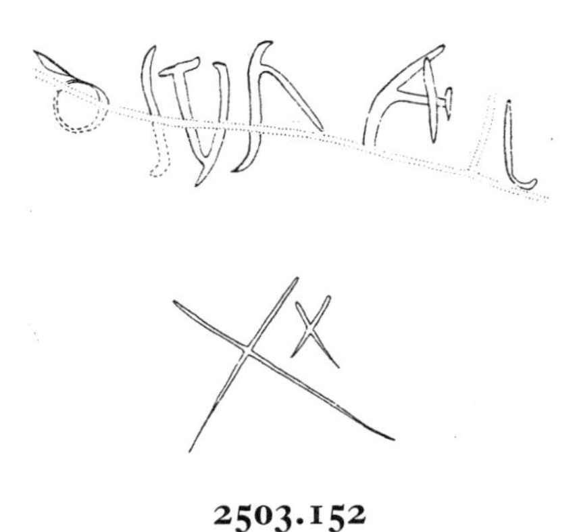

2503.152

2503.153. Colchester (*Camulodunum*), Essex. Small grey-ware carinated bowl (½) of Camulodunum form 227, containing a cremation. Found before 1891 inside another urn containing bones. Colchester Museum. Drawn by R.G.C., 1928.

EE ix 1351 b. Haverfield, *Arch. J.* xlix (1892), 189. T. May, *Cat.* (1930), 20 No. 33 with pl. IV.33 and 245 No. 5 with fig. 9.5 (with inscription wrongly shown retrograde).

graffito on the neck: PVIIRORVM
Puerorum
'(Ashes) of the boys'

Compare *RIB* 2503. 574, 575 and *CIL* xiii 10017.57.

It is uncertain whether *pueri* here means 'slaves' or literally 'boys'; the word is also found used more generally for 'children'. Evidently the larger vessel contained a multiple cremation, which perhaps suggests small children rather than adult slaves.

2503.153

2503.154. St. Albans (*Verulamium*), Hertfordshire. Plate (½) of imported micaceous terra nigra (Camulodunum form 4) of late Augustan to Tiberian date, found in 1968 in Burial 123 during excavation of the pre-conquest cremation cemetery at King Harry Lane. Verulamium Museum. Reproduced from Stead and Rigby.

Britannia xix (1988), 501 No. 63. I.M. Stead and V. Rigby, *Verulamium: The King Harry Lane Site* (1989), 202 No. 2 with fig. 55.2, and 306.123 with fig. 110.123.

graffito beneath the base: R with cross

2503.154

2503.155. (?) London *or* Verulamium (St. Albans). Complete reeded-rim jar (¼ and ½) containing a cremation, found before 1683, when it entered the collections of the Ashmolean Museum, Oxford. The vessel is of a type well represented at London and Verulamium and was probably made at kilns in the Verulamium region, for instance at Brockley Hill, Middlesex. The find-spot is not recorded, but is likely to have been as stated. Drawing: Ashmolean Museum.

Britannia xii (1981), 387 No. 43. A. MacGregor, *Tradescant Rarities* (1983), 272 No. 211 with fig.

graffito on the wall: SΛTTONIS
Sattonis
'(Property *or* Ashes) of Satto'

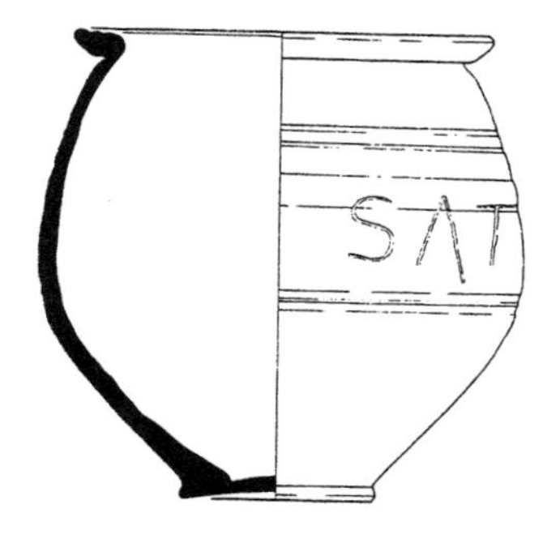

2503.155

It seems reasonable to take the graffito as the name of the deceased in the genitive. The writing is acceptably Roman: the open Λ would have been a sophisticated touch by a 17th-century improver. The name *Satto* is not likely to have occurred to such a person: it has been found in Roman Britain only as a samian stamp; as a cognomen it occurs principally at Trier and in upper Germany. R.S.O.T., *Britannia*.

2503.156. Newington near Sittingbourne, Kent. Funnel-necked beaker with cordon (? ½), found in or before 1633 in a Roman cemetery, associated with samian and a colour-coated beaker. Now lost. Traced by R.P.W. from Casaubon.

CIL vii 19. Taylor et al., *VCH* Kent iii (1932), 162. M. Casaubon, *Marcus Aurelius Antoninus . . . his meditations translated* (1634), Notes, pp. 31–32, with pl. W. Burton, *Commentary on Antoninus . . .* (1658), 180, 183. Gale in Leland, *Itinerary* (ed. T. Hearne, 1711), vi 103, ed. 3 (1769), 128. Battely, *Antiquitates Rutupinae* (1745), 107. Gough's Camden (1789) i, pl. facing p. cxlix, No. 1; (1806), i, pl. facing p. ccvi, No. 1.

graffito around the neck: SEVERIANVS·PATER·D·OLA· IO.[. . .]·V·FELLIΛ

SEVERIANVS . . . OL(L)A, Casaubon.

OLA·IOV . . . . OV·FFLLIA, Huebner, *CIL*.

For *ola* compare *RIB* 2503.112 with note.

The letters of Casaubon's careful transcript ('as neere as they could bee imitated') occupy two lines because of the width of his page, but from his drawing of the vessel it is clear that the text was continuous. Thus where it starts is uncertain. R.P.W. understands the text to be *Severianus pater d(at) ola(m) . . . fillia(e)*, '(Her) father Severianus gives (this) jar . . . to (his) daughter (?)', but this is not very convincing. Possibly there was a funeral text beginning D[M], followed by the name of the deceased, a description (FEMIN[A] ?), and concluding with SEVERIANVS PATER, but this puzzling question seems beyond conjecture.

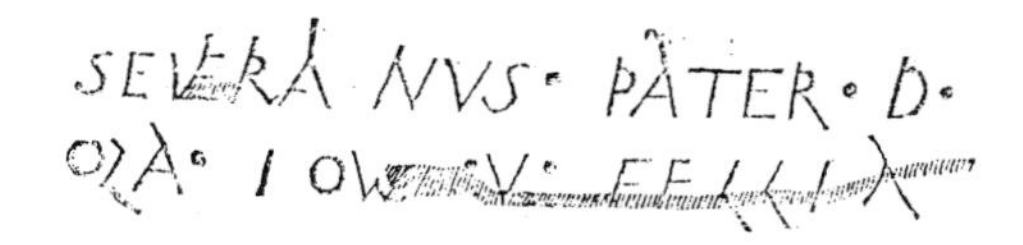

2503.156

2503.157. Colchester (*Camulodunum*), Essex. Narrow-necked jar (¼) in 'fumed grey clay', containing a cremation, height 381 mm, diameter 279 mm, found before 1890 in an unrecorded location. Colchester Museum ex Jarmin collection. Drawn by R.P.W., 1954.

EE ix 1351 a. Haverfield, *Arch. J.* xlvii (1890), 241. *Archaeological Review* iii (1889), 275 with fig. T. May, *Cat.* (1930), 245 No. 3 with fig. 9.3.

graffito around the bulge: THALIVS VASSV

The reading is certain, but not the interpretation. The handwriting of each word is different (note the difference in A, V and S), which suggests that they are the names of successive owners, one of them presumably the deceased. *Th* is un-Latin, being used for a Celtic consonant and for Greek θ, which may become *t* in Vulgar Latin. Thus *Thalius*, which seems to be unattested (though Holder notes *Thaliacum*), may be cognate with *Talio* (see *RIB* 2415.47, 2501.532, 2503.591, and *CIL* iii 1640.4). The name *Vassu(s)*, though hardly attested, would seem to be derived from Celtic **vassos* ('servant', 'vassal') like *Vassius*; compare *Britannia* xviii (1987), 360–3 No. 1, (b) 10–11, *Vasianus* (with note).

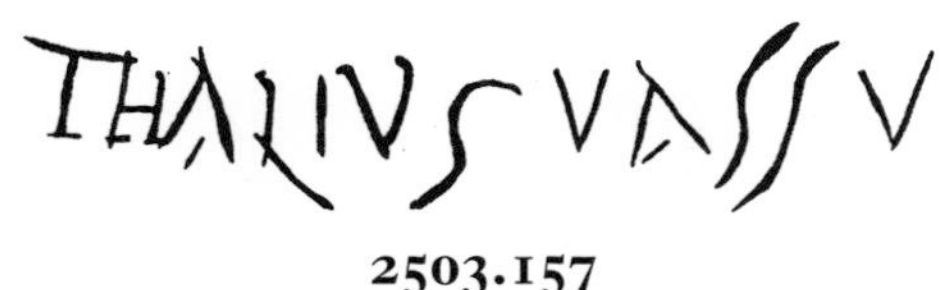

2503.157

2503.158. Barnwood, Gloucestershire. Part of a Black-burnished cooking pot (½), resembling Gillam form 117, found before 1930 during excavations at a Roman cemetery. Cheltenham Museum. Drawn by R.P.W., 1968.

Clifford, *TBGAS* lii (1930), 248 with fig. 39.

graffito above the lattice decoration: VIIRIIC
Verec(undi)
'(Property) of Verecundus'

Verec(us) or *Verec(undus)*, Clifford.

2503.158

2503.159. Ospringe, Kent. Globular grey jug with narrow flanged neck (½), found in 1925 in a burial. Ospringe Museum. Drawn by R.P.W., 1961.

W. Whiting, W. Hawley and T. May, *Ospringe* (1931), 63 No. 472 with pl. LII.472.

graffito on the shoulder: VICTORIANVS

VICTORIANVS, May, loc. cit.

Compare *RIB* 2501.307 for *Victoricus* and *Victorina* from this site.

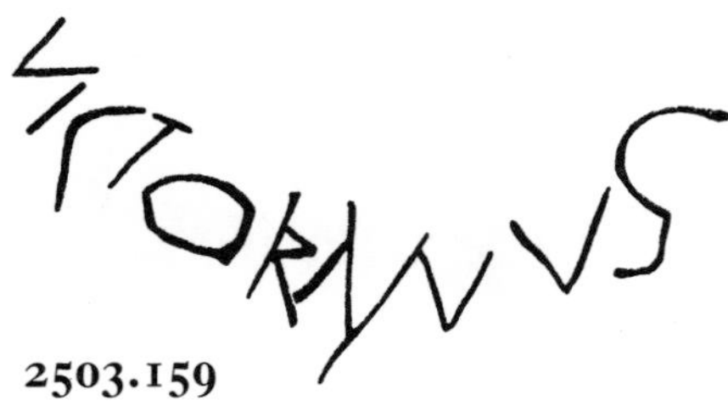

2503.159

2503.160. Beckfoot (? *Bibra*), Cumbria [Cumberland]. Early fourth-century grey cooking pot used as a cremation urn ($\frac{1}{2}$), restored from fragments, found in 1952 at a point 200 m south of the south-west angle of the fort. In private possession. Drawn by R.P.W., 1952.

JRS xliii (1953), 131 No. 21.

graffito on the shoulder: [. . .]VROCATAE
Perhaps *V(i)rocatae*
'(Property *or* Ashes) of Virocata'

The Celtic name *Virocata* seems to be unattested, but *Cat(t)us* and its compounds, and names in *Viro-*, are common. Also compare *Virocantus*, *CIL* v 5883.

2503.160

2503.161. Wroxeter (*Viroconium*), Shropshire. Fragment from the side of a grey urn (scale uncertain), found in 1974 in the 'cemetery field' in line with two other cremations on the south side of Watling Street (Horseshoes Lane) on the east side of the Roman city. In private possession. Drawn by S.S.F. from a sketch by R.P.W.

Britannia vii (1976), 390 No. 60.

graffito on the wall: [. . .]VRVṢ[. . .]

'S' looks more like C or O, R.S.O.T.

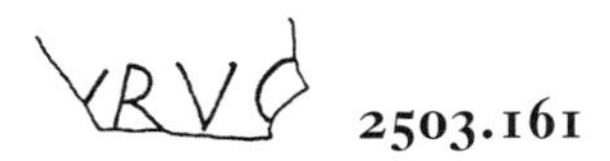

2503.161

(i) Alphabets (*RIB* 2503.162–168)

2503.162. Little Chester, Derbyshire. Neck of a red jug ($\frac{1}{1}$) of the late third to fourth century, found in 1966 during excavation of a water-pipe trench on the south side of the north rampart of the fort. Derby Museum. Drawn by S.S.F. from rubbings by R.P.W., 1966.

JRS lvii (1967), 209 No. 45.

graffito around the flange on the neck:
ABCDEFGHIKLPNIMOQXTSV

The lower part of ABCD is abraded. The second half of the alphabet is in confused sequence with I apparently repeated instead of R.

2503.162

2503.163. Colchester (*Camulodunum*), Essex. Sherd from a white-coated grey-ware one-handled jug ($\frac{1}{2}$), found in 1928 during excavations in Holly Tree Meadow (Insula 15). Colchester Museum. Drawn by R.P.W., 1954.

graffito on the shoulder: ABCDẸF̣G[. . .]

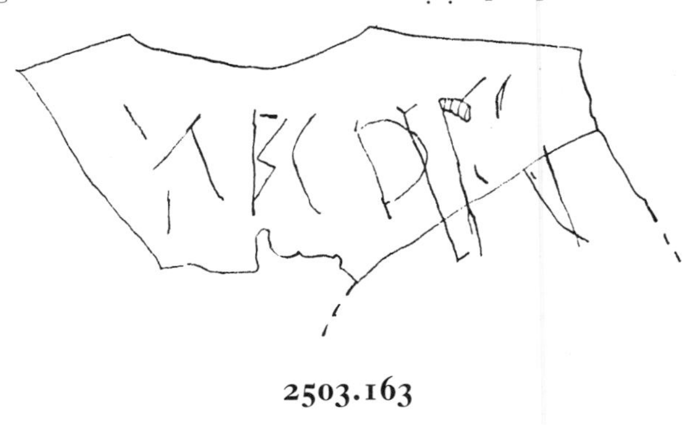

2503.163

2503.164. Chichester (*Noviomagus*), West Sussex. Small jug ($\frac{1}{2}$), found in 1895–6 during excavations at a Roman cremation cemetery at Alexandra Terrace, beside Stane Street, *c.* 300 m east of the East Gate of the Roman city. Formerly in Chichester Museum (ex Butler collection) but now lost. Vessel (after Clark) and two incomplete sketches (by R.P.W.) drawn by Nicholas Griffiths, 1993.

Collingwood in Clark, *Suss. AC* lxxx (1939), 172 with fig. 3.163.

two graffiti: (a) on the shoulder, part of an alphabet: .AXBXCX followed by some small meaningless signs
(b) below the shoulder: IIIOPHIOAN and a large KN

We print R.G.C.'s transcription of (a) and (b). In (a) each X spaces two letters. In (b) the alphabetic sequence perhaps continues, G(?), H, I, K, each separated by another letter (?).

2503.164

2503.167

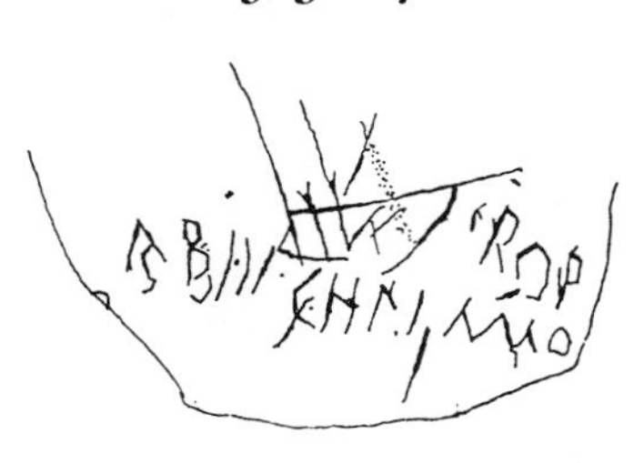

2503.168

2503.165. Chelmsford (*Caesaromagus*), Essex. Sherd from a jar ($\frac{1}{2}$). Chelmsford Museum. Reproduced from Going.

C.J. Going, *The Mansio . . .: The Roman Pottery* (1987), 102 with fig. 50.31.

graffito on the wall: ABCDẸ[. . .]

There is part of another (?) graffito above, and scoring is also visible.

2503.165

2503.166. Chedworth, Gloucestershire. Fragment of a flanged bowl copying Dr. 38 ($\frac{1}{1}$), found in 1954 in Roman debris outside the south wall of the Roman villa. Chedworth Museum. Drawn by R.P.W., 1955.

JRS xlv (1955), 149 No. 27. Rutter, *TBGAS* lxxvi (1957), 163.

2503.166

graffito below the inside of the rim: ΛBCDEFGHI[. . .?]

Since the alphabet begins with the edge of the fragment, and there is a short space after I, it may be that this graffito was cut after the bowl was broken.

2503.167. Binsted Wyck, Hampshire. Part of a red colour-coated bowl ($\frac{1}{2}$) imitating a Dr. 18, found in 1975 during excavation of a late third- to early fourth-century rubbish deposit in the stoke-room of the bath-house at the Roman villa. The flange and footstand have been removed and the scars rubbed down. Farnham Museum. Drawn by S.S.F. from a tracing by M.W.C.H.

Britannia vii (1976), 384 No. 24.

graffito below the scar of the flange: ABCDḶ

2503.168. Scole (? *Villa Faustini*), Norfolk. Part of the base of a grey-ware dish ($\frac{1}{2}$), found in 1983 with a group of second-century pottery at the Long Meadow Estate. Norwich Museum. Drawn by M.W.C.H.

Britannia xv (1984), 345 No. 51.

graffito: X͡VTṢRQP | ABIIFGHIL͡MNO | C̣Ḍ

After breakage the sherd was used for an alphabet; C and D were at first omitted in error and later, rather hesitantly, were added below A and B. Lack of space compelled the writer to continue the sequence from P to X retrograde above the first thirteen letters.

(j) Personal Names (*RIB* 2503.169–466)

2503.169. Nettleton Scrubb, West Kington, Wiltshire. Fragment from the wall of a grey vessel (½), found in 1967 while excavating Building XVIII. Bristol Museum. Drawn by S.S.F. from a rubbing by R.P.W., 1968.

JRS lix (1969), 244 No. 62. Wright in W.J. Wedlake, *The Excavation of the Shrine of Apollo at Nettleton, Wiltshire, 1956–71* (1982), 177 No. 7 with fig. 110.435.

graffito on the wall: ΛBE[. . .]

2503.169

2503.170. Canterbury (*Durovernum*), Kent. Part of a jar in coarse light grey ware (¼), found in 1949 during excavations at the Bus Station in St. George's Lane. Canterbury Museum. Drawn by M.G. Wilson.

S.S. Frere and S. Stow, *The Archaeology of Canterbury* vii (1983), 283 No. 731 with fig. 124.731.

graffito on the shoulder: ABIT[. . .]
Abit[i]
'(Property) of Abitus'

For *Abitus*, presumably the cognomen *Habitus* unaspirated, compare Oswald *Index*, s.v.

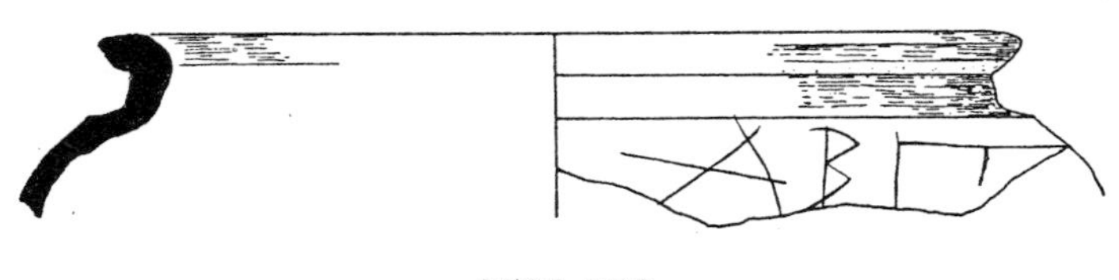

2503.170

2503.171. London (*Londinium*). Globular jug (½) in dull red ware, height 224 mm, found before 1915. British Museum ex W. Ransom collection. Drawn by R.G.C.

2503.171

two graffiti: (a) ΛDIVTORIS
Adiutoris
'(Property) of Adiutor'
(b) below the base, ⋇, a mark of ownership

2503.172. Castleford (*Lagentium*), West Yorkshire. Two conjoining sherds (½) from the base of a dish in grey fabric with a black finish, found in 1981 during excavations at the fort. West Yorkshire Archaeology Service. Drawn by R.S.O.T.

Britannia xviii (1987), 377 No. 55.

graffito beneath the base: [. . .]Λ̣DIVTOR[. . .]
Adiutor[is]
'(Property) of Adiutor'

Compare *RIB* 2501.22 (also from Castleford), ADIVITO, perhaps *Adiu⟨i⟩to[r]*.

2503.172

2503.173. Bodiam, East Sussex. Part of the rim of a coarse-ware bowl (½), found in 1959 *c.* 300 m north of Bodiam railway station on the west side of the Ockham House to Bodiam Bridge road. Present whereabouts unknown. Drawn by S.S.F. from a rubbing by R.P.W., 1960.

JRS l (1960), 242 No. 42.

graffito below the rim: ADIṾ[. . .]
Perhaps *Adiu[tor]*

ADIẸ[. . .], R.P.W.

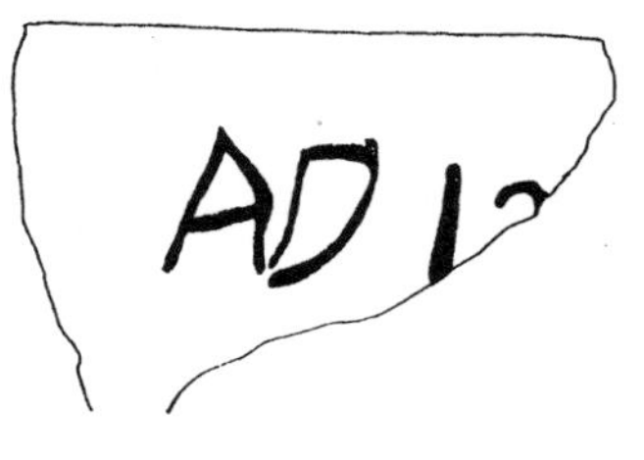

2503.173

2503.174. Brough on Humber (*Petuaria*), Humberside [Yorkshire]. Part of a two-handled storage jar (½), height *c.* 495 mm, found during excavations in 1935. Hull Museum. Drawn by R.P.W., 1951.

P. Corder and T. Romans, *Excavations at the Roman Town at Brough, East Yorkshire 1935* (1936), 34–5 without a reading.

graffito on a handle: ΛIIḶIVS
Aelius

For *Aelius* as a cognomen compare *RIB* 2501.30.

2503.174

2503.175. Colchester (*Camulodunum*), Essex. Base (½) of a grey-ware jar, 70 mm in diameter and cut down to form a lid or large counter, found in 1985 during excavations in Culver Street. Colchester Museum. Drawn by M.W.C.H.

Britannia xxi (1990), 367 No. 18.

graffito beneath the base: ẠẸṢṚIA.LIṆXI

The reading is uncertain. For commentary see *Britannia* loc. cit., note 23.

2503.175

2503.176. Kingscote, Gloucestershire. Fragment (½) from a storage jar in grey fabric with orange surface, found in 1974–5 during excavation of a Roman building at The Chessalls. Corinium Museum, Cirencester. Drawn by M.W.C.H.

Britannia viii (1977), 441 No. 81.

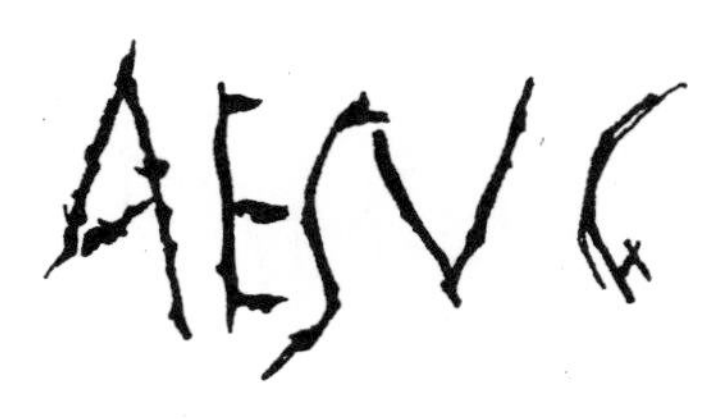

2503.176

graffito on the shoulder: AESVC

Presumably a name derived from the god *Esus* (*Aesus*); compare *Esuccus* (*CIL* xiii 5366a), *Esico* (*RIB* 2501.172). But also note *esox* (*-ocis*), 'salmon', a Celtic word.

2503.177. Newport, Isle of Wight. Sherd (½) from the grooved lid of a Vectis-ware vessel, found shortly before 1987. Isle of Wight Archaeological Service. Drawn by R.S.O.T., 1990. See also PL.V A.

Britannia xxii (1991), 303 No. 38 with fig. 9. D.J. Tomalin, *Roman Wight* (1987), 34 with pl. 3.

graffito: ALAṬVCCA

ALANCCA, Tomalin, loc. cit.

Alatucca is presumably a personal name hitherto unattested, cognate with the Celtic name *Tucca* (whence the nomen *Tuccius*); compare also *Paltucca* at Bath (Tomlin, *Tab. Sulis* 98.21).

2503.177

2503.178. Dorchester (*Durnovaria*), Dorset. Rim-sherd from a Black-burnished jar (½), found in 1984 during excavations at Greyhound Yard. Dorchester Museum. Drawn by R.S.O.T., 1989.

Britannia xx (1989), 336 No. 21. P.J. Woodward et al., *Excavations at Greyhound Yard, Dorchester, 1981–4* (1993), 284 No. 6.

graffito below the rim: Λ̣ḶḄIḶΛ̣[. . .]

Possibly *Albila*, a variant of *Albilla*, derived from *Alba*. For the masculine form *Albillus* see Oswald, *Index*, s.v.

2503.178

2503.179. St. Albans (*Verulamium*), Hertfordshire. Sherd (½) from a jug in red fabric with a cream slip, found in 1959 unstratified during excavation of the city's defences. Verulamium Museum. Drawn by M.G. Wilson.

S.S. Frere, *Verulamium Excavations* iii (1984), 278 No. 9 with fig. 115.9.

graffito on the shoulder below the handle: AL[. . .]

There is possibly the beginning of a third letter, but it looks too close to L to be deliberate.

2503.179

2503.180–82. Slonk Hill, East Sussex. Sherds from three separate jars (½), found in 1970 during excavations at the settlement. Present whereabouts unrecorded. Drawn by R. Hartridge.

Britannia vi (1975), 289 Nos. 29 a–c.

180: graffito inverted in relation to the rim: ΛMB
181: graffito: [.]MB[. . .]
182: graffito: [.]MB

The graffiti are significant as coming from a downland peasant settlement. The abbreviated owner's name probably contained the Celtic element *Ambi-*.

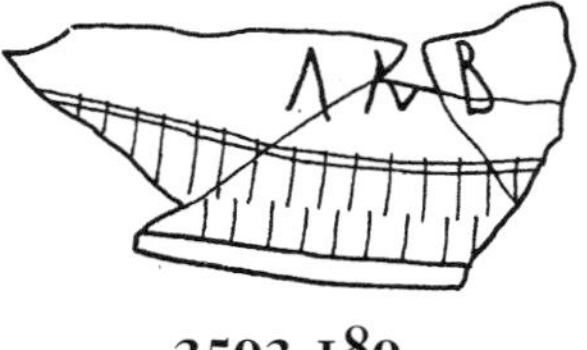

2503.180

2503.181

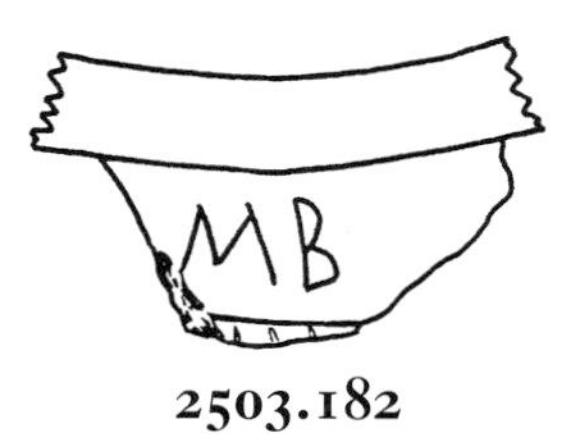

2503.182

2503.183. London (*Londinium*). Fragments of a straight-sided black dish with lattice pattern (½), of Antonine date, found in 1955 at Nos. 28–35 The Minories. In private possession. Drawn by R.P.W., 1956.

JRS xlvi (1956), 151 No. 37.

graffiti on two fragments of the wall, within ansate frames: (a) ΛMB
(b) [.]MB

Compare Nos. 180–2. The abbreviated owner's name probably contained the Celtic element *Ambi-*.

2503.183

2503.184. Housesteads (*Vercovicium*), Northumberland. Base of a grey cooking-pot (½), found before 1936. Housesteads Museum. Drawn by R.P.W., 1940.

graffito: ΛND[. . .]

Many Celtic names begin with the intensive prefix *ande-*, e.g. *Andecarus* (*Tab. Vindol.* ii, No. 182).

2503.184

2503.185. Winterton, Humberside [Lincolnshire]. Part of the side of a grey dish (½), found in 1963 unstratified during excavations at the Roman villa. Scunthorpe Museum. Drawn by S.S.F. from rubbings by R.P.W., 1968.

JRS lix (1969), 245 No. 64. I.M. Stead, *Excavations at Winterton Roman Villa* . . . (1976), 191 No. 5 with fig. 95.5.

graffito, inverted, on the inner face of the wall: ANI

Perhaps *Ani(cetus)* (compare *RIB* 148), but there are other possibilities.

2503.185

2503.186. Shakenoak Farm, Oxfordshire. Base of a bowl ($\frac{1}{2}$) in red colour-coated ware stamped AT[. . .]ḌAI, found in 1970 in a fourth-century context on Site C during excavations at the Roman villa. Ashmolean Museum, Oxford. Rubbings by A.R. Hands. Reproduced from Brodribb et al.

Britannia ii (1971), 301 No. 78. A.C.C. Brodribb et al., *Excavations* at *Shakenoak* iv (1973), 88 No. 10 with fig. 46.

graffito within the footstand: ΛNNΛ

As text, R.S.O.T. after autopsy. MINΛ, *Britannia*; this is a possible alternative reading despite the unconvincing M; but *Mina* is only doubtfully attested elsewhere (*CIL* viii 8771), whereas the feminine personal name *Anna* is fairly common.

The fabric resembles East Gaulish samian ware, but the rouletting is too coarse and the stamp not recognised by Brenda Dickinson. The vessel is probably from the Oxfordshire kilns.

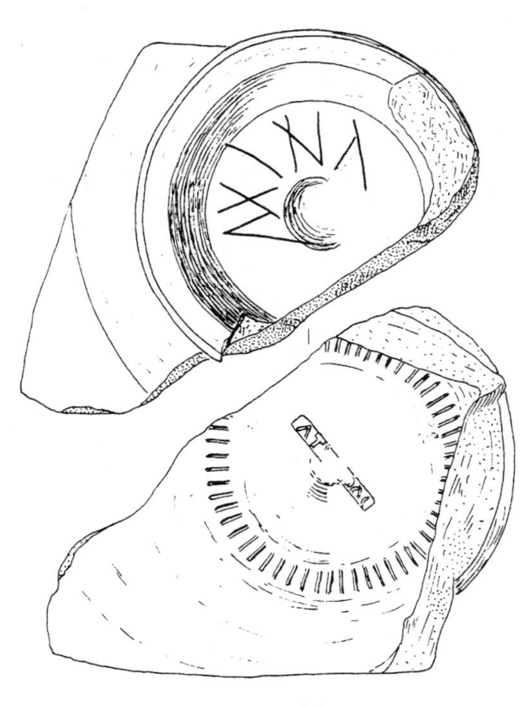

2503.186

2503.187. Gadebridge Park, Hemel Hempstead, Hertfordshire. Part of the rim and wall of a buff segmental bowl ($\frac{1}{2}$), resembling Gillam type 293, found in 1968 in a ditch during excavations at the Roman villa. Dacorum District Council. Rubbings by R.P.W., 1970. Reproduced from Neal.

Britannia i (1970), 314 No. 42. Wright in D.S. Neal, *Gadebridge Park* (1974), 255 No. j with fig. 113 j.

graffito, inverted, on the wall: ΛNN

The second and third letters have extra cuts, R.P.W.

2503.187

2503.188. Housesteads (*Vercovicium*), Northumberland. Part of a matt red bowl ($\frac{1}{2}$), found in 1931 in Building IV in the *vicus*. Housesteads Museum. Drawn by R.P.W., 1946.

graffito below the rim: ΛNṾ[. . .]

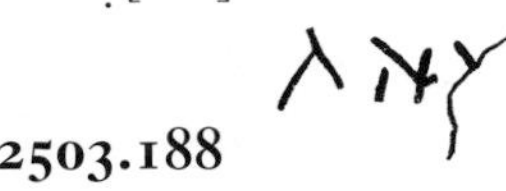

2503.188

2503.189. Exeter (*Isca Dumnoniorum*), Devon. Sherd in dark brown fabric ($\frac{1}{2}$) with burnished lattice pattern, found in 1972 during excavations at the Cathedral Green. Exeter Museum. Reproduced from Bidwell.

Britannia ix (1978), 476 No. 21. Hassall in P.T. Bidwell, *The Legionary Bath-house and Basilica and Forum at Exeter* (1979), 243 No. 4 with fig. 77.4.

graffito on the shoulder: [. . .]ΛP̣RI[. . .]
Probably *Apri* or *Apri[lis]*
'(Property) of Aper *or* Aprilis'

2503.189

2503.190. Caistor St. Edmund (*Venta Icenorum*), Norfolk. Base of a red colour-coated vessel of grey fabric ($\frac{1}{1}$), found in 1931 in the street north of the forum. Norwich Museum. Drawn by R.P.W. from a rubbing by R. Goodburn, 1971.

graffito on the base: ΛSΛḅΛ

The fourth letter is a cursive form.

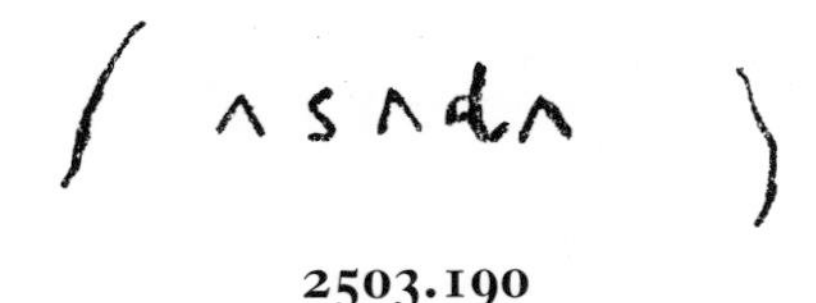

2503.190

2503.191. Housesteads (*Vercovicium*), Northumberland. Part of a bowl with a red slip (½), found in or before 1936. Housesteads Museum. Drawn by R.P.W., 1940.

graffito below the rim: ΛSCVLI
Asculi
'(Property) of Asculus'

The name *Asculus* seems to be unattested, but is perhaps derived from the place-name *Asculum* in Picenum. *[M]asculi* must have been excluded by R.P.W.

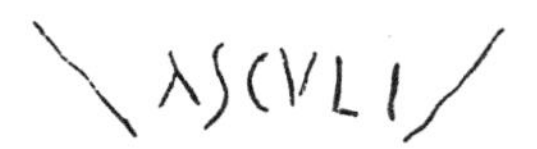

2503.191

2503.192. Silchester (*Calleva*), Hampshire. Part of the base (½) of a terra nigra dish, found in 1982 in a pre-Flavian context at the basilica. Reading Museum. Drawn by M.W.C.H.

Britannia xxi (1990), 368 No. 19.

graffito on the upper face of the base: ΛSRÎOL[. . .]

For comment on the reading see M.W.C.H., *Britannia* loc. cit., note 23.

2503.192

2503.193. Canterbury (*Durovernum*), Kent. Base (1/1) of a small jar or beaker in hard orange fabric, found in 1980 in a late second-century context at the Marlowe III site. Canterbury Museum. Drawn by M.W.C.H.

Britannia xiii (1982), 415 No. 39.

two graffiti partially superimposed beneath the base:
(a) lightly cut, [. . .]ITV
(b) boldly cut, ΛTE[. . .]

(a) is partially obscured by (b).

2503.193

2503.194. Silchester (*Calleva*) Hampshire. A large grey to black two-handled jar (½), height 318 mm, found before 1916. Reading Museum. Drawn by R.P.W. from a rubbing by R.G.C.

T. May, *Silchester* (1916), 195 No. B; 284 No. 22.

graffito on the shoulder: ATINIONIS
Atinionis
'(Property) of Atinio'

ATINIONVS, May.

The nomen *Atinius* is well attested, but for *Atinio* compare *ICUR* 6143.

2503.194

2503.195. Corbridge (? *Coria*), Northumberland. Small buff jug (½), found in 1938 in a pre-Hadrianic level beneath the apsidal building on Site 40T. Department of Archaeology, Durham University. Drawn by R.P.W., 1939.

JRS xxix (1939), 229 No. 14.

graffito: ΛTTITIIRTI
Atti Terti
'(Property) of Attius Tertius'

2503.195

2503.196. Cirencester (*Corinium*), Gloucestershire. Part of a grey jar (1/1). Corinium Museum ex Cripps collection. Drawn by R.P.W., 1952.

graffito on the wall: ΛTVNAT̂I
Atunati
'(Property) of Atunatus'

Perhaps [FO]RTVNAT(I), R.S.O.T. conject. But the name may be a derivative of Atunus (*CIL* iii 4952).

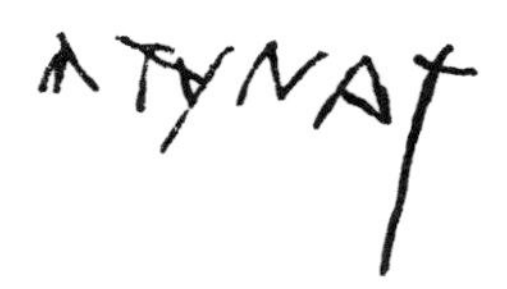

2503.196

2503.197. Colchester (*Camulodunum*), Essex. Brown bowl of Belgic type (½), height 83 mm, found in 1885 in Culver Street. Colchester Museum. Drawn by R.P.W., 1954.

T. May, *Cat.* (1930), 247 with fig. 9.7.

graffito within the footstand: AVEDO

For the cognomen *Avedo* compare *CIL* v 4304. Compare also *RIB* 2489.6, AVE | DO | MI | NA.

2503.197

2503.198. Unknown provenance, said to have been found in the river Thames. Base of a grey-ware vessel (½), purchased in 1984 in Charing Cross Market. In private possession. Drawn by M.W.C.H.

Britannia xv (1984), 344 No. 38.

graffito below the base: ΛVIINT
Probably *Avent(ini)*
'(Property) of Aventinus'

2503.198

2503.199. Exeter (*Isca Dumnoniorum*), Devon. Base (⅟) of a bowl in céramique à l'éponge, found in 1978 in a fourth-century deposit. Exeter Museum. Drawn by M.W.C.H.

Britannia x (1979), 347 No. 18. Hassall in N. Holbrook and P.T. Bidwell, *Roman Finds from Exeter* (1991), 280 No. 7.

graffito on the underside of the base:
[. . .]VITAE | P. . . . .
Perhaps *[A]vitae*
'(Property) of Avita'

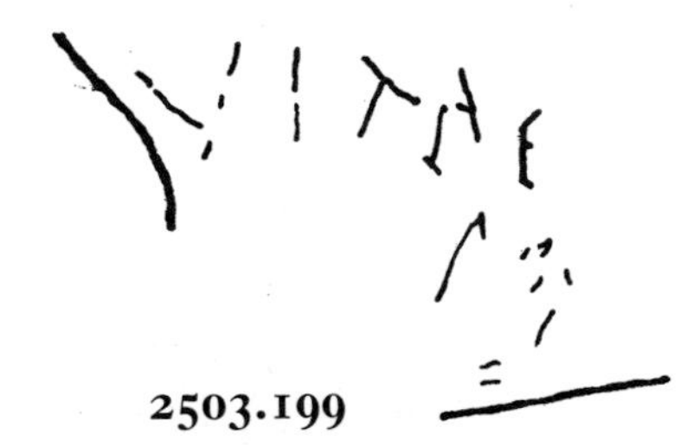

2503.199

2503.200. Carlisle (*Luguvalium*), Cumbria [Cumberland]. Part of the base of a Black-burnished vessel (½), found in 1978 during excavations at Keays Lane, Scotch Street. Tullie House Museum. Drawn by R.S.O.T., 1993.

Britannia xi (1980), 409 No. 16.

graffito on the base: [. . .]ΛVITIVS[. . .]
Probably *Avitius*

[. . .]AVITIIR[. . .], R.S.O.T., *Britannia*. As text, R.S.O.T., 1993.

Avitius is a nomen 'manufactured' from *Avitus* and well attested in *CIL* xiii.

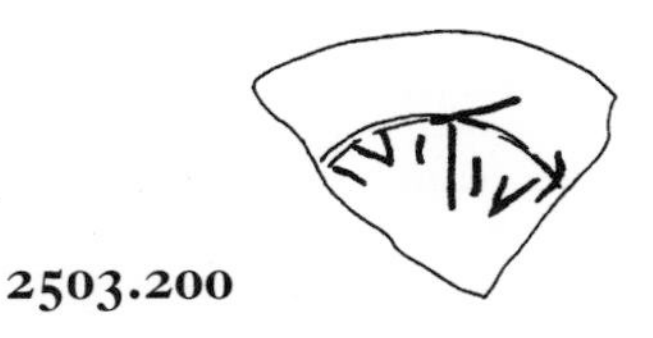

2503.200

2503.201. Shakenoak Farm, Oxfordshire. Part of the base of a bowl (½) in red colour-coated Oxfordshire ware, found in 1970 in a late fourth-century deposit above Fishpond No. 1 during excavations at the Roman villa. Ashmolean Museum, Oxford. Reproduced from Brodribb et al.

A.C.C. Brodribb et al., *Excavations at Shakenoak* iv (1973), 88 No. 6 with fig. 45.6.

graffito on the base: [. . . ?]AX

Possibly *[M]ax(imi)*; but if it was centred the graffito is complete. A and a mark of identification is a possible interpretation.

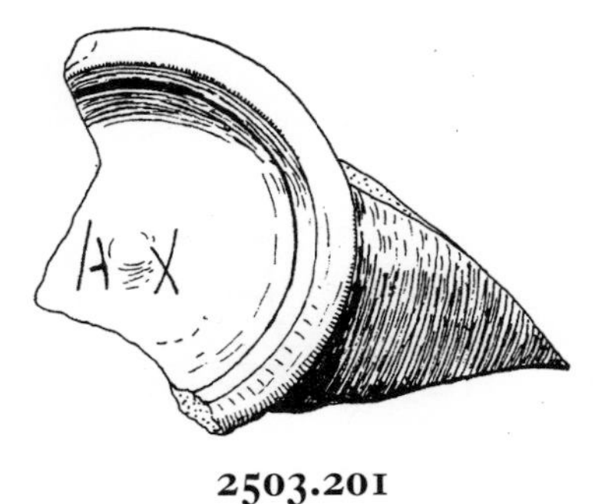

2503.201

2503.202. Caerleon (*Isca*), Gwent [Monmouthshire]. Part of a flanged bowl of 'Caerleon ware' (½), found in 1927–29 during excavations in the Prysg Field. National Museum, Cardiff. Traced by R.P.W. from Nash-Williams.

Nash-Williams, *AC* lxxxvii (1932), 66 fig. 15.1.

graffito on the wall: BAS[. . .]
Perhaps *Bas[si]*
'(Property) of Bassus'

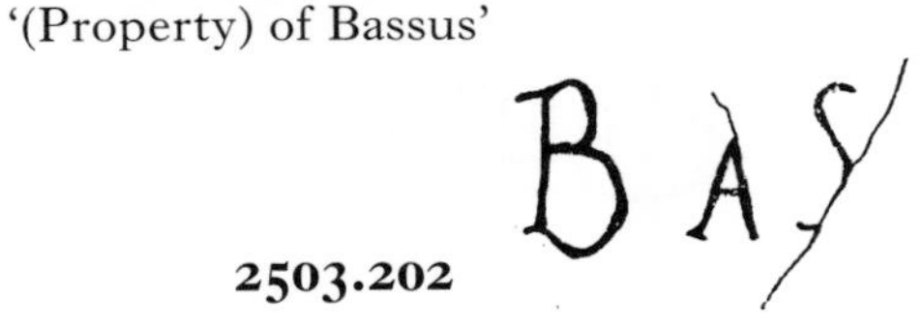

2503.202

2503.203. Brougham (*Brocavum*), Cumbria [Westmorland]. Black-burnished cooking pot of Gillam type 145 (½), found in 1967 while excavating Grave 75 in the Roman cemetery north-east of the fort. Department of the Environment. Drawn by S.S.F. from rubbings by R.P.W., 1970.

Britannia i (1970), 314 No. 43.

graffito above the lattice on the shoulder: BΛTΛ

Bata is perhaps a feminine variant of the name *Bato*, well attested in Pannonia and notably among the Breuci (A. Mócsy, *Pannonia and Upper Moesia* (1974), 59).

2503.203

2503.204. Canterbury (*Durovernum*), Kent. Sherd (½) from the upper part of a grog-tempered Belgic butt beaker, found in 1978 in the filling of a ditch dated *c.* A.D. 40–70 during excavations at No. 16 Watling Street. Canterbury Museum. Drawn by M.W.C.H.

Britannia xiii (1982), 414 No. 32.

graffito on the shoulder: BE

The graffito appears to be complete.

2503.204

2503.205. Maryport (*Alauna*), Cumbria [Cumberland]. Sherd of thick coarse ware (*c.* ¼), found in or before 1794 at the fort. Now lost. Drawn by R.P.W. from Hutchinson.

CIL vii 1336.142 (erroneously classifying it as a samian stamp). Hutchinson, *Cumb.* ii (1794), pl. VI.14 facing p. 284, without a text. Bailey, *CW*² xv (1915), 165.

2503.205

graffito: BELEṆỊ[. . .]
Perhaps *Beleni[ci]*
'(Property) of Belenicus'

BELEA[. . .], Hutchinson. BELENI[. . .] 'with half of I broken off at the edge', Bailey. A name *Belea*[. . .] is not attested. For *Belenicus* see Oswald, *Index*, s.v.

2503.206. Housesteads (*Vercovicium*), Northumberland. Part of a Black-burnished 2 vessel (½), dated to the late second or early third century, found in 1979. Newcastle upon Tyne University. Drawn by Miriam Daniels.

Britannia xiv (1983), 349 No. 51.

graffito: BELICIΛNI
Beliciani
'(Property) of Belicianus'

This 'Celtic' personal name is usually spelt *Bellicianus* (compare *RIB* 2491.80, 2501.102), but the present spelling is also found (compare *RIB* 375).

2503.206

2503.207. Heronbridge, Cheshire. Black-burnished dish (Collingwood type 44), (½), found in 1930. Grosvenor Museum, Chester. Drawn by R.P.W., 1947.

graffito on the rim: BIIBI
B(a)ebi
'(Property) of Baebius'

For the 'Vulgar' spelling compare *RIB* 671, *L. Bebius Crescens*.

2503.207

2503.208. Camelon (? *Colania*), Central Region [Stirlingshire]. Part of a lid in coarse ware, found in 1975–9 during excavations at the fort. Falkirk Museum. Drawing by courtesy of Dr. V.A. Maxfield.

Britannia xxiv (1993), 321 No. 29.

graffito: [. . .]BLII[. . .]
Probably *Ble[. . .]*

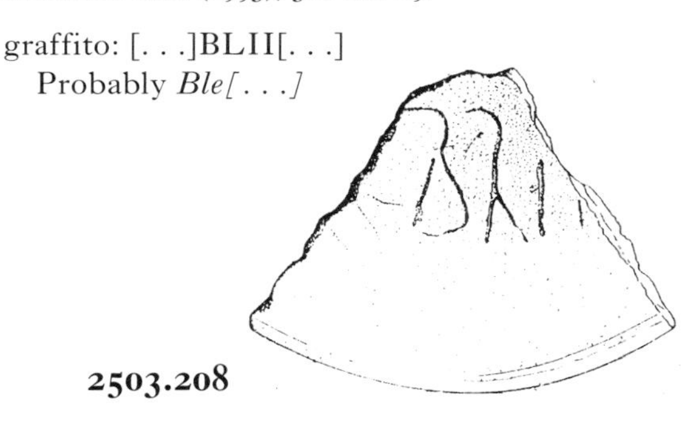

2503.208

2503.209. Colchester (*Camulodunum*), Essex. Part of a grey-ware vessel ($\frac{1}{2}$) imitating samian form Déchelette 65, found before 1925. Colchester Museum. Drawn by R.P.W., 1954.

T. May, *Cat.* (1930), 247 with fig. 9.8.

graffito on the shoulder: BLLA
  Probably *B(e)lla*

B.LΛ, May. As text, R.P.W.

For *Bellus/a* see Kajanto, *Cognomina* 231, who suggests that the name may be 'largely Celtic'.

2503.209

2503.210. East Dean, Hampshire. Part of a black cooking-pot ($\frac{1}{2}$), found in 1869 in a Roman building near Holbury. Salisbury Museum. Drawn by R.P.W., 1940.

Master, *WAM* xiii (1872), 40.

graffito: BERA͡E
  Perhaps '(Property) of Bera'

Probably complete at the end; there is no trace of the top horizontal of the E, R.P.W. The name is otherwise attested, but compare *CIL* v 8115, 20 (Milan), *Berra*.

2503.210

2503.211. Wallsend (*Segedunum*), Tyne and Wear [Northumberland]. Sherd ($\frac{1}{2}$) from a vessel in Black-burnished 2 ware, found in 1975 during excavations at the fort. Wallsend Museum. Drawn by R.S.O.T., 1992.

Britannia vii (1976), 389 No. 55.

graffito: BIDIVS

BLDIVS, *Britannia*.

The name is otherwise unattested.

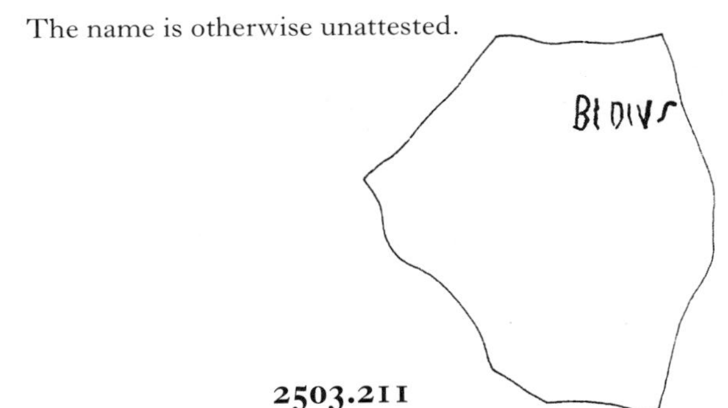

2503.211

2503.212. Bainbridge (? *Virosidum*), North Yorkshire. Black-burnished jar ($\frac{1}{2}$) of the late third or early fourth century, found in 1928 in the inner ditch at the north-east angle of the fort. Leeds University. Drawn by R.P.W., 1960.

JRS li (1961), 197 No. 41.

graffito on the shoulder: BIṆIS

Complete at each end, R.P.W. Compare *RIB* 1806, *Binius*.

2503.212

2503.213. Alcester, Warwickshire. Part of a storage jar ($\frac{1}{4}$), found in 1964–66 in a late fourth-century context during excavations in the extramural area. Warwickshire Museum. Drawing by courtesy of Nicholas Palmer.

S. Cracknell and C. Mahany (eds.), *Roman Alcester* i: *The Southern Extramural Area* (1994), fig. 57 No. 11.

graffito on the shoulder: ḄR

RR, Cracknell and Mahany.

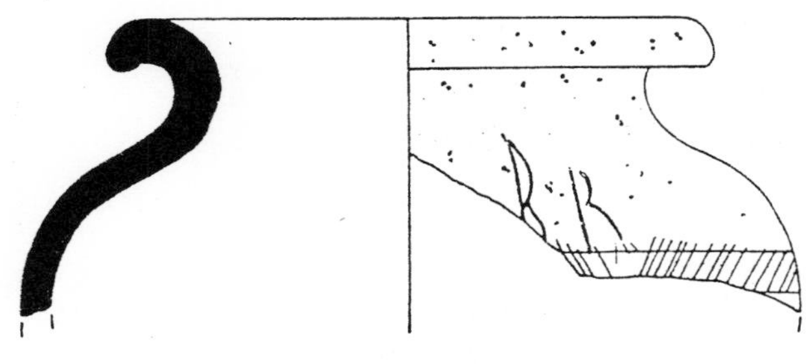

2503.213

2503.214. Newstead (*Trimontium*), Borders Region [Roxburghshire]. Part of a Black-burnished dish with lattice decoration (Gillam form 221), found in 1905–9 during excavations at the fort. National Museums of Scotland, Queen Street, Edinburgh. Drawn by R.G.C., 1936.

J. Curle, *Newstead* (1911), 230 with fig. 22.7.

two graffiti: (a) BRVT
  Perhaps *Brut(us)*
(b) overriding part of (a), V

For *Brutus* and related cognomina see Kajanto, *Cognomina*, 264.

2503.214 

2503.215. Colchester (*Camulodunum*), Essex. Bowl ($\frac{1}{4}$) in Black-burnished 2 ware, found in 1927–29 during excavation of the 'Mithraeum' in the Holly Trees Meadow (Insula 15). Colchester Museum. Reproduced from Hull.

M.R. Hull, *Roman Colchester* (1958), 139 No. 40 with fig. 67.90.

two graffiti, (a) on the rim: IX or XI
'Nine' *or* 'Eleven'
(b) inverted on the wall: BV

2503.215

2503.216. Holt, Clwyd [Denbighshire]. Part of a buff jar ($\frac{1}{2}$), found in 1907–15 during excavations at the legionary works depot. National Museum, Cardiff. Drawn by R.P.W., 1953.

W.F. Grimes, *Holt* (1930), 134 No. 35.

graffito below the rim: BVTṚ[. . .]
Perhaps *Butr[io]*

For the name *Butrio* see Oswald, *Index*, s.v.

2503.216

2503.217. Scole (? *Villa Faustini*), Norfolk. Base of a coarse-ware vessel ($\frac{1}{2}$) in a local fabric, found in 1983, during excavations at Scole House, in a Roman well disused towards the end of the second century. Norwich Museum. Drawn by M.W.C.H.

Britannia xv (1984), 347 No. 52.

graffito within the footstand: CAN
Probably *Can(didi)*
'(Property) of Candidus'

2503.217

2503.218. Exeter (*Isca Dumnoniorum*), Devon. Rim of a late first- or second-century South-Western Black-burnished 1 cooking pot ($\frac{1}{2}$), found in 1977–8 during excavations in Mermaid Yard. Exeter Museum. Drawn by M.W.C.H.

Britannia xx (1989), 335 No. 17. Hassall in N. Holbrook and P.T. Bidwell, *Roman Finds from Exeter* (1991), 280 No. 8.

graffito on the shoulder: [. . .]CANDỊ[. . .]
Probably *Candi[di]*
'(Property) of Candidus'

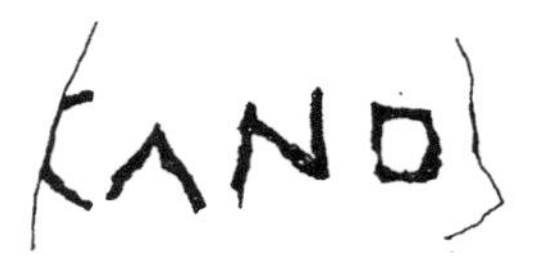

2503.218

2503.219. Cirencester (*Corinium*), Gloucestershire. Part of the base ($\frac{1}{2}$) of a Black-burnished dish, found in 1974 unstratified at St. Michael's Field (Insula VI). Corinium Museum. Drawn by M.W.C.H.

Britannia xiv (1983), 343 No. 24.

cursive graffito on the wall: [. . .]ṆDIDIΛẸ
[Ca]ndidiae
'(Property) of Candida'

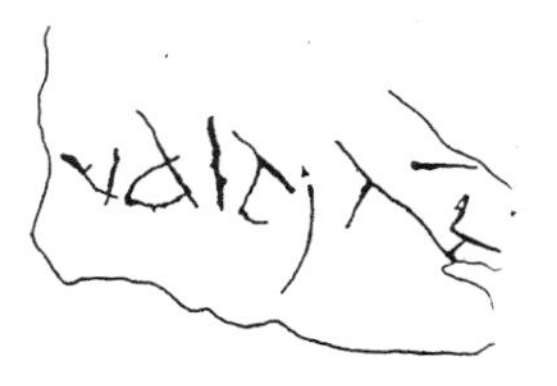

2503.219

2503.220. Silchester (*Calleva*), Hampshire. Fragment of a buff jug ($\frac{1}{2}$), found in 1955 during excavations in Insulae XXII A/XXIII. Reading Museum. Drawn by R.P.W., 1956.

JRS xlvi (1956), 151 No. 39. Boon, *Arch.* cii (1970), 68 with fig. 8 c, No. 104. G.C. Boon, *Silchester: the Roman Town of Calleva* (1974), 131.

graffito on the shoulder: CARṾ[. . .]
Probably *Caru[s]*

Boon, *Silchester*, loc. cit., notes the 'speculative' restoration of the graffito as *(oleum) carv[inum]*, 'oil of walnuts'; compare Pliny, *NH* xv, 28. This seems unlikely; the word in any case is *caryinum*.

2503.220

2503.221. Langton, North Yorkshire. Part of a colour-coated beaker ($\frac{1}{2}$) of Lower Nene Valley ware, found in 1930 during excavation of the Roman villa. Malton Museum. Drawn by R.P.W., 1951.

graffito below the lip: CAS[. . .]

Probably *Cas[sius]* or *Cas[tus]* or derived names.

2503.221

2503.222. Olney, Buckinghamshire. Fragment from the shoulder of a grey jar ($\frac{1}{2}$), found in 1961–2 without associated material in the Emberton gravel pit south of the village. Aylesbury Museum. Drawn by S.S.F. from rubbings by R.P.W., 1963.

JRS liv (1964), 184 No. 42.

graffito on the shoulder: CΛVS

Perhaps for *Ca(v)us*; compare *RIB* 94 and 2492.10.

2503.222

2503.223. Wilderspool, Cheshire. Part of a storage jar ($\frac{1}{2}$), found in 1900. Warrington Museum. Drawn by R.P.W., 1952.

May, *T. Lancs. & Chesh. Hist. Soc.* lii (1900), 51.

graffito on the shoulder: CIILΛ[. . .]
Probably *Cela[ti]*
'(Property) of Celatus'

'Probably 102 *lagenae*', May.

For *Celatus* compare *RIB* 274 and Holder s.v.

2503.223

2503.224. St. Albans (*Verulamium*), Hertfordshire. Fragment of a beaker ($\frac{1}{1}$) in orange-red paste with a dark brown colour-coat, showing part of the arm of a charioteer. Found in 1957 in a late pit outside Building XIV.1. Verulamium Museum. Drawn by M.G. Wilson.

JRS xlviii (1958), 154 No. 39. S.S. Frere, *Verulamium Excavations* i (1972), 364 No. 7 with fig. 140.7.

cursive graffito above the arm: CIILIIR
Celer

The cognomen *Celer* is frequent (see Kajanto, *Cognomina*, 248), but may also be intended literally as 'swift' when applied to a charioteer; indeed, it was also a typical dog's name (Columella vii 12.13).

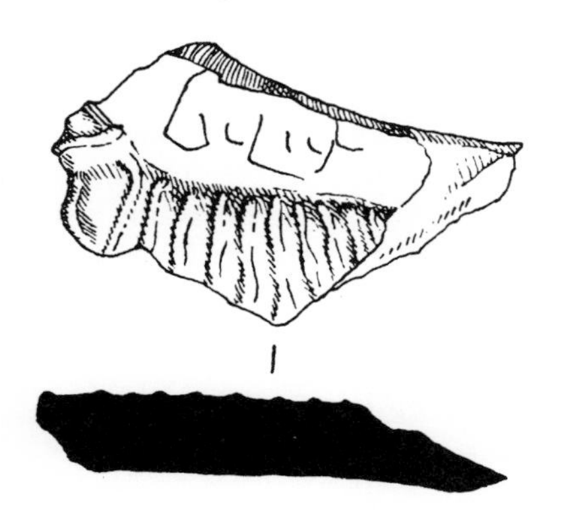

2503.224

2503.225. Braughing, Hertfordshire. Part of a large late Iron Age storage vessel ($\frac{1}{2}$) decorated with rough combing, found in 1979 in a late Iron Age pit of Augustan date during excavations at the Gatesbury Track. Hertford Museum. Drawn by M.W.C.H.

Britannia x (1979), 349 No. 25. Partridge, *Herts. Arch*, vii (1979), 117 with fig. 35.

graffito: CIINΛṬIṆ[. . .]

CIINΛṬẠ[. . .] is also possible. The name (?) may be cognate with *Cennatus*, for which see Oswald, *Index*, s.v. Compare *RIB* 2503.271 with note.

2503.225

2503.226. Ware, Hertfordshire. Fragment (½) from the base of a grey-ware dish, found in 1978 on the early Roman land-surface, sealed by third-century timber buildings at the Allen and Hanbury site. Hertford Museum. Drawn by M.W.C.H.

Britannia x (1979), 350 No. 28.

graffito below the base: CIINNIO
Cennio

For the nomen *Cennius* see *CIL* ix 5209; and compare Oswald, *Index*, s.v. *Cennatus* and *Cenno*.

2503.226

2503.227. Southwark, south London. Fragment from the wall of a buff jar (½), found in 1962 during excavations at No. 199 Borough High Street. Cuming Museum. Drawn by S.S.F. from rubbings by R.P.W., 1968.

JRS lix (1969), 245 No. 65.

graffito on the wall: CEVS[. . .]
Probably *Cens[orinus]*

For *Censorinus* compare *RIB* 98, 218, 2045; for *Censorina*, *RIB* 670. *Censor* (*RIB* 605) is also possible. Compare also *RIB* 2503.509.

2503.227

2503.228. Unrecorded provenance. Graffito (½) found before 1956. Yorkshire Museum, York. Drawn by R.P.W., but without giving description or context.

graffito: CIVILIS
Civilis
'(Property) of Civilis'

2503.228

2503.229. Catterick (*Cataractonium*), North Yorkshire. Two conjoining sherds (½) of a buff jug dated by associated material to the Flavian-Trajanic period, found in 1959 during excavations on the line of the new A1 road. Yorkshire Museum, York. Drawn by R.S.O.T., 1990.

Britannia xxi (1990), 376 No. 66.

graffito on the shoulder: CLAV[. . .]
Probably *Clau[dius . . . ?]*

2503.229

2503.230. Cambridge (*Duroliponte*). Fragment (½) from the wall of a Black-burnished bowl with bead rim, found in 1974 in the demolition-level of a shrine at Ridgeons Garden. Museum of Archaeology and Anthropology, Cambridge. Drawn by M.W.C.H.

Britannia x (1979), 347 No. 15.

graffito on the wall: COCCA

For the feminine name *Cocca* compare *CIL* xii 1924.

2503.230

2503.231. Colchester (*Camulodunum*), Essex. Part of a grey handled jar (½), found in 1927–29 in the Holly Trees Meadow (Insula 15). Colchester Museum. Drawn by R.P.W., 1954.

JRS xxxiv (1944), 91 No. 24.

graffito around the shoulder:
[. . .]COMINIFAMILIARIS.[. . .]TITISCX[. . .]|
IIII[. . .]ENI

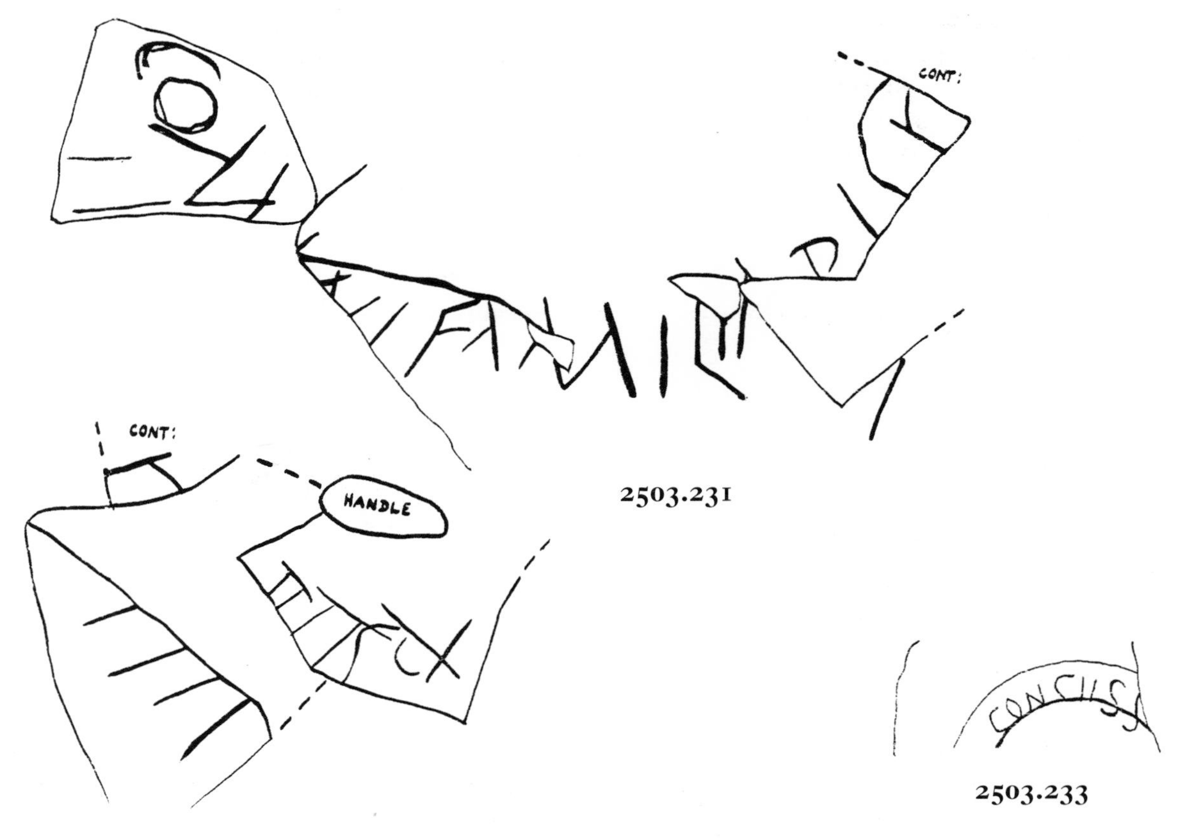

2503.231

Comini Familiaris [. . .]TITISCX[. . .] IIII
[. . .]ENI
'(Property ?) of Cominius Familiaris . . . .'

l.2. [. . .]IIII[. . .]ENI, *JRS*, but [. . .]ENI is not on the drawing. Cominius is a common nomen; compare also *RIB* 2411.120–2.

2503.232. Dorchester (*Durnovaria*), Dorset. Two conjoining fragments ($\frac{1}{2}$) of an orange-coated vessel in buff fabric, found in 1961 during excavations at the Colliton Park Roman house. Dorchester Museum. Drawn by S.S.F. from rubbings by R.P.W., 1961.

JRS lii (1962), 199 No. 52; liii (1963), 167 corrigendum.

graffito, inverted, on the lower part of the wall:

2503.232

2503.233

COMVNỊ[. . .] | [. . .]C̣ΛV.[. . .]
Perhaps *Com(m)uni[s]*

The writer's instrument appears to have slipped when making the left-hand side of O.

For the common cognomen *Communis* see Kajanto, *Cognomina* 256; compare also *RIB* 2501.140.

2503.233. Saunderton, Buckinghamshire. Part of the base of a coarse grey jar ($\frac{1}{2}$), found in 1938 during excavations at the Roman villa. Aylesbury Museum. Drawn by R.P.W.

JRS xxix (1939), 229 No. 15.2 with fig. 21.2. Ashcroft, *Records of Bucks.* xiii (1939), 411 with pl. 6.

graffito around the base: CONCIISS[. . .]
Concess[i]
'(Property) of Concessus'

CONGIVS S(emis), Oswald in Ashcroft, loc. cit.

As text, R.G.C. (*JRS*), who notes that the thin lines of Oswald's G and V are minute scratches not comparable with the deliberate incisions; they are shown on the *JRS* fig., but are omitted by R.P.W.

For the common cognomen *Concessus* see Kajanto, *Cognomina* 350.

2503.234. Leicester (*Ratae*). Fragment ($\frac{1}{1}$) from a (?) jug in orange-buff ware, found in 1965 unstratified during excavations in Castle Street. Leicester Museum. Drawn by M.W.C.H.

Britannia xvii (1986), 444 No. 58.

graffito on the wall: CONNE
  Perhaps *Conn(a)e*
  '(Property) of Conna'

Connus and *Conna* are not apparently attested, although *Connius* occurs both as nomen and cognomen. It is derived by Holder from Celtic *Connos*, a name occurring on Gaulish coins and which would in its closest Latinized form become *Connus/a*. M.W.C.H.

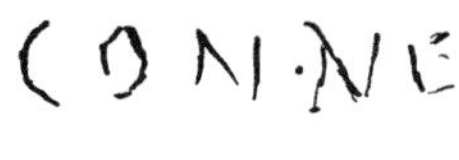

2503.234

2503.235. St. Albans (*Verulamium*), Hertfordshire. Part of a colour-coated Lower Nene Valley ware beaker ($\frac{1}{4}$ and $\frac{1}{2}$), found in 1974 during excavation of the extramural Baths in Branch Road. Verulamium Museum. Reproduced from Greep.

Greep, *Herts. Arch.* viii (1980–82), 207 No. 5 with figs. 1.5 and 2.5.

graffito below the rim: CV

Probably an abbreviated name such as *Cu(pitus)*, not a numeral. Compare *RIB* 2501.152, *Cupit[i]*, also from St. Albans.

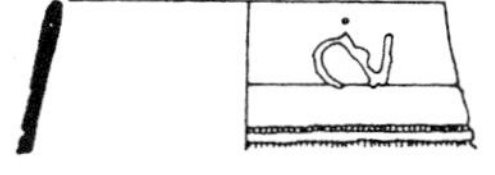

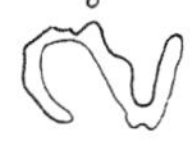

2503.235

2503.236. Caerleon (*Isca*), Gwent [Monmouthshire]. Part of a soft brownish-grey cooking pot ($\frac{1}{2}$), found in 1954 during excavations south-west of the fortress. National Museum, Cardiff. Drawn by G.C. Boon, 1992.

JRS l (1960), 242 No. 43 c.

graffito on the wall: [. . .]ÇVNICATI[. . .]
  Cunicati
  '(Property) of Cunicatus'

ṾNKATI, R.P.W., *JRS*, G.C. Boon, 1960. As text, R.P.W. from a rubbing, 1977.

The name *Cunicatus* seems to be unattested, but the Celtic name-elements *Cuno-* and *-catus* are quite common.

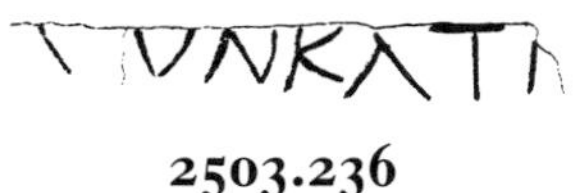

2503.236

2503.237. Lincoln (*Lindum*). Part of a bulbous colour-coated beaker ($\frac{1}{2}$) in buff fabric with black slip, rouletted, found in 1972 during excavations at the Holmes Grain Warehouse site. Lincoln Archaeological Trust. Drawn by S.S.F. from a rubbing by M.W.C.H.

Britannia v (1974), 465 No. 29.

graffito on the neck: CVИ

Cuno- ('hound') is a frequent Celtic name-element.

2503.237

2503.238. Bower Chalke, Wiltshire. Part of the rim of a grey sandy flanged bowl ($\frac{1}{2}$), found in 1959 in the upper levels of a cross-ridge dyke known as Middle Chase Ditch. Salisbury Museum. Drawn by Philip Rahtz.

Britannia xviii (1987), 372 No. 29.

graffito beneath the rim: CVN[. . .]

It is unclear whether the graffito is complete, but presumably a personal name in *Cuno-*. Compare No. 237.

2503.238

2503.239. Winchester (*Venta Belgarum*), Hampshire. Fragment from a Black-burnished dish ($\frac{1}{2}$), found in 1968 in a late third- or fourth-century context during excavations at Wolvesey Palace. Winchester Museum. Drawn by R.P.W.

Britannia vii (1976), 385 No. 29.

graffito on the wall: CVNI[. . .]

Perhaps *Cunitus*: compare *RIB* 2416.2 and 3.

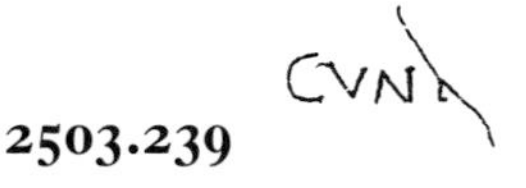

2503.239

2503.240. Caves Inn (*Tripontium*), Warwickshire. Part of the base of a Black-burnished dish of Gillam type 322 ($\frac{1}{2}$), found in 1962 during excavation of a defensive ditch on the east side of Watling Street.

2503.240

Warwickshire Museum. Drawn by S.S.F. from rubbings by R.P.W., 1963.

JRS liii (1963), 167 No. 54. Cameron and Lucas, *T. Birm. AS* lxxxiii (1969), 177 No. 11 with fig. 28.11.

graffito on the base: DIICVMA
Decuma

Decuma is a variant of *Decima*, R.P.W.

2503.241. Corbridge (? *Coria*), Northumberland. Part of the rim of a grey cooking pot ($\frac{1}{2}$), found in 1952 in Temple III immediately below the debris of late second-century destruction. Corbridge Museum. Drawn by R.P.W., 1964.

graffito on the inner surface of the rim: DIIMII[. . .]
Probably *Deme[trius]*

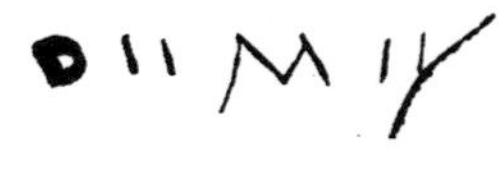

2503.241

2503.242. Wilderspool, Cheshire. Two conjoining sherds of a storage jar ($\frac{1}{4}$), found in 1900. Warrington Museum. Drawn by R.P.W., 1952.

May, *T. Lancs & Chesh. Hist. Soc.* lii (1900), 51.

graffito on the shoulder: DIINSIBALI
Densibali
'(Property) of Densibalus'

L is reversed. The name seems to be otherwise unknown; possibly a variant of *Decebalus*: compare *RIB* 1920 and 2501.156.

2503.243. Silchester (*Calleva*), Hampshire. Part of a small bead-rim cooking pot in native hand-made gritted ware ($\frac{1}{2}$), height 83 mm, diameter 95 mm, found before 1952. Reading Museum. Drawn by R.P.W., 1952.

two graffiti on the wall: (a) DEṢIM
(b) DESIMIINIΛ|Λ

Apparently *Desimena*, a name otherwise unknown; possibly *Decimina* was intended.

2503.243

2503.244. Chelmsford (*Caesaromagus*), Essex. Fragments of so-called 'Romano-Saxon' pot ($\frac{1}{2}$ and $\frac{1}{4}$), decorated with two rows of bosses pressed out from within, triangular settings of dimples, and incised cruciform motifs. Found unstratified during excavations at the site of Orchard Street Hall. Chelmsford Museum. Rubbings by W.J. Rodwell. Reproduced from Rodwell. See also PL. IV B.

JRS lix (1969), 245 No. 66. Rodwell, *Antiq. J.* l (1970), 262–5 with fig. 2 and pl. XXXVII. Both these references give the find-spot as Kelvedon, corrected in *Britannia* xiii (1982), 421 corrigendum (b). C.J. Going, *The Mansio . . .: The Roman Pottery* (1987), 57 Group 20 with fig. 32.390, and 102.3 with fig. 50.38.

graffito on the shoulder: DISETE
Diset(a)e
'(Property) of Diseta'

Since the pot is incomplete, a vocative of *Disetus* cannot be excluded, but seems unlikely. *Diseta* would be the feminine form of the Celtic name *Disetus* or *Diseto* (see Oswald, *Index*, s.v.), although *Diseto* is also found as a woman's name (*CIL* v 6025, xii 3603).

The vessel was unstratified but associated with material most probably derived from a late fourth-century context. There is no evidence to suggest that it came from a burial.

For a discussion of 'Romano-Saxon' pottery see J.P. Gillam in P.J. Casey (ed.), *The End of Roman Britain* (1979), 103–18: he concludes that it is not 'in any sense a hybrid between Roman and Saxon pottery'.

2503.242

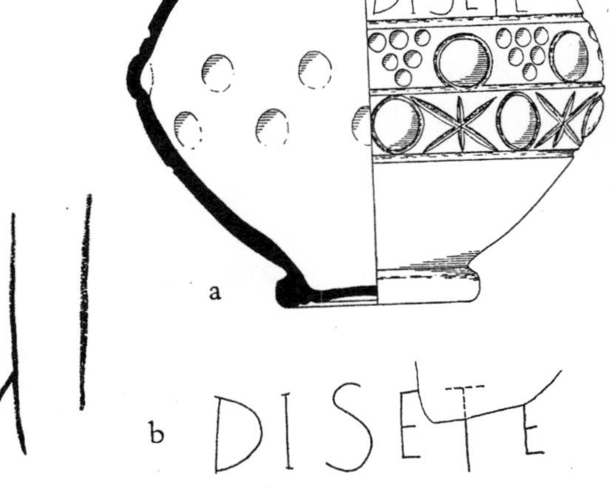

2503.244

2503.245. Springhead (? *Vagniacis*), Kent. Part of a grey jar ($\frac{1}{2}$), found in 1952 during excavations. Gravesend Museum. Drawn by R.P.W., 1954.

Penn, *Arch. Cant.* lxv (1952), 173; lxxi (1957), 104 with fig. 17.10.

graffito on the shoulder: DMR
Perhaps *D(ecimus) M(. . .) R(. . .)*

2503.245

2503.246. London (*Londinium*). Fragment from a grey colour-coated narrow-necked beaker ($\frac{1}{2}$), found in 1956 during excavations at the White Tower, Tower of London. Department of the Environment. Drawn by R.P.W., 1964.

JRS liv (1964), 184 No. 43.

graffito below rouletting: DOM
Probably *Dom(itii)* or *Dom(itiani)*
'(Property) of Domitius *or* Domitianus'

2503.246

2503.247. Elmswell, Humberside [Yorkshire]. Fragment of grey Crambeck ware ($\frac{1}{2}$), found in 1955 on a chalk-and-cobble pavement on Bramble Hill. In private possession. Drawn by R.P.W., 1956.

JRS xlvi (1956), 151 No. 38 b.

graffito on the inside face: DOMỊ[. . .]
Probably *Domi[tii]* or *Domi[tiani]*
'(Property) of Domitius *or* Domitianus'

2503.247

2503.248. Baldock, Hertfordshire. Sherd ($\frac{1}{2}$) from a small vessel in a fabric imitating *terra nigra*, found in 1972 in the filling of a pit complex in Walls Field. Letchworth Museum. Reproduced from Stead and Rigby.

Britannia xi (1980), 412 No. 42. Hassall in I.M. Stead and V. Rigby, *Baldock* (1986), 189 No. 838 with fig. 82.838.

graffito: [. . .]ḌON.[. . .]
Perhaps *Dona[tus]*

2503.248

2503.249. Caerleon (*Isca*), Gwent [Monmouthshire]. Fragment ($\frac{1}{2}$) of a Black-burnished dish of Antonine date, found in 1956 during excavation of Building VII outside the fortress. National Museum, Cardiff. Drawn by G.C. Boon, 1992.

graffito: EFF[. . .]

The only possibility seems to be *Efficax*, which occurs ten times in *CIL* (Kajanto, *Cognomina*, 259).

2503.249

2503.250. Gloucester (*Glevum*). Fragment ($\frac{1}{2}$) from a coarse-ware jar in micaceous orange-brown fabric, found in 1974 in the filling of the late Roman city ditch. Gloucester Museum. Drawn by L.V. Marley.

Britannia xiv (1983), 344 No. 29. Hassall in C. Heighway, *The East and North Gates of Gloucester* (1983), 199 No. G 3 with fig. 114.G 3.

graffito: IIPIΛ
Epia

Perhaps a variant of *Eppius/a*.

2503.250

2503.251. Chesters (*Cilurnum*), Northumberland. Part of a black cooking pot ($\frac{1}{2}$) of fourth-century date found before 1886. Chesters Museum. Drawn by R.P.W., 1943.

EE vii 1180. *IG* xiv 2577.12. Anon., *PSAN*[2] ii (1886), 203, fig.

graffito on the wall in Greek letters: [. . .]ẸΠΩṂ[. . .]

Compare *RIB* 2503.124. Here, however, *Epona* is not a possibility since Juvenal viii 157 shows that the *o* in *Epona* is short.

2503.251

2503.252. South Shields (*Arbeia*), Tyne and Wear [Durham]. Part of a shallow dish (½) in Black-burnished ware with lattice decoration, height 45 mm, diameter 286 mm, found in the 19th century. Museum of Antiquities, Newcastle upon Tyne, ex T. Stephens collection. Drawn by R.P.W., 1940.

two graffiti, (a) on the inside of the base: ER palm branch
(b) on the underside of the base ẸṚ

This item may be the same as *RIB* 2494.125 (South Shields, now lost), which Bruce describes as 'an amphora or wine-jar', noting that 'the letters ER have been scratched both on the inside and outside'. His drawing (ibid.) should be compared with R.P.W.'s of *RIB* 2503.252: the graffito is the same, except that the bottom edge of the sherd has since been lost. Nevertheless, the fabric of 2503.252 could hardly be confused with that of an amphora, and the possibility remains that both vessels bore the mark of a single owner.

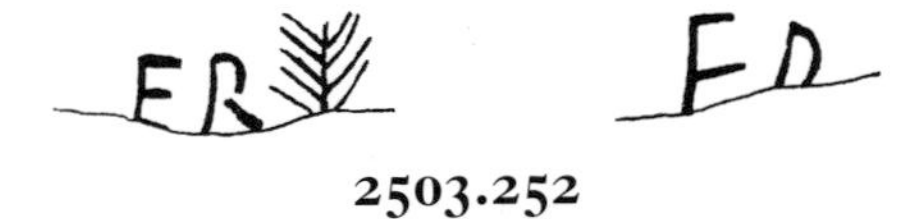

2503.252

2503.253. Caerleon (*Isca*), Gwent [Monmouthshire]. Part of a buff flanged bowl imitating Dr. 38 (½), found in 1954 in the Bear House Field. National Museum, Cardiff. Drawn by R.P.W.

JRS l (1960), 242 No. 43a.

graffito on the lower part of the wall: [. . .]ERRIṾ[. . .]
Perhaps *[. . .V]errius[. . .]*

ERRA͡V[. . .], R.P.W., *JRS*. As text, R.S.O.T.

R.P.W. (archive) conjectures *errav[isti]*, 'you have made a mistake', but this seems unlikely.

2503.253

The nomen *Verrius* is well attested in Gallia Narbonensis, from which Legio ii Augusta drew recruits (e.g. *RIB* 361, and compare *Britannia* xix (1988), 490 No. 4 with note).

2503.254. Colchester (*Camulodunum*), Essex. Part of a white jug (½), found before 1939. Colchester Museum. Drawn by R.P.W., 1943.

JRS xxxiv (1944), 91 No. 27.

graffito on the shoulder: IIRRVMOLLIES[. . .]

IIRRVMOLIIIS[. . .], R.P.W., *JRS*, suggesting . . . *l(ibrae) iii s(emis)*, '3½ pounds'. As text, R.P.W., 1976, *RIB* archive.

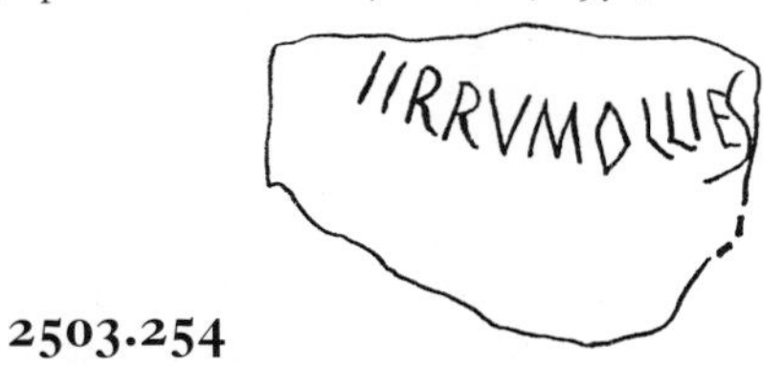

2503.254

2503.255. Cirencester (*Corinium*), Gloucestershire. Fragment (½) of a Black-burnished dish, found in 1972 unstratified at St. Michael's Field (Insula VI). Corinium Museum. Drawn by M.W.C.H.

Britannia xiv (1983), 344 No. 25.

graffito in Greek letters on the wall: [. . .]YTY[. . .]
Probably [E]ὐτύ[χης]
'Eutyches'

This Greek name is very common: compare Solin, *Namenbuch*, 796–801 and *RIB* 2501.174.

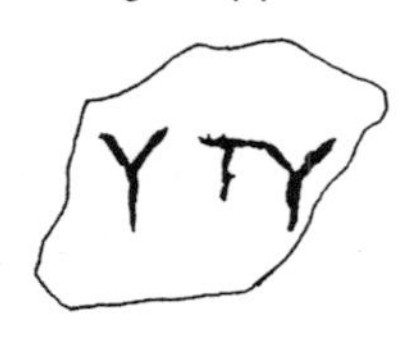

2503.255

2503.256. Chesterholm (*Vindolanda*), Northumberland. Two conjoined fragments from a Black-burnished cooking pot (½), found in 1970 on Site XXIV in a rubbish-deposit of *c.* A.D. 300. Vindolanda Museum. Drawn by S.S.F. from rubbings by R.P.W., 1970.

Britannia ii (1971), 301 No. 74.

graffito: EXVPERATVS
Ex(s)uperatus

For the name compare *RIB* 369, where the same spelling is found.

2503.256

2503.257. Old Kilpatrick, Strathclyde [Dunbartonshire]. Part of a Black-burnished ware dish (½), found in 1923–24 during excavations at the Antonine Wall fort. Hunterian Museum. Drawn by R.P.W., 1956.

S.N. Miller, *The Roman Fort at Old Kilpatrick* (1928), 50 No. 6 with pl. XVII.6.

two graffiti on the upper surface of the base: (a) X, a mark of ownership
(b) FAV

Fau(stus) or *Fau(stinus)* is likely, but there are other possibilities.

2503.257

2503.258. Chester (*Deva*). Graffito (½), found before 1956. Grosvenor Museum. Drawn by R.P.W.

graffito: FELI[. . .]
Feli[cis]
'(Property) of Felix'

2503.258

2503.259. Chesterholm (*Vindolanda*), Northumberland. Part of the wall of a fourth-century cooking pot (½), found in 1970 unstratified in the south-east corner of the bath-house in the *vicus*. Vindolanda Museum. Drawn by S.S.F. from rubbings by R.P.W., 1970.

Britannia ii (1971), 301 No. 75.

graffito on the wall: FELIC[. . .]
Felic[is]
'(Property) of Felix'

2503.259

2503.260. Chalk, Kent. Sherd from a Black-burnished vessel with lattice decoration (½), burnt red, found in 1961 during excavation of a Roman building. Present whereabouts unrecorded. Drawn by S.S.F. from a rubbing by R.P.W., 1964.

JRS liv (1964), 184 No. 44 a. Woodhead in Johnston, *Britannia* iii (1972), 144 No. 3 with fig. 19.3.

graffito in Greek letters on the shoulder, above the lattice: ΦΗΛΙΚΙ[. . .]

Apparently a transliteration of *felici[. . .]*, either *felici[ter]* or the genitive of *Felix* (i.e. *Felici[s]*) or of a cognate name.

2503.260

2503.261. Fishbourne, West Sussex. Jar (½) found in 1961–69 during excavations at the Roman palace in an occupation-layer of Period I. Fishbourne Museum. Reproduced from Cunliffe.

B.W. Cunliffe, *Excavations at Fishbourne 1961–69* ii (1971), 369 No. 5 with fig. 145.5.

graffito on the shoulder: F·F

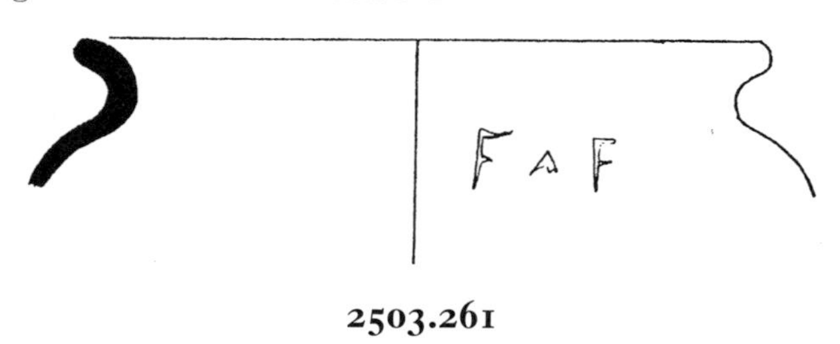

2503.261

2503.262. Colchester (*Camulodunum*), Essex. Part of a grey jar (½), found in 1929 in the Holly Trees Meadow (Insula 15). Colchester Museum. Drawn by R.P.W., 1943.

JRS xxxiv (1944), 91 No. 25.

graffito on the shoulder: FIDE[. . .]
Fide[lis]
'(Property) of Fidelis'

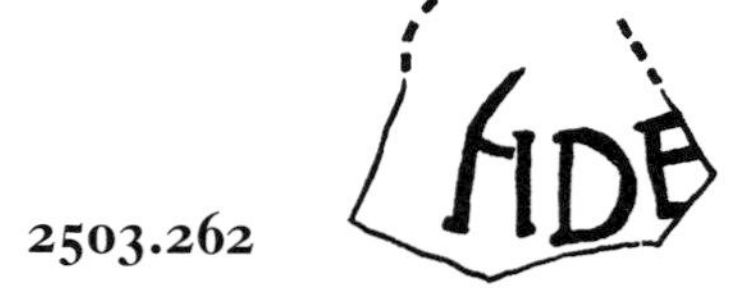

2503.262

2503.263. Corbridge (? *Coria*), Northumberland. Part of a white costrel (½) of second-century date, found in 1907 during excavation of Pit 3, *c.* 50 m west of the rampart on Site 45. Corbridge Museum. Drawn by R.P.W., 1955.

Forster, *Arch. Ael.*[3] iv (1908), 295 (repr. 91).

graffito on the shoulder: [. . .]IRMANV
Perhaps *[F]irmanu(s)*

2503.263

2503.264. Colchester (*Camulodunum*), Essex. Part of a buff jug (½), found in 1929 in the main room of 'the Mithraeum' in Holly Trees Meadow (Insula 15). Colchester Museum. Drawn by R.P.W., 1943.

graffito on the shoulder: FLΛ.[. . .]

Flav[ius] cannot be read. The possibilities are *Fl(avius) M(?)[. . .]* or *Fla.[. . .]*, presumably *Fla[minius]*.

2503.264

2503.265. Corbridge (? *Coria*), Northumberland. Part of a black flat-rimmed dish (½) of Antonine date, found in 1941 inside the West Gate of the West Compound. Corbridge Museum. Drawn by R.P.W., 1948.

JRS xxxviii (1948), 104 No. 24.

graffito below the rim: FLΛV[. . .]
Probably *Flav[ius . . .?]*

The derived cognomina *Flavianus, Flavinus* or *Flavus* are also possible.

2503.265

2503.266. Brancaster (*Branodunum*), Norfolk. Fragment (1/1) from the base of a colour-coated beaker, found in 1977 in the settlement outside the fort. Norwich Museum. Drawn by M.W.C.H.

Britannia ix (1978), 480 No. 59.

graffito beneath the base: FOR
Perhaps *For(tunati)*
'(Property) of Fortunatus'

2503.266

2503.267. Canterbury (*Durovernum*), Kent. Fragment (½) of a narrow-mouthed jar with a burnished buff surface, found in 1979 during the excavation of early Roman timber buildings at the Marlowe Street Car Park, Site II. Canterbury Museum. Drawn by M.W.C.H.

Britannia xi (1980), 413 No. 46.

graffito on the neck: [. . .]NIΛLS
[Ge]nial(i)s
'(Property) of Genialis'

2503.267

2503.268. Catterick (*Cataractonium*), North Yorkshire. Rim of a grey-ware jar (½) dated to the first or early second century, found in 1959 during excavations on the line of the new A1 road. Yorkshire Museum, York. Drawn by R.S.O.T., 1990.

Britannia xxi (1990), 376 No. 67.

graffito in Greek letters below the rim: ΓΕΡ
Γερ(οντιος)
'Gerontius'

An abbreviated Greek personal name, the only possibility being *Gerontius* and its cognates: see Solin *Namenbuch*, Index.

Gerontius is well attested in *CIL* xiii and was current in Britain at the end of the Roman period (Zosimus vi 2.4), which it survived as *Geraint*.

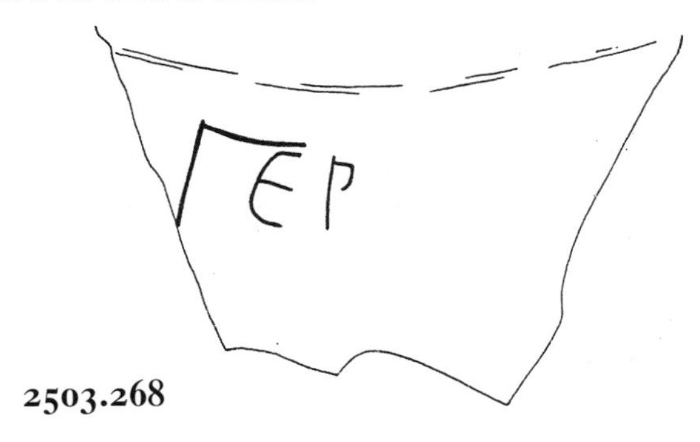

2503.268

2503.269. London (*Londinium*). Part of a coarse jug (½), found in 1872–73 at the National Safe Deposit Co. Museum of London. Drawn by R.P.W., 1954.

graffito on the shoulder: GIITL
Perhaps *G(a)et(u)l(us)* or *G(a)et(u)l(icus)*

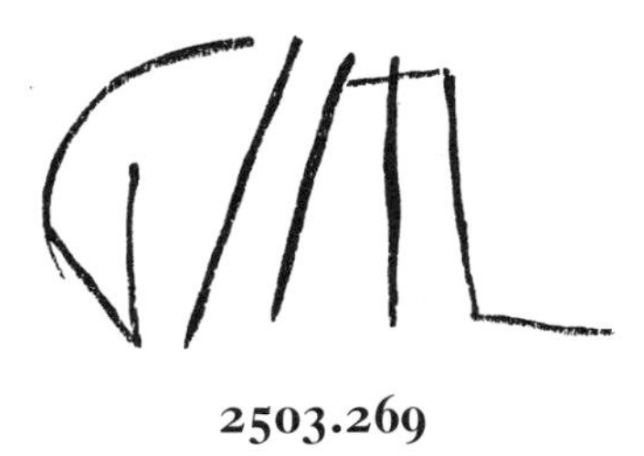

2503.269

2503.270. Chester (*Deva*). Fragment from a mica-coated bowl (½), imitating Dr. 24/25, found in 1967 during excavations at the Old Market Hall site. Grosvenor Museum. Drawn by S.S.F. from a rubbing by R.P.W., 1970.

Britannia ii (1971), 294 No. 32.

graffito inside the bowl: GIS
Perhaps *G(aius) I(. . .) S(. . .)*

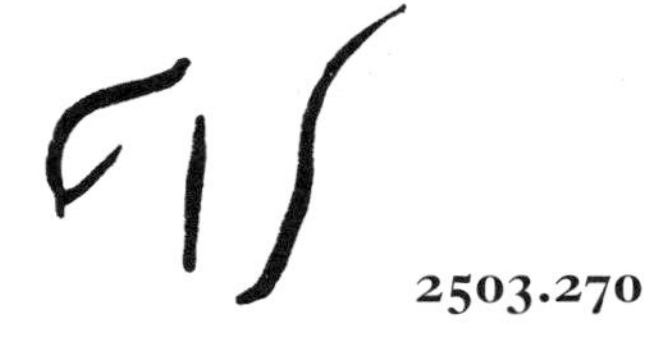

2503.270

2503.271. Skeleton Green, Puckeridge, Hertfordshire. Part of the base of a terra rubra plate (½), stamped ATTISSV (twice), found in 1972 in a pit of Period I Phase iii, dated *c.* A.D. 15–25, during excavation of the pre-Roman settlement. Hertford Museum. Drawn by S.S.F. from a rubbing by M.W.C.H.

Britannia v (1974), 464 No. 20. Partridge, *Britannia* xiii (1982), 325–6 with fig. 12.1.

graffito on the underside of the base: GRAECVS
Graecus

The name is probably that of a slave or freedman of a merchant trading in pre-Roman Britain. Compare Kajanto, *Cognomina*, 204. Compare also *RIB* 2503.225.

2503.271

2503.272. Holt, Clwyd [Denbighshire]. Fragment of a thin-walled beaker (½) in buff ware with a buff slip, found in 1907–15 during excavations at the legionary works-depot. National Museum, Cardiff. Drawn by S.S.F. from a rubbing by R.G.C.

W.F. Grimes, *Holt* (1930), 134 No. 33.

graffito: [. . .]ERMES·.[. . .]
[H]ermes [. . . ?]

2503.272

2503.273. Caerleon (*Isca*), Gwent [Monmouthshire]. Conjoined fragments (½) from the rim and shoulder of a grey cooking pot with lattice decoration, found in 1970 in a Flavian level in Barrack XII in the Prysg Field. Caerleon Museum. Drawn by S.S.F. from rubbings by R.P.W., 1971.

Britannia ii (1971), 304 No. 94.

graffito above the lattice: [. . .]ỊBERNA[. . .]
[H]iberna or *[Hiberna[lis]*

The name may not have been aspirated: compare *RIB* 377 (Caerleon), *[?Flavi]a Iberna*. Neither cognomen is common (see Kajanto, *Cognomina*, 218), so *[H]iberna/(H)iberna* is perhaps to be preferred.

2503.273

2503.274. Ibid. Bowl in Caerleon ware (½), found before 1939. Caerleon Museum. Drawn by R.P.W., from a rubbing by G.C. Boon, 1968.

JRS lix (1969), 245 No. 67.

graffito below the flange of the rim: HIL
Hil(arus) or a cognate name

2503.274 HIL

2503.275. Maidstone, Kent. Grey bowl (¼) found in 1972–8 in a deposit of late second- to mid third-century date during excavation of The Mount Roman Villa. Maidstone Museum. Reproduced from Kelly.

Kelly, *Arch. Cant.* cx (1992), 221 No. 23 with fig. 14.23.

graffito on the shoulder: IΛ

If the graffito is an abbreviated personal name, the most probable expansion is *Ianuarius*.

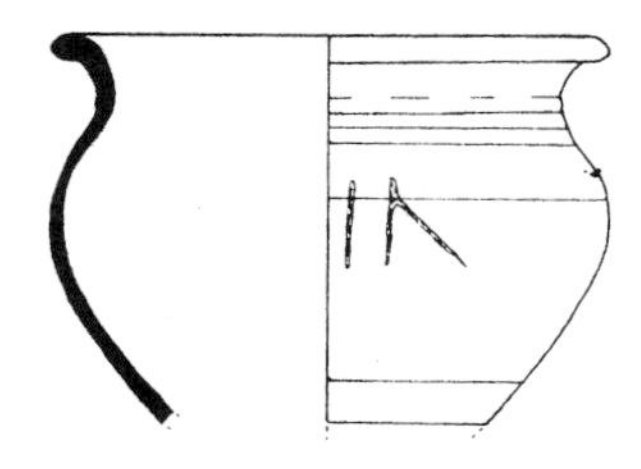

2503.275

2503.276. Nanstallon, Cornwall. Fragment from the wall of a buff jug ($\frac{1}{1}$), found in 1968 during excavations at the fort. Bodmin Museum. Drawn by S.S.F. from rubbings by R.P.W., 1968.

JRS lix (1969), 245 No. 68.

graffito on the wall: IA͡N
Probably *Ian(uarii)*
'(Property) of Ianuarius'

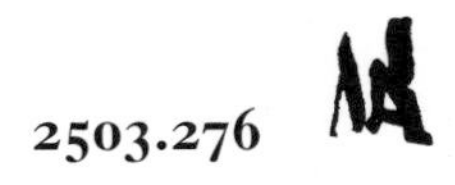

2503.276

2503.277. St. Albans (*Verulamium*), Hertfordshire. Part of a straight-sided flanged black bowl ($\frac{1}{2}$) of late third- or fourth-century type, found in 1930–34 in Pit 2, Insula IV.7. Verulamium Museum. Drawn by R.P.W., 1954.

graffiti on the base: (a) IΛ̣SI
(b) CVNOḶ[. . .]ṾII

(b) CVNOB[. . .] is less likely, R.P.W.

For *Iasus* compare Oswald, *Index*, and Roxan *RMD* i, 108 (*M. Sentilius Iasus*, witness to military diplomata in the period A.D. 140–58). As *Iassus* it is frequent in Oswald, *Index* and *CIL* xiii. *Cuno-* ('hound') is a frequent Celtic name element, but *Cunovendi*, the best-attested in Britain, does not seem to fit here.

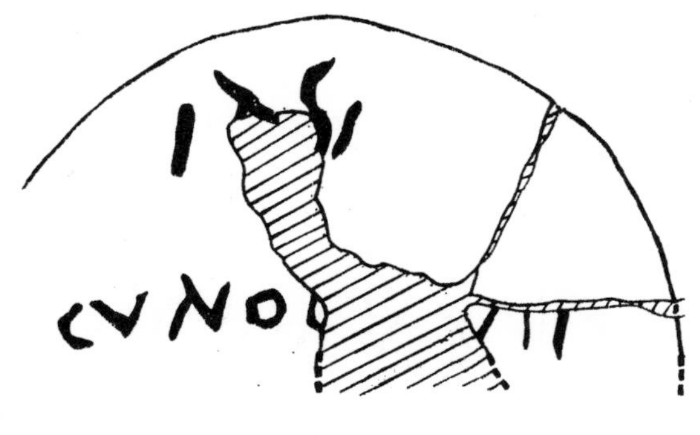

2503.277

2503.278. Chelmsford (*Caesaromagus*), Essex. Sherd from a beaker ($\frac{1}{1}$). Chelmsford Museum. Reproduced from Going.

C.J. Going, *The Mansio . . .: The Roman Pottery* (1987), 102 with fig. 50.34 (inverted).

two graffiti: (a) A
(b) ỊM

2503.278

2503.279. St. Albans (*Verulamium*), Hertfordshire. Part of a colour-coated beaker ($\frac{1}{4}$ and $\frac{1}{1}$) in hard grey fabric with a silver-grey exterior slip spilling over onto the inside of the rim. Found in 1974 during excavation of the extramural Baths in Branch Road. Verulamium Museum. Reproduced from Greep.

Greep, *Herts. Arch.* viii (1980–82), 207 No. 8 with figs. 1.8 and 2.8.

graffito inside the lip: IM *or* VVI

2503.279

2503.280. Canterbury (*Durovernum*), Kent. Part of a grey beaker ($\frac{1}{2}$), found in 1957 during excavations at Whitehall Road. Canterbury Museum. Drawn by S.S.F. from a rubbing by R.P.W., 1958.

JRS xlix (1959), 138 No. 28.

graffito on the shoulder: INT

2503.280

2503.281

2503.281. Colchester (*Camulodunum*), Essex. Part of a grey flask ($\frac{1}{2}$), found in 1928 in the Holly Trees Meadow (Insula 15). Colchester Museum. Drawn by S.S.F. from a draft by R.P.W., 1954.

two graffiti on the wall: (a) [. . .]S
(b) I (*or* L)OM

2503.282. Caistor St. Edmund (*Venta Icenorum*), Norfolk. Part of a grey dish ($\frac{1}{2}$), found in 1931 at the south end of the drainage ditch on the east side of the forum. Norwich Museum. Drawn by R. Goodburn, 1971.

Britannia ii (1971), 300 No. 69. Atkinson, *Norfolk Arch.* xxvi (1936–8), 226 No. 8 with pl. W.8.

graffito on the wall: IOVINI
Iovini
'(Property) of Iovinus'

A crack has damaged the I.

2503.282

2503.283. Traprain Law, Lothian Region [East Lothian]. Sherd of grey ware ($\frac{1}{1}$), found in 1914 during excavations at the hill-fort. National Museums of Scotland, Queen Street, Edinburgh. Drawn by S.S.F. from a photograph in Curle.

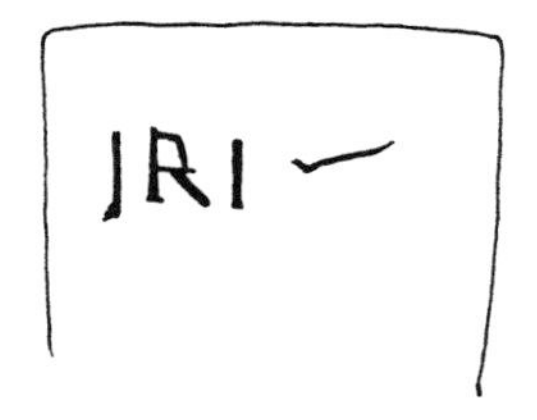

2503.283

Haverfield, *Roman Britain in 1914*, 30 No. 2. Curle, *PSAS* lxvi (1931–32), 358 with fig. 42.

graffito on the inner face: IRI stop.

CRIC, R.P.W. from three rubbings, 1976. His drawing is missing, but the published photograph does not support this reading. As text, Curle, loc. cit.

2503.284. Gloucester (*Glevum*). Part of a Black-burnished jar ($\frac{1}{2}$), found in 1974 in an early fourth-century context at the East Gate. Gloucester Museum. Drawn by L.V. Marley.

Hassall in C. Heighway, *The East and North Gates of Gloucester* (1983), 199 No. G.6 with fig. 114.G.6.

graffito: [. . .]IṢIΛṢ[. . .]
Perhaps *Isias*

[. . .]ISIΛI[. . .], Hassall, loc. cit. As text, R.S.O.T.

Theophoric feminine name *Isias* (from *Isis*) is well attested: see Solin, *Griechischen Personennamen*, 375–6.

2503.284

2503.285. (?) London (*Londinium*). Part of the rim of a Lower Nene Valley ware colour-coated beaker ($\frac{1}{2}$), found before 1856 probably in London. British Museum ex Roach Smith collection. Drawn by R.P.W., 1962.

H.B. Walters, *Cat.* (1908), No. M2506.

graffito below the rim: [. . .]ITALVṢ[. . .]
Italus

2503.285

2503.286. Wilderspool, Cheshire. Part of a storage jar ($\frac{1}{2}$) found in 1898. Warrington Museum. Drawn by R.P.W., 1952.

graffito on the shoulder: IVCVNDI[. . .]
Iucundi
'(Property) of Iucundus'

Compare *RIB* 2503.288, perhaps the same owner.

2503.286

2503.287. London (*Londinium*). Inkpot in buff ware with brown coating ($\frac{1}{4}$ and $\frac{1}{2}$), height 54 mm, diameter 76 mm, found in 1868 in Canon Street. British Museum. Drawn by R.P.W., 1952, and reproduced from *Guide*.

JRS xlii (1952), 108 No. 34. BM, *Guide Rom. Brit.* (1951), 31 fig. 15.

graffito on the wall: IVCVNDI | NDI
Iucundi | ⟨*ndi*⟩
'(Property) of Iucundus'

In l.1 the letters NDI are more deeply incised but less carefully cut, as if they were a secondary addition to replace the letters in l.2., R.P.W.

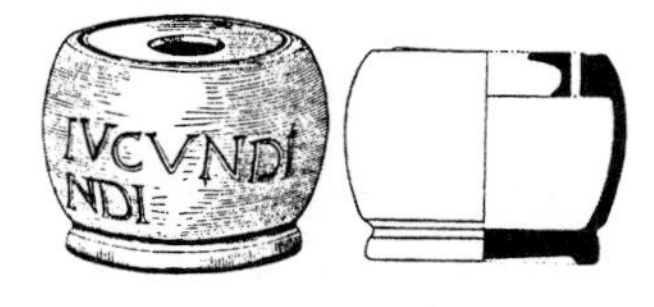

2503.287

2503.288. Wilderspool, Cheshire. Part of a storage jar ($\frac{1}{2}$), found in 1898–1900. Warrington Museum. Drawn by R.P.W., 1952.

May, *T. Lancs. & Chesh. Hist. Soc.* lii (1900), 51.

graffito on the shoulder: IVCVNDVS
Iucundus

DV have been inserted in narrower lettering by a second hand, R.P.W.

IVCVNS, May.

Compare *RIB* 2503.286, perhaps the same owner.

2503.288

2503.289. Dorchester (*Durnovaria*), Dorset. Rim sherd from a Black-burnished jar ($\frac{1}{2}$), found in 1984 during excavations in The Greyhound Yard. Dorchester Museum. Drawn by R.S.O.T.

Britannia xx (1989), 336 No. 24. P.J. Woodward et al., *Excavations at Greyhound Yard, Dorchester, 1981–4* (1993), 284 No. 7.

graffito below the rim: IVLΛ
Perhaps *Iul(i)a* or *Iul(l)a*

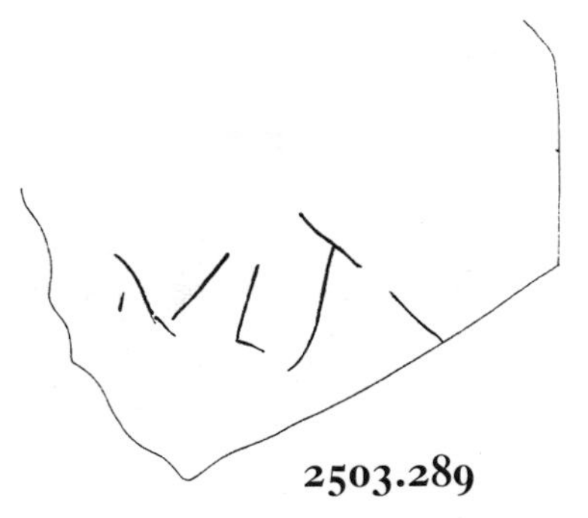

2503.289

2503.290. Ilkley, North Yorkshire. Part of a grey jar ($\frac{1}{2}$), found in 1919–21 during excavations at the fort. Ilkley Museum. Reproduced from Woodward.

Woodward, *YAJ* xxviii (1925), 258, fig. 40.8 and 275 No. 16.

graffito: IVL[. . .]
Probably *Iul[ius . . .?]*

2503.290

2503.291. Corbridge (? *Coria*), Northumberland. Part of the rim of a flat-rimmed black bowl ($\frac{1}{2}$), without recorded provenance. Corbridge Museum. Drawn by R.P.W., 1964.

graffito on the flat rim: IVL[. . .]
Probably *Iul[ius . . .?]*

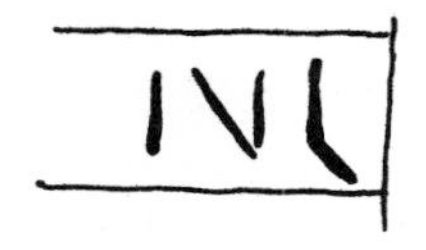

2503.291

2503.292. Colchester (*Camulodunum*), Essex. Part of a jug in red ware with a white slip ($\frac{1}{2}$), found in 1929 in the Holly Trees Meadow (Insula 15). Colchester Museum. Drawn by R.P.W., 1943.

JRS xxxiv (1944), 91 No. 28.

graffito on the wall: [. . .] leaf-stop IVL· | [. . .] leaf-stop SIVE leaf-stop TΛV[. . .]
[. . .] Iul(ius)· | *(. . . ?)· sive Tau[rus]* or *Tau[rinus]*
'Iulius (. . .?) or Taurus/Taurinus'

The spacing each side of the leaf-stops suggests the possibility that another name may have preceded *Iul(ius)* and that three (or more) alternatives were shown. More probably, however, *Iul(ius)* is the new name of the former *Tau(rus)*: for this use of *sive* see Dessau, *ILS* iii p. 928.

2503.292

2503.293. South Shields (*Arbeia*), Tyne and Wear [Durham]. Part of the rim of a third-century Black-burnished dish ($\frac{1}{2}$), found in 1885. Museum of Antiquities, Newcastle-upon-Tyne. Drawn by R.P.W., 1961.

graffito below the rim: IVLỊ[. . .]
Probably *Iuli[us]*

2503.293

2503.294. Brecon (? *Cicucium*), Powys [Brecknockshire]. Part of a black everted-rim dish ($\frac{1}{2}$), found in 1924–25 during excavations at the fort. National Museum, Cardiff. Drawn by R.P.W., after Wheeler.

R.E.M. Wheeler, *Brecon* (1926), 248 with fig. 105.9.

graffito below the rim: IVLIṾ[. . .]
Iuliu[s]

2503.294

2503.295. Cumberland. A flanged bowl bequeathed in 1926 to Tullie House Museum, Carlisle as part of the Mawson collection; it presumably came from Kirkby Thore or perhaps some other Cumbrian site. Drawn by R.P.W., 1952.

JRS xliii (1953), 131 No. 18.

graffito on the upper part of the wall:
IVLVICTORINI
Iul(i) Victorini
'(Property) of Iulius Victorinus'

2503.295

2503.296. Brompton on Swale, North Yorkshire. Two conjoining sherds ($\frac{1}{2}$) from a narrow-necked coarse-ware jar, found in 1972 during excavations beside the line of the new A1 road. Yorkshire Museum, York. Drawn by R.S.O.T., 1990.

Britannia xxii (1991), 307 No. 56 (cited under Catterick).

two graffiti, (a) on the shoulder: IVNIΛ
Iunia
(b) (not illustrated), on the rim: [. . .]. .VI IIII

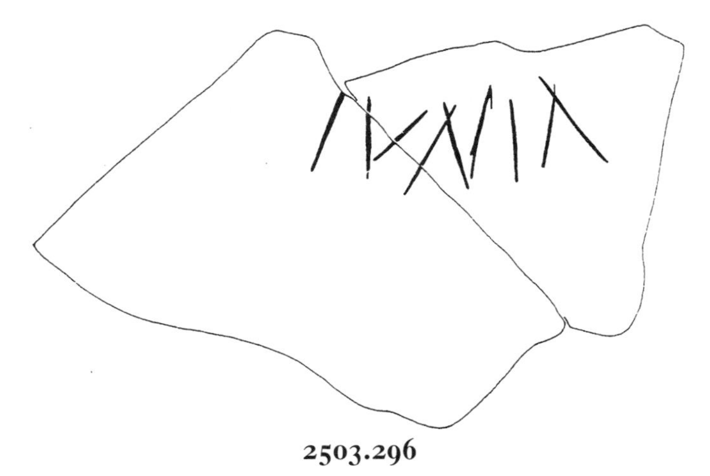

2503.296

2503.297. Tiddington, Warwickshire. Part of a Severn Valley ware jar ($\frac{1}{2}$), found in 1981–3 in a late third- or fourth-century context during excavations at the settlement. Warwickshire Museum. Drawing by courtesy of Nicholas Palmer.

Booth in N. Palmer, *Tiddington Roman Settlement, Warwickshire* (forthcoming), No. 166 and No. 658.

graffito on the neck: IVN
Probably *Iun(ii)*
'(Property) of Iunius'

IVNỌ, Booth, loc. cit.

There is a void in the surface of the vessel after N.

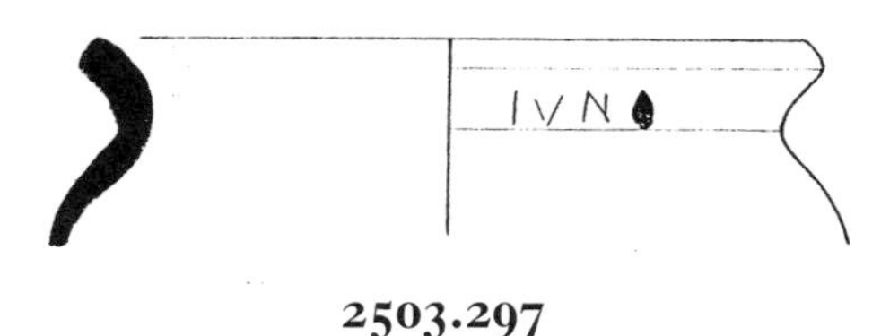

2503.297

2503.298. Dorchester (*Durnovaria*), Dorset. Base of a black-ware vessel ($\frac{1}{2}$), found in 1971 in a late first- or early second-century context at No. 34 Trinity Street. Dorchester Museum. Drawn by S.S.F. from a tracing by B.J. O'Connor.

Britannia iv (1973), 330 No. 14.

graffito on the base: IVṆ
Perhaps *Iun(ii)*
'(Property) of Iunius'

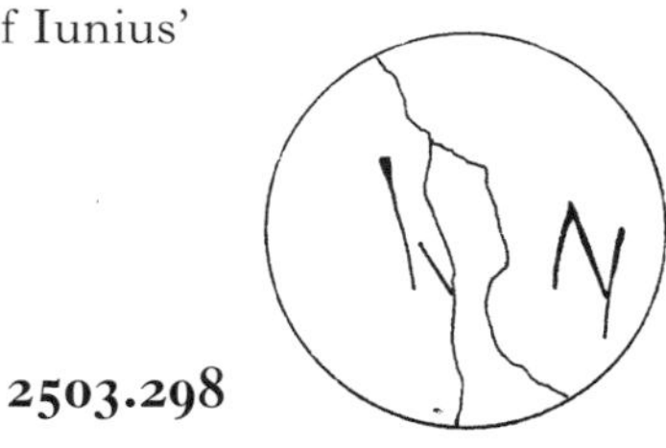

2503.298

2503.299. Caistor St. Edmund (*Venta Icenorum*), Norfolk. Base of a grey jar (½), found in 1933 unstratified in the north colonnade of the forum. Norwich Museum. Drawn by R. Goodburn.

Britannia ii (1971), 300 No. 70.

graffito on the base: IVSTI
Iusti
'(Property) of Iustus'

2503.299

2503.300. Haslingfield, Cambridgeshire. Narrow-necked grey jar (½), height 279 mm, diameter at mouth 133 mm, found some years before 1952. Museum of Archaeology and Anthropology, Cambridge (1952), ex Letchworth Museum. Drawn by R.P.W.

graffito, inverted, on the shoulder: IVSTINI
Iustini
'(Property) of Iustinus'

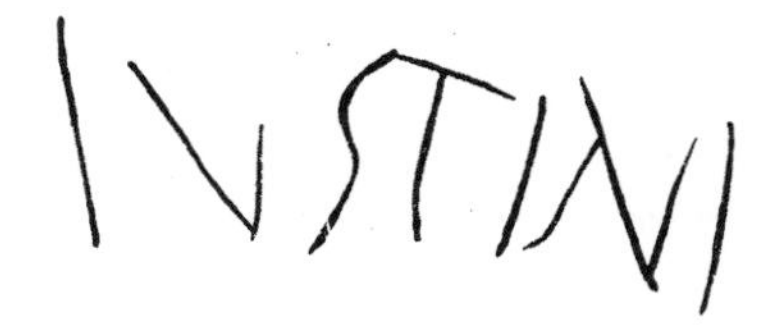

2503.300

2503.301. Gatcombe, Somerset. Part of a Black-burnished 1 jar (½), found in 1966–76 in occupation-debris during the excavation of Building 19. Bristol Museum. Reproduced from Branigan.

K. Branigan, *Gatcombe Roman Villa* (1977), 109 No. 369 with fig. 23.369.

two graffiti, (a) on the inside of the rim: IX+
(b) on the shoulder: X

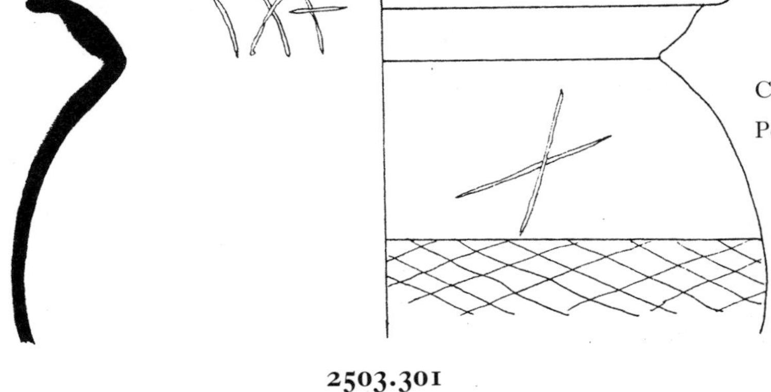

2503.301

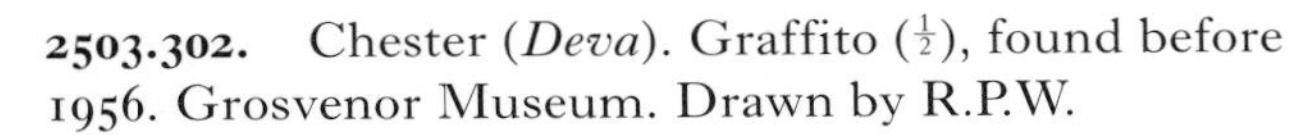

2503.302. Chester (*Deva*). Graffito (½), found before 1956. Grosvenor Museum. Drawn by R.P.W.

graffito: LΛΛ | LṾΛ̣[. . .]
Perhaps *L(ucius) V(. . .) A(. . .)*

LΛΛ | LVP̣, R.P.W., archive.

2503.302

2503.303. Winchester (*Venta Belgarum*), Hampshire. Fragment (½) from the top of a small everted-rim jar in dark red colour-coat, found in 1969 in a third- to fourth-century context at the Cathedral Green. Winchester Museum. Drawn by M.W.C.H.

Britannia viii (1977), 441 No. 87.

graffito at the girth: [. . .]LΛT

The graffito is possibly complete: if so, then probably *Lat(inus)*.

2503.303

2503.304. London (*Londinium*). Two conjoining fragments (½) of a grey jar, found in 1957 during excavations in Noble Street, outside the west gate of the Cripplegate fort. Museum of London. Drawn by S.S.F. from a rubbing by R.P.W., 1958.

JRS xlviii (1958), 155 No. 41.

graffito on the wall below a wavy line:
[. . .]OLLIṾ[. . .]
Perhaps *(L)olliu[s. . . ?]*

Compare *RIB* 2501.295.

Possibly OLLΛ[. . .], S.S.F.

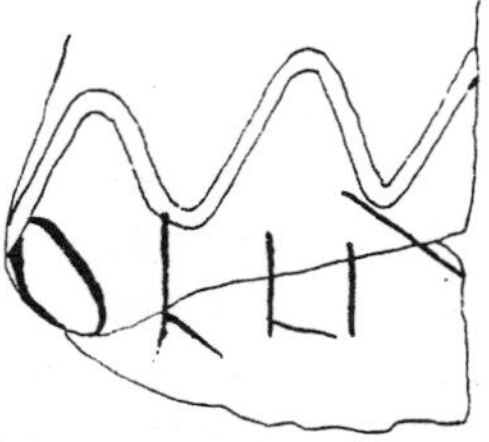

2503.304

2503.305. Cirencester (*Corinium*), Gloucestershire. Sherd from a black dish (½), found in 1959 during excavations at the Parsonage Field, Watermoor Road. Corinium Museum. Drawn by S.S.F. from a rubbing by R.P.W., 1962.

JRS lii (1962), 199 No. 55.

graffito on the wall: [. . .]ḶVCANVS[. . .]
Probably *Lucanus*

2503.305

2503.306. Old Harlow, Essex. Fragment from the wall of a grey bowl (½), found in 1970 at Holbrooks. Harlow Museum. Drawn by S.S.F. from a rubbing by R.P.W., 1971.

Britannia ii (1971), 295 No. 41.

graffito on the wall: LVCI
Luci
'(Property) of Lucius'

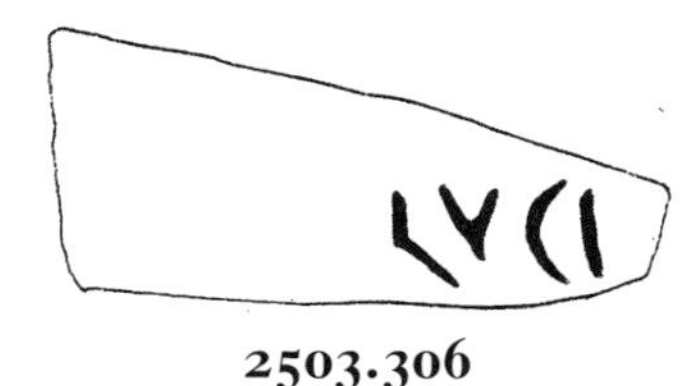

2503.306

2503.307. Canvey Island, Essex. Fragment of a grey rouletted beaker (½), badly burnt and worn, found in 1968 at Leigh Beck on the surface. Southend Museum. Drawn by S.S.F. from a rubbing by R.P.W., 1968.

JRS lix (1969), 245 No. 69.

graffito: LVCI[. . .]

Luci, Luci[us], or a cognate name.

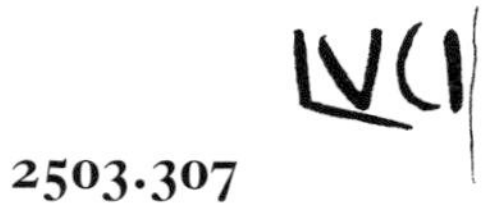

2503.307

2503.308. Droitwich (*Salinae*), Hereford and Worcester [Worcestershire]. Part of a large cordoned storage jar (½) in a pink-buff ware, found in 1938 at Dodderhill in ditch-filling about half way along the east side of the fort and associated with mid first-century pottery. In private possession. Drawn by R.P.W. from a tracing by J.K. St. Joseph.

JRS xxix (1939), 227 No. 13. St. Joseph, *T. Birm. AS* lxii (1938), 30 with fig. 2.

graffito on the shoulder: LVCOṆ[. . .]

Perhaps *Lucon[ianus]*; compare *CIL* xii 2205. Otherwise a variant spelling of *Lucco (Lucconis)* or *Lucconius (Lucconi)*, for which see Holder, s.v.

2503.308

2503.309. Springhead (*Vagniacis*), Kent. Part of the wall of an orange-coloured jar (½), found in 1970 south-west of Temple III. Gravesend Museum. Drawn by S.S.F. from rubbings by R.P.W., 1970.

Britannia ii (1971), 299 No. 58.

graffito on the wall: [. . .]MAIICI
Maeci
'(Property) of Maecius'

The nomen is fairly common, e.g. *ILS* 1025 (tribune of Legio ix Hispana). A praenomen may have been lost.

2503.309

2503.310. Mucking, Essex. Two conjoining fragments from a straight-sided dish (½) of grey burnished ware, found in 1968 during excavations. Department of the Environment. Drawn by S.S.F. from a rubbing by W.J. Rodwell, 1967.

JRS lix (1969), 245 No. 70.

graffito: MAGNV[. . .]
Magnu[s]

2503.310

2503.311. Turret 34 A, Hadrian's Wall, Northumberland. Fragment from the wall of a black narrow-mouthed jar (½), found in 1971 during consolidation-work. Museum of Antiquities, Newcastle upon Tyne. Drawn by S.S.F. from rubbings by R.P.W., 1971.

Britannia iii (1972), 360 No. 42 b.

graffito on the wall: [. . .]MΛSVIITVS
Ma(n)suetus

For other instances of this Vulgar assimilation of *ns* to *s* see Colin Smith, *ANRW* xxix.2, 920–1.

2503.311

2503.312. Leicester (*Ratae*). Part of a jug (½) in white fabric, found in 1968 with material of the late first to early second centuries in the filling of a timber-lined cellar at Southgate Street. Leicester Museum. Drawn by M.W.C.H.

Britannia xx (1989), 340 No. 48.

graffito on the shoulder: [. . .]MAPORIGIS[. . .]
Presumably *Maporigis*
'(Property) of Maporix'

The name appears to be unattested; it is composed of the two elements **mapos* and -*rix* ('youthful king').

2503.312

2503.313. Gestingthorpe, Essex. Base of a grey jar (½), found in 1965 in a fourth-century deposit in a ditch while excavating an industrial site at Hill Farm. In private possession. Drawn by S.S.F. from rubbings by R.P.W., 1970.

2503.313

Britannia i (1970), 314 No. 44 a. J. Draper, *Excavations by Mr. H.P. Cooper on the Roman Site at Hill Farm, Gestingthorpe, Essex* (1985), 89 with fig. 44.528.

graffito on the base: MΛP

If the jar itself is fourth-century, the graffito is an abbreviated personal name *Map(. . .)* incorporating **mapos* (compare *RIB* 2503.312 with note), not an abbreviated *tria nomina*; but the date is very uncertain.

Compare No. 314.

2503.314. Ibid. Base of a grey jar found 3.5 m from *RIB* 2503.313. In private possession. Drawn by S.S.F. from rubbings by R.P.W., 1970.

Britannia i (1970), 314 No. 44 b. J. Draper, op. cit. 89 with fig. 43.493.

graffito on the base: MΛP

Compare No. 313 with note.

2503.314

2503.315. London (*Londinium*). Base of a grey jar (½), found in 1962 in a pit during excavations in the Cripplegate fort at St. Albans, Wood Street. Museum of London. Drawn by S.S.F. from rubbings by M.W.C.H.

Britannia vi (1975), 287 No. 17.

lightly scratched graffito on the base: MΛRCI
Marci
'(Property) of Marcus'

For *Marcus* as a cognomen, compare *RIB* 2298 and 2501.328–330.

2503.315

2503.316. Doncaster (*Danum*), South Yorkshire. Part of a dish (½) in Black-burnished ware, found in *c.* 1911 at Frenchgate. Doncaster Museum. Drawn by S.S.F. from a rubbing by Dr. P.C. Buckland.

Britannia xiii (1982), 420 No. 82.

graffito on the rim: MΛRCI
Marci
'(Property) of Marcus'

See note to *RIB* 2503.315 and compare *RIB* 2494.178, *T(iti) Fl(avi) Mar[. . .]* also from Doncaster.

2503.316

2503.317. Middlewich, Cheshire. Part of a grey cooking pot (½) with lattice-decoration, found in 1966 during road-works near the centre of the Roman settlement. Middlewich Archaeological Society. Drawn by S.S.F. from rubbings by J.D. Bestwick, 1967.

JRS lviii (1968), 213 No. 73.

graffito: MARCVRI

The name *Marcurus* or *Marcurius* seems to be unattested, and it is possible that *Mercurius* was meant.

2503.317

2503.318. London (*Londinium*). Part of a pinch-neck jug (¼), found in 1974–78 during excavations at New Fresh Wharf, Lower Thames Street. Museum of London. Reproduced from Dyson.

Britannia xviii (1987), 371 No. 22. T. Dyson (ed.), *The Roman Quay at St. Magnus House, London* (1986), 108 with fig. 1.46.

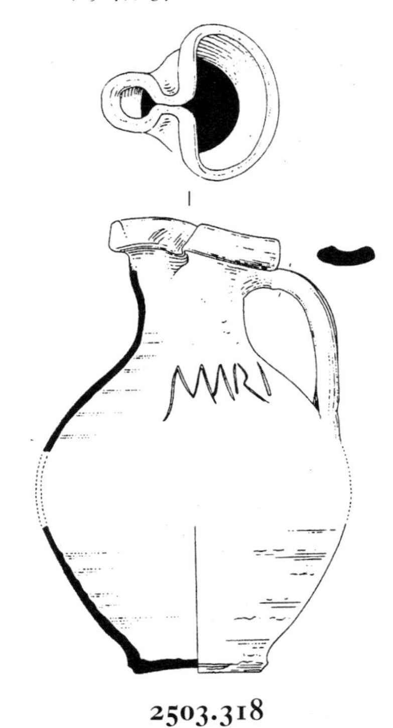

2503.318

graffito on the shoulder: MARI
Mari
Probably '(Property) of Marius'

Marius is a common nomen and cognomen, but M.W.C.H., *Britannia*, loc. cit., points out that *Marus* is occasionally found and is cognate with the Celtic name-element *-marus* ('great').

2503.319. Ibid. Two conjoining fragments from the base of a black cooking pot (½), found in 1966 unstratified on the Dyers' Arms site just east of Cannon Street Station. Museum of London. Drawn by S.S.F. from rubbings by R.P.W., 1966.

JRS lvii (1967), 210 No. 51.

graffito on the base: [. . .]ARIṆỊ[. . .]
Perhaps *[M]arini*
'(Property) of Marinus'

[. . .]ARIIẠ[. . .], R.P.W. The last three letters are hard to make out on the rubbings, but appear to read as text.

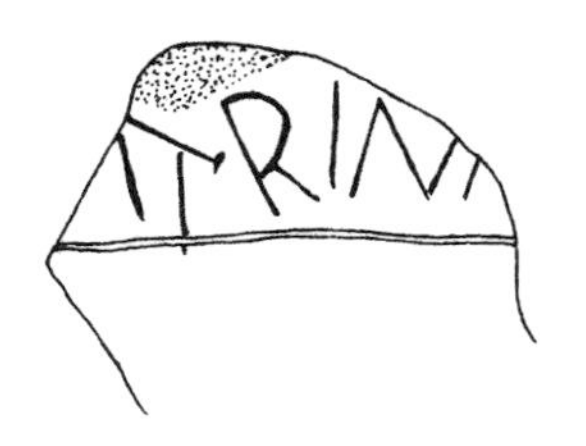

2503.319

2503.320. Bierton, Buckinghamshire. Fragment of coarse pottery (½), found in 1979 during excavations at the settlement. Aylesbury Museum. Drawn by M.W.C.H.

Britannia xi (1980), 407 No. 8.

graffito: MARINVS
Marinus

2503.320

2503.321. Eccles, Kent. Sherds (½) from a grey storage jar, found in 1964 and 1966 in the filling of a late Antonine ditch at the Roman villa. Maidstone Museum. Drawn by S.S.F. from a rubbing by R.P.W., 1967.

JRS lvii (1967), 210 No. 52.

graffito below the shoulder: [. . .]ARIṆ[. . .]
   Perhaps *[. . .M]arin[us]*

[. . .]ARIṂ[. . .], R.P.W.

[C]arinus is also possible, but is much less common.

2503.321

2503.322. Tiddington, Warwickshire. Fragment (½) from a flagon found in 1981–83 during excavations at the settlement. Warwickshire Museum. Drawing by courtesy of Nicholas Palmer.

Booth in N. Palmer, *Tiddington Roman Settlement, Warwickshire* (forthcoming), No. 165 with fig.

graffito: MAR
   Mar(tialis) or similar

2503.322

2503.323. Alcester, Warwickshire. Part of a grey storage jar (¼), found in 1964–66 during excavations in the extramural area. Warwickshire Museum. Drawing by courtesy of Nicholas Palmer.

S. Cracknell and C. Mahany (eds.), *Roman Alcester* i: *The Southern Extramural Area* (1994), fig. 57, No. 10.

two graffiti: (a) on the shoulder: MΛR
   Mar(tialis) or similar
(b) on the rim, VI beside III (erased)

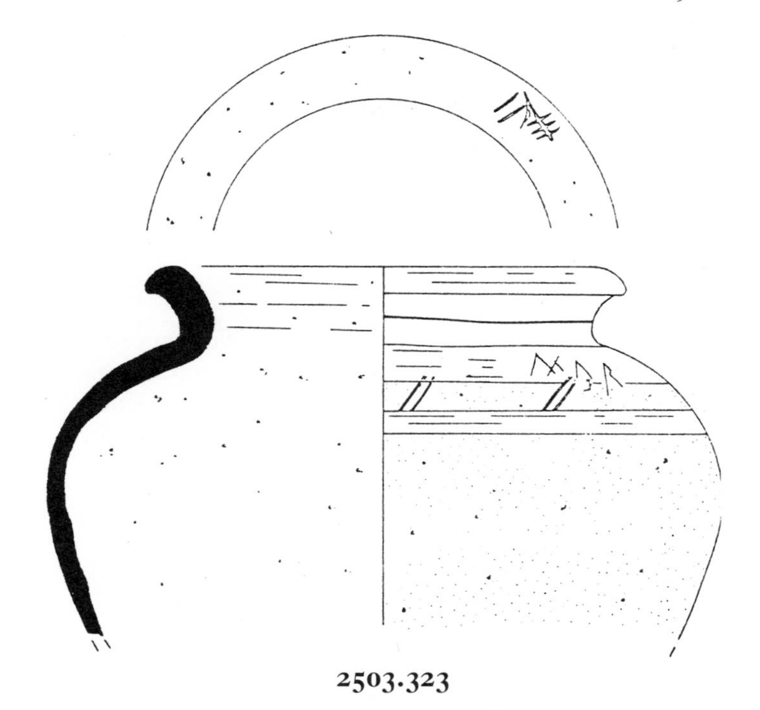

2503.323

2503.324. Chelmsford (*Caesaromagus*), Essex. Sherd (½) from the base of a shallow bowl in grey-brown fabric, found in 1975 in a late second-century context near the *mansio*. Chelmsford Museum. Reproduced from Going.

Britannia viii (1977), 437 No. 50. C.J. Going, *The Mansio . . .: The Roman Pottery* (1987), 102 with fig. 49.21.

graffito on the base: MΛR[. . . ?]
   Probably *Mar(tialis)* or similar

[. . .]Λ̣MΛR, *Britannia*.

There is trace of another (?) graffito to the left.

2503.324

2503.325. Bath (*Aquae Sulis*), Avon [Somerset]. Fragment (½) from the base of a dish in grey fabric and darker grey burnished surface, found in 1970 in a mid second-century context during excavations at Citizen House. Roman Baths Museum. Drawn by M.W.C.H.

Britannia viii (1977), 444 No. 99.

graffito beneath the base: MΛRTIṆṾS
   Martinus

2503.325

2503.326. Wroxeter (*Viroconium*), Shropshire. Part of a dish (½), found in 1913 during excavations. Sought in vain by R.P.W., 1953. Drawn by R.G.C.

J.P. Bushe-Fox, *Wroxeter 1913*, 23 with fig. 14.

graffito on the rim: MΛRTINVS

2503.326

2503.327. Chesterholm (*Vindolanda*), Northumberland. Part of the side of a grey dish (½), found in 1972 unstratified on Site XXXIII in the *vicus*. Vindolanda Museum. Drawn by S.S.F. from rubbings by R.P.W., 1972.

Britannia iv (1973), 332 No. 29.

graffito on the wall: [. . .]ṂΛRTINV[. . .]
Martinu[s]

2503.327

2503.328. Ibid. Part of the wall (½) of a grey vessel, found in 1971 unstratified in Building XI in the *vicus*. Vindolanda Museum. Drawn by S.S.F. from rubbings by R.P.W., 1972.

Britannia iii (1972), 360 No. 50.

graffito on the wall: MΛRṬ[. . .]
Probably *Mart[inus]* (compare No. 327) or *Mart[ialis]*

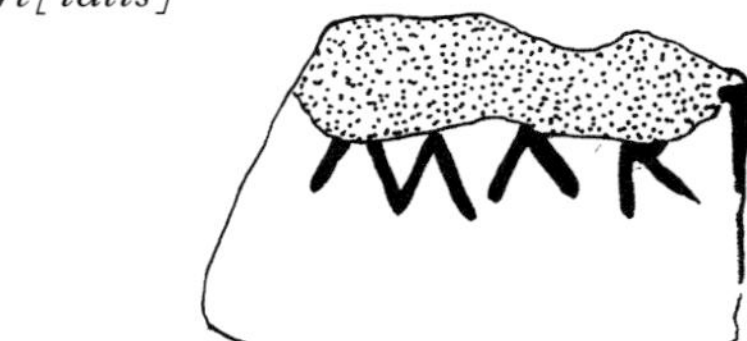

2503.328

2503.329. Corbridge (? *Coria*), Northumberland. Grey third-century cooking pot (½), found before 1914. Corbridge Museum. Drawn by R.P.W., 1940.

graffito on the base: MAS
Perhaps *M(arcus) A(. . .) S(. . .)*

2503.329 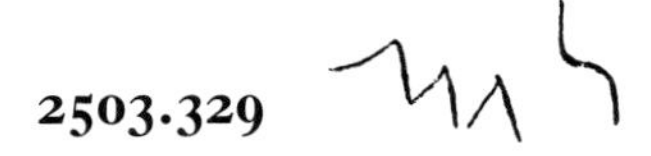

2503.330. London (*Londinium*). Black carinated beaker (½), height 127 mm, diameter at the mouth 83 mm, found in 1950 in Walbrook. Museum of London. Drawn by R.P.W., 1951.

JRS xli (1951), 144 No. 25.

graffito around the base: MΛT

Compare *RIB* 2501.353, 355, 359.

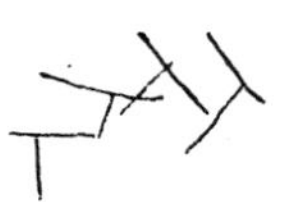

2503.330

2503.331. Richborough (*Rutupiae*), Kent. Part of a buff storage jar (½), found in 1931–38 during excavations at the fort. In store at Dover Castle. Drawn by R.P.W.

B.W. Cunliffe (ed.), *Richborough* v (1968), 184 No. 2 with fig.

graffito on the shoulder: [. . .?]MΛT

2503.331

2503.332. Winchester (*Venta Belgarum*), Hampshire. Part of a vessel with flared mouth and beaded rim (½), found in 1967 with mid fourth-century material during excavations at Wolvesey Palace. Winchester Museum. Drawn by M.W.C.H.

Britannia vii (1976), 384 No. 28.

graffito below the rim: [. . .]MΛT
Perhaps *Mat(erni)*
'(Property) of Maternus'

The graffito is probably complete.

2503.332

2503.333. Colchester (*Camulodunum*), Essex. Buff-coated jug (½), found in 1929 in Holly Trees Meadow (Insula 15). Colchester Museum. Drawn by R.P.W., 1943.

JRS xxxiv (1944), 91 No. 30.

graffito on the wall: [. . .]ṂATEṚ[. . .]
Probably *Mater[ni]*
'(Property) of Maternus'

2503.333

2503.334. Unrecorded provenance. Graffito (½) found before 1956, drawn by R.P.W., but without giving description or context.

graffito: M͡AT͡R
Probably *Matr(onae)*
'(Property) of Matrona'

2503.334

2503.335. Neatham, Hampshire. Part of a flanged bowl (½) in burnished grey ware, found in 1974 in the filling of a well containing late third-century pottery and coins. Alton Museum. Drawn by S.S.F. from rubbings by M.W.C.H.

Britannia vi (1975), 286 No. 10. M. Millett and D. Graham, *Excavations . . . . at Neatham, Hampshire, 1969–79* (1986), 67 fig. 48.24.

graffito below the flange: MΛTVGIINΛ̣[. . .]
Matugena

For the masculine form *Matugenus*, see *RIB* 2409.22, 2411.297, 2501.363, 2503.336 and Oswald, *Index*, s.v; compare also the Verulamium-region mortarium-maker (Hartley in S.S. Frere, *Verulamium Excavations* iii (1984), 286).

2503.335

2503.336. Chesterholm (*Vindolanda*), Northumberland. Two conjoining fragments from the rim of a black jar, found in 1983. Vindolanda Museum. Drawing: the Vindolanda Trust.

Britannia xix (1988), 503 No. 80. E., R., and A. Birley, *Vindolanda* ii (1993), 98 No. 5 with fig. 12.3.

graffito beneath the rim: [. . .]MΛTVGENVS

See note to *RIB* 2503.335, and in particular compare *RIB* 2501.363 (Chesterholm).

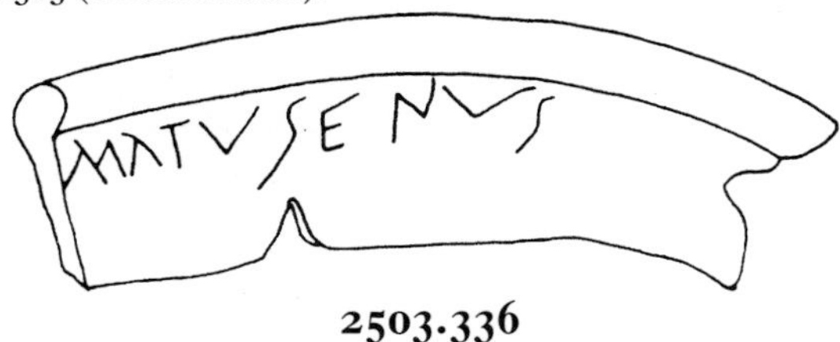

2503.336

2503.337. St. Albans (*Verulamium*), Hertfordshire. Base of a small red-coated jar or beaker (½), found in 1956 unstratified in Building XXI.1. Verulamium Museum. Drawn by M.G. Wilson.

Britannia viii (1977), 442 No. 91. S.S. Frere, *Verulamium Excavations* iii (1984), 277 No. 4 with fig. 115.4.

two graffiti, (a) beneath the base: MΛṾ | ILODVO
a lightly cut V has been inserted between D and O
Maviloduo
'For Maviloduus'
(b) on the wall, just above the base: INI

We print R.P.W.'s transcript, but the drawing suggests (a) MΛI | BODC, B being of cursive form. For BODC compare Nash-Williams, *ECMW* No. 229, Boduoc, Oswald *Index* s.v. *Boduocus*, and R.P. Mack, *The Coinage of Ancient Britain* (1964), Nos. 395–6, BODVOC.

2503.337

2503.338. Usk (*Burrium*), Gwent [Monmouthshire]. Part of a storage jar in soft orange fabric (½), found in 1973 during excavations at the pre-Flavian fortress. National Museum, Cardiff. Reproduced from Hassall.

Britannia viii (1977), 446 No. 109. Hassall in G.C. Boon and M. Hassall, *Usk* (1982), 58 No. 48 with fig. 5.48.

graffito lightly cut on the wall: MΛVṚI
'(Property) of Maurus'

MΛVGI, M.W.C.H. locc. citt. As text, M.W.C.H. 1993.

2503.338

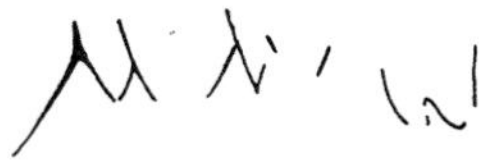

2503.339. Canterbury (*Durovernum*), Kent. Part of a colour-coated beaker (½) in orange fabric and black slip (Lower Nene Valley ware), found in a context dated *c.* A.D. 290–350 at the Marlowe IV site. Canterbury Museum. Drawn by M.W.C.H.

Britannia xiii (1982), 415 No. 46.

graffito on the neck: [. . .]ṂΛ·VR·.[. . .]
Probably *Maur[i]*
'(Property) of Maurus'

A name developed from *Maurus* is also possible (see Kajanto, *Cognomina*, 266).

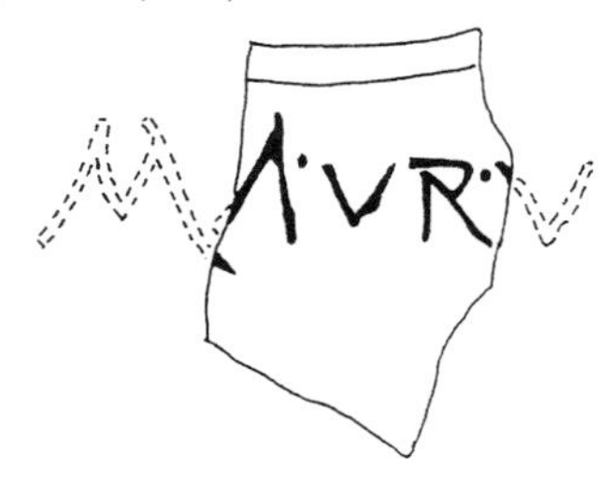

2503.339

2503.340. Templebrough, South Yorkshire. Jug (½), height 197 mm, found in 1917 during excavations at the fort. Rotherham Museum. Drawn by R.P.W., 1952.

T. May, *Templebrough* (1922), 111 with pl. XXX b.

graffito on the shoulder: MΛVRVCIVS
Maurucius

MΛVRICIVS, May.

The name seems to be unattested, but is presumably another of those developed from *Maurus* (see Kajanto, *Cognomina*, 206).

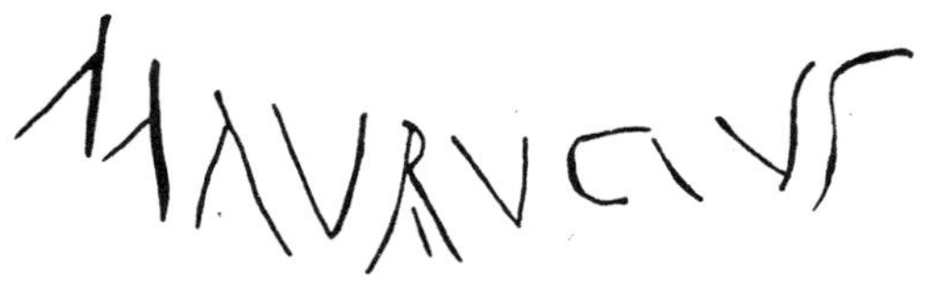

2503.340

2503.341. Old Ford, east London. Part of a colour-coated beaker (½), found in 1970 with second-century material in the filling of a ditch during excavations at Lefevre Road. Museum of London. Drawn by S.S.F. from rubbings by M.W.C.H.

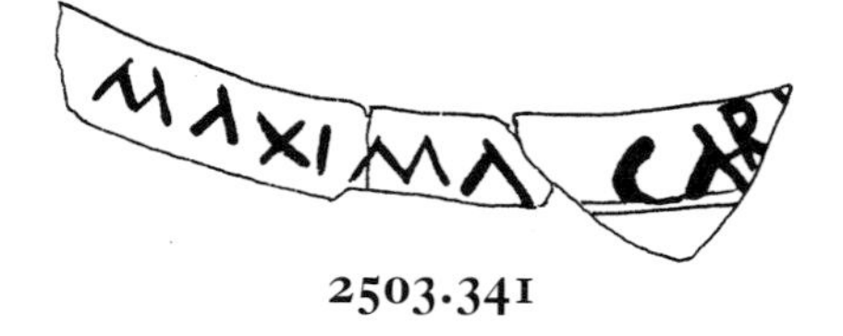

2503.341

Britannia vi (1975), 287 No. 18.

graffito below the rim: MΛXIMΛ CAR.[. . .]
Perhaps *Maxima Car[i]*
'Maxima (wife *or* daughter) of Carus'

2503.342. Dicket Mead, Welwyn, Hertfordshire. Part of the base (½) of a Black-burnished dish, found in 1969–70 in a gully behind Building 2 during excavations at the Roman villa. Welwyn Archaeological Society. Reproduced from Rook.

Britannia xi (1980), 412 No. 44. Rook, *Herts. Arch.* ix (1983–6), 142 No. 6 with fig. 55.6.

graffito on the underside of the base:
ME[. . .] | TỊṆE
Probably *Me[li]tine*

This Greek feminine personal name is properly spelled *Melitene*.

2503.342

2503.343. Gloucester (*Glevum*). Two conjoining fragments (½) from the top of a Black-burnished 1 cooking pot with lattice decoration, found in 1978 in an early fourth-century context at the East Gate. Gloucester Museum. Drawn by L.V. Marley.

Britannia xiv (1983), 344 No. 30. Hassall in C. Heighway, *The East and North Gates of Gloucester* (1983), 199 No. G.4 with fig. 114.G.4.

graffito below the rim: MIIMOR
Memor

2503.343

2503.344. London (*Londinium*). Two conjoining sherds (½) from a roughcast beaker in orange fabric and dark grey colour-coat, found in 1981 with late second-century material in the filling of a Roman drain during excavations at Pudding Lane and Lower Thames Street. Museum of London. Drawn by M.W.C.H.

Britannia xiii (1982), 418 No. 65.

graffito below the cornice rim: MER and, at right-angles to it, M

Mercator or *Mercurius/alis* are the most likely names.

2503.344

2503.345. Richborough (*Rutupiae*), Kent. Part of a thin black bowl (½). In store at Dover Castle. Drawn by R.P.W., 1954.

graffito: [. . .]ṂIISSṾ.[. . .]
Perhaps *Messu[s]*

The nomen *Messius* is quite well attested (Schulze, 33), but for *Messus* compare *CIL* iii 10135.

2503.345

2503.346. Chesterholm (*Vindolanda*), Northumberland. Part of a grey burnished dish (½), found in 1968 in excavations west of the stone fort. Vindolanda Museum. Drawn by S.S.F. from rubbings by R.P.W., 1969.

JRS lix (1969), 245 No. 71. E., R. and A. Birley, *Vindolanda* ii (1993), 99 No. 10 with fig. 12.9.

graffito on the upper side of the base: MIN͡EṚ[. . .]

2503.346

Miner[valis] or *Miner[vini]*
'(Property) of Minervalis *or* Minervinus'

Miner[vinus] or a similar name, Birley loc. cit.

2503.347. Colchester (*Camulodunum*), Essex. Part of a grey cooking pot (½) of Camulodunum form 267. Colchester Museum. Drawn by R.P.W., 1954.

graffito on the shoulder: [. . .]ṂENERVINVS
Minervinus

For the Vulgar spelling compare *RIB* 1200, *deae Menervae*.

2503.347

2503.348. Lincoln (*Lindum*). Black vessel with the figure of a man fighting an animal, probably a dog, height 203 mm. British Museum ex A. Trollope, 1866. Sought in vain by R.P.W. Reprinted from *CIL*.

CIL vii 1338.15.

graffito on the lower part of the wall: MIN

2503.349. Silchester (*Calleva*), Hampshire. Buff jar (½), height 152 mm, diameter 127 mm, found in 1891 during excavations in Insula III. Reading Museum. Drawn by R.P.W., 1951.

T. May, *Silchester* (1916), 285 No. 27 with pl. LXXXV.27.

graffito on the shoulder: MINVTIONIS
Minutionis
'(Property) of Minutio'

The final letter could alternatively be I, R.P.W.

MINVTIONII, May.

Minutio seems to be unattested, but is presumably elaborated from *Minutus* (for which see Kajanto, *Cognomina*, 243).

2503.349

2503.350. London (*Londinium*). Lower half of a buff beaker with narrow pedestalled base (½), found before 1854 'in the Thames'. British Museum ex Roach Smith. Drawn by R.P.W., 1961.

CIL vii 1338.16 (wrongly described as samian). Roach Smith, *Cat.* (1854), 47; *Rom. Lond.* (1859), 108. H.B. Walters, *Cat.* (1908), 436 No. M.2837.

two graffiti, (a) on the wall: MOMVVL
(b) on the base (not illustrated): CÎBOVVI

(b) The first letter was inscribed as I, altered to C.

2503.350

2503.351. York (*Eboracum*). Part of a grey-ware dish (½) of late second- to early third-century date, found in 1950 during excavations in Hungate, *c.* 213 m south-east of the South-East Gate of the fortress. Yorkshire Museum. Drawn by R.P.W., 1965.

JRS lii (1962), 199 No. 57. Richardson, *Arch. J.* cxvi (1959), 54, 74 No. 20 with fig. 12.20.

graffito on the wall: MONTIṾS

The drawing in *Arch. J.*, loc. cit., supports the reading MONTIVS. The nomen is rare and not in Schulze, but see *CIL* viii 17, 112; compare also Oswald *Index* s.v. *Monticus*.

2503.351

2503.352. Ribchester (*Bremetennacum*), Lancashire. Part of a beaker (½) in Black-burnished 1 ware found in 1977 in a mid Antonine occupation-layer in a stone building in the *vicus*. Ribchester Museum. Traced by M.W.C.H. from a drawing by Paul Gibbons.

Britannia xii (1981), 388 No. 55.

graffito: NAT SVM·F[. . .]
Perhaps *Nat(alis) sum. F[eliciter]*
'I am (the property of) Natalis. Good Luck!'

Compare *RIB* 2501.119 and 2502.2, and for the restoration *f[eliciter]* with a personal name compare *RIB* 2491.114 and 2503.102.

2503.352

2503.353. Gadebridge Park, Hemel Hempstead, Hertfordshire. Conjoining sherds (½) from the neck of a colour-coated beaker, found in 1966 beneath an early fourth-century tessellated floor in Building A, Room 28 during excavations at the Roman Villa. Dacorum District Council. Drawn by S.S.F. from rubbings by R.P.W., 1970.

Britannia ii (1971), 296 No. 46. Wright in D.S. Neal *Gadebridge Park* (1974), 254 No. e with fig. 113.e.

graffito on the neck: NATV[. . .]
Perhaps *Natu[s]*

The V has been cut twice.

For *Natus* as a cognomen see Kajanto, *Cognomina* 304.

2503.353

2503.354. Canterbury (*Durovernum*), Kent. Two sherds (½) from the base and upper part of a globular grey-ware jar, found in 1978 with late second- to late third-century material during excavations at No. 16 Watling Street. Canterbury Museum. Drawn by M.W.C.H.

Britannia xiii (1982), 414 No. 34.

two graffiti: (a) beneath the base, NX or (inverted) XN
(b) faintly on the shoulder: [. . .]ṆAVMẠ[. . .]

(b) This combination of letters does not occur in I. Marriott's *Analytical Index of Personal Names*. It might perhaps be part of the rare Greek name *Naumachus* (*IG* xii 8 No. 277, l. 119). Compare *Naumachius* (*PLRE*, 618), M.W.C.H.

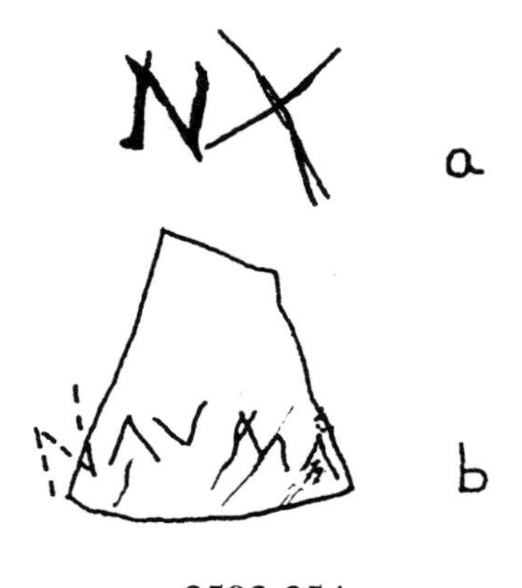

2503.354

2503.355. Housesteads (*Vercovicium*), Northumberland. Two conjoining fragments (½) of a Black-burnished 2 bowl of the late second to early third century, found in 1980. Newcastle upon Tyne University. Drawn by Miriam Daniels, 1994.

Britannia xiv (1983), 349 No. 52.

graffito: NỊIVTỌ[. . .]
Neuto

Neuto may be a Tungrian personal name: compare *AE* 1975, 644 from the shrine of Nehalennia (P. Stuart and J.E. Bogaers, *Deae Nehalenniae* (1971), No. 30), and *CIL* xiii 3628, *Neutto*. Cohors i Tungrorum was stationed at Housesteads after the abandonment of the Antonine Wall.

2503.355

2503.356. Chelmsford (*Caesaromagus*), Essex. Sherd from a jar (½). Chelmsford Museum. Reproduced from Going.

C.J. Going, *The Mansio . . .: The Roman Pottery* (1987), 102 with fig. 50.29.

graffito: NII[. . .]

2503.356

2503.357. Colchester (*Camulodunum*), Essex. Fragment of a grey-ware jar (½), found in 1973 in a residual context at Lion Walk. Colchester Museum. Drawn by M.W.C.H.

Britannia viii (1977), 438 No. 62.

graffito, lightly incised on the shoulder: NICA[. . .]

Perhaps *Nica[nor]* (compare *RIB* 970), but there are other possibilities.

2503.357

2503.358. Usk (*Burrium*), Gwent [Monmouthshire]. Part of a grey-ware jar (½), found in 1973 in a latrine pit during excavations at the pre-Flavian fortress. National Museum, Cardiff. Reproduced from Hassall.

Britannia ix (1978), 483 No. 88. Hassall in G.C. Boon and M. Hassall, *Usk* (1982), 55 No. 43 with fig. 5.43.

graffito below the base: NICIIFỌRO, altered to NICIIFỌRI
Nicefori
'(Property) of Niceforus'

The Greek personal name *Nicephoros* is not uncommonly spelt *Niceforus*: see *CIL* vi, part 2, fasc. 4.

2503.358

2503.359. Gloucester (*Glevum*). Sherd of dark grey ware (½), found in 1958 unstratified during excavations at the Bon Marché site, St. Aldate Street. Gloucester Museum. Drawn by S.S.F. from rubbings and a cast by A.G. Hunter, 1962.

JRS lii (1962), 199 No. 58.

graffito: [. . .]ṆIIVIṾ[. . .]

Perhaps *N(a)eviu[s. . . .]*, but there are other possibilities including *Neuṭọ* (compare *RIB* 2503.355).

2503.359

2503.360. South Shields (*Arbeia*), Tyne and Wear [Durham]. Fragment (½) of a late second-century Black-burnished bowl, found in 1967 during excavations at the fort. South Shields Museum. Drawn by S.S.F. from rubbings by R.P.W., 1971.

Britannia ii (1971), 295 No. 36.

graffito below the rim: NOBIḶ[. . .]
Probably *Nobil[is]*

2503.360

2503.361. Richborough (*Rutupiae*), Kent. Graffito ($\frac{1}{2}$), found before 1956. In store at Dover Castle. Drawn by R.P.W.

graffito: NVAB

Perhaps two graffiti, N and VAB; or IVVAB, possibly *Iu(li) Vab(ri)*. For *Vabrius* compare *RIB* 1633.

2503.361

2503.362. Dorchester (*Durnovaria*), Dorset. Buff jug ($\frac{1}{2}$), broken but largely complete, found in 1984 during excavations in The Greyhound Yard. Dorchester Museum. Drawn by R.S.O.T. See also PL. IVA.

Britannia xx (1989), 336 No. 25. P.J. Woodward et al., *Excavations at Greyhound Yard, Dorchester*, 1981–4 (1993), 284 No. 3.

graffito on the shoulder between the two handles:
NVT͡RICIS
Nutricis
'(Property) of Nutrix'

Nutrix, meaning 'wet-nurse', as a proper name is more often that of the goddess (see *ILS* iii, p. 547, s.v.) than a human being: Kajanto, *Cognomina*, 323 cites only *CIL* xii 4742. But the dative case might have been expected of a vessel dedicated to a goddess, so we take this to be a (human) personal name.

2503.362

2503.363. St. Albans (*Verulamium*), Hertfordshire. Base of a red beaker ($\frac{1}{2}$), found in 1956 in Insula XXI in the area between Buildings 1 and 2. Verulamium Museum. Drawn by R.P.W., 1970.

Britannia ii (1971), 296 No. 49. S.S. Frere, *Verulamium Excavations* iii (1984), 278 No. 6.

graffito on the base: OCTOB | R͡IΛN͡I
Perhaps *Octobriani*
'(Property) of Octobrianus'

The name is a plausible formation from *October* (see Kajanto, *Cognomina*, 219), but seems to be unattested. The ligatures proposed in l.2 are not convincing, R.S.O.T.

2503.363

2503.364. Gayton Thorpe, Norfolk. Base of a buff jar ($\frac{1}{1}$) found in 1983 during field-walking at the site of the Roman villa. In private possession. Drawn by M.W.C.H.

Britannia xv (1984), 344 No. 41.

graffito in Greek letters: οδευcυc
By metathesis for 'Οδυσ(σ)εύς
'Odysseus'

2503.364

2503.365. Puckeridge, Hertfordshire. Two sherds ($\frac{1}{2}$) from a carinated beaker in dark grey ware, found in 1972 during excavation of a pit containing material of the second half of the second century. Hertford Museum. Reproduced from Hassall.

Britannia xvii (1986), 443 No. 53. Hassall, *Herts. Arch.* x (1988), 147 No. 2 with fig. 67.2.

graffiti on the neck:
(a) [. . .]ΛI | [. . .]OPTΛT[. . .] | [. . .]S.[. . .]
(b) [. . .]OMIICO̧[. . .]

Perhaps a list of personal names including *Optat[us]* and a Celtic name *[. . .]omeco*.

2503.365

2503.366. Caernarvon (*Segontium*), Gwynedd. Part of a black jar ($\frac{1}{2}$) of the early second century, found in 1923 in the covered drain traversing Building 1. Segontium Museum. Drawn by R.P.W., 1954.

R.E.M. Wheeler, *Segontium* (1924), 163 with fig. 76.29.

graffito on the shoulder: OPTIO

For *Optio* as a cognomen see Kajanto, *Cognomina*, 320.

2503.366 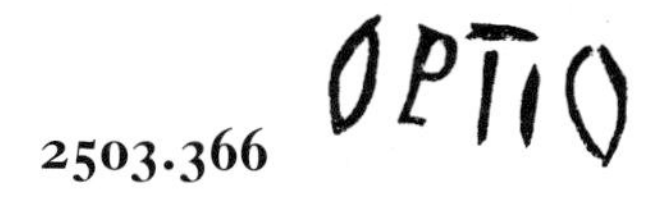

2503.367. Binchester (*Vinovia*), Durham. Six sherds, two adjoining, from the shoulder of a buff jug (½), found in 1977 and 1978, three of them in levelling material of the late first and early second century on the site of the late bath-house within the fort. Bowes Museum. Barnard Castle. Not illustrated.

Britannia ix (1978), 477 No. 30; x (1979), 355 No. 50.

graffito: PΛCΛTI
Pacati
'(Property) of Pacatus'

For *Pacatus* compare *RIB* 1786.

2503.368. Felixstowe, Suffolk. Indented pedestal beaker (½), height 197 mm, diameter 133 mm, found in 1920. Ipswich Museum. Drawn by R.P.W., 1951.

JRS xlii (1952), 108 No. 35. Moore, *P. Suffolk IA* xxiv (1948), 172 with fig. 6.vii.

graffito below the rim: PACΛTVṢ[. . .]
Pacatus

Compare *RIB* 2503.367 with note.

2503.368

2503.369. Housesteads (*Vercovicium*), Northumberland. Part of the rim (½) of a Black-burnished 2 bowl of the late second to early third century, found in 1978. Newcastle upon Tyne University. Drawn by Miriam Daniels.

Britannia xiv (1983), 349 No. 53.

graffito: PΛIΛTIVṢ

The name, unless a mistake for e.g. *Pacatius*, seems to be unattested. It may be cognate with the rare cognomen *Paius* (see *AE* 1976.392 with note, citing *CIL* v 1956).

2503.369

2503.370. Richborough (*Rutupiae*), Kent. Graffito (½), found before 1956. In store at Dover Castle. Drawn by R.P.W.

graffito: PAT

Probably *Pat(ernus)* or a derived name, though there are other possibilities.

2503.370

2503.371. St. Albans (*Verulamium*), Hertfordshire. Late third-century funnel-necked jug (½) in orange-coloured ware with a smooth slip, found in 1930–34 in Pit 5 at Insula IV.7. Sought in vain by P. Corder at the Verulamium Museum, 1942. Reproduced from Wheeler.

Wheeler, *Verulamium* (1936), 199 No. 78 with figs. 38 and 39.

graffito: PΛTERNI
Paterni
'(Property) of Paternus'

2503.371

2503.372. Silchester (*Calleva*), Hampshire. Part of a jar in light buff ware (½). Reading Museum. Drawn by R.P.W., 1951.

T. May, *Silchester* (1916), 284 No. 24 with pl. LXXXV.24.

graffito on the wall: PAVLATI[. . .]
Presumably *Paulati*
'(Property) of Paulatus'

There is a fracture before the V.

PANIA[. . .] or PANTA, May.

Paulatus seems to be unattested, but like *Paulins* must be developed from *Paul(l)us*.

2503.372

2503.373. Dicket Mead, Welwyn, Hertfordshire. Part of a dish (¼) in Black-burnished ware, found in 1969–70 during excavations at the Roman villa. Welwyn Archaeological Society. Reproduced from Rook.

Rook, *Herts. Arch.* ix (1983–6), 120 No. 164 with fig. 37.164.

grafito on the wall: PAVL[. . .]
Paul[i] or *Paul[ini]*
'(Property) of Paulus *or* Paulinus'

2503.373

2503.374. Barburgh Mill, Dumfries and Galloway [Dumfriesshire]. Part of the rim and shoulder of a Black-burnished 1 cooking pot (½), found in 1971 in the ditch of the fortlet. Dumfries Museum. Drawn by S.S.F. from rubbings by R.P.W., 1973.

Britannia iv (1973), 335 No. 41. Breeze, *Britannia* v (1974), 154 No. 2 with fig. 6.2.

graffito on the shoulder: [. . .]PAVL·Ṃ[. . .]
[. . .]Paul(inius) M[. . .]

Possibly [A]PRILIṾ[S] or even [A]PRILỊ[S], R.S.O.T. conject.
M. The letter N is less likely, R.P.W.

2503.374

2503.375. Gadebridge Park, Hemel Hempstead, Hertfordshire. Part of the base of a dish (½) in dark grey fabric, found in 1963 in the stoke-hole in Room 10 during excavations at the Roman villa. Dacorum District Council. Rubbings by R.P.W., 1964. Reproduced from Neal.

JRS liv (1964), 185 No. 48. Wright in D.S. Neal, *Gadebridge Park* (1974), 254 No. (a), with fig. 113 a.

cursive graffito on the upper surface of the base: [. . .]ITHOVS[. . .]

The name *Peirithous* would fit and probably belonged to a Greek slave, compare *IG* iii 1169. R.P.W.

2503.375

2503.376. North Warnborough, Hampshire. Part of a grey jar (½), found in 1929–30 during excavation of a Roman villa at Lodge Farm. Present whereabouts unknown. Drawn by R.G.C.

Liddell, *P. Hants. FC* x (1931), 13 with pl. XVII.

graffito on the shoulder: PERỊGRINẠ[. . .]
Perigrina

PERIGRINI, Liddell. As text, R.P.W.

For *Peregrina* by Vulgar confusion between unstressed *ĕ* and *ĭ*.

2503.376

2503.377. Rocester, Staffordshire. Two conjoining sherds (½) in buff fabric, found in 1985 unstratified during excavations at the fort. Stoke on Trent Museum. Drawn by Sarah Butler, 1985.

Britannia xvii (1986), 449 No. 74.

graffito: PIIRII
Probably *Pere(grinus)*

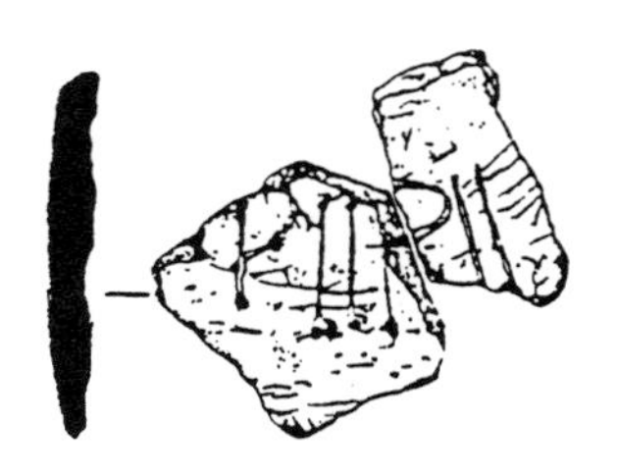

2503.377

2503.378. Wroxeter (*Viroconium*), Shropshire. Jar of buff ware (½), restored from fragments, height 330 mm, found in 1924–27 in Pit 12 of Flavian date. Rowley's House Museum, Shrewsbury. Drawn by R.P.W., 1953.

JRS xxxiii (1943), 81 No. 18. D. Atkinson, *Wroxeter* (1942), 284 with fig. 42.A2.

graffito in Greek letters on the shoulder: ΦΙΛΟC
φίλος
The Greek name *Philos*

ΦΙΑΟΣ, *JRS*, Atkinson. As text, R.P.W., 1976.

Compare *RIB* 110, *Philus*, and 2494.158.

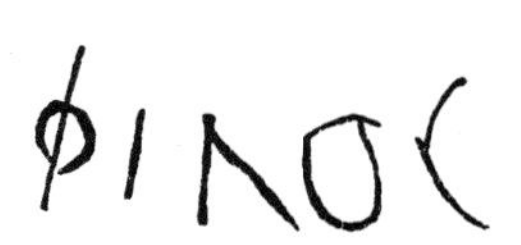

2503.378

2503.379. Porcupine Bank, 150 miles (240 km) off the west coast of Ireland. Grey-ware jar (¼ and ½), not likely to be later than the second century, dredged up from a depth of 170 fathoms (311 m) in 1934 by a trawler from Penarth. National Museum, Cardiff. Drawings: National Museum of Wales, 1993.

JRS xxiv (1934), 220 No. 8 with pl. XXV. O'Ríordáin, *Proc. R. Irish Academy* li (1947), 65 with pl. VI. Boon, *Antiq. J.* lvii (1977), 25 with note 103.

graffito on the base: CPISCI | FAGI above the figure of an otter.

G(ai) Pisci Fagi

'(Property) of Gaius Piscius Fagus' *or* 'of Gaius the Fish-eater'

The figure is identified as 'possibly a bear' by Nash-Williams (*JRS* loc. cit.), but as an otter by J.A. Bateman, Keeper of Zoology at the National Museum (quoted by Boon, loc. cit.). The nomen *Piscius* and the cognomen *Fagus* seem to be unparalleled (FAGO in *CIL* xiii 33 being the name of a god). Therefore, in view of the likely derivation of *Piscius* from *piscis* ('fish') and the possibility that *Fagus* is not *fagus* ('beech-tree') but Greek φάγος ('glutton', compare φάγειν 'to eat'), we follow Boon (loc. cit.) in understanding the graffito as a visual pun. In his words, 'despite the linguistic *mésalliance*, C PISCI|FAGI must surely be rendered 'Gaius the Fish-eater'. This gives point to the drawing of the otter. Whether the pot actually belonged to a Gaius Piscius Fagus, or the graffito is only a shipboard joke, is uncertain. Probably the latter, since nomina and cognomina were humorously manufactured from words for food and drink; compare Suetonius, *Tiberius* 42.1; *ILS* 8761 (note *Multivorus*, 'glutton'); perhaps *CIL* ix 2689; and the *Testamentum Porcelli* (in F. Buecheler (ed.), *Petronii Saturae* at end).

'The jar is not Romano-British', Boon, loc. cit. There is some resemblance to vessels from Aquitaine (compare J. Santot, *Céramiques communes Gallo-Romaines d'Aquitaine* (1979); information from Professor M.G. Fulford.

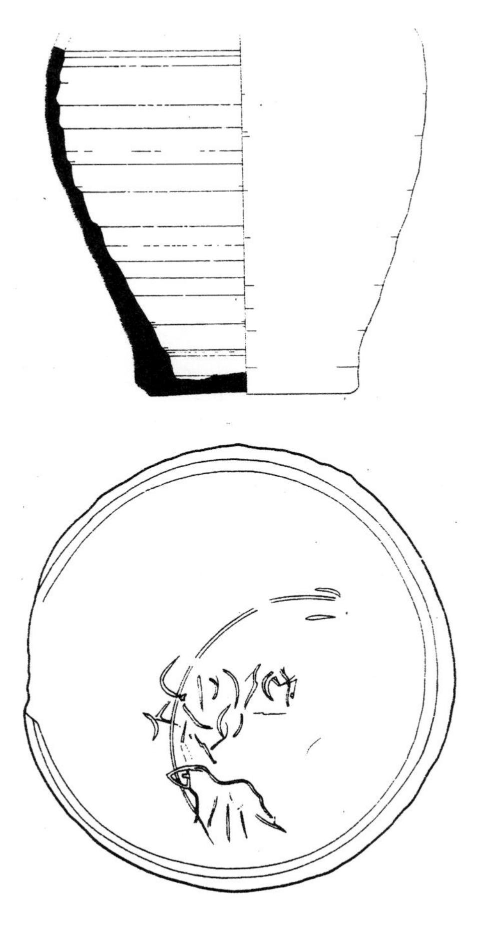

2503.379

2503.380. London (*Londinium*). Two-handled storage jar (½), height 380 mm, found in 1959 with *RIB* 2442.14 in a first-century well at Whitechapel, Aldgate. British Museum. Drawn by S.S.F. from rubbings by R.P.W., 1960.

JRS li (1961), 197 No. 45.

two graffiti, (a) between the handles: POERI
(b) lightly cut below the left-hand handle: HICẸSI

(a) *Poerus* is not attested as a name. Perhaps *Pueri* was meant (compare *RIB* 2503.153). This might be a Vulgarism; compare *Appendix Probi* 131, 'puella' non 'poella'.

2503.380

2503.381. Shakenoak Farm, Oxfordshire. Fragment from a dark grey storage jar found in 1970 in a fourth-century deposit on Site C during excavations at the Roman villa. Ashmolean Museum, Oxford. Drawn by R.S.O.T., 1993.

Britannia ii (1971), 301 No. 79. A.C.C. Brodribb et al., *Excavations at Shakenoak* iv (1973), 88 No. 9. with fig. 45.9.

graffito lightly incised on the wall:
PONIỌ | [. . .]IỊRII.ṾNDIṢ

Perhaps part of a hexameter.

PONIO | [. . .]IPRII IVNDIS, *Britannia*. As text R.S.O.T., 1993, after autopsy.

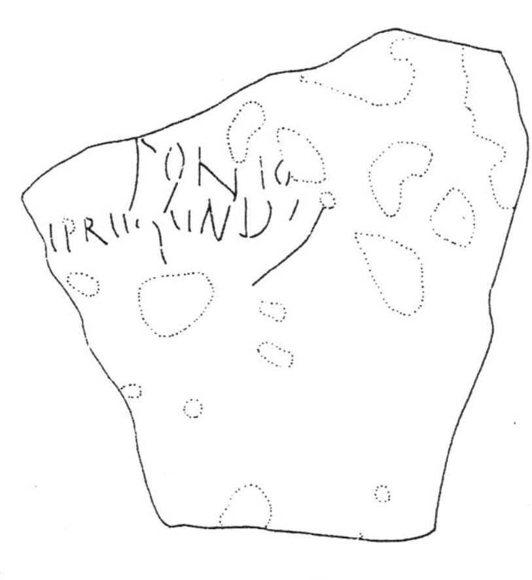

2503.381

2503.382. Stebbing, Essex. Part of a grey jar (½), found in 1956 in a pit at the site of the Roman villa at Blake Farm. In private possession. Drawn by R.P.W., 1957.

JRS xlviii (1958), 155 No. 42.

graffito on the base: POSTIMIA
Presumably for *Postumia*

A fracture crosses TI.

2503.382

2503.383. Silchester (*Calleva*), Hampshire. Black jar with lattice pattern (½), found before 1900. Reading Museum. Drawn by R.P.W., 1951.

Haverfield, *VCH* Hampshire i (1900), 284 No. 19 f. T. May, *Silchester* (1916), 284 No. 21 with pl. LXXXIV.21.

graffito on the wall overlapping the lattice:
POSTVMII
Postumii
'(Property) of Postumius'

2503.383

2503.384. Castleford (*Lagentium*), West Yorkshire. Sherd from a pot in grey ware (½), found in 1981 during excavations at the fort. West Yorkshire Archaeology Service. Drawn by R.S.O.T.

graffito on the wall: PP

2503.384

2503.385. Lullingstone, Kent. Grey hemispherical bowl (½), with rope-pattern at the neck, found in 1950–51 in Room 15 of the Roman villa, in a late third-century deposit. Lullingstone Villa Museum. Drawn by R.P.W., 1954.

JRS xlv (1955), 149 No. 32. Meates, *Arch. Cant.* lxv (1952), 56 No. 60 with fig. 11.60 (without a reading).

graffito on the shoulder: PPD
Perhaps *P(ublius) P(. . .) D(. . .)*

The second letter is P not F or E, R.P.W.

2503.385

2503.386. Silchester (*Calleva*), Hampshire. Base of a small buff vessel (½), found in 1975 during field-walking in Insula IV. Reading Museum. Drawn by M.W.C.H.

Britannia vii (1976), 384 No. 27.

graffito above a grid of two pairs of lines intersecting at right angles: PRIMΛ

The sherd was possibly used as a gaming counter: compare *RIB* 2439.

2503.386

2503.387. Lullingstone, Kent. Three conjoined fragments of a buff storage jar (½), found in 1958 during excavations at the Roman villa. Lullingstone Villa Museum. Rubbings (two sherds) by R.P.W., 1959. Reproduced from Pollard.

JRS xlix (1959), 138 No. 29 a. Pollard in G.W. Meates, *The Lullingstone Roman Villa* ii (1987), 280 No. ii with fig. 89.429 (three sherds).

graffito on the shoulder: [. . .]ṚIMA[. . .] | VII.[. . .]

[P]RIMA | VII O, Pollard. [P]RIMA[. . .] | [. . .]S [. . . *and* . . .]V[. . .], R.P.W. (before the fragments were assembled).

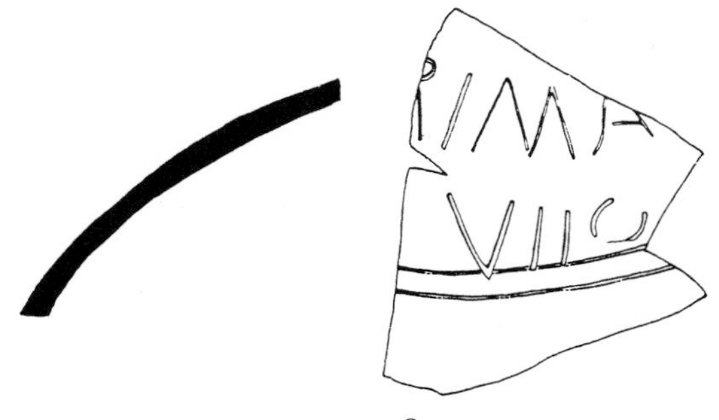

2503.387

2503.388. Mucking, Essex. Part of a Black-burnished dish (½), found in 1967 during excavations. Department of the Environment. Drawn by S.S.F. from a rubbing by W.J. Rodwell.

JRS lix (1969), 245 No. 72.

graffito: PRI

Probably *Pri(mus)* or a cognate name.

2503.388

2503.389. York (*Eboracum*). Bowl in buff ware (½) imitating Dr. 37, found in 1955 during excavations at St. Mary's Abbey. Yorkshire Museum. Drawn by R.P.W., 1955.

JRS xlvi (1956), 152 No. 42.

graffito on the base: PRIṂ[.]

Prim[i]

'(Property) of Primus'

There is room for only one letter after Ṃ.

2503.389

2503.390. Corbridge (? *Coria*), Northumberland. Part of a grey cooking pot with cross-hatching (½), of mid second-century date, found in 1946 in an unrecorded context. Corbridge Museum. Drawn by A. Kühne.

graffito on the shoulder above the lattice pattern: PRISC̣Ị[. . .]

Prisci

'(Property) of Priscus'

Possibly a name derived from *Priscus*, but *Priscus* is very common.

2503.390

2503.391. Winterton, Humberside [Lincolnshire]. Part of a grey dish (½), found in 1963 during excavations at the Roman villa. Scunthorpe Museum. Drawn by S.S.F. from rubbings by R.P.W., 1968.

JRS lix (1969), 245 No. 73. I.M. Stead, *Excavations at Winterton Roman Villa . . .* (1976), 191 No. 7 with fig. 95.7.

graffito on the wall: PV͡Λ

PV͡M, R.P.W., *JRS*. More likely PA[. . .], R.S.O.T. As text, R.P.W., archive.

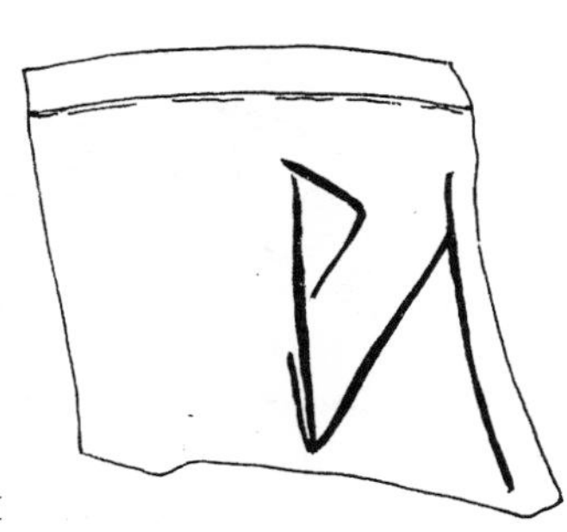

2503.391

2503.392. Ibid. Base of a beaker with orange slip (½), found in 1972 in the aisled Building P during excavations at the Roman villa. Scunthorpe Museum. Drawn by S.S.F. from rubbings by R.P.W., 1975.

Britannia vi (1975), 287 No. 15.

graffito on the base: PVN

Unless this is the initials *P(ubli) V(. . .) N(. . .)*, *Pun(ici)* is likely, '(Property) of Punicus'.

2503.392

2503.393. Great Dunmow, Essex. Sherds of a grey jar (½), found in 1971 during the excavation of a ditch apparently forming the rear boundary of a plot facing the Roman Stane Street within the settlement. Essex Archaeological Society. Drawn by S.S.F. from rubbings by P.J. Drury.

Britannia iii (1972), 356 No. 24.

graffito:
[. . .]QVI·IITVS[·].ỊIMVS·H͡C·ỊIB͡ṂIIRAVI[. . .]

QVI·IITVS[·]RIIMVS·IC·IIB͡MIIRAVIṬ for *Quietus Remus (h)ic emperavit*, 'Quietus Remus ordered this', R.P.W., *Britannia*, taking *(h)ic* as a mistake for *hoc*.

Quietus is easy, the medial point having been inserted to separate I from II (i.e. E), but otherwise both reading and interpretation are difficult. The *Britannia* reading requires two difficult ligatures, two forms apparently of R, and *emberavit* for *imperavit*.

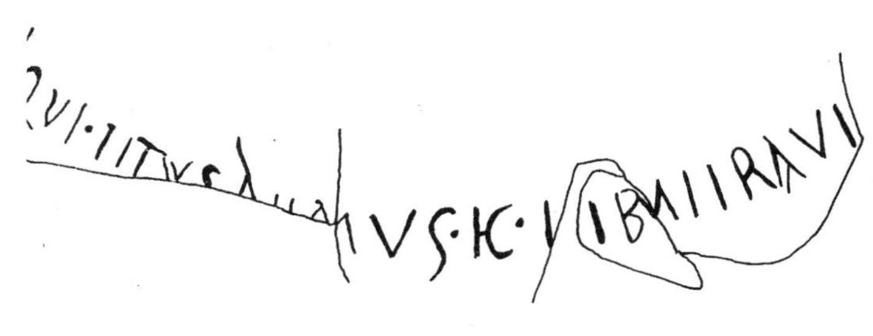

2503.393

2503.394. Leicester (*Ratae*). Black-burnished dish (½) of Gillam form 221, found in 1874 during excavations for the new Municipal Buildings on the site of the old Cattle Market, Horsefair Street. Leicester Museum. Drawn by R.P.W., 1948.

graffito on the wall: QVIN
Quin(ti)
'(Property) of Quintus'

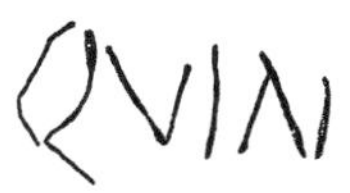

2503.394

2503.395. Rivenhall, Essex. Part of a Black-burnished dish (½) with lattice decoration, found in 1972 in a late second-century deposit at Building 2 of the Roman villa. Present whereabouts not recorded. Drawn by M.W.C.H.

Britannia viii (1977), 439 No. 69.

graffito: QVINTES[. . .]

Presumably a name derived from *quintus* but **Quinte(n)sis* is not attested (compare *Quintane(n)sis*, Kajanto, *Cognomina*, 204); perhaps a variant of *Quintasius* (ibid., 174, but only African).

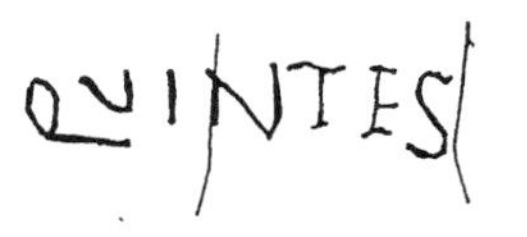

2503.395

2503.396. Holt, Clwyd [Denbighshire]. Part of a large red flanged jar (½), diameter *c.* 255 mm, found in 1907–15 during excavations at the legionary works depot. National Museum, Cardiff. Drawn by R.P.W., 1953.

W.F. Grimes, *Holt* (1930), 134 No. 36.

graffito on the shoulder: QVINTIẠ[. . .]
Quintia[ni]
'(Property) of Quintianus'

QVINTI M(ANV), Grimes. QVINTIṂ[. . .], *Quinti M[. . .]*, R.P.W. As text, R.S.O.T.

Quinti M[. . .] is a possible reading, but one might have expected a gap after I and trace of the second apex of M. *Quintianus* is a common cognomen; for a legionary example see *RIB* 1031.

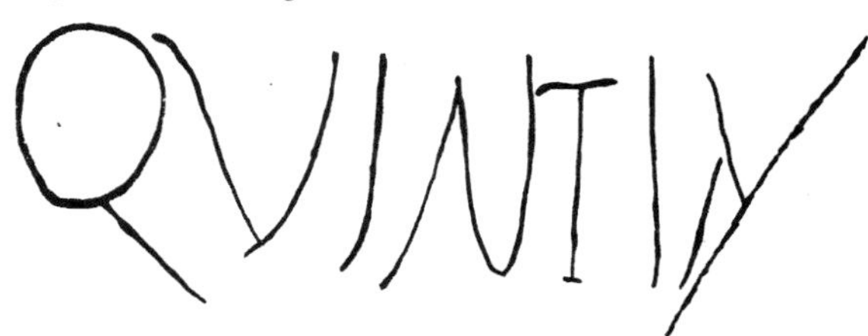

2503.396

2503.397. Caernarvon (*Segontium*), Gwynedd. Part of a grey-ware carinated bowl (½), found in 1923 in an unrecorded context. Segontium Museum. Drawn by R.P.W., 1954.

graffito on the lower part of the wall: REG[. . .]

Most likely a cognomen derived from *rex*, e.g. *Regulus* (see Kajanto, *Cognomina*, 317); or the Celtic-derived *Reginus* (compare *RIB* 1065, Oswald *Index* and Holder s.v.). Compare *RIB* 2503.578.

2503.397

2503.398. St. Albans (*Verulamium*), Hertfordshire. Funnel-necked buff jug (½), found in 1932 in Pit 5 of the late third century during excavation of Building IV.7. Verulamium Museum. Drawn by R.P.W., 1954.

Wheeler, *Verulamium* (1936), 199 No. 79 with fig. 38.79 and 200, fig. 39.79 a.

graffito on the lower part of the wall:
Leaf stop SΛCER leaf stop.

Although *Sacer* is a Latin adjective ('holy'), it evidently contained a Celtic name-element since it is common in the Gallic provinces (Kajanto, *Cognomina*, 211 and compare Oswald, *Index*, s.v. *Sacco*).

2503.398

2503.399. Colchester (*Camulodunum*), Essex. Part of a colander (½) in Hadham ware, found in 1964 in a residual context south of the precinct wall of the temple of Claudius. Colchester Museum. Drawn by M.W.C.H.

Britannia xi (1980), 410 No. 29.

graffito: SAL

Presumably part of a personal name, perhaps *Salvianus* (compare *RIB* 1062, 1215, 1234) or *Salvius* (compare *RIB* 968, 978).

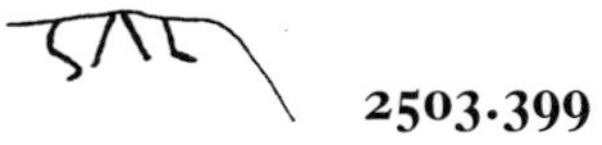

2503.399

2503.400. London (*Londinium*). Pottery vessel found before 1859. British Museum ex Roach Smith, but not located by R.P.W. Reprinted from *CIL*.

CIL vii 1335.6. Roach Smith, *Rom. Lond.* (1859), 106, wrongly listed as a samian stamp, SALV.F. RCHM, *Roman London* (1928), 177 No. 103.

two graffiti, (a) on the base: SΛLVE
(b) 'on the back': ⋏

Perhaps *Salv(a)e*, '(Property) of Salva', but since *Salvius* is many times more common than *Salvus*, more likely to be a misreading of SALVII.

2503.401. Lullingstone, Kent. Part of a late second-century Black-burnished cooking pot (½), height 254 mm, diameter at the mouth 178 mm, found in 1958 in the tannery pit on the west side of the Roman villa. Lullingstone Villa Museum. Drawn by S.S.F. from a rubbing by R.P.W., 1959.

JRS xlix (1959), 139 No. 30. Pollard in G.W. Meates, *The Lullingstone Roman Villa* ii (1987), 280 No. iv and 238 with fig. 75.160.

graffito on the shoulder: SΛS

Compare *RIB* 2501.490.

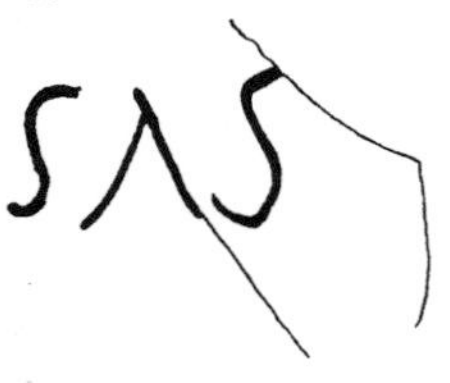

2503.401

2503.402. Dorchester (*Durnovaria*), Dorset. Base (½) in Black-burnished ware, found in 1971 in a late first- or early second-century context at No. 34 Trinity Street. Dorchester Museum. Drawn by S.S.F. from a tracing by B.J. O'Connor.

Britannia iv (1973), 330 No. 15.

graffito on the base, which was subsequently pierced: SAT

Probably *Sat(urnini)*
'(Property) of Saturninus'

2503.402

2503.403. Maryport (*Alauna*), Cumbria [Cumberland]. Fragment from the wall of a grey bowl (½), found in 1966 unstratified during excavations at the fort. Senhouse Museum, Maryport. Drawn by S.S.F. from rubbings by R.P.W., 1972.

Britannia iii (1972), 355 No. 19.

graffito below the rim: SΛT
  Probably *Sat(urnini)*
  '(Property) of Saturninus'

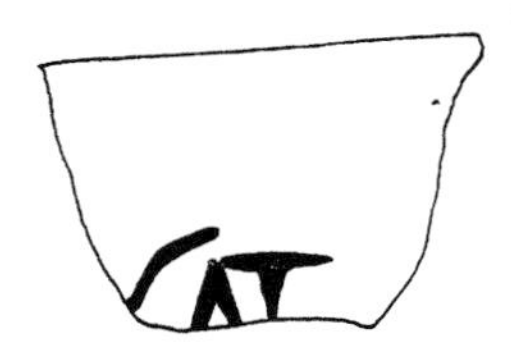

2503.403

2503.404. St. Albans (*Verulamium*), Hertfordshire. Part of a jar (½) in coarse granulated dark grey ware, found in 1958 in a deposit dated *c.* A.D. 75–85 outside Room 14 of Period II A in Insula XIV. Verulamium Museum. Drawn by S.S.F. from a rubbing by R.P.W., 1959.

JRS xlix (1959), 139 No. 31. S.S. Frere, *Verulamium Excavations* i (1972), 286 No. 296 with fig. 108.296 and 364 No. 4 with fig. 140.4.

graffito on the shoulder: SΛX
  Perhaps *Sax(ae)*
  '(Property) of Saxa'

The Latin cognomen *Saxa* is not in Kajanto's index, but is well attested (see Schulze, 369, and *ILS* 1104); also compare *RIB* 1918. Another possibility is the Celtic name *Saxamus* (Oswald, *Index* and Holder s.v.). Compare No. 405.

2503.404

2503.405. Canterbury (*Durovernum*), Kent. Fragment (½) from a jar in fine buff fabric with grey surface, found in 1977 in the late third-century rampart of the city wall at St. Radigund's. Canterbury Museum. Drawn by M.W.C.H.

2503.405

Britannia xiii (1982), 415 No. 51.

graffito on the wall: SΛX̣[. . .]
  Perhaps *Sax[ae]*
  '(Property) of Saxa'

Compare *RIB* 2503.404 with note.

2503.406. Billericay, Essex. Base of a grey vessel (½), found in 1971 in a pit or well at Billericay School, School Road, with late second- to early third-century material. Present whereabouts unrecorded. Drawn by S.S.F. from rubbings by S.G.P. Weller, 1973.

Britannia iv (1973), 330 No. 19.

graffito around the base: SECVNDΛ.VỊ

Perhaps SECVNDΛṆVṢ, R.S.O.T. conject.

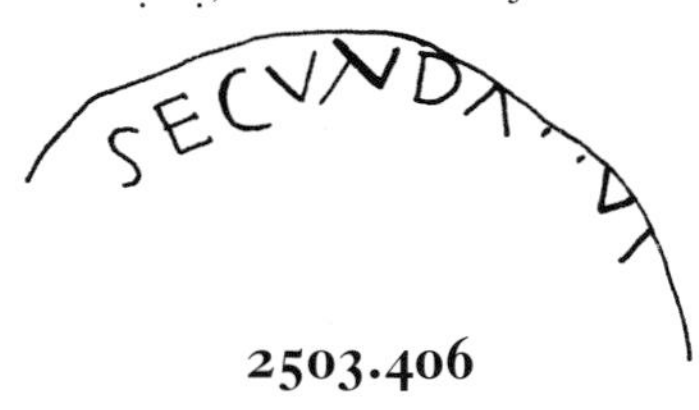

2503.406

2503.407. Chester (*Deva*). Piece of pottery or tile (½) in buff fabric, found in 1976 in a residual context at Abbey Green. Grosvenor Museum. Drawn by M.W.C.H.

Britannia viii (1977), 436 No. 47.

graffito: [. . .]DΛI[. . .] | SIICVṆ[. . .]
  [. . .]dai[. . .] | *Secun[dus]*

2503.407

2503.408. Richborough (*Rutupiae*), Kent. Sherd (½) from a rouletted beaker of polished dark grey ware, found in 1928–32 unstratified in Area XVI. In store at Dover Castle. Drawn by R.P.W.

J.P. Bushe-Fox, *Richborough* iv (1949), 255 No. 7 with pl. LXXII.4.

graffito above the rouletting: [. . .]C̣VRΛ[. . .]
  Perhaps *[Se]cura*

2503.408

2503.409. London (*Londinium*). Fragment of a buff jar ($\frac{1}{2}$), found in 1928–34 on the site of the Bank of England. Museum of London. Drawn by R.P.W., 1953.

JRS xliv (1954), 111 No. 49.

graffito on the lower part of the wall: SIICVR[. . .]
Probably *Secur[i]*
'(Property) of Securus'

The final letter is R not N, R.P.W.

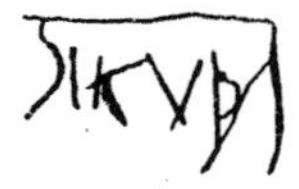

2503.409

2503.410. St. Albans (*Verulamium*), Hertfordshire. Fragment of a jug in red ware ($\frac{1}{2}$), found in 1956 in a fourth-century deposit south-west of Building XXVII.1. Verulamium Museum. Drawn by M.G. Wilson.

JRS xlvii (1957), 234 No. 40. S.S. Frere, *Verulamium Excavations* iii (1984), 278 No. 10 with fig. 115. 10.

graffito on the wall: [. . .]SEṆ[. . .]
Probably *Sen[. . .]*

[. . .]SEM[. . .], R.P.W., *JRS*.

The larger size of the S suggests that the graffito is complete at the beginning. Names in *Sen-* (e.g. *Senecianus*) are much more common than *Sempronius* in Britain and Gaul.

2503.410

2503.411. Carlisle (*Luguvalium*), Cumbria [Cumberland]. Base of a Black-burnished 1 cooking pot ($\frac{1}{2}$), found in 1981–84 unstratified during excavations at Annetwell Street. Tullie House Museum. Drawn by Ian Caruana.

2503.411

Britannia xxi (1990), 367 No. 17.

two graffiti beneath the base: (a) SIINNΛ
Senna
(b) X

Senna is a (masculine) Celtic personal name since it is found in *CIL* xiii and *CIL* v, and must be cognate with *S(a)enus* (*RIB* 67, 685 and *AE* 1956.249, *civis Dumnonius*). For the developed form *Sennianus* see *RIB* 2495.1 and 2501.501.

2503.412. Shakenoak Farm, Oxfordshire. Two conjoining fragments ($\frac{1}{2}$) from the base of a Black-burnished cooking pot, found respectively in 1962 in a deposit dated *c.* A.D. 120–250 and in 1964 in a deposit dated *c.* A.D. 200–350 during excavations at the Roman villa. Ashmolean Museum, Oxford. Drawn by R.S.O.T., 1993.

JRS lv (1965), 227 No. 46. A.C.C. Brodribb et al., *Excavations at Shakenoak* i (1968), 40 No. 1 with fig. 12.1.

graffito on the inside surface of the base:
SIINT[.]CΛ
Sent[i]ca

VLIXIIS (read inverted), R.P.W. As text, R.S.O.T. by autopsy.

For *Sentica* compare *Britannia* xxiii (1992), 312 No. 8 (Low Borrow Bridge), with note.

2503.412

2503.413. Pakenham, Suffolk. Base of a (?) jar in micaceous grey ware ($\frac{1}{2}$), found in 1985 in a pit dated to the late second century. Ipswich Museum. Drawn by M.W.C.H.

Britannia xxi (1990), 372 No. 38.

graffito beneath the base: SIIR
Ser(. . .)

2503.413

2503.414. Housesteads (*Vercovicium*), Northumberland. Two conjoining fragments (½) of the base of a Black-burnished bowl, found in 1971 in the room in the south-west corner of the hospital in the fort. Museum of Antiquities, Newcastle upon Tyne. Drawn by S.S.F. from rubbings by R.P.W., 1971.

Britannia iii (1972), 360 No. 44.

graffito on the base: [. . .]RIINA

Perhaps *[Se]rena*

'The final letter is cursive in form', R.P.W.

R.P.W. apparently envisaged a New Roman Cursive (fourth-century) form, which seems unlikely here. The final letter may be a blundered I, for *[Se]reni*, R.S.O.T.

2503.414

2503.415. Eccles, Kent. Two conjoining fragments (½) from the wall and base of a buff storage jar in Patch Grove ware, found in 1967 during excavations at the Roman villa. Maidstone Museum. Drawn by S.S.F. from rubbings by R.P.W., 1967.

JRS lviii (1968), 213 No. 74.

graffito on the base: SILTII

A nomen *Siltius*, of which this would be the uncontracted genitive, is not attested. The reading seems open to doubt.

2503.415

2503.416. Colchester (*Camulodunum*), Essex. Grey carinated bowl of Camulodunum form 227 (½), height 111 mm, diameter 127 mm, found in or before 1924 without recorded provenance. Colchester Museum ex Laver collection. Drawn by R.P.W. from a rubbing by R.G.C., 1928. See also PL. VI B.

T. May, *Cat.* (1930), 246 No. 6 with fig. 9.6.

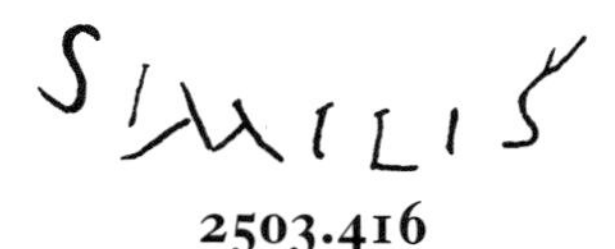

2503.416

two graffiti, (a) below the base: a cross (mark of ownership) (*not illustrated*)

(b) above the carination: SIMILIS

'(Property) of Similis'

2503.417. Camelon (?*Colania*), Central Region [Stirlingshire]. Part of a grey dish (½) with lattice decoration and a flat rim, found in 1899–1900 during excavations at the fort. National Museums of Scotland, Queen Street, Edinburgh. Drawn by R.G.C., 1936.

graffito below the base: SIMILIS

'(Property) of Similis'

2503.417

2503.418. Corbridge (?*Coria*), Northumberland. Part of a Black-burnished cooking pot (½), found before 1940. Corbridge Museum. Drawn by R.P.W., 1940.

graffito below the base: SQVNDEX

Perhaps *S(extus) Q(. . .) V(i)ndex*

S(exti) Qu(i)n(ti) Dex(tri), R.P.W.

There is no room for more than one letter for the praenomen, R.P.W. The praenomina *Sex(tus)* and *Sp(urius)* are both occasionally abbreviated to S, but the result is ambiguous.

2503.418

2503.419. Colchester (*Camulodunum*), Essex. Part of a grey jar (½), found in 1929 in Holly Trees Meadow (Insula 15). Colchester Museum. Drawn by R.P.W., 1943.

JRS xxxiv (1944), 91 No. 31.

graffito on the shoulder below a wavy line:

[. . .]PICI ET EVRI

Perhaps *[Sul]pici et Euri*

'(Property) of Sulpicius and Eurus'

Eurus, the (Greek) east wind, is doubtfully attested as a personal name in *CIL* ii 443.

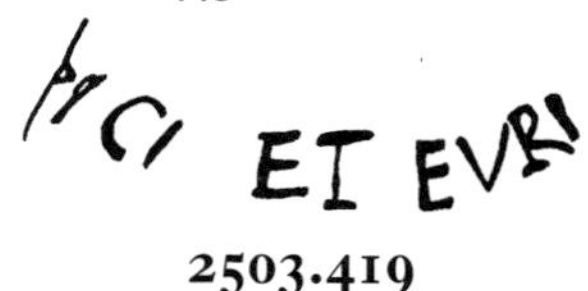

2503.419

2503.420. Caerleon (*Isca*), Gwent [Monmouthshire]. Part of a grey jar ($\frac{2}{3}$), found in 1928 during excavation of the amphitheatre. Drawn by R.G.C., 1928.

graffito on the base: SYMPHORVS

This Greek name is quite common in the western provinces (see Mócsy, *Nomenclator*, s.v. *Synphorus*)

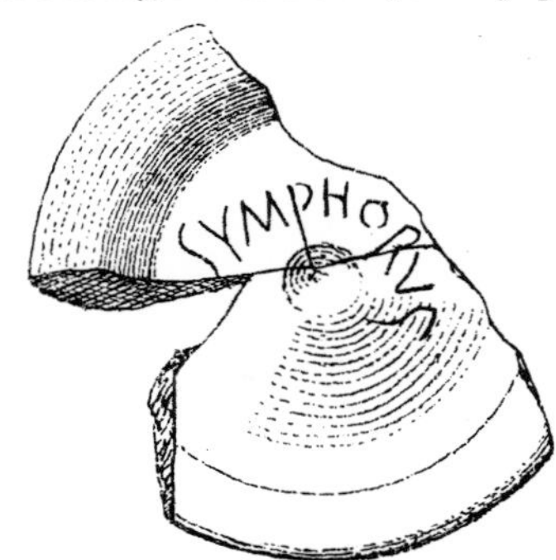

2503.420

2503.421. Wanborough (*?Durocornovium*), Wiltshire. Fragment from the rim of a black-cooking pot ($\frac{1}{2}$), found in 1969 during the excavation of Roman buildings in the settlement. Swindon Museum. Drawn by S.S.F. from rubbings by R.P.W., 1970.

Britannia i (1970), 314 No. 46.

graffito: TAMM[. . .]
Tamm[o] or *Tamm[onius]*

Compare *RIB* 67 and 87.

2503.421

2503.422. Gadebridge Park, Hemel Hempstead, Hertfordshire. Fragment from the wall of a grey bowl ($\frac{1}{2}$), found in 1967 in the hypocaust channel of Room 35 during excavations at the Roman villa. Dacorum District Council. Drawn by S.S.F. from rubbings by R.P.W., 1970.

Britannia ii (1971), 296 No. 47. Wright in D.S. Neal, *Gadebridge Park* (1974), 254 No. c with fig. 113.c.

graffito on the wall: ṬAR Ẹ[. . .]

R.P.W. suggests *Tare[ntinus]*, but it is not certain that the graffito is continuous.

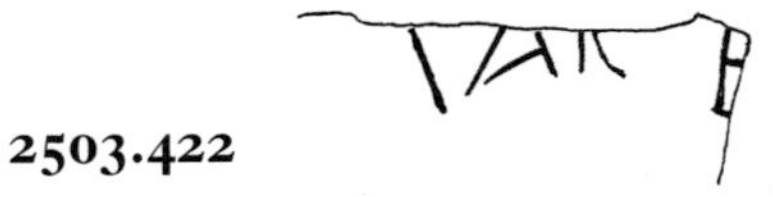

2503.422

2503.423. Stebbing, Essex. Fragment of a black flanged bowl ($\frac{1}{2}$), of late third- or fourth-century date, found in 1951 on a Roman metal-working site. In private possession. Drawn by R.P.W., 1951.

JRS xlii (1952), 108 No. 36.

graffito on the inner face of the wall: TA͡VRỊ[. . .]
Tauri or *Tauri[ni]*
'(Property) of Taurus *or* Taurinus'

2503.423

2503.424. Tarrant Hinton, Dorset. Conjoining sherds ($\frac{1}{2}$) from a Black-burnished ware dish, found in 1976 at the Roman villa at Barton Field. Wimborne Archaeological Group. Drawn by M.W.C.H.

Britannia xii (1981), 383 No. 31.

graffito beneath the base: TER
Perhaps *Ter(entii)*
'(Property) of Terentius'

2503.424

2503.425. Wilderspool, Cheshire. Two conjoining sherds of a storage jar ($\frac{1}{2}$), found in 1900. Warrington Museum. Drawn by R.P.W., 1952.

May, *T. Lancs & Chesh. Hist. Soc.* lii (1900), 51.

graffito on the shoulder: T ITẠITR

'indecipherable', May.

The reading seems certain except for Λ, with its vertical second stroke; but the alternative possibilities of II (i.e. E) with casual damage or reversed L (compare *RIB* 2503.242, also from Wilderspool) make no better sense. Possibly a blundered TIIRTI, *Terti*, '(Property) of Tertius'.

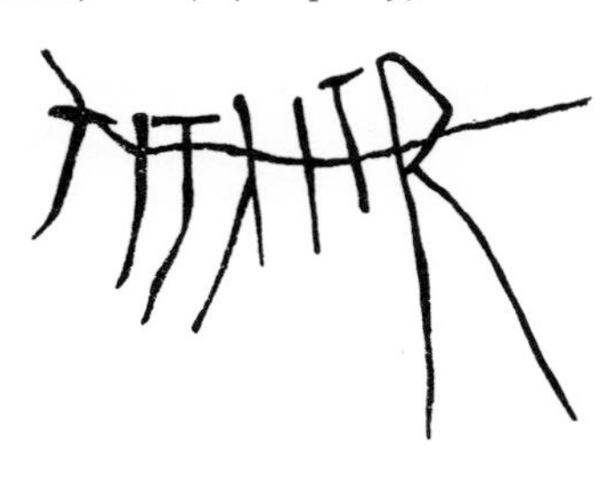

2503.425

2503.426. Southwark, south London. Part of the base of a first-century grey-ware beaker (1/1), found in 1978 in a late-Roman pit during excavations at No. 199 Borough High Street. Museum of London. Reproduced from Hassall.

Britannia x (1979), 354 No. 41. Hassall in P. Hinton (ed.), *Excavations in Southwark 1973–6 and Lambeth 1973–9* (1988), 365 No. 12 with fig. 164.12.

graffito around the base: [. . .]IΛTITI ΛTILI[. . .]

Perhaps *Titi Atili* (or *Atili[ani]*) *[. . .]ia*, '. . . (wife *or* daughter) of Titus Atilius *or* Titius Atilianus'; otherwise perhaps *Atili [. . .]iatiti*, '(Property) or Atilius[. . .]iatitus'.

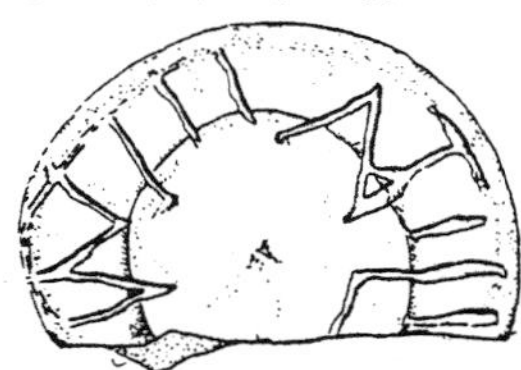

2503.426

2503.427. Fishbourne, West Sussex. Jar (1/2), found in 1961–69 during excavations at the Roman palace. Fishbourne Museum. Reproduced from Cunliffe.

B.W. Cunliffe, *Excavations at Fishbourne, 1961–69* ii (1971), 369 No. 6 with fig. 145.6.

graffito on the shoulder: TL

The graffito appears to be complete.

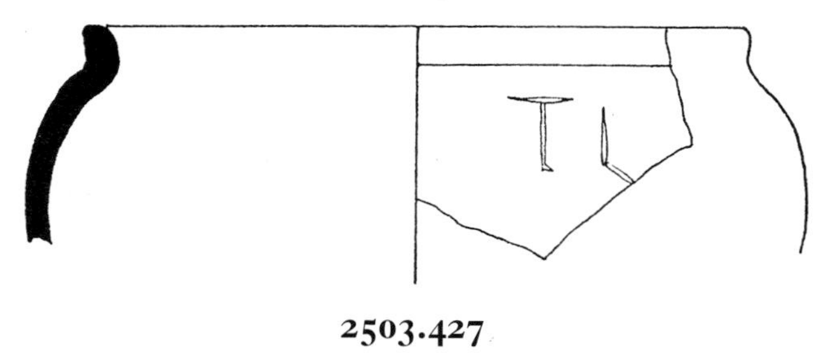

2503.427

2503.428. Collyweston, Northamptonshire. Part of the base of a pinkish-buff jar (1/2), found in 1953 unstratified during excavations *c.* 40 m south of Roman buildings examined in the Great Wood. Burghley Estate Office, Stamford. Reproduced from Knocker.

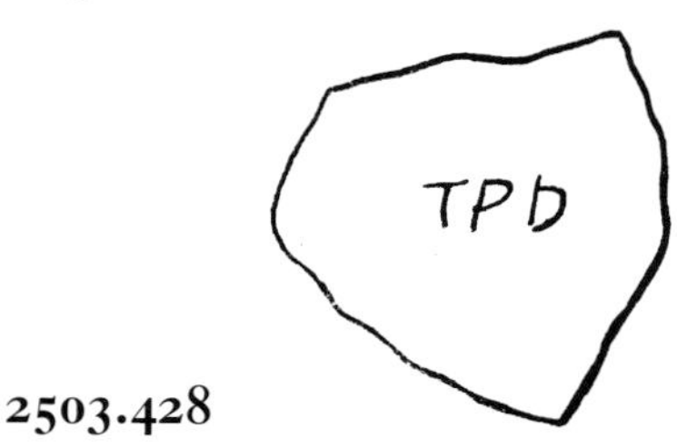

2503.428

JRS lix (1969), 245 No. 74. Knocker, *Arch. J.* cxxii (1965), 67 No. 8 with fig. 8.8.

graffito on the base: TPD

Perhaps *T(itus) P(. . .) D(. . .)* or even *t(esta) p(ondo)* $\bar{V}$ misunderstood (compare *RIB* 2503.14), but this is an unlikely place for a note of weight.

2503.429. Southwark, south London. Fragment of a grey-ware beaker (1/1), found in 1975 in a ditch with second-century material during excavations at No. 199 Borough High Street. Museum of London. Reproduced from Hassall.

Britannia x (1979), 354 No. 40. Hassall in P. Hinton (ed.), *Excavations in Southwark 1973–76 and Lambeth 1973–9* (1988), 365 No. 4 with fig. 164.4.

graffito: TRIẠ

TRII or less probably TIVI, M.W.C.H., *Britannia*. As text, Hassall in Hinton.

2503.429 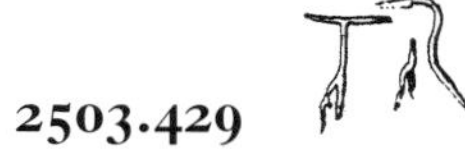

2503.430. St. Albans (*Verulamium*), Hertfordshire. Part of a brown dish (1/2), found in 1964 in Insula XIII. Verulamium Museum. Drawn by S.S.F. from a rubbing by R.P.W., 1968.

JRS lix (1969), 245 No. 75.

graffito on the wall: TRO
Perhaps *Tro(phimi)*
'(Property) or Trophimus'

This Greek name is frequent in Italy and the western provinces (see Móscy, *Nomenclator* s.v.); compare *RIB* 2501.550 and *Tab. Vindol.* ii No. 341. Alternatively *T(itus) R(. . .) O(. . .)*.

2503.430

2503.431. Cambridge (*Duroliponte*). Fragment (1/2) from the upper part of a beaker with lustrous surface, found in 1975 with late third-century material covering the gravel yard of a shrine at Ridgeons Garden. Museum of Archaeology and Anthropology, Cambridge. Drawn by M.W.C.H.

Britannia x (1979), 347 No. 14.

graffito on the neck: TVA
Probably *T(itus) V(. . .) A(. . .)*

Tua, perhaps 'Yours', *Britannia*.

2503.431

2503.432. St. Albans (*Verulamium*), Hertfordshire. Part of a beaker ($\frac{1}{4}$ and $\frac{1}{2}$) in greyish fabric with a very dark grey slip. Unprovenanced. Verulamium Museum. Reproduced from Greep.

Greep, *Herts. Arch.* viii (1980–82), 207 No. 1 with figs. 1.1 and 2.1.

graffito below the rim: VACỊ.[. . .]

VACV[. . .], perhaps part of a personal name or *vacu[a]* (*olla*), Greep. As text, R.S.O.T.

Possibly *Vacia* (compare *RIB* 961, 1742), the second A clumsily crossed.

2503.432

2503.433. Chesterholm (*Vindolanda*), Northumberland. Part of the rim of a Black-burnished bowl ($\frac{1}{2}$), found in 1968 in a context dated *c.* A.D. 120–130 or a little later. Vindolanda Museum. Drawing: the Vindolanda Trust.

Britannia xix (1988), 503 No. 81. E., R., and A. Birley, *Vindolanda* ii (1993), 98 No. 4 with fig. 12.3.

two graffiti: (a) [. . .]IΛ
(b) VALIINTIṆ[. . .]
Valentin[i]
'(Property) of Valentinus'

2503.433

2503.434. Colchester (*Camulodunum*), Essex. Part of a grey flask ($\frac{1}{2}$), found in 1928 unstratified in the Holly Trees Meadow (Insula 15). Colchester Museum. Drawn by R.P.W., 1954.

graffito on the shoulder: V.[.]ỊỊRI
Perhaps *V[al]eri*
'(Property) of Valerius'

2503.434

2503.435. Caerleon (*Isca*), Gwent [Monmouthshire]. Part of a bowl ($\frac{1}{2}$) in orange coarse ware (Caerleon ware) imitating Dr. 37, found in 1927 during excavation of Entrance D at the amphitheatre. Caerleon Museum. Drawn by G.C. Boon, 1992.

graffito: [. . .]LERI
Probably *[Va]leri*
'(Property) of Valerius'

2503.435

2503.436. Wall (*Letocetum*), Staffordshire. Part of a coarse-ware cup ($\frac{1}{2}$) of red fabric with buff slip, found in 1951 in a spoil-heap from the excavations of 1912–14 on the west side of the bath-house. Wall Museum. Drawn by R.P.W., 1951.

JRS xlii (1952), 108 No. 37.

graffito on the wall: VΛRI
Vari
'(Property) of Varus'

VIIRI, *Veri*, *JRS*. As text, R.P.W., archive.

'The two strokes after V converge towards the top, and make possible the reading *Vari*, instead of *Veri*', *JRS*.

VIIRI is perfectly acceptable and, since *Verus* and its cognate are so frequent in Britain and Gaul, probably to be preferred. R.S.O.T.

2503.436

2503.437. Eccles, Kent. Fragment of a black bowl (½) with zig-zag scoring on the wall, found in 1968 immediately north-east of the main house at the Roman villa. Maidstone Museum. Drawn by S.S.F. from rubbings by R.P.W., 1969.

JRS lix (1969), 245 No. 76.

graffito on the rim: V̂AR

Compare *RIB* 2501.568.

2503.437

2503.438. Unknown provenance. Black flanged dish (½) with a wavy line inside found in the 19th century probably in Cambridgeshire or Essex and perhaps at Great Chesterford. Museum of Archaeology and Anthropology, Cambridge, ex Braybrooke collection. Drawn by R.P.W., 1951.

graffito on the wall: [. . .]VΛRRIΛTVS
Varriatus

Probably complete, R.P.W.

The name is not otherwise attested.

2503.438

2503.439. Colchester (*Camulodunum*), Essex. Fine polished grey beaker (½ and ¼) found in 1927–29 in the main chamber of the 'Mithraeum' in the Holly Trees Meadow (Insula 15). Colchester Museum. Graffito drawn by R.P.W., 1954, and vessel reproduced from Hull. See also PL. VI A.

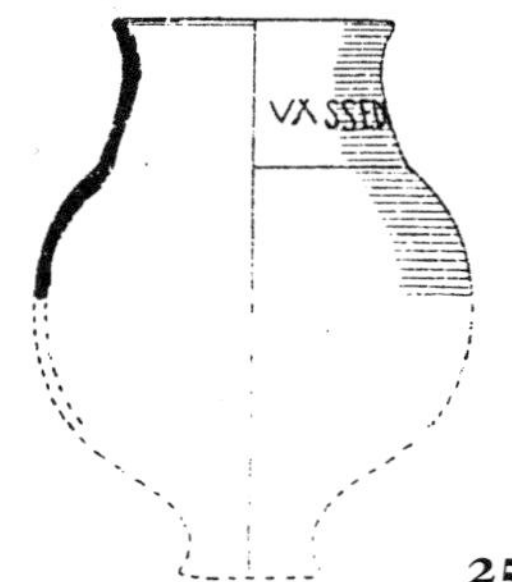

2503.439

JRS xxxiv (1944), 91 No. 32. M.R. Hull, *Roman Colchester* (1958), 144 No. 147 with fig. 71.147.

graffito on the neck: ỤΛSSEDO
Vassedo

This Celtic name is attested in Narbonensis: see Holder s.v.

2503.440. Piddington, Northamptonshire. Fragment (½) from a mica-gilt dish in fawn-coloured fabric, found in 1986 with material dated to the first half of the second century during excavations at the Roman villa. Upper Nene Valley Archaeological Society. Drawn by M.W.C.H.

Britannia xviii (1987), 372 No. 26.

graffito on the wall: VΛTINIII
Vatini(a)e or possibly *Vatinii⟨i⟩*
'(Property) of Vatina *or* Vatinius'

2503.440

2503.441. Leicester (*Ratae*). Part of the base (½) of a micaceous terra nigra plate (Camulodunum form 1), found in 1965 in a context dated to the first half of the first century during excavations at St. Nicholas Circle. Leicester Museum. Traced by M.W.C.H. from a drawing by Richard Pollard.

Britannia xvii (1986), 445 No. 60.

graffito beneath the base: [. . .]IILVGNA
[V]elugna

Compare *CIL* xiii 6221 from Worms, *Amandus Velugni f(ilius) Devas* (i.e. from Chester).

2503.441

2503.442. Colchesther (*Camulodunum*), Essex. Part of a black bowl (½) of second-century date, found before 1928. Colchester Museum. Drawn by R.P.W., 1943.

2503.442

graffito on the wall: VIIN
Ven(. . .)

NIIA, *Nea*, R.P.W. (archive). As text, R.G.C.

R.G.C.'s reading is preferred here because IIN looks better that way up (assuming V to have a double stroke or casual damage), and because *Venustus* (or similar) is far more likely a name than the Greek noun *Nea*.

2503.443. Castleford (*Lagentium*), West Yorkshire. Part of a pinkish-buff jug (½), found in 1978. West Yorkshire Archaeology Service. Drawn by R.S.O.T., 1988.

Britannia xix (1988), 505 No. 101.

graffito on the shoulder: VVẸRI
probably *⟨V⟩Veri*
'(Property) of Verus'

R is cursive but the E is a capital letter, assuming that a faint horizontal stroke belongs to it. The graffito seems to be complete, but since no personal name *Uverus* is known, V was probably repeated in error for the common name *Verus*.

2503.443

2503.444. Ilchester (? *Lindinis*), Somerset. Jug (¼ and ½) in buff fabric with a cream slip, found in 1975 during excavations west of the Fosse Way and south of the Roman town, at Little Spittle in a suggested votive context. Taunton Museum. Vessel reproduced from Leach, graffito drawn by M.W.C.H.

Britannia viii (1977), 444 No. 101. P. Leach, *Ilchester* i: *Excavations 1974–5* (1982), 74 and 159 No. 220 with fig. 71.220.

graffito around the body:
MVIỊRINA VṚILVCOLOPAṚBO·COMTṂ

M Verina Urilucolo parbo COMTM, 'Verina for little Urilucolus . . .' M.W.C.H. But reading and interpretation both seem to be uncertain.

2503.445. Camelon (? *Colania*), Central Region [Stirlingshire]. Two conjoining sherds of a grey dish with lattice decoration (½), found in 1899–1900 during excavations at the fort. National Museums of Scotland, Queen Street, Edinburgh. Drawn by R.P.W., 1954.

Anderson, *PSAS* xxxv (1901), 389.

graffito on the wall: VESTΛLỊS
Vestalis
'(Property) of Vestalis'

For this Latin cognomen derived from the goddess *Vesta* see Kajanto, *Cognomina*, 214.

2503.445

2503.446. Pakenham, Suffolk. One of two grey bowls (½), one upturned on the other (see *RIB* 2503.447), found in 1953 during excavations at the Roman villa at Redcastle Farm. Diameter at the base 165 mm, height 102 mm. Ipswich Museum. Drawn by R.P.W., 1954.

JRS xliv (1954), 111 No. 51 a.

graffito on the base: VIITVLA
Vetula

Vetula is pejorative (e.g. Juvenal, *Sat.* i 39) but it is occasionally found as a cognomen (Kajanto, *Cognomina*, 302); compare *RIB* 2503.447, evidently the same owner.

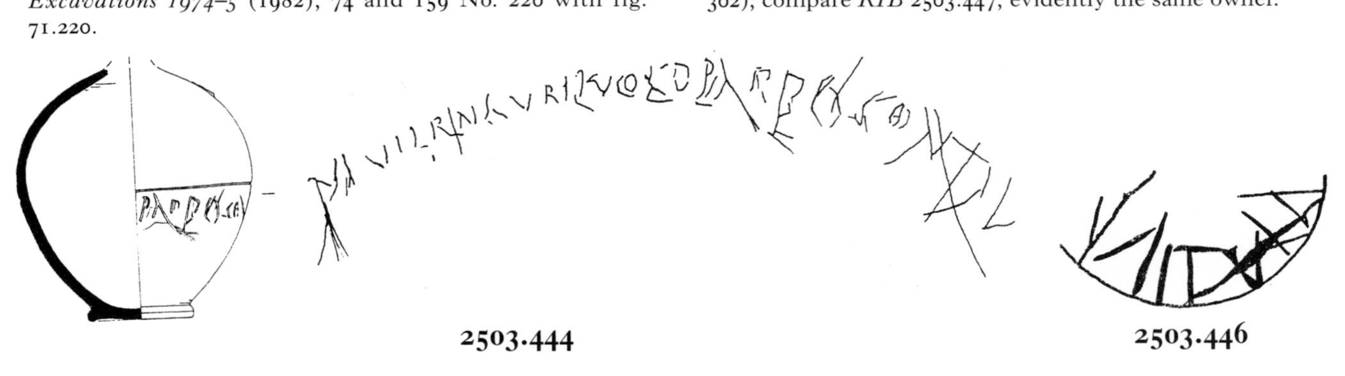

2503.444 **2503.446**

2503.447. Ibid. One of two grey bowls (½), one upturned on the other (see *RIB* 2503.446), found in 1953 during excavations at the Roman villa at Redcastle Farm. Diameter at the base 179 mm, height 89 mm. Ipswich Museum. Drawn by R.P.W., 1954.

JRS xliv (1954), 111 No. 51 b.

graffito on the base: VIITV
Vetu(la)

Compare No. 446 with note.

2503.447

2503.448. Corbridge (? *Coria*), Northumberland. Part of a black bowl (½), without recorded provenance. Corbridge Museum. Drawn by R.P.W., 1964.

graffito on the wall: VIẠ[. . .]
Perhaps *Via[tor]*

For this common cognomen compare *RIB* 617, 1817, 2031; and, abbreviated thus, *RIB* 2501.604, 605.

2503.448

2503.449. Silchester (*Calleva*), Hampshire. Part of the base (scale uncertain) of a vessel in red ware with a white slip, found before 1951. Reading Museum. Drawn by S.S.F. from a sketch by R.P.W., 1951.

graffito below the base: VICARỊ
'(Property) of Vicarius'

Vicarius ('deputy') is uncommon as a personal name: see Kajanto, *Cognomina*, 314.

2503.449

2503.450. Richborough (*Rutupiae*), Kent. Part of a buff jug (½), found in 1928–32 during excavations at Site VI with first- and second-century pottery. In store at Dover Castle. Drawn by R.P.W.

J.P. Bushe-Fox, *Richborough* iv (1949), 255 No. 8 with pl. LXX b.

graffito on the shoulder: VICTOR[. . .]
Victor[is] or a cognate name
'(Property) of Victor'

2503.450

2503.451. Holt, Clwyd [Denbighshire]. Part of a red jug (½), found in 1907–15 during excavations at the legionary works depot. National Museum, Cardiff. Drawn by R.P.W., 1953.

W.F. Grimes, *Holt* (1930), 134 No. 34.

graffito at the base of the neck: VICTORI[. . .]
Victori[s] or a cognate name
'(Property) of Victor'

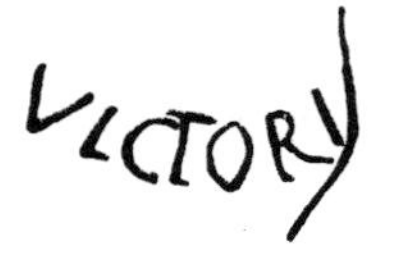

2503.451

2503.452. Colchester (*Camulodunum*), Essex. Fragment from the shoulder of a grey flask (½), found in 1929 in Holly Trees Meadow (Insula 15). Colchester Museum. Drawn by R.P.W., 1943.

JRS xxxiv (1944), 90 No. 21.

graffito: [. . .]1–2 VICT
Probably . . . *Vict(oris)*

[. . .]C VICT, *Vict(oris)*, R.P.W. Possibly [IV]L or [IV]LI VICT with casual damage, *[Iu]li Vict(oris)*, R.S.O.T.

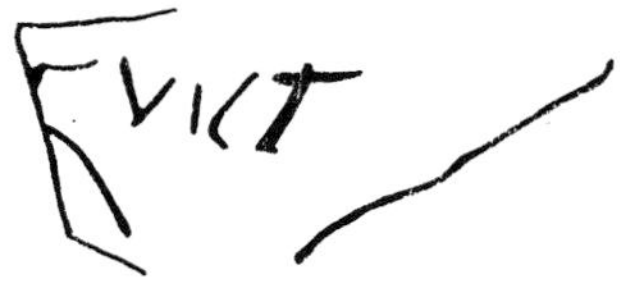

2503.452

2503.453. Canterbury (*Durovernum*), Kent. Base of a black jar (½), found in 1951 during excavations at Nos. 10–11 Castle Street. Canterbury Museum. Drawn by R.P.W., 1952.

JRS xliii (1953), 131 No. 20.

graffito on the base: VIDI
'(Property) of Vidius'

For the nomen *Vidius* see *ILS* 4650, *CIL* iii 5861 and Oswald, *Index*, s.v.

2503.453

2503.454. London (*Londinium*). Fragment of the rim of a colour-coated bag-shaped beaker with devolved cornice rim (½), found in 1955 during excavations at the Jewel House site, Tower of London. Department of the Environment. Drawn by R.P.W., 1964.

JRS liv (1964), 185 No. 45.

graffito below the lip: [. . .]·VIDIC̣[. . .]

Possibly *Vidi C[. . .]*, or blundered *Vi(n)dic[is]*

Compare *RIB* 2503.603.

2503.454

2503.455. Gadebridge Park, Hemel Hempstead, Hertfordshire. Fragment from the shoulder of a whitish jar (½), found in 1968 in a ditch below the Roman villa. Dacorum District Council. Drawn by S.S.F. from rubbings by R.P.W., 1970.

Britannia i (1970), 314 No. 47. Wright in D.S. Neal, *Gadebridge Park* (1974), 255 No. h with fig. 113 h.

graffito on the shoulder: VINB[. . .]

2503.455

2503.456. Ibid. Base of a reddish pot (½), found in 1967 in the filling of a chalk quarry in a fourth-century context during excavations at the Roman villa. Dacorum District Council. Reproduced from Neal.

Britannia ii (1971), 296 No. 45. D.S. Neal, *Gadebridge Park* (1974), 255 No. l with fig. 113 l.

graffito on the base: [. . .]INCENTI
[V]incenti
'(Property) of Vincentius'

[. . .]INGENTI, *Ingenti*, R.P.W. As text, R.S.O.T.

Ingentius (from *ingens*) and *Vincentius* (from *vincens*) are both typically 'late' formations (third/fourth century), but *Ingentius* is very rare and *Vincentius* quite common. See Kajanto, *Cognomina*, 275 and 278, and in Britain *RIB* 1533 and 2491.78. Moreover C not G seems to have been inscribed.

2503.456

2503.457. Gloucester (*Glevum*). Complete white-slipped jug (½), found in 1974 in a timber building thought to be a guard-chamber at the North Gate of the fortress. Gloucester Museum. Drawn by L.V. Marley.

Britannia xiv (1983), 344 No. 32. Hassall in C. Heighway, *The East and North Gates of Gloucester* (1983), 199 No. G.1 with fig. 114.G1.

graffito below the handle: VIPSASSVI
'(Property) of Vipsassuus' (?)

The name is otherwise unattested.

2503.457

2503.458. Rockbourne, Hampshire. Base of New Forest buff ware (½), found before 1963 during excavations at the Roman villa. In store with Hampshire Museums Service. Drawn by S.S.F. from a rubbing by R.P.W., 1965.

graffito on the base: VITAL
Vital(is)
'(Property) of Vitalis'

2503.458

2503.459. Caerleon (*Isca*), Gwent [Monmouthshire]. Part of a two-handled pink jug (½), dated *c.* A.D. 70–110, found in 1926 in Room 24 of the *fabrica* in Jenkin's Field. Caerleon Museum. Drawn by R.P.W., 1953.

Nash-Williams, *AC* lxxxiv (1929), 255 (repr. 21), fig. 15.2.

graffito on the shouler: VITΛḶ[. . .]
Vital[is]
'(Property) of Vitalis'

2503.459

2503.460. Darenth, Kent. Base of a grey jar (½), found in 1969 in association with fourth-century coins in Room 2 during excavations at the Roman villa. Maidstone Museum. Drawn by S.S.F. from rubbings by R.P.W., 1971.

Britannia ii (1971), 298 No. 54. B. Philp, *Excavations in West Kent, 1960–1970* (1973), 153 No. 458 with fig. 46.458.

graffiti: (a) VITIΛ
(b) owner's mark
'Vitia, (her mark)'

For *Vitia* compare *CIL* iii 7912 and vi 28523, 29095 and 34259.

The two graffiti do not appear to be successive.

2503.460

2503.461. Lincoln (*Lindum*). Sherd from the upper part of a colour-coated bulbous beaker (½), in orange fabric with a hard red slip on the inside and a black slip outside, found in 1972 during excavations at the Holmes Grain Warehouse. Lincoln Archaeological Trust. Drawn by S.S.F. from a rubbing by M.W.C.H.

Britannia v (1974), 466 No. 30.

graffito on the neck: [. . .]ḶỊVSVITRẠ[. . .]
Probably *[. . .]lius Vitra[. . .]*

[. . .]ẠIVSVITRẠ[. . .], M.W.C.H. As text, R.S.O.T.

Possibly *[Iu]lius Vitra[sianus]*. *Iulius* is a likely nomen at a legionary colonia, but there are other possibilities. For the cognomen *Vitrasianus* compare *CIL* x 4657.

2503.461

2503.462. Brecon (? *Cicucium*), Powys [Brecknockshire]. Base of a buff jar (½), found in 1925 during excavations at the fort. National Museum, Cardiff. Drawn by R.G.C., 1925.

graffito on the base: VITV

Probably *Vitu(lus)*: see Kajanto, *Cognomina*, 329; but compare *Vitus* (ibid., 347).

2503.462

2503.463. Keynsham, Avon [Somerset]. Part of a dish of coarse black ware (½), found in 1922–23 on the site of the Roman villa at Keynsham cemetery. J.S. Fry and Son's Museum, Somerdale. Drawn by R.P.W.

Horne, *Antiq. J.* iv (1924), 157. Bullard and Horne, *Arch.* lxxv (1926), 132. *TBGAS* xlvi (1924), 2.

graffito on the upper surface of the base: VNICA

Unicus/a as a name is very rare: see Kajanto, *Cognomina*, 294.

2503.463

2503.464. Middlewich (*Salinae*), Cheshire. Part of a large storage jar (½), found in 1968–69 set in the floor of a Roman workshop. Middlewich Archaeological Society. Drawn by S.S.F. from rubbings by J.D. Bestwick.

Britannia i (1970), 313 No. 37.

two graffiti: (a) M (partly recut)
(b) VRCA

(a) M͡A (b) A͡MVRCA, R.P.W. As text, R.S.O.T.

2503.464

For the name *Urca*, otherwise unattested, compare *RIB* 2501.635. For R.P.W.'s reading and interpretation see *Britannia* loc. cit., note 47. These assume a ligatured open A and barred A in the same graffito, and that *amurca* (which always means the watery lees of olive-pressing) means 'waste from brine' here.

2503.465. Colchester (*Camulodunum*), Essex. Part of a cream-ware jug ($\frac{1}{2}$), found in 1976 in a gully containing late third-century material, during excavations in the suburb outside the Balkerne Gate. Colchester Museum. Drawn by M.W.C.H.

Britannia xi (1980), 411 No. 32.

graffito on the shoulder: [. . .]ṾRSIC[. . .]
Probably *Ursic[ini]*
'(Property) of Ursicinus'

Ursicius is also possible (compare *CIL* xiii 4152), but *Ursicinus* is more common (see Kajanto, *Cognomina*, 330), It tends to be late Roman (ibid. and *PLRE* s.v.).

2503.465

2503.466. Ribchester (*Bremetennacum*), Lancashire. Fragment ($\frac{1}{2}$) from a jug in white fabric, found in 1977 in a Hadrianic or early Antonine context in the *vicus* of the fort. Ribchester Museum. Traced by M.W.C.H. from a drawing by Paul Gibbons.

Britannia xii (1981), 388 No. 54.

graffito: X̂ỊΛSTI

The first letter might be a blundered C, giving *Casti*, '(property) of Castus'.

2503.466

(k) Acephalous and uninterpreted graffiti
(*RIB* 2503.467–619)

2503.467. Little Chester, Derbyshire. Fragment of the shoulder of a buff jug ($\frac{1}{1}$), found in 1960 during excavations at the fort. Derby Museum. Drawn by S.S.F. from a rubbing by R.P.W., 1960.

JRS li (1961), 197 No. 46. Webster, *Derbys. AJ* lxxxi (1961), 104 No. 51 with fig. 9.51.

graffito on the shoulder: [. . .]Λ̣BRIKΛ[. . .]

Neither *Fabrica* nor *Fabricator* is attested as a personal name, and *fabrikavit* would be expected to be cut before firing; but compare *RIB* 2503.596.

Perhaps [V]ṂBRI KA[RI] (two names) or similar. R.S.O.T.

2503.467

2503.468. Titsey, Surrey. Fragment from a bluish-grey flat-bottomed vessel ($\frac{1}{2}$), found in 1864–65 during excavations at the Roman villa. Now lost. Drawn by R.P.W. after Leveson-Gower.

Leveson-Gower, *Surrey AC* iv (1869), 225 with pl. II.5.

graffito on the base: [. . .]Λ̣BVST[. . .]

BVSP, Leveson-Gower. As text, R.P.W.

The first letter could also be M or R. For *Arbustus* (two instances) see Kajanto, *Cognomina*, 334.

2503.468

2503.469. Wiggonholt, West Sussex. Part of a grey beaker ($\frac{1}{2}$) with rouletted decoration, found in 1964 in a pit south of the Roman bath-house. Worthing Museum. Drawn by S.S.F. from rubbings by R.P.W., 1965.

JRS lv (1965), 227 No. 48 a. Evans, *Suss. AC* cxii (1974), 127 No. 10 with fig. 9.10.

graffito on the shoulder: [. . .]Λ̣CCΛ

Perhaps *[V]acca* (compare *RIB* 2501.556), or *[M]acca* (compare *Maccus*, *RIB* 2491.105, 2501.314).

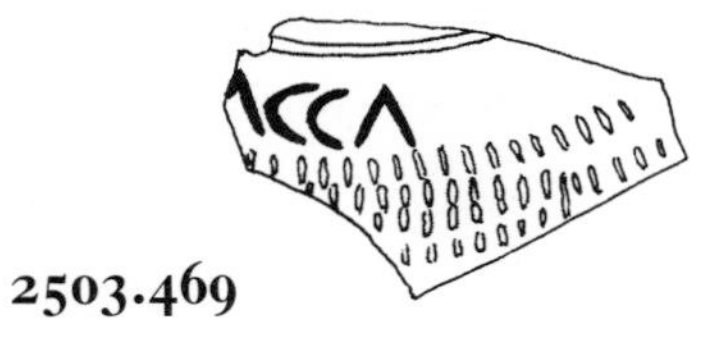

2503.469

2503.470. St. Albans (*Verulamium*), Hertfordshire. Part of a colour-coated beaker (¼ and ½) in a dense grey fabric with lead-grey 'metallic' surfaces, decorated with barbotine scrolls under the colour-coat, with a band of rouletting above. Found in 1956 in Insula XIII during excavations in the car-park of the Museum. Verulamium Museum. Reproduced from Greep.

Greep, *Herts. Arch.* viii (1980–82), 207 No. 4 with figs. 1.4 and 2.4.

graffito below the rim: [. . .]Ạ CI

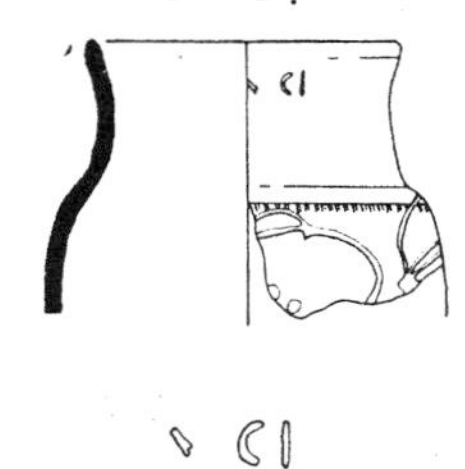

2503.470

2503.471. Saham Toney, Norfolk. Base of a coarse-ware jar (½), found in 1978 during field-walking at the settlement at Woodcock Hall. In private possession. Drawn by M.W.C.H.

Britannia x (1979), 355 No. 45.

graffito below the base: [. . .]ACVS

P. de Schaetzen, *Index des terminaisions des marques de potiers . . . . sur terra sigillata* (1956), 44–5, lists twenty-seven names with this common Celtic suffix.

2503.471

2503.472. Canterbury (*Durovernum*), Kent. Part of a jar (½) in dark grey fabric, found in 1980 in a context dated *c.* A.D. 100–125 during excavations at the Marlowe IV site. Canterbury Museum. Drawn by M.W.C.H.

Britannia xiii (1982), 415 No. 44.

graffito on the inside of the rim: [. . .]ẠḌDVA[. . .]

The reading of the first two letters is very uncertain.

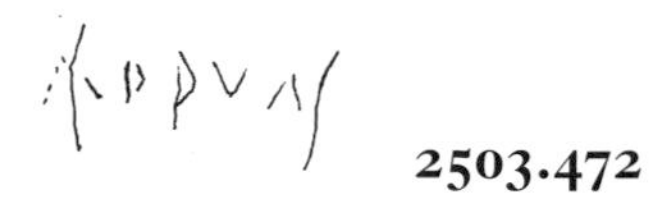

2503.472

2503.473. Chesterholm (*Vindolanda*), Northumberland. Fragment of a fawn-coloured bowl (½), found before 1986 in the outer ditch of the stone fort. Vindolanda Museum. Drawing: the Vindolanda Trust.

E., R., and A. Birley, *Vindolanda* ii (1993), 99 No. 8 with fig. 12.7.

graffito: [. . .]ALIS

AC̣IS, Birley. As text, R.S.O.T.

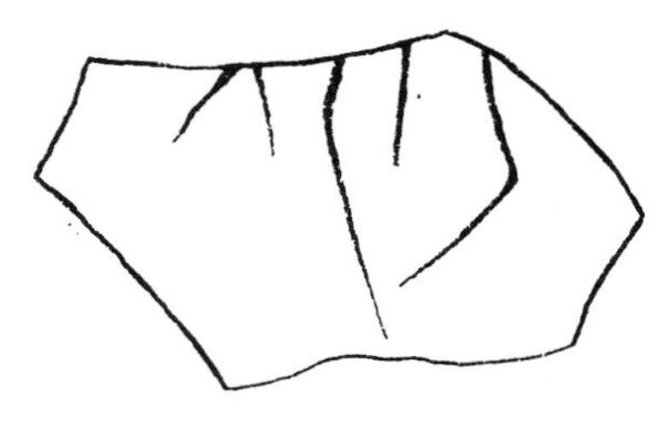

2503.473

2503.474. Canterbury (*Durovernum*), Kent. Fragment of a buff vessel (½), found in 1947 in a first-century pit at No. 5 Watling Street. Canterbury Museum. Drawn by R.P.W., 1952.

JRS xliii (1953), 131 No. 22 a. Jenkins, *Arch. Cant.* lxv (1952), 129 with fig. 6.16.

graffito: [. . .]ALIS

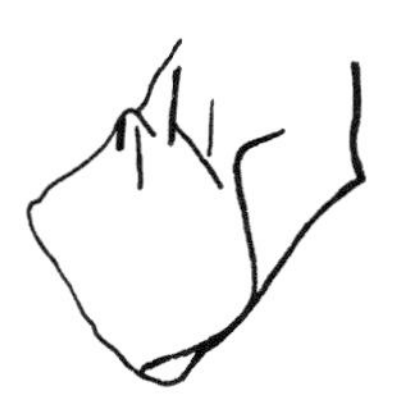

2503.474

2503.475. Wall (*Letocetum*), Staffordshire. Four conjoining sherds from a grey storage jar (½), found in 1979–87 in a context dated to the first half of the second century. Wall Museum. Drawn by R.S.O.T.

Britannia xxi (1990), 371 No. 33.

graffito on the wall: [. . .]2–3ALIS XVI
'. . .alis sixteen'

Compare *RIB* 2503.493.

2503.476. Colchester (*Camulodunum*), Essex. Part of the lip of a white jug ($\frac{1}{2}$), found in 1929 in the Holly Trees Meadow (Insula 15). Colchester Museum. Drawn by R.P.W., 1943.

graffito on the inside of the lip: [. . .]ΛND[. . .]

2503.476

2503.477. Cirencester (*Corinium*), Gloucestershire. Part of a vessel ($\frac{1}{1}$), with orange surface and grey core, found in 1974 in a late first-century context during excavations in St. Michael's Field (Insula VI). Corinium Museum. Drawn by M.W.C.H.

Britannia xiv (1983), 343 No. 23.

graffito: [. . .]R[. . .] | [. . .]S | [. . .]ΛNỊṢ[. . .]

[. . .]R[. . .|. . .]ẠNỊÇ[. . .], *Britannia*

2503.477

2503.478. Canterbury (*Durovernum*), Kent. Six fragments from a bowl imitating Dr. 38 ($\frac{1}{2}$) in grey fabric with orange surface, found in 1980 in a residual context in St. Margaret's Street. Canterbury Museum. Drawn by M.W.C.H.

Britannia xiii (1982), 415 No. 45; xx (1989), 339 No. 42.

graffito above the flange: [. . .]ANI[. . .]

The letters are widely spaced, and there would have been a maximum of seven; perhaps therefore a name ending in *-anus* in the genitive case.

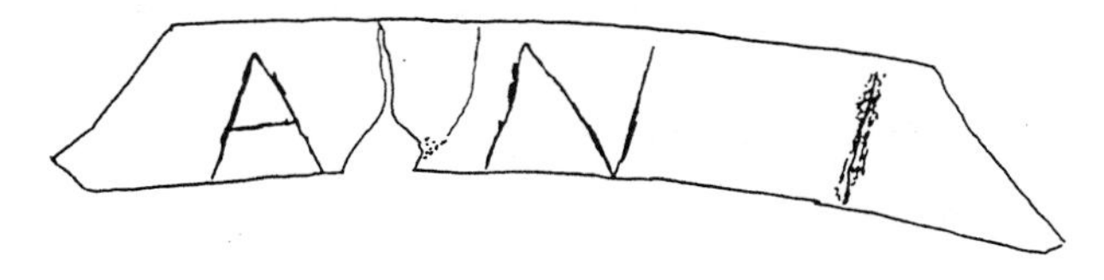

2503.478

2503.479. Birrens (*Blatobulgium*), Dumfries and Galloway [Dumfriesshire]. Part of the rim of a Black-burnished bowl ($\frac{1}{2}$), found in 1969 at a depth of 3.6 m in clearing a well in the courtyard of Building IX/X at the west end of the central buildings in the fort. Hunterian Museum, Glasgow. Drawn by S.S.F. from rubbings by R.P.W., 1969.

Britannia i (1970), 314 No. 48.

graffito on the rim: [. . .].A͡NT[. . .]

[. . .]ANT[. . .], R.P.W. [. . .]ONT[. . .] or [. . .]ṢƆ A͡NT[. . .] are other possibilities. The cross-bar of an A ligatured to N is clear on the rubbings.

2503.479

2503.480. Margate, Kent. Fragment from the shoulder of a buff jug ($\frac{1}{2}$), found in 1959 during excavations at a settlement-site at Drapers Mills School. Margate Museum. Drawn by S.S.F. from rubbings by R.P.W., 1964.

JRS liv (1964), 185 No. 46.

graffito on the shoulder: [. . .]ΛRA[. . .]

2503.480

2503.481. Eccles, Kent. Part of a dark grey beaker ($\frac{1}{2}$), found in 1963 during excavations at the Roman villa. Maidstone Museum. Drawn by S.S.F. from rubbings by R.P.W., 1964.

JRS liv (1964), 185 No. 47 a.

graffito on the shoulder: [. . .]ẠRI.[. . .]

2503.481

2503.482. Canterbury (*Durovernum*), Kent. Fragment from the wall of a black dish with lattice decoration ($\frac{1}{2}$), found in 1953 in a fourth-century deposit over the bank of the city wall near the Castle. Canterbury Museum. Drawn by R.P.W., 1961.

JRS li (1961), 197 No. 47. S.S. Frere et al., *The Archaeology of Canterbury* ii (1982), 141 No. 4 with fig. 77.4.

graffito below the rim: [. . .]AR.[. . .]

[. . .]ARỊ[. . .], R.P.W.

2503.482

2503.483. Strageath, Tayside Region [Perthshire]. Sherd ($\frac{1}{2}$) from a dark orange-brown jug, found in 1974 during excavations at the *principia* of the fort. National Museums of Scotland, Queen Street, Edinburgh. Drawn by M.G. Wilson.

S.S. Frere and J.J. Wilkes, *Strageath* (1989), 267 No. 2 with fig. 133.2.

graffito: [. . .]ẠTE[. . .]

AIV, Frere and Wilkes, loc. cit. As text, R.S.O.T.

2503.483

2503.484. Canterbury (*Durovernum*), Kent. Part of the shoulder of a burnished black jar of third-century type ($\frac{1}{2}$), found in 1947 at No. 5 Watling Street. Canterbury Museum. Drawn by R.P.W., 1952.

JRS xliii (1953), 131 No. 22 b. Jenkins, *Arch. Cant.* lxv (1952), 129 with fig. 6.17.

graffito below a band of rouletting: [. . .]ẠTIO

2503.484

2503.485. Corbridge (? *Coria*), Northumberland. Lower part of an orange-coloured jug with white slip ($\frac{1}{2}$), found in 1970 to the north of Site 39 in a pre-Antonine level. Corbridge Museum. Drawn by S.S.F. from rubbings by R.P.W., 1970.

Britannia ii (1971), 301 No. 77.

graffito on the wall: [. . .]ATTI

Perhaps *Atti*, but there are other possibilities, such as *[M]atti*.

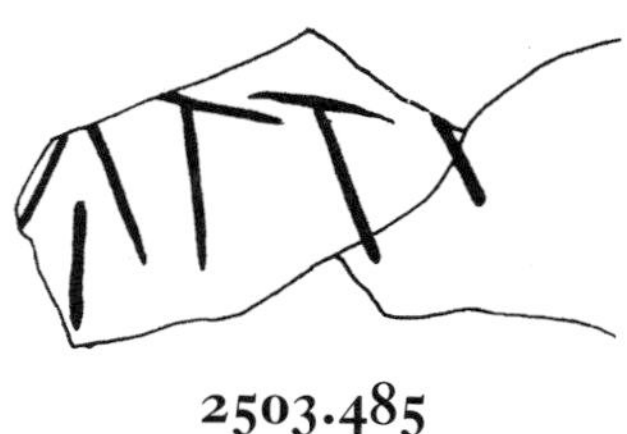

2503.485

2503.486. Waddon Hill, Dorset. Fragment from a vessel in black native ware ($\frac{1}{1}$), found during excavations at the pre-Flavian fort. Bridport Museum. Reproduced from Webster.

Webster, *P. Dorset NHAS* ci (1979), 85 No. 3 with fig. 41.3 (shown inverted).

graffito: [. . .]AVI

2503.486

2503.487. Chesterholm (*Vindolanda*), Northumberland. Part of the shoulder ($\frac{1}{2}$) of a grey storage jar, found in 1987 in a context dated *c.* A.D. 97–103 during excavations at the early forts. Vindolanda Museum. Drawing: the Vindolanda Trust.

Britannia xix (1988), 503 No. 84. E., R., and A. Birley, *Vindolanda* ii (1993), 98 No. 6 with fig. 12.5.

graffito: [. . .]A[. . .]ṾMI

[. . .]M[. . .] and [. . .]ṾMI, R.S.O.T., *Britannia* loc. cit. As text, Birley.

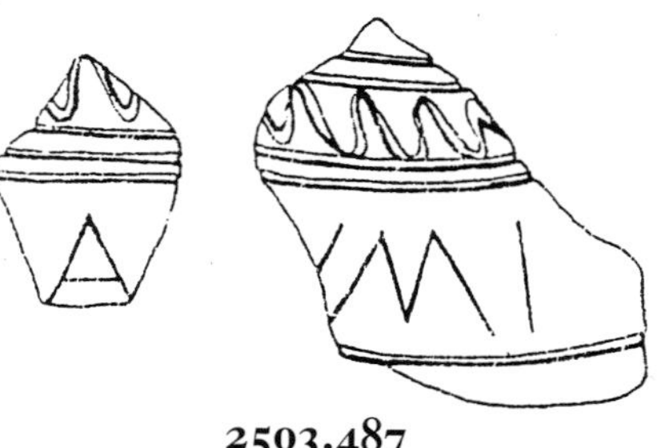

2503.487

2503.488. Caerleon (*Isca*), Gwent [Monmouthshire]. Sherd (½) in orange-buff 'Caerleon ware' with dark orange slip, found in 1926–27 during excavations in Jenkin's Field. Caerleon Museum. Drawn by R.P.W., 1953.

Nash-Williams, *AC* lxxxiv (1929), 255 with fig. 15.3 (omitting the first stroke of A).

graffito: [. . .]ẠVTI[. . .]

Compare *RIB* 2497.28. Perhaps *[Pl]auti*, but there are other possibilities.

2503.488

2503.489. Silchester (*Calleva*), Hampshire. Part of a coarse grey-ware jar (scale uncertain), found before 1900. Reading Museum. Reproduced from May.

Haverfield, *VCH* Hampshire i (1900), 284 No. 19 g. T. May, *Silchester* (1916), 284 No. 25 with pl. LXXXV.25.

graffito on the wall within a cartouche:
[. . .]. .BRIVS

wVBRIVS, Haverfield. [. . .]NVBRIVS, May for (?) [MA]NVBRIVS.

2503.489

2503.490. Wiggonholt, West Sussex. Part of a colour-coated beaker (½) in Lower Nene Valley ware, found in 1964 in a pit south of the Roman bath-house. Worthing Museum. Drawn by S.S.F. from a rubbing by R.P.W., 1965.

JRS lv (1965), 227 No. 48 b. Evans, *Suss. AC* cxii (1974), 127 No. 11 with fig. 9.11.

graffito below the lip: [. . .]CΛḌ[. . .]

2503.490

2503.491. Canterbury (*Durovernum*), Kent. Part of a black jar (½), found in 1950 in a third-century deposit at the Roman Theatre. Canterbury Museum. Reproduced from Frere.

JRS xli (1951), 144 No. 22. Frere, *Britannia* i (1970), 112 No. 2 with fig. 13.2.

graffito on the wall: [. . .]ÇΛṬ[. . .]

The first letter might be K, R.P.W.

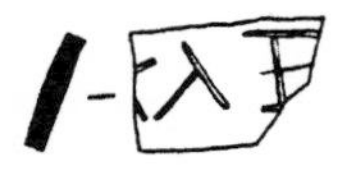

2503.491

2503.492. Ardoch, Tayside Region [Perthshire]. Part of a grey bowl (½) with lattice decoration, found in 1896–97 during excavations at the fort. National Museums of Scotland, Queen Street, Edinburgh. Drawn by R.P.W., 1954.

graffito on the wall: [. . .]CAT

2503.492

2503.493. Park Street, Hertfordshire. Part of a dark grey jar (½), found in 1943 in a fourth-century deposit behind the west wall of the cellar in the Roman villa. Verulamium Museum, St. Albans. Drawn by R.P.W., 1943.

JRS xxxiv (1944), 90 No. 18. O'Neil and Corder, *Arch. J.* cii (1947), 96 with fig. 22.5.

two graffiti on the wall, (a) [. . .]ÇIA
(b) XVI

(b) 'Sixteen'

Compare *RIB* 2503.475.

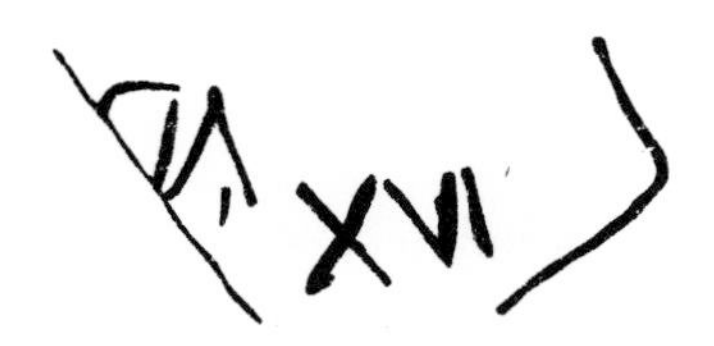

2503.493

2503.494. Cambridge (*Duroliponte*). Two-handled vessel with globular body above a tall and probably hollow pedestal, containing 'a few coins', found in 1802 in digging the foundations of the new gaol. Now lost. Reprinted from *Gent. Mag.*

EE iii 141. *Gent. Mag.* November 1802, 1000–1 with pl. II, fig. 1.

graffito: . . .C.ICC.M*IA*PCE

'The letters are extremely imperfect', *Gent. Mag.*

2503.495. Caerleon (*Isca*), Gwent [Monmouthshire]. Fragment (½) of a Black-burnished dish of Antonine date, found in 1956 during excavation of Building VII outside the fortress. Caerleon Museum. Drawn by G.C. Boon.

graffito, inverted, below the rim: [. . .]C̣IR

Possibly CIR, *G(aius) I(ulius) R*(. . .).

2503.495

2503.496. Springhead (*Vagniacis*), Kent. Fragment from the wall of a black cooking pot (½), found in 1965 unstratified on the south side of a new carriageway of the A2 road. Gravesend Museum. Drawn by S.S.F. from rubbings by R.P.W., 1970.

Britannia ii (1971), 299 No. 57.

graffito on the wall: [. . .]CỌCC[. . .]

'Letter 2 seems to be O rather than E or V', R.P.W., loc. cit.

2503.496

2503.497. Chesterholm (*Vindolanda*), Northumberland. Sherd from a Black-burnished 1 vessel (½), found in 1980 during excavations at the stone fort. Vindolanda Museum. Reproduced from Bidwell.

Britannia xiii (1982), 419 No. 75. Tomlin in P.T. Bidwell, *The Roman Fort of Vindolanda* (1985), 215 No. 2 with fig. 79.2.

graffito on the wall: [. . .]CORI.[. . .] | [. . .]ACO | F[. . .]

There is trace of another letter (perhaps I) after CORI, not drawn.

2503.497

2503.498. Ibid. Fragment from the lip of a black bowl (½), found in 1973 unstratified on Site XXXIII in the *vicus*. Vindolanda Museum. Drawn by S.S.F. from rubbings by R.P.W., 1974.

Britannia v (1974), 467 No. 45.

graffito below the lip: [. . .]CVṂ[. . .]

2503.498

2503.499. St. Albans (*Verulamium*), Hertfordshire. Fragment (½) from a necked jar in local grey ware, found in 1968 with second-century pottery in the cellar of an extramural building at King Harry Lane. Verulamium Museum. Drawn by M.W.C.H.

Britannia xix (1988), 501 No. 64.

graffito: [. . .]CVN[. . .]

Probably *[Se]cun[dus]*, but there are other possibilities.

2503.499

2503.500. Unrecorded provenance. Graffito (½), found before 1956, drawn by R.P.W., but without description or context.

graffito: [. . .]. .CVNI[. . .]

Possibly [S]ỊICVNḌ[VS]

2503.500

2503.501. Caerleon (*Isca*). Part of a buff pot-lid in Caerleon ware (½), found probably in 1936 during excavations in Jenkin's Field. National Museum, Cardiff. Drawn by R.G.C.

graffito on the outside below the rim in Greek letters: [. . .]ΔΑΦΟΚΡΑ[. . .]

ΑΛΦΟΚΡΜ̣[. . .], R.P.W. As text, R.S.O.T.

2503.501

2503.502. Canterbury (*Durovernum*), Kent. Part of a Black-burnished dish or bowl (½), with lattice decoration, found in 1978 in a residual context during excavations at No. 16 Watling Street. Canterbury Museum. Drawn by M.W.C.H.

Britannia xiii (1982), 414 No. 35.

two graffiti: (a) on the wall, [. . .]Λ *or* [. . .]M
(b) along the flange of the rim: [. . .]ḌIIRVΛLI[. . .]

[MI]NERVALI[S] is excluded by the first surviving letter, but there seems to be no other possibility.

2503.502

2503.503. Richborough (*Rutupiae*), Kent. Part of a storage jar (½), found during excavations west of the outer Claudian ditch. In store at Dover Castle. Drawn by R.P.W., 1954.

graffito: [. . .]DIA[. . .]

2503.503

2503.504. Caernarvon (*Segontium*), Gwynedd. Part of the shoulder of a black jar (½) 'of the early second century' found in 1923 in the covered drain crossing Building I. Segontium Museum. Drawn by R.P.W., 1954.

R.E.M. Wheeler, *Segontium* (1924), 163 with fig. 76.30.

graffito on the shoulder: [. . .]ḌIVO[. . .]

'It may or may not be VXOR', Wheeler. 'The first letter seems to be D: the loop is too large for P, R or B. The third letter is not X; there is a casual shallower cut near the bottom', R.P.W.

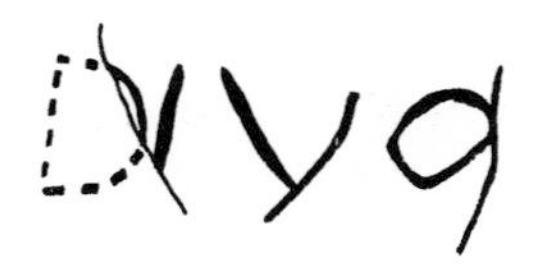

2503.504

2503.505. Melandra Castle, Derbyshire. Part of a white jar (½), found before 1951. Buxton Museum. Drawn by R.P.W., 1951.

two graffiti on the wall: (a) [. . .]I(*or* N)IDI
(b) .[. . .]

(b) could read G, O or Q. R.P.W.

2503.505

2503.506. Brecon (? *Cicucium*), Powys [Brecknockshire]. Buff bowl (½), found in 1924–25 during excavations at the fort. National Museum, Cardiff. Drawn by R.P.W., 1960.

R.E.M. Wheeler, *Brecon* (1926), 248 No. 8 with fig. 105.8.

graffito below the rim: [. . .]IIGISA .[. . .]

[. . .]EGISA or [A]VCISA (?), Wheeler, loc. cit.

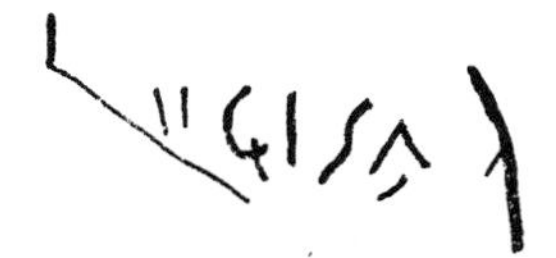

2503.506

2503.507. London (*Londinium*). Carinated beaker in fine black micaceous ware (½), imitating Camulodunum form 120, found in 1980 in dumped material behind the second-period Roman quay constructed *c.* A.D. 70. Museum of London. Drawn by M.W.C.H.

Britannia xiii (1982), 418 No. 66.

graffito below the rim: [. . .]ẸḶIC̣MẠ

2503.507

2503.508. Richborough (*Rutupiae*), Kent. Fragment (½) from a jar in hard red ware, found before 1940. In store at Dover Castle. Drawn by S.S.F. from a tracing by R.G.C.

J.P. Bushe-Fox, *Richborough* iv (1949), 255 No. 4 with fig. (inverted).

graffito: [. . .]IIIISIS

Perhaps *[. . .]ensis* with the oblique stroke of the N lost or not noted.

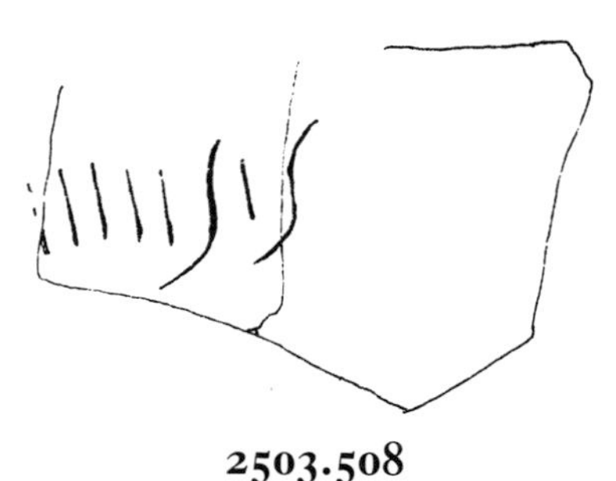

2503.508

2503.509. Chesterholm (*Vindolanda*), Northumberland. Fragment (½) from a greyish-white vessel, found in 1987 in a floor of Period IV (*c.* A.D. 104–120) during excavations in the early forts. Vindolanda Museum. Drawing reproduced from Birley.

Britannia xix (1988), 503 No. 82. E., R., and A. Birley, *Vindolanda* ii (1993), 98 No. 3 with fig. 12.2.

graffito: [. . .]ẸNSỌ[. . .]

Perhaps *[C]enso[rinus]*

[. . .]NSỌ[. . .], Tomlin, *Britannia* loc. cit. As text, Birley.

Compare *RIB* 2503.227 with note.

2503.509

2503.510. Ware, Hertfordshire. Fragment (½) from a grey-ware dish, found in 1976 in a residual context during excavations at the Allen and Hanbury site. Hertford Museum. Drawn by M.W.C.H.

Britannia x (1979), 350 No. 29.

graffito on the wall: [. . .]IINT[. . .]

2503.510

2503.511. Colchester (*Camulodunum*), Essex. Sherd from a grey vessel (scale uncertain), found in 1929 in the Holly Trees Meadow (Insula 15). Colchester Museum. Traced by S.S.F. from a sketch by R.P.W., 1943.

graffito on the wall: [. . .].ERṬ[. . .]

The first letter may be C, G or S.

2503.511

2503.512. Chesterholm (*Vindolanda*), Northumberland. part of the base of a Black-burnished dish (½), found unstratified in the *vicus*. Vindolanda Museum. Drawn by S.S.F. from a sketch by R.S.O.T.

graffito beneath the base: [. . .]F̣EL[. . .]

2503.512

2503.513. Usk (*Burrium*), Gwent [Monmouthshire]. Fragment (½) in buff fabric, found in 1973 in a pre-Flavian pit during excavations at the pre-Flavian fortress. National Museum, Cardiff. Drawn by M.W.C.H.

Britannia xiv (1983), 349 No. 58.

graffito: [. . .]F̣ỊDẸ or [. . .]ṬỊDẸ

2503.513

2503.514. Wilderspool, Cheshire. Part of a storage jar (½), found in or before 1902. Warrington Museum. Drawn by R.P.W.

graffito: [. . .]F̣IDI[. . .]
Probably FIDI[ILIS] i.e. *Fide[lis]*
'(Property) of Fidelis'

[. . .]ADI[. . .], R.P.W. As text, R.S.O.T.

2503.514

2503.515. Chichester (*Noviomagus*), West Sussex. Part of a black flanged dish (½), found in 1935 unstratified at the site of Marks and Spencer, East Street. Chichester Museum. Drawn by S.S.F. from a sketch by R.P.W., 1952.

graffito on the wall: [. . .]F̣ILVMI

Perhaps ṢILVAṆI misunderstood, R.S.O.T.

2503.515

2503.516. Leicester (*Ratae*). Fragment of a buff jar (½), found in 1953 on an excavation in Blue Boar Lane. Leicester Museum. Drawn by R.P.W., 1954.

JRS xliv (1954), 110 No. 48. Clarke, *T. Leics. AS* xxx (1954), 117 fig. 2.

graffito on the shoulder: [. . .]FLATVẠ

The last letter seems to be A not R; a feminine name in *-flatua* is reasonable, whereas a verb *flatur* is unlikely in this context, R.P.W.

2503.516

2503.517. Colchester (*Camulodunum*), Essex. Part of a grey-ware jar (½), found in 1978 in a robber-trench outside the Roman North Gate. Colchester Museum. Drawn by M.W.C.H.

Britannia xi (1980), 411 No. 30.

graffito on the shoulder above a zone of lattice:
[. . .]ḤOINIC̣[. . .]
Perhaps *[P]hoinic[is]*
'(Property) of Phoinix'

[. . .]HOINI S[. . .], *Britannia*. As text, M.W.C.H., 1994.

For examples of this Greek name, typical of slaves and freedmen, see Solin, *Namenbuch*, 1301.

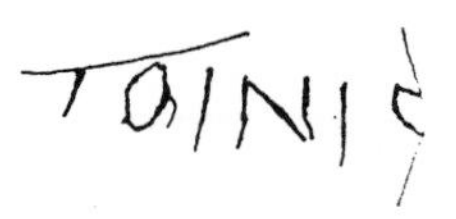

2503.517

2503.518. Brecon (*? Cicucium*), Powys [Brecknockshire]. Fragment (½) from the lower part of a small orange-buff jug of the first century, found in 1925 during excavations at the fort. National Museum, Cardiff. Drawn by G.C. Boon, 1992.

graffito: [. . .].ỊC̣VNI

Perhaps [L]ICVNI or [. . .]IICVNI, Boon. Or possibly [VIIR]IICVND[VS], R.S.O.T.

2503.518

2503.519. Silchester (*Calleva*), Hampshire. Part of a jar in grey ware (½). Reading Museum. Drawn by R.P.W., 1951.

graffito on the shoulder: [. . .]IMIỊ[. . .]

2503.519

2503.520. Usk (*Burrium*), Gwent [Monmouthshire]. Part of a buff vessel with a shallow footstand (½), found in 1969 during excavations at the pre-Flavian fortress. National Museum, Cardiff, Drawn by S.S.F. from rubbings by M.W.C.H.

Britannia vi (1975), 293 No. 48. Hassall in G.C. Boon and M. Hassall, *Usk* (1982), 58 No. 47 with fig. 5.47.

graffito within the footstand: [. . .]ỊMOΛVI

2503.520

2503.521. York (*Eboracum*). Sherd (½), found before 1962. Drawn by R.P.W.

RCHM, *York* i (1962), 134, fig. 87.31.

graffito: [. . .] .IMON. .[. . .]

2503.521

2503.522. Canterbury (*Durovernum*), Kent. Fragment (½) from a vessel in reduced fabric and a slipped brown surface, found in 1982 in a pit with material of the late first to early second century during excavations in St Margaret's Street. Canterbury Museum. Drawn by M.W.C.H.

Britannia xx (1989), 339 No. 43.

graffito on the wall: [. . .]INΛ[. . .]

If inverted, VṆI or VỊṾI could be read.

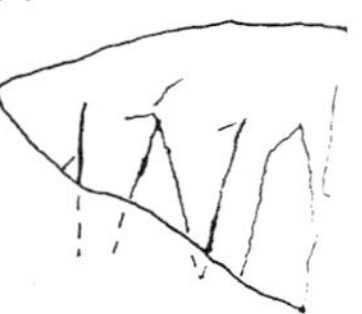

2503.522

2503.523. Ibid. Part of a colour-coated beaker (½) in buff fabric and dark brown slip, found in 1978 in a residual context at No. 16 Watling Street. Canterbury Museum. Drawn by M.W.C.H.

Britannia xiii (1982), 414 No. 36.

graffito: [. . .]INE[. . .]

2503.523

2503.524. Manchester (*Mamucium*). Two conjoining sherds (½) from a white jar, found in or before 1909. City Art Gallery ex Queen's Park Museum, Manchester. Drawn by R.P.W., 1952.

graffito on the wall: [. . .]INI

2503.524

2503.525. Unrecorded provenance. Graffito (½) found before 1956, drawn by R.P.W., but without giving description or provenance.

cursive graffito: [. . .].IṆVS̩[. . .]

The first letter may by N, *[. . .]ninus*, e.g. *[Satur]ninus*.

2503.525

2503.526. Exeter (*Isca Dumnoniorum*), Devon. Fragment (½) in buff fabric, found in 1976 in a residual context at the Cathedral Green. Exeter Museum. Drawn by M.W.C.H.

Britannia ix (1978), 476 No. 22. Hassall in N. Holbrook and P.T. Bidwell, *Roman Finds from Exeter* (1991), 79 No. 2.

graffito: [. . .]IRC[. . .]

Possibly [MI]IRC[ATOR] or [MI]IRC[VRIALIS] etc.

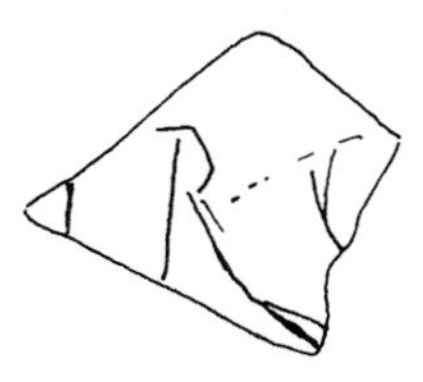

2503.526

2503.527. St Albans (*Verulamium*), Hertfordshire. Part of a narrow-necked grey jar (½), found in 1956 in Insula XVII, stratified above a Flavian building. Verulamium Museum. Drawn by M.G. Wilson.

S.S. Frere, *Verulamium Excavations* iii (1984), 278 No. 8 with fig. 115.8.

graffito on the neck: [. . .]ỊSA

The first letter could also be N or V.

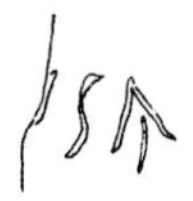

2503.527

2503.528. Dorchester (*Durnovaria*), Dorset. Sherd (½) from a Black-burnished vessel found in 1971 in a late first- or early second-century context at No. 34 Trinity Street. Dorchester Museum. Drawn by S.S.F. from a tracing by B.J. O'Connor.

Britannia iv (1973), 330 No. 16.

graffito below the rim: [. . .]ỊTΛ[. . .]

'It seems impossible to read *[V]ita[lis]*' R.P.W. He suggests perhaps *Ita[lici]*.

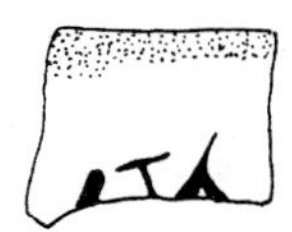

2503.528

2503.529. London (*Londinium*). Two conjoining fragments (½) from a colour-coated beaker in Colchester fabric, found in 1979 in the late Roman demolition layers of a Roman building at Peninsular House, Lower Thames Street. Drawn by M.W.C.H.

Britannia xii (1981), 389 No. 65.

graffito on the neck: [. . .]ỊVI MΛ̣R·BOR·Λ̣IF̣·

The letter B was originally cut as R.

2503.529

2503.530. Caersws, Powys [Montgomeryshire]. Fragment (½) in orange fabric, found in 1985–86 during excavations in the *vicus* of the fort. Clwyd-Powys Archaeological Trust. Drawn by M.W.C.H.

Britannia xx (1989), 344 No. 65.

graffito on the wall: [. . .].ỊVS Λ[. . .]

At the beginning is the top part of a rounded letter, B, C, D, G, P or R. The last surviving letter could be part of Λ, or M or N. The space between this and the preceding S is not large, but probably represents a division between a nomen and cognomen. M.W.C.H.

2503.530

2503.531. Gorhambury, Hertfordshire. Part of a grey-ware lid or base (½), found in 1973 in a small pit on the west side of the Roman villa. Verulamium Museum, St Albans. Drawn by M.W.C.H.

Britannia xiii (1982), 413 No. 25. D.S. Neal et al., *Excavation of the Iron Age, Roman and medieval settlement at Gorhambury, St Albans* (1990), 184.

graffito on the underside: [. . .]LΛỊONVS IΛΛ̣[. . .]

As text, and perhaps *Ian[uarius Be]latonus*, M.W.C.H. This text would have been continuous, but does not look long enough to fill the circumference; moreover *Ianuarius* is usually a cognomen. In view of the damage to 4–5 successive letters, any reading is uncertain; *[.Pl]atorius Ia[nuarius]*, for example could also be read. R.S.O.T.

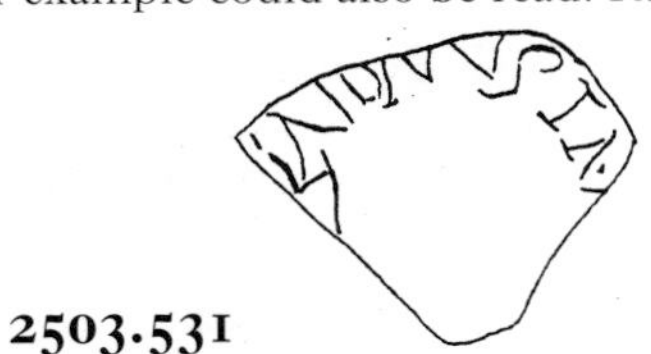

2503.531

2503.532. Piercebridge, Durham. Sherd from the base of a cooking pot (½), discoloured pink through burning, found in 1933–34 in the culvert at the north-east angle of the fort. Bowes Museum, Barnard Castle. Drawn by R.G.C., 1936.

graffito on the base: [. . .]LICI[. . .]

2503.532

2503.533. Canvey Island, Essex. Sherd from a grey jar (½), found in 1961 unstratified at a 'red hill' on the east coast of the island. Southend Museum. Drawn by S.S.F. from a rubbing by R.P.W., 1961.

JRS lii (1962), 199 No. 54.

graffito on the wall: [. . .].LIVS

The first letter could be I, N, or V.

2503.533

2503.534. Housesteads (*Vercovicium*), Northumberland. Black-burnished jar of third-century type (½), found before 1936. Housesteads Museum. Drawn by R.G.C., 1936.

graffito on the shoulder: [. . .]LRVṢ[. . .]

2503.534

2503.535. Eccles, Kent. Fragment from the shoulder of a grey beaker (½), found in 1964 during excavations at the Roman villa. Maidstone Museum. Drawn by S.S.F. from rubbings by R.P.W., 1965.

JRS lv (1965), 227 No. 49.

graffito on the shoulder: [. . .]. | [. . .].MΛ̣

[. . .]ṂMΛ or [. . .]ẠMΛ, R.P.W., loc. cit.

2503.535

2503.536. London (*Londinium*). Part of a black dish (½), found in 1950 in Walbrook. Museum of London. Drawn by R.P.W., 1951.

JRS xli (1951), 144 No. 24.

graffito on the wall: [. . .]ṂANTỊ

[. . .]manti

2503.536

2503.537. Amerden, Buckinghamshire. Urn in rough dark grey ware (½), found in the bed of the river Thames before 1899, when it was presented to the British Museum. Drawn by R.P.W., 1959.

EE ix 1003 a. H.B. Walters, *Cat.* (1908), 436 No. M. 2838. Wright, *Britannia* viii (1977), 279–82 with fig.

graffito in Greek letters on the lower part of the wall:
[. . .]. . .[. . .] | [. . .]ṂANTIOCMYΛOΦIC̣Ị [. . .] | EP̣ PΨ
[. . .]μάντιος μυλοφισι[κός] | EP̣ PΨ
[. . .]mantios mulophysi[kos]
'[. . .]mantius the mule-physician'

μυλοφισικός is taken to be a hitherto unattested Latin-Greek compound of *mulus* (a mule) and *physicus* (physician), equivalent to *mulomedicus*, R.P.W.

The vessel was recognised by Dr C.J. Young as being a normal Romano-British coarse ware, and is unlikely to be an import.

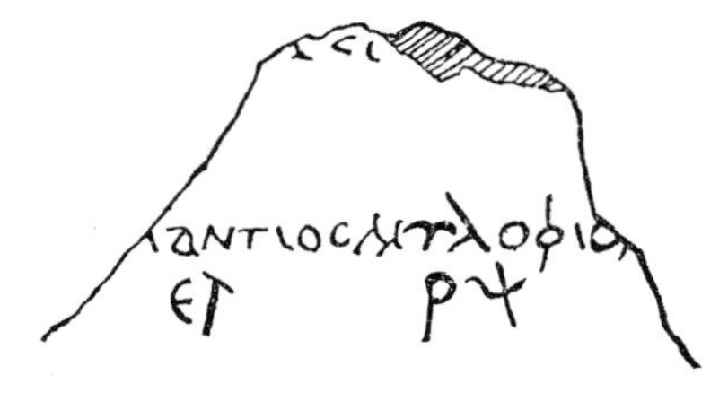

2503.537

2503.538. Richborough (*Rutupiae*), Kent. Sherd from a rouletted beaker (¼) in a dark grey clay, found in 1928–32 unstratified to the south of Site IV. In store at Dover Castle. Traced by S.S.F. from a photograph.

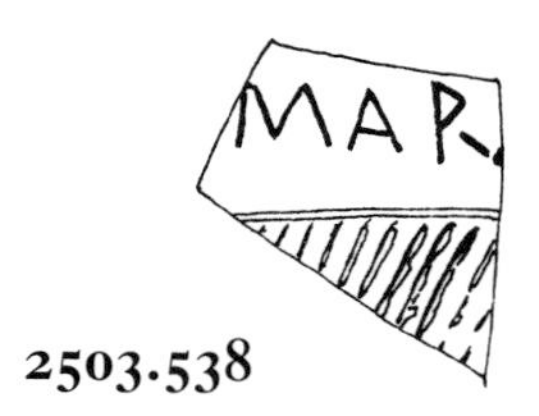

2503.538

J.P. Bushe-Fox, *Richborough* iv (1949), 255 No. 6 with pl. LXXII.5.

graffito above the rouletting: [. . .]MAR[. . .]

Perhaps *Mar[tialis]* or a cognate name

2503.539. Caerleon (*Isca*), Gwent [Monmouthshire]. Part of a grey cooking pot (½), found in 1931–33 in Golledge's Field. National Museum, Cardiff. Drawn by R.P.W., 1965.

JRS lvi (1966), 225 No. 59.

graffito on the shoulder: [. . .]M͡AR[. . .]

Perhaps *Mar[tialis]* or a cognate name.

2503.539

2503.539a. Ibid. Part of a cup in Caerleon ware imitating Dr. 33, found in 1931–33 in Golledge's Field. National Museum, Cardiff. Not illustrated.

JRS lvi (1966), 224 No. 50

graffito on the wall: [. . .]MΛRI.[. . .]

2503.540. Dorchester (*Durnovaria*), Dorset. Fragment (½) with an orange colour-coat, found in 1969 during excavation of a probably fourth-century pit at Hospital Site C. Dorchester Museum. Drawn by M.W.C.H.

Britannia xvi (1985), 326 No. 17.

graffito: [. . .].ARC[. . .]

Probably for *Ṃarc[i]* or possibly *Ṇarc[issi]*, M.W.C.H., *Britannia*.

2503.540

2503.541. Beauport Park, East Sussex. Two sherds (½) perhaps from the same grey-ware vessel, found in 1980 during excavations near the bath-house of the *classis Britannica* workshop. In store awaiting a site museum. Drawn by M.W.C.H.

Britannia xii (1981), 384 No. 34.

two graffiti: (a) [. . .]MΛṬV[. . .] or [. . .]ṂTV[. . .]
(b) [. . .]TΛ MO[. . .]

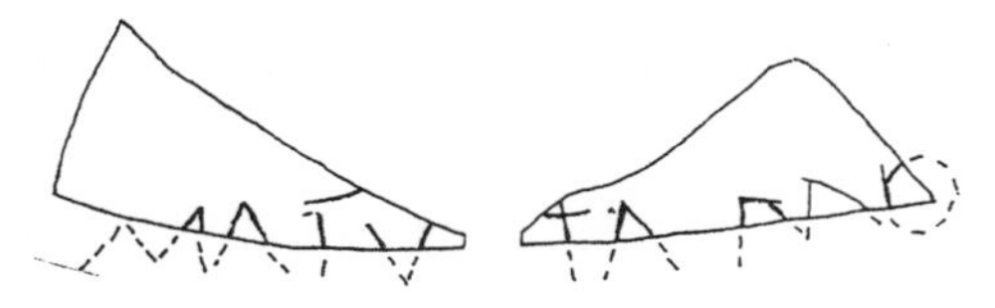

2503.541

2503.542. Colchester (*Camulodunum*), Essex. Part of a handled beaker in grey ware (½), found in 1929 unstratified at the Union House. Colchester Museum. Drawn by R.P.W., 1954.

graffito on the wall: [. . .]MΛV[. . .]

2503.542

2503.543. Credenhill Camp, Hereford and Worcester [Herefordshire]. Part of a buff single-handled jug (½), found in 1963 in a fire-pit during excavations in the hill-fort. Hereford Museum. Drawn by S.S.F. from rubbings by R.P.W., 1969.

Britannia i (1970), 314 No. 49. Stanford, *Arch. J.* cxxvii (1970), 116 No. P.14 with fig. 19. P.14.

graffito on the lower part of the wall:
[. . .]M[. . .] | [. . .]MEṆ[. . .]

2503.543

2503.544. London (*Londinium*). Part of a small grey jar or beaker (½) of late first- to second-century date, found in 1954–55 during the Walbrook excavations on a wooden floor-surface west of the temple of Mithras. Museum of London. Drawn by R.P.W. from a rubbing by Miss J. Morris.

Britannia ii (1971), 300 No. 63.

graffito on the base: [. . .]MIIR

If an abbreviated personal name, *Mercator* or *Mercurius/alis* are the most likely.

2503.544

2503.545. Chalk, Kent. Fragment of a dark grey dish (½), found in 1961 during excavation of a Roman building. Present whereabouts unrecorded. Drawn by S.S.F. from rubbings by R.P.W., 1964.

JRS liv (1964), 184 No. 44 b. Woodhead in Johnston, *Britannia* iii (1972), 144 No. 2 with fig. 19.2

graffito, inverted, on the wall: [. . .]ṂIΛ

Perhaps VII (not inverted), Woodhead. As text, R.P.W.

2503.545

2503.546. Kingscote, Gloucestershire. Part of a beaker (½) in orange fabric with a reduced grey core, found in 1976 in the demolition-level of a Roman building. Corinium Museum, Cirencester. Drawn by M.W.C.H.

Britannia viii (1977), 441 No. 82.

graffito below the rim: [. . .]MINI

2503.546

2503.547. Ribchester (*Bremetennacum*), Lancashire. Part of a beaker (½) in Black-burnished I ware, found in 1977 in a Hadrianic or early Antonine context during excavations in the *vicus*. Ribchester Museum. Traced by M.W.C.H. from a drawing by Paul Gibbons.

Britannia xii (1981), 388 No. 56.

graffito: [. . .]ṂINI

2503.547

2503.548. Barnsley Park, Gloucestershire. Part of the base (½) of a Black-burnished jar, found in 1967 during excavations at the Roman villa. Corinium Museum, Cirencester. Drawn by R.S.O.T.

Britannia xiii (1982), 413 No. 23.

graffito beneath the base: [. . .]MIṆI
Perhaps *[Fir]mini*
'(Property) of Firminus'

A building stone inscribed FIRMINI was found in the same excavation (ibid., note 37), but there are other possibilities.

2503.548

2503.549. Lincoln (*Lindum*). Sherd from the upper part of a colour-coated bulbous beaker (½) in light orange fabric with a deep orange slip inside and a brown slip outside, found in 1972 during excavations at the Holmes Grain Warehouse. Lincoln Archaeological Trust. Drawn by S.S.F. from a rubbing by M.W.C.H.

Britannia v (1974), 466 No. 31.

graffito below the rim: [. . .]ṂINV

2503.549

2503.550. Fishbourne, West Sussex. Fragment of a dish (½), found in 1961–69 during excavations at the Roman palace. Fishbourne Museum. Reproduced from Cunliffe.

Wright in B.W. Cunliffe, *Excavations at Fishbourne 1961–69* ii (1971), 369 No. 7 with fig. 145.7.

graffito on the wall: [. . .]ṂPẠ[. . .]

[. . .]V͡P[. . .], R.P.W. in Cunliffe, loc. cit. As text, R.S.O.T. Possibly *[Ca]mpa[nus]*, but too little survives for confidence. For *Campanus/a* compare *RIB* 2491.148, 2503.140.

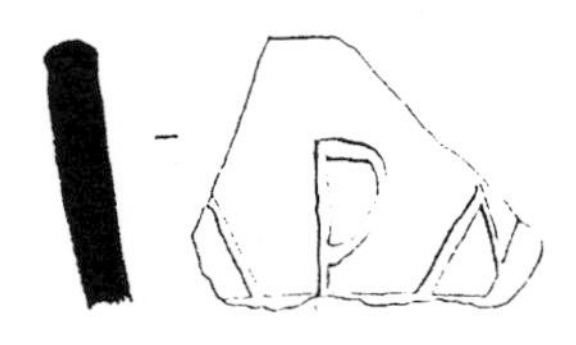

2503.550

2503.551. Binchester (*Vinovia*), Durham. Upper part of a jar in light grey fabric (½), found in 1977 in the foundation-trench of a building erected after AD 335/45. Bowes Museum, Barnard Castle. Drawing by courtesy of the Bowes Museum.

Britannia ix (1978), 477 No. 29.

two graffiti on the shoulder: (a) [. . .]ṆDRVS
(b) in a second hand, APXH
ἀρχή
'Beginning' (?)

(a) For names ending in the common Greek suffix -ανδρος see F. Bechtel, *Historischen Personennamen des Griechischen* (1917), 49–52.

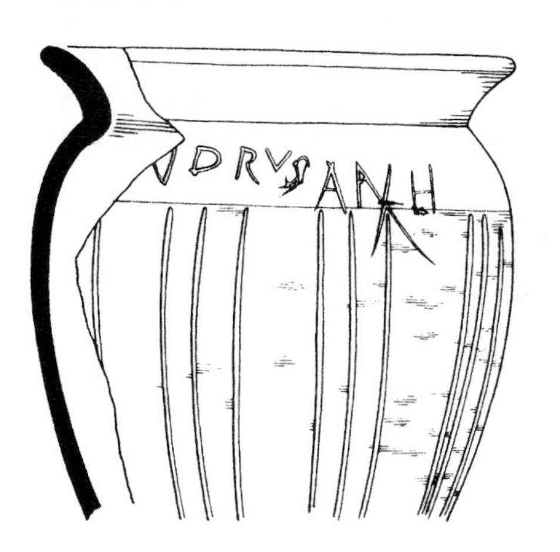

2503.551

2503.552. St Albans (*Verulamium*), Hertfordshire. Part of a colour-coated beaker (¼ and ½) in pale orange-brown fabric with a greyish-brown slip, decorated with a white barbotine scroll below a band of rouletting. Found in 1934 during excavations on the intended Museum site at Insula XIII.1. Reproduced from Greep.

Lowther, *Antiq. J.* xvii (1937), 48 No. 9 with fig. 9.9. Greep, *Herts. Arch.* viii (1980–82), 207 No. 2 with figs. 1.2 and 2.2.

graffito below the rim: [. . .].NICIANI

Probably *[Vi]niciani* or *[Mi]niciani*, but there are other possibilities.

[. . .]IVICIANI, Greep.

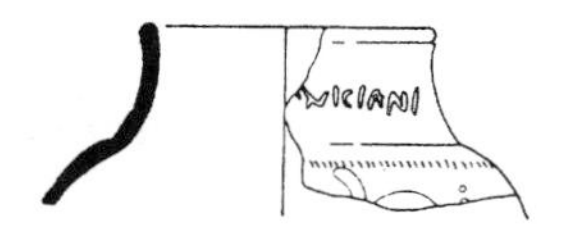

2503.552

2503.553. Park Street, Hertfordshire. Two conjoined sherds (½) from a buff jar, found in 1943–44 during excavations at the Roman villa. Verulamium Museum, St Albans. Reproduced from O'Neil with amendment by R.P.W.

O'Neil, *Arch. J.* cii (1947), 96 with fig. 22.6.

graffito: [: . .]NIỊṂ[. . .]

2503.553

2503.554. Gelligaer, Mid Glamorgan. Part of the base of a red-ware jar (½), found in 1899–1901 during excavations at the fort. National Museum, Cardiff. Reproduced from Ward.

J. Ward, *The Roman Fort of Gellygaer* (1903), 92 (repr. 42) with fig. 18.

graffito: [. . .]NII

2503.554

2503.555. Canterbury (*Durovernum*), Kent. Part of a black poppy-head beaker (½), found in 1950 at the site of the Roman theatre, St Margaret's Street. Canterbury Museum. Drawn by R.P.W., 1951.

JRS xli (1951), 144 No. 26. Frere, *Britannia* i (1970), 112 No. 3 with fig. 13.3

graffito on the shoulder: [. . .]ṆICAṆ[. . .]

The name might be *Nicanius*, *Nicander*, *Nicanor* or *Nicandus*, R.P.W.

Vicanus might be added to these possibilities: compare *RIB* 2499.4 with note.

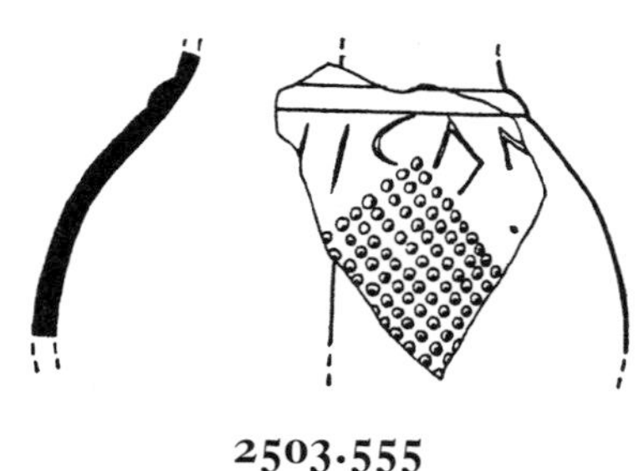

2503.555

2503.556. Ibid. Part of fourth-century grey beaker (½), found in 1946 unstratified in the courtyard of the Roman house in Butchery Lane. Canterbury Museum. Drawn by R.P.W., 1946.

JRS xxxvii (1947), 182 No. 19.

graffito on the shoulder: [. . .]NITVS.[. . .]

The last letter may be I or L or less probably T, R.P.W.

Perhaps two graffiti, the first ending [. . .]NITVS.

2503.556

2503.557. Gloucester (*Glevum*). Fragment (½) from a jar in orange fabric with specks of mica, found in 1974 in the construction-trench for the early fourth-century widening of the city wall at Nos. 38–44 Eastgate Street. Gloucester Museum. Drawn by L.V. Marley.

2503.557

Britannia xiv (1983), 344 No. 31. Hassall in C. Heighway, *The East and North Gates of Gloucester* (1983), 199 No. G.5 with fig. 114.G.5.

graffito: [. . .]NLO

The graffito is perhaps complete at the beginning, M.W.C.H., *Britannia*.

2503.558. London (*Londinium*). Part of a large storage jar in grey-buff ware (½), found before 1925 in Tokenhouse Yard. Museum of London. Drawn by R.P.W.

graffito on the shoulder: [. . .]N MΛN

Perhaps [. . .]Ṇ MARỊ, R.S.O.T. As text, R.P.W.

2503.558

2503.559. Colchester (*Camulodunum*), Essex, Butt-beaker (½) in off-white fabric of Camulodunum form 113, found in 1971 unstratified during the levelling of a school playing-field at Holly Field, Sheepen. Colchester Museum. Drawn by M.W.C.H.

Britannia viii (1977), 438 No. 63.

graffito: +N NIIM

2503.559

2503.560. Brougham (*Brocavum*), Cumbria [Westmorland]. Part of the wall of a dark grey cooking pot (½), found in 1967 during road-construction east of the fort. Department of the Environment. Drawn by S.S.F. from rubbings by R.P.W., 1968.

JRS lviii (1968), 214 No. 76.

graffito on the wall: [. . .]ṆOṂ[. . .]

2503.560

2503.561. Leicester (*Ratae*). Part of a Black-burnished dish (½), found in 1980 in a residual context at Causeway Lane. Leicester Museum. Drawn by M.W.C.H.

Britannia xiii (1982), 416 No. 53.

graffito on the wall: [. . .].NOSIINΛ[. . .]

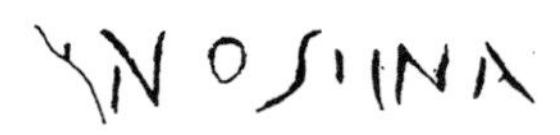

2503.561

2503.562. Colchester (*Camulodunum*), Essex. Part of a black dish found before 1873. Sought in vain by R.P.W. in Colchester Museum. Reprinted from *CIL*.

CIL vii 1338.19

graffito: [. . .]ИPL[. . .]

2503.563. Great Dunmow, Essex. Fragment (½) from a grey-ware dish, found in 1985 at No. 44 New Street. In private possession. Drawn by M.W.C.H.

Britannia xvii (1986), 442 No. 46.

graffito on the upper side of the base:
[. . .]NTIΛ̣[. . .]

2503.563

2503.564. Colchester (*Camulodunum*), Essex. Part of a rough-cast beaker with cornice-rim (½), in orange fabric and dark colour-coat, found in 1971 in a pit with late third- or fourth-century material at Lion Walk. Colchester Museum. Drawn by M.W.C.H.

Britannia viii (1977), 438 No. 66.

graffito: [. . .]NVS

2503.564

2503.565. Camelon (? *Colania*), Central Region [Stirlingshire]. Part of a bowl or dish in Black-burnished 1 ware (½), found in 1976 during excavations at the fort. Falkirk Museum. Drawing by courtesy of Dr V.A. Maxfield.

Britannia xxiv (1993), 321 No. 28.

graffito deeply cut on both base and wall with the same instrument and apparently intended as a continuous text: [. . .].NVT[. . .]

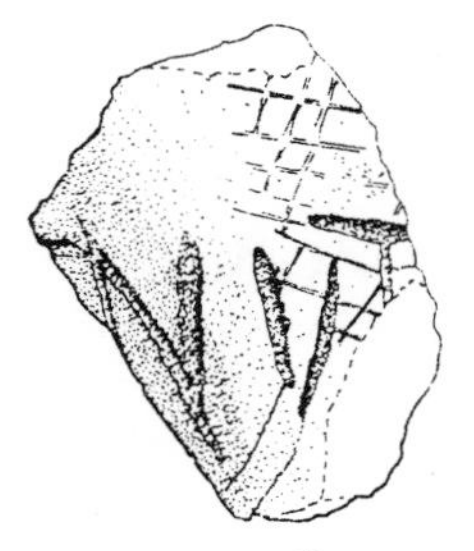

2503.565

2503.566. Canterbury (*Durovernum*), Kent. Fragment of a dark grey-buff coarse-ware Belgic jar (½), found in 1955 in a pre-Roman Belgic deposit sealed by the Roman Watling Street at the Whitehall Road site west of the river Stour. Canterbury Museum. Drawn by R.P.W., 1960.

JRS l (1960), 242 No. 45. S.S. Frere et al., *The Archaeology of Canterbury* viii (1987), 208 No. 2 with fig. 79.2.

graffito cut on the shoulder diagonally towards the rim above the combed decoration: [. . .]ṆVX̣

N is reversed, and X has one extra cut.

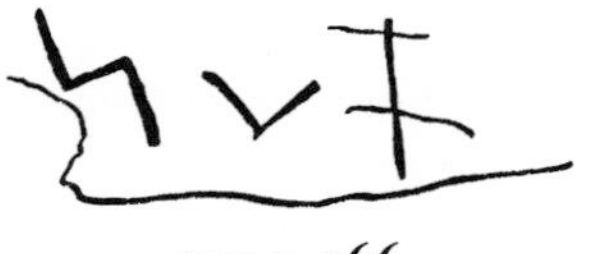

2503.566

2503.567. Unrecorded provenance. Graffito (½), found before 1956. Drawn by R.P.W., but without giving description or provenance.

graffito: [. . .].NX[. . .]

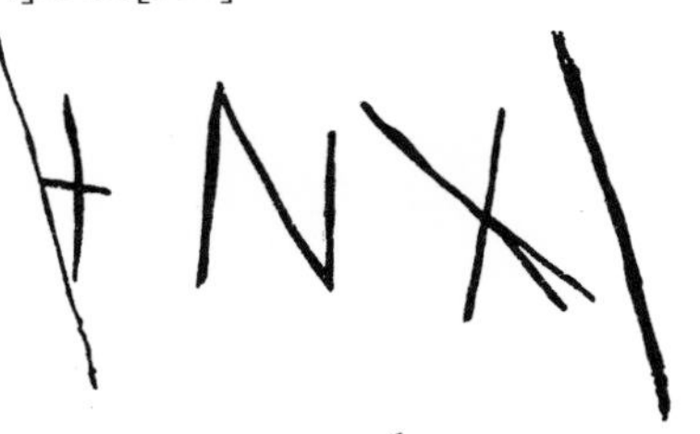

2503.567

2503.568. Rockbourne, Hampshire. Fragment from a black cooking pot in New Forest ware (½), found in or before 1963 in Room X of the West Park Roman villa. Hampshire Museum service. Drawn by S.S.F. from a rubbing by R.P.W., 1965.

JRS lvi (1966), 225 No. 60.

graffito: [. . .]OLΛ

Agricola is the only common name in *-ola*, but compare also *Ertola* (RIB 1181) and *Silvicola* (*Britannia* xviii (1987), 362 No. 1(b), and the Hoxne Treasure (ibid. xxv (1994), 308 Nos. 84–7). For *ola*, if the graffito is complete, compare *RIB* 2503.112, 113 with note.

2503.568

2503.569. Eccles, Kent. Part of the wall of a grey bowl (½), found in 1967 during excavations at the Roman villa. Maidstone Museum. Drawn by S.S.F. from rubbings by R.P.W., 1967.

JRS lviii (1968), 213 No. 75.

graffito on the wall below a groove: [. . .]ỌḶIS[. . .]

Perhaps a Greek personal name in *-polis*.

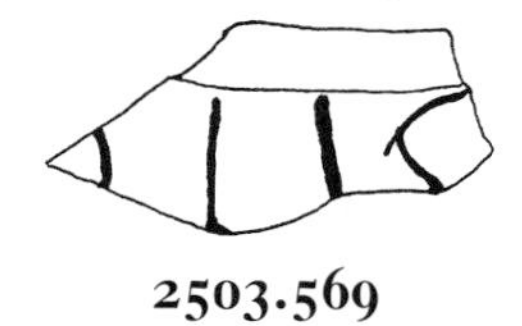

2503.569

2503.570. Canterbury (*Durovernum*), Kent. Part of a narrow-mouthed vessel (½) in grey fabric, found in 1976 in a residual context at Nos. 77–79 Castle Street. Canterbury Museum. Drawn by M.W.C.H.

Britannia xx (1989), 339 No. 44.

graffito on the wall above rouletting:
[. . .]ỌṂỊṂỊ[. . .] | [. . .]ABḄ[. . .]

l.2. The last letter could also be D, F, P or R.

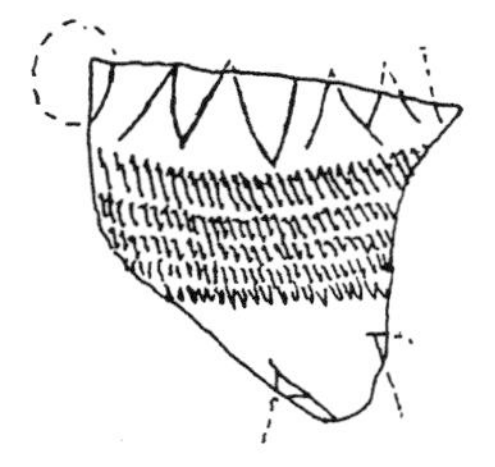

2503.570

2503.571. Winchester (*Venta Belgarum*), Hampshire. Fragment from the shoulder of a Black-burnished vessel (½), found in 1971 in a residual context at Wolvesey Palace. Winchester Museum. Drawn by M.W.C.H.

Britannia vii (1976), 385 No. 30.

graffito on the shoulder: [. . .]OMI·[. . .]

Perhaps *[D]omi(tius)* or *[D]omi(tianus)*, but there are other possibilities, such as *Comitianus* (*RIB* 154).

2503.571

2503.572. Caistor St. Edmund (*Venta Icenorum*), Norfolk. Fragment of a grey vessel (½), found in 1931 during excavation of the forum. Norwich Museum. Drawn by S.S.F. from a sketch by R.P.W.

Britannia ii (1971), 300 No. 71.

graffito: [. . .]ỌNΛ

2503.572

2503.573. Caerleon (*Isca*), Gwent [Monmouthshire]. Part of a jar (¼) in hard orange fabric, found in 1964–81 during excavation of the legionary bath-house. Caerleon Museum. Reproduced from Zienkiewicz.

J.D. Zienkiewicz, *The Legionary Fortress Baths at Caerleon* ii (1986), 23 No. 6 with fig. 4.6.

graffito on the shoulder: [. . .]OP̣P̣[. . .]

The second letter could be R or B and the third R, B, or O.

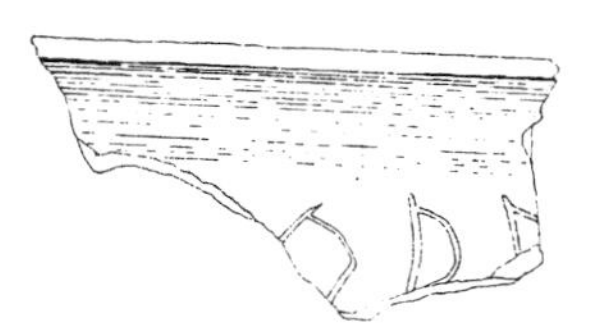

2503.573

2503.574. Piercebridge, Durham. Fragment from the wall of a Black-burnished cooking pot (½), found in 1964 unstratified in a barrack *c.* 50 m south of the East Gate of the fort. Bowes Museum, Barnard Castle. Drawn by S.S.F. from a rubbing by R.P.W., 1964.

JRS lv (1965), 227 No. 50.

graffito below the lattice decoration:
[. . .]ORVM | [. . .]. . .
'(Property) of . . . (*plural*)'

Compare *RIB* 2503.153, *puerorum*, and 575 with note.

2503.574

2503.575. Ilkley, North Yorkshire. Fragmentary base of 'a colour-coated unguent pot' (½), found in 1919–21 in the lowest level of Room F in the *praetorium* of the fort. Ilkley Museum. Drawn by R.P.W. after Woodward.

Woodward, *YAJ* xxviii (1925), 175, 256, 258 with figs. 38.4 and 40.7.

graffito on the base: [. . .].RVM | N.[. . .]

Perhaps two graffiti, one of plural owners ending in -*[o]rum*; or else N.[. . .].RVM.

2503.575

2503.576. Hackeston, Suffolk. Fragment of fine orange ware (½), found in 1974 during excavations at the settlement. Ipswich Museum. Drawn by S.S.F. from rubbings by M.W.C.H.

Britannia vi (1975), 288 No. 27.

graffito on the wall: [. . .]P̣E·TIỊ[. . .]

Perhaps [LVC]RETIA[NVS] or similar, R.S.O.T. As text, M.W.C.H.

2503.576

2503.577. St. Albans (*Verulamium*), Hertfordshire. Part of the base of a plate (½) in Terra Rubra I ware, found in 1958 in a residual context in Room 26 of Period IIB in Insula XIV. Verulamium Museum. Rubbings by R.P.W., 1960. Drawn by M.G. Wilson.

JRS li (1961), 197 No. 43. S.S. Frere, *Verulamium Excavations* i (1972), 364 No. 3 with fig. 140.3.

graffito on the upper side of the base:
[. . .].PIIO | [. . .].

The first letter might be A or M.

2503.577

2503.578. Colchester (*Camulodunum*), Essex. Part of a jug (½) in fine polished red ware, found in 1929 in the Holly Trees Meadow (Insula 15). Colchester Museum. Drawn by R.P.W., 1943.

graffito (inverted) on the neck: [. . .]REG[. . .]

Possibly *Reg[ulus]* or *Reg[inus]*; compare *RIB* 2503.397 with note.

2503.578

2503.579. Chesters (*Cilurnum*). Fragment (⅔) in yellow ware with two narrow brown bands below the graffito, found in 1892 during excavations at the fort. Sought in vain by R.P.W. Reproduced from Blair.

Blair, *PSAN*[2] (1892), 162, 166 with fig.

graffito: [. . .]ṚEPO[. . .]

Apparently not part of an AREPO word-square (compare *RIB* 2447.20).

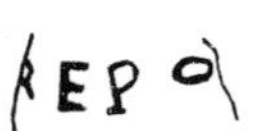

2503.579

2503.580. Caerleon (*Isca*), Gwent [Monmouthshire]. Part of a cooking pot (½) in coarse ware, found in 1927 during excavations at the amphitheatre. National Museum, Cardiff. Drawn by R.P.W., 1965.

JRS lvi (1966), 225 No. 61.

graffito on the shoulder: [. . .]RẸṢ[. . .]

The first letter is likely to be B. Possibly *Res[pectus]* or *Res[titutus]*.

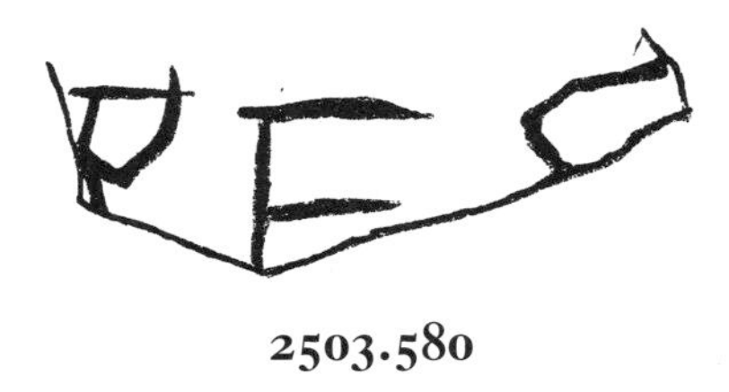

2503.580

2503.581. Eccles, Kent. Three non-joining parts of a grey bowl (½), found in 1964 while excavating a rubbish-deposit dated *c.* A.D. 100–150 in Room 33 of the Roman villa. Maidstone Museum. Drawn by S.S.F. from rubbings by R.P.W., 1965.

JRS lv (1965), 228 No. 51.

three graffiti: (a) below the rim: [. . .]ṚINṾ[. . .]
(b) on the wall: V̂AṚ[. . .]
(c) on the upper surface of the base:
[. . .]V | X[. . .] | Ẹ[. . .]

(c) [. . .]V[. . . ?] | X[. . . ?] | [. . .]ỊṬ[. . .], R.S.O.T.

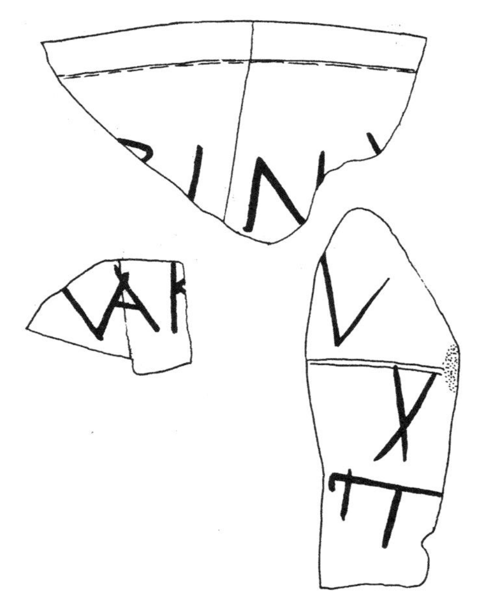

2503.581

2503.582. Canterbury (*Durovernum*), Kent. Fragment of Black-burnished ware (½), found in 1978 during excavations at No. 16 Watling Street. Canterbury Museum. Drawn by M.W.C.H.

Britannia xi (1980), 413 No. 47.

graffito: [. . .]RIN[. . .]

2503.582

2503.583. Lullingstone, Kent. Three fragments, not joining, of a Black-burnished jar (½), found in 1958 during excavations at the Roman villa. Lullingstone Villa Museum. Drawn by S.S.F. from rubbings by R.P.W., 1959.

JRS xlix (1959), 139 No. 29b. Pollard in G.W. Meates, *The Lullingstone Roman Villa* ii (1987), 280 No. 1 with fig. 88.428.

three graffiti: (a) [. . .]RIVS.[. . .]
(b) [. . .]ṚPVO.[. . .]
(c) [. . .]T

(a) [. . .]RIVSZ[. . .], R.P.W., *JRS*. [. . .]RIVSV[. . .], Pollard.

(c) VT, Pollard.

2503.583

2503.584. Corbridge (*? Coria*), Northumberland. Part of a jug (½), found in 1906–14 during excavations. Corbridge Museum. Drawn by S.S.F. from a tracing by R.P.W.

graffito on the wall: [. . .]ṚOTI

The most probable names are either *Crotus* or *Protus*, both of which are attested elsewhere in Britain.

2503.584

2503.585. Wilderspool, Cheshire. Fragment of dull red ware (scale uncertain), found in or before 1910. Warrington Museum. Drawn by S.S.F. from a sketch by R.P.W., 1952.

graffito: [. . .]RTIS[. . .]

2503.585

2503.586. Barnsley Park, Gloucestershire. Fragment from a reddish vessel (½), found in 1968 unstratified during excavations at the Roman villa. Corinium Museum, Cirencester. Drawn by S.S.F. from rubbings by R.P.W., 1970.

Britannia i (1970), 315 No. 50.

graffito: [. . .]SΛ̣IṆI

'The diagonal stroke of N is only dotted,' R.P.W., *Britannia*; however, the rubbings show a continuous connecting sulcus.

2503.586

2503.587. Eccles, Kent. Fragment from a brown colour-coated beaker in cream-coloured fabric (½), found in 1970 in a mid third-century rubbish deposit in Ditch VII during excavations at the Roman villa. Maidstone Museum. Drawn by S.S.F. from rubbings by R.P.W., 1970.

Britannia ii (1971), 297 No. 51.

graffito below the rim: [. . .]ṢNA[. . .]

2503.587

2503.588. Chesterholm (*Vindolanda*), Northumberland. Fragment of a dark grey vessel (½), found before 1987 unstratified during excavations. Vindolanda Museum. Drawing: the Vindolanda Trust.

E., R., and A. Birley, *Vindolanda* ii (1993), 98 No. 7 with fig. 12.6.

graffito on the shoulder:
[. . .]ṢṬION[. . .]

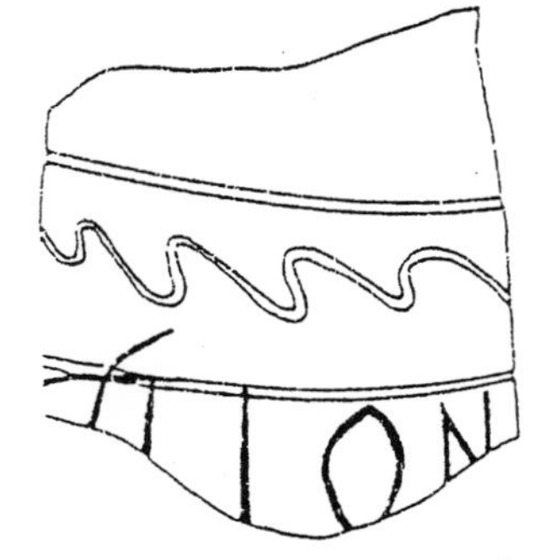

2503.588

2503.589. Silchester (*Calleva*), Hampshire. Jar (¼) 'coated with black bitumen' and carrying a lattice band, height 178 mm, diameter at mouth 124 mm, found in 1901 during excavation of Pit XXV in Building XXVII.1. Reading Museum. Drawn by R.P.W., 1951.

T. May, *Silchester* (1916), 285 No. 28 with pl. LXXXV.28.

graffito around the shoulder:
SVMS⟨S⟩EER P CTVI RMIIV

The third S is deleted: perhaps *sum se⟨e⟩r(vus)*. . ., R.P.W.

PCTVIRMITV NMSFEER, 'perhaps a writing exercise,' May.

2503.589

2503.590. Dicket Mead, Welwyn, Hertfordshire. Part of the neck of a colour-coated beaker (½), found in 1969 in a gully behind Building 2 during excavations at the Roman villa. Welwyn Archaeological Society. Reproduced from Rook.

Britannia iv (1973), 331 No. 24. Rook, *Herts. Arch.* ix (1983–6), 142 No. 2 with fig. 55.2.

graffito below the rim: [. . .]ṢX̣͡X̣

Perhaps SΛ͡X was intended; compare *RIB* 2503.404–5, S.S.F.

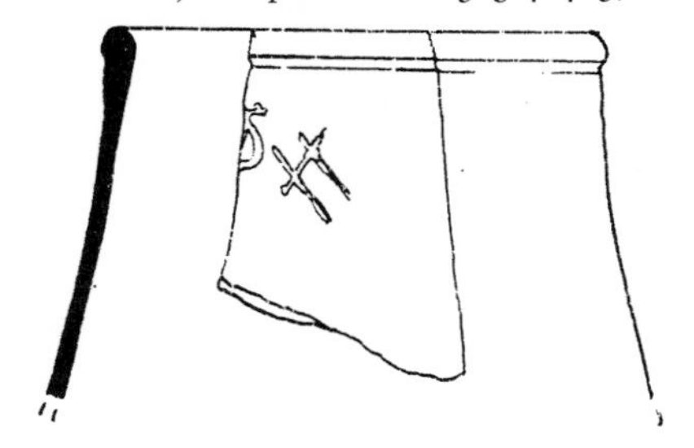

2503.590

2503.591. Canterbury (*Durovernum*), Kent. Fragment ($\frac{1}{2}$) from the upper part of a grey-ware jar, found in 1979 with second- and third-century material in a drain at the St. Margaret's Street Baths. Canterbury Museum. Drawn by M.W.C.H.

Britannia xiii (1982), 414 No. 38.

graffito: [. . .]TALIS

Probably *[Vi]talis* or *[Na]talis*, but there are other possibilities.

2503.591

2503.592. Ibid. Fragment ($\frac{1}{1}$) from a poppy-head beaker in smooth grey ware, found in 1978 during excavations at No. 16 Watling Street. Canterbury Museum. Drawn by M.W.C.H.

Britannia xi (1980), 413 No. 48.

graffito on the shoulder: [. . .]TARI[. . .]

2503.592

2503.593. Colchester (*Camulodunum*), Essex. Fragment of a colour-coated beaker ($\frac{1}{2}$), found in 1929 during excavations in Holly Trees Meadow (Insula 15). Colchester Museum. Drawn by R.P.W., 1943.

graffito between bands of rouletting: [. . .]TEM.[. . .]

The final letter could be P or less probably B, D, E, F, I or R, R.P.W.

2503.593

2503.594. Dorchester (*Durnovaria*), Dorset. Part of a large Black-burnished jar ($\frac{1}{2}$), found in 1984 during excavations in Greyhound Yard. Dorchester Museum. Drawn by R.S.O.T., 1994.

Britannia xx (1989), 336 No. 27. P.J. Woodward et al., *Excavations at Greyhound Yard, Dorchester, 1981–4* (1993), 284 No. 15.

graffito below the rim: [. . .]ṬEOṚ

The final letter is taken to be cursive R rather than Λ, but no restoration presents itself.

2503.594

2503.595. Rocester, Staffordshire. Part of a Black-burnished bowl ($\frac{1}{2}$) with lattice decoration, found in 1960 unstratified in a sewer-trench in Church Lane. In private possession. Drawn by S.S.F. from a rubbing by R.P.W., 1960.

JRS li (1961), 198 No. 48.

graffito on the rim: [. . .]THΛ[.]I
  Probably [. . .]THΛ[I]I
  [. . .]thae

There is no trace of a digit at the fracture-point, but sense requires [I]I for . . .*thae*, R.P.W. Compare *RIB* 2503.157 with note.

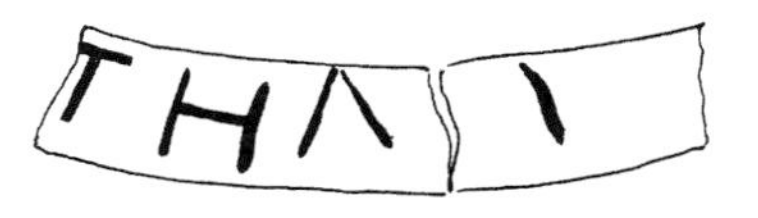

2503.595

2503.596. Scole (*? Villa Faustini*), Norfolk. Grey-ware fragment ($\frac{1}{2}$), found in 1973 in an early second-century context. Norwich Museum. Drawn by M.W.C.H.

Britannia vii (1976), 388 No. 45.

graffito: [. . .]TICOFỊICI[. . .]
  Perhaps *[. . .]tico feci[t]*
  '. . .tico made (this)'

The graffito was cut after firing, Britannia loc. cit. Compare *RIB* 2503.467.

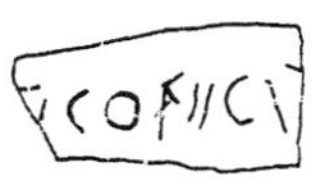

2503.596

2503.597. Baldock, Hertfordshire. Fragment from the base of a grey burnished vessel (½), found in 1968 in a pit with fourth-century pottery during excavation of trial trenches along Clothall Road. Letchworth Museum. Reproduced from Stead and Rigby.

Britannia xi (1980), 412 No. 43. Hassall in I.M. Stead and V. Rigby, *Baldock* (1986), 189 No. 839 with fig. 82.839.

graffito on the base: [. . .]TOḶỊ[. . .]

2503.597

2503.598. Old Winteringham, Humberside [Lincolnshire]. Fragment from the wall of a buff jug (½), found in 1964 during excavations at the settlement. Scunthorpe Museum. Drawn by S.S.F. from a rubbing by R.P.W., 1968.

JRS lix (1969), 246 No. 77. I.M. Stead, *Excavations at Winterton Roman Villa* . . . (1976), 191 with fig. 95.1.

graffito on the wall: [. . .]ṾΛT

2503.598

2503.599. Corbridge (? *Coria*), Northumberland. Part of a jug (½), found before 1940. Corbridge Museum. Drawn by R.P.W., 1940.

graffito on the shoulder: [. . .]VΛTI[. . .]

[Pri]vatus, [Ser]vatus, or a similar name.

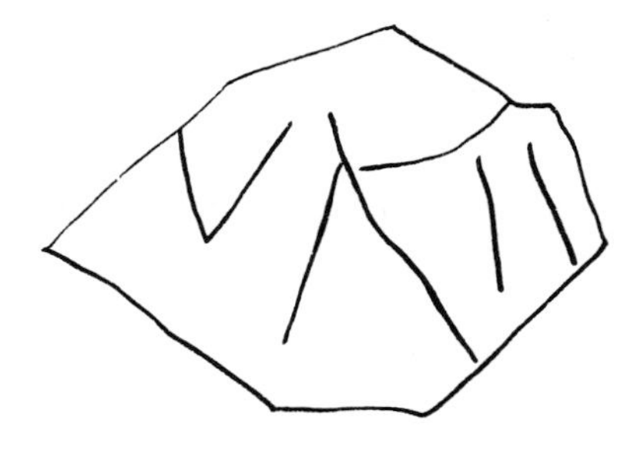

2503.599

2503.600. Hacheston, Suffolk. Part of the base of a grey-ware vessel oxidized orange on the surface (½), found in 1973 during excavations at the settlement. Ipswich Museum. Drawn by S.S.F. from a rubbing by M.W.C.H.

Britannia v (1974), 468 No. 54.

graffito on the upper (?) surface of the base:
[. . .]ṾCA[. . .]

2503.600

2503.601. Chesterholm (*Vindolanda*), Northumberland. Fragment from the wall of a Black-burnished 1 vessel (½), found in 1973 in the ditch near the south-western angle of the stone fort. Vindolanda Museum. Drawn by S.S.F. from rubbings by R.P.W., 1974.

Britannia v (1974), 468 No. 48.

graffito: [. . .]ṾCIV[. . .]
Presumably *[. . .]uciu[s]*

Perhaps *[L]uciu[s]*, but there are other possibilities.

2503.601

2503.602. Canterbury (*Durovernum*), Kent. Part of a (?) beaker (½) in fine hard grey fabric with a shiny slipped shoulder above rouletting, found in 1980 in a late second- or third-century context at the Marlowe IV site. Canterbury Museum. Drawn by M.W.C.H.

Britannia xiii (1982), 415 No. 47.

graffito: [. . .]ṾIDE[. . .]

2503.602

2503.603. Dicket Mead, Welwyn, Hertfordshire. Sherd (½) from the base of a Black-burnished dish, found in 1970 in a pit with third-century material during excavations at the Roman villa. Welwyn Archaeological Society. Reproduced from Rook.

Britannia iv (1973), 332 No. 25; x (1979), 350 No. 27. Rook, *Herts. Arch.* ix (1983–6), 142 No. 5 with fig. 55.5.

graffito on the underside of the base:
[. . .]VIDIO̩[. . .]

If a personal name, almost certainly *Avidius* in the dative, since the only other possibilities are excessively rare, M.W.C.H. But VI(N)DIC[IS] is possible. Compare however No. 454.

2503.603

2503.604. Gadebridge Park, Hemel Hempstead, Hertfordshire. Fragment from the rim of a grey flanged dish (½), found in 1965 in a second-century gully associated with the baths of the Roman villa. Dacorum District Council. Drawn by S.S.F. from rubbings by R.P.W., 1970.

Britannia i (1970), 315 No. 51. D.S. Neal, *Gadebridge Park* (1974), 255 No. i with fig. 113 i.

graffito below the rim: [. . .]V̩IN[. . .]

2503.604

2503.605. Canterbury (*Durovernum*), Kent. Fragment (½) from the base of a Black-burnished dish, found in 1978 during excavations at No. 16 Watling Street. Canterbury Museum. Drawn by M.W.C.H.

Britannia xi (1980), 413 No. 49.

graffito on the upper side of the base:
[. . .]VIRO.[. . .]

[. . .]VIRO I[. . .], M.W.C.H., *Britannia*.

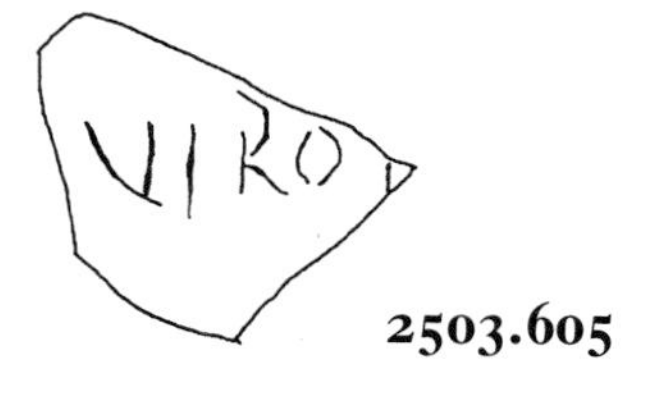

2503.605

2503.606. Colchester (*Camulodunum*), Essex. Fragment (½) from a grey-ware jar, found in 1975 in a pit with mid second- to mid third-century material during excavations in the suburbs outside the Balkerne Gate. Colchester Museum. Drawn by M.W.C.H.

Britannia xi (1980), 411 No. 31.

graffito on the shoulder above a zone of lattice:
[. . .].VLEN[. . .]

2503.606

2503.607. Castleford (*Lagentium*), West Yorkshire. Sherd from a cream-coloured jar (½), found in 1985 during excavations at the fort. West Yorkshire Archaeology Service. Drawn by R.S.O.T., 1986.

Britannia xviii (1987), 377 No. 58.

graffito on the wall: [. . .].VLICI

[Gaet]ulici could be restored if T had a curving downstroke, but this is uncertain.

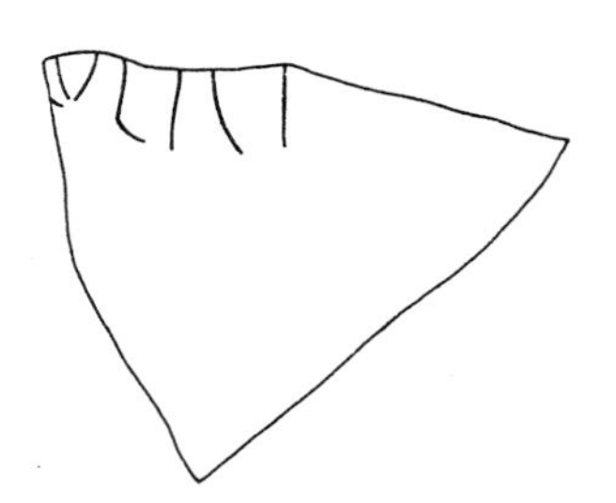

2503.607

2503.608. Colchester (*Camulodunum*), Essex. Part of a white-coated jug (scale uncertain), found before 1943. Colchester Museum. Drawn by S.S.F. from a sketch by R.P.W., 1943.

JRS xxxiv (1944), 91 No. 33.

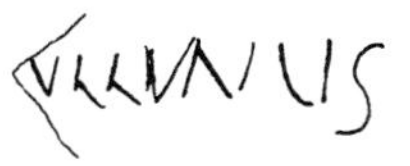

2503.608

graffito on the wall: [. . .]VLLVNVS

[. . .]VLLINVS, *JRS*. As text, R.P.W., 1977. It is possible that the fourth letter has been corrected.

2503.609. Malton (*Derventio*), North Yorkshire. Fragment of a cream-coloured jug of red fabric (½), found in 1970 in the *vicus* south of the fort. Malton Museum. Drawn by S.S.F. from rubbings by R.P.W., 1971.

Britannia ii (1971), 303 No. 90.

graffito: [. . .]ṾLX̣ | [. . .]T

The X has an extra stroke and may represent a stop. R.P.W., *RIB* archive.

2503.609

2503.610. Dicket Mead, Welwyn, Hertfordshire. Two sherds (½) from the base of a Black-burnished dish, found in 1969–70 in rubble inside Building 3 during excavations at the Roman villa. Welwyn Archaeological Society. Reproduced from Rook.

Britannia xii (1981), 386 No. 41. Rook, *Herts. Arch.* ix (1983–6), 142 No. 7 with fig. 55.7.

two graffiti on the underside of the base:
(a) [. . .]ṾMINE[. . .]
(b) [. . .EṬ Ṃ[. . .]

(a) The first letter could just possibly be I preceded by the tail of an R or part of an X (not shown on the drawing). If V is the correct reading *[Post]umin(a)e* could be restored, M.W.C.H., *Britannia*.

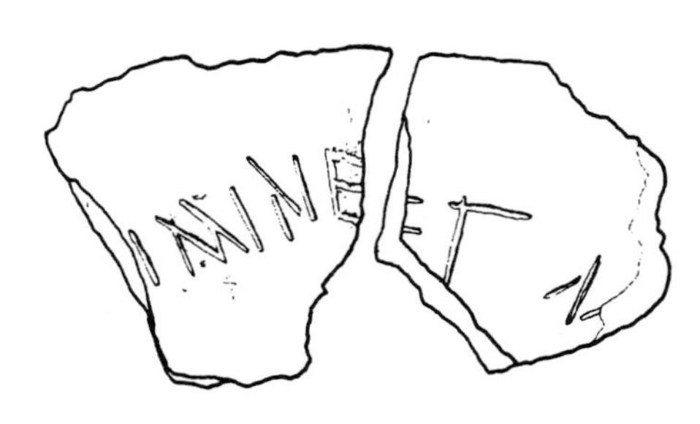

2503.610

2503.611. Wiggonholt, West Sussex. Part of a dark grey cooking pot (½), found in 1964 during excavations at the Roman bath-house. Worthing Museum. Drawn by S.S.F. from rubbings by R.P.W., 1967.

JRS lviii (1968), 214 No. 78. Evans, *Suss. AC* cxii (1974), 127 No. 14 with fig. 9.14.

graffito on the shoulder: [. . .]ṾRE

2503.611

2503.612. Eccles, Kent. Two conjoining fragments from a grey cooking pot (½) with acute lattice decoration, found in 1966 in the filling of a late Antonine ditch at the Roman villa. Maidstone Museum. Drawn by S.S.F. from rubbings by R.P.W., 1967.

JRS lvii (1967), 210 No. 53.

graffito on the wall, over the lattice: [. . .]VRIII

2503.612

2503.613. Colchester (*Camulodunum*), Essex. Fragment of a grey jar (scale uncertain), found before 1943. Colchester Museum. Drawn by S.S.F. from a sketch by R.P.W., 1943.

graffito on the shoulder: [. . .]ṾRIVS

Perhaps *[Merc]urius*, but there are other possibilities.

2503.613

2503.614. London (*Londinium*). Sherd from a segmented bowl (½), found in 1975 in a residual context during excavations at New Fresh Wharf. Museum of London. Drawn by M.W.C.H.

Britannia xiii (1982), 418 No. 67.

graffito below the rim: [. . .]VS·ASPRI[. . .]

Variants of the cognomen *Asper* in *Aspri-* are very rare (Kajanto, *Cognomina*, 265); if therefore ASPRI is complete and the genitive of *Asper*, it is a patronymic, or even, perhaps, a possessive preceded by the name of the vessel. See M.W.C.H.'s note ad loc.

2503.614

2503.615. Ibid. Fragment from the rim of a dark grey beaker (½), found in 1968 in the ash of the stoke-hole of a bath-building north of Lower Thames Street. Museum of London. Drawn by S.S.F. from rubbings by R.P.W., 1969.

JRS lix (1969), 246 No. 78.

graffito below the rim: [. . .]ṾSVLI

[. . .]ṆSVLI also seems possible, compare *Tab. Sulis* 98, 12, *Gunsula*.

2503.615

2503.616. Chalk, Kent. Fragment from the rolled rim of a polished grey dish (½), found in 1961 during excavation of a Roman building. Present whereabouts unrecorded. Drawn by S.S.F. from rubbings by R.P.W., 1964.

JRS liv (1964), 185 No. 44 c. Woodhead in Johnston, *Britannia* iii (1972), 145 No. 5 with fig. 19.5.

graffito on the rim: [. . .]ṾTO.[. . .]

[. . .]ṆTO[. . .] is less likely, R.P.W.

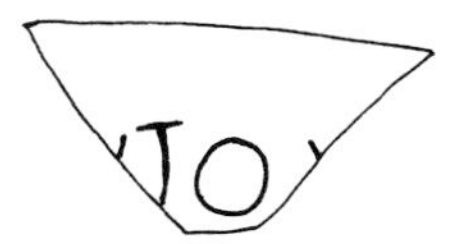

2503.616

2503.616a. Binchester (*Vinovia*), Durham. Fragments from a large orange-coloured jug (½), found in 1978 amongst levelling material of the late first and early second centuries on the site of the later bath-house within the fort. Bowes Museum, Barnard Castle. Drawn by R.S.O.T. from a photograph.

Britannia x (1979), 349 No. 21.

graffito in flowing capitals: [. . .].VTTONIS
 Probably *[S]uttonis*
 '(Property) of Sutto'

What remains of the first surviving letter suggests C or G, but more likely S or T. The attested names *Butto* and *Neutto* are therefore not possible, but for **Sutto* compare *Satto* (*RIB* 2503.155) and *Suttonius* (*CIL* v 8110, 325) and *Suttius* (v 1779).

2503.616 a

2503.617. Usk (*Burrium*), Gwent [Monmouthshire]. Fragment (½) of a vessel in coarse buff fabric, found in 1974 during excavations at the pre-Flavian fortress. National Museum, Cardiff. Drawn by S.S.F. from rubbings by M.W.C.H.

Britannia vi (1975), 293 No. 49. Hassall in G.C. Boon and M. Hassall, *Usk* (1982), 58 No. 50 with fig. 5.50.

graffito: [. . .]ṾXAṂ[. . .]

Perhaps two graffiti, (i) IX; (ii) AṆ[. . .], R.S.O.T.

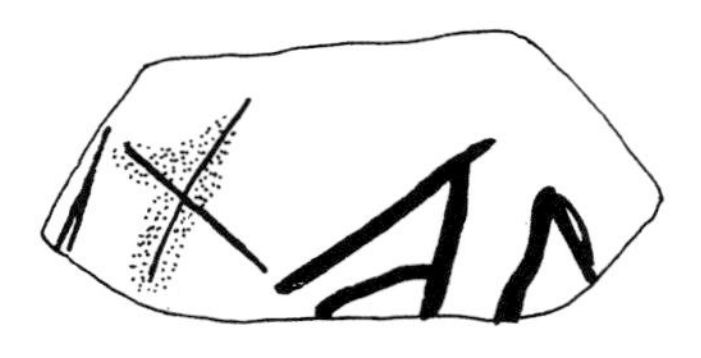

2503.617

2503.618. Caersws, Powys [Montgomeryshire]. Fragment (½) from a Black-burnished vessel with traces of burnished decoration on the inside, found in 1985–6 during excavations in the *vicus* of the fort. Clwyd-Powys Archaeological Trust. Drawn by M.W.C.H.

Britannia xx (1989), 344 No. 66.

graffito on the wall: [. . .]XIINIC[. . .]

2503.618

2503.619. Harlton, Cambridgeshire. Fragment of Hornsey ware (½), found in 1938 by James Money. Present whereabouts unknown. Drawn by R.S.O.T., 1994, from photographs. See also PL. II B.

graffito: [. . .].[. . .] | [. . .]ANT INIO.[. . .] | [. . .]VSEST.[. . .] | [. . .]LAV.[. . .] | [. . .].T[. . .]

l. 4 'The tail of the first S seems to merge into what may be the top of a C,' Money, *RIB* archive.

R.G.C. doubted the genuineness of this graffito, but the letter-forms and content do not suggest that it is *falsum*.

2503.619

FALSA

2503.620.* Spong Hill, North Elmham, Norfolk. Anglo-Saxon cremation-urn (scale uncertain), found in or before 1760 when it was given by Mrs Milles to Bryan Faussett; later, after entering the Mayer collection, it passed to Liverpool Museum where it was destroyed by enemy bombing during the Second World War. Reproduced from Roach Smith. See also PL. VIII.

CIL vii 94. *EE* iii p. 116; ix p. 523. C. Roach Smith, *Coll. Ant.* v (1861), 115–6 with pl. X, quoting (p. 121) a memorandum by Faussett. Haverfield, *VCH* Norfolk i (1901), 312 with fig. 27 (photograph). C. Hills, *The Anglo-Saxon Cemetery at Spong Hill, North Elmham* (East Anglian Archaeology, Report No. 6), i (1977), 32.

2503.620*

two graffiti: (a) on the shoulder above the decoration: D(is) M(anibus)

(b) below (a), within a panel forming a compartment in the decorated band: *Laeliae* | *Rufinae* | *vixit a(nnos) xiii* | *m(enses) iii d(ies) vi*

'To the spirits of the departed (and) of Laelia Rufina; (she lived) thirteen years, three months, six days'

For the identification of the find-spot see Roach Smith, loc. cit., 116. Mistakenly assuming the inscription to be genuine and a pointer to continuity between Roman and Anglo-Saxon burial rites, he expressed surprise that Faussett had not noted its presence. But the absence of comment by Faussett suggests that the graffito was cut after the vessel had left his collection. The letters are 'rude and not altogether Roman', and the inscription is of a type 'common enough in Rome', as Haverfield noted, *VCH* loc. cit. This would an anachronism on a sixth-century hand-made vessel; the graffito must be a modern forgery based on a genuine inscription apparently unpublished.

2503.621.* Mount Batten, Plymouth, Devon. Part of the rim of a vessel found in 1939. Now lost. Traced by S.S.F. from a sketch by R.P.W., 1940 (scale uncertain).

JRS xxxi (1941), 148 No. 21. Judge, *Antiq. J.* xx (1940), 381 with photograph.

graffito on the rim: LMANQ

The reading was by C.F.C. Hawkes, but R.G.C. (*JRS*) considered the markings to be fortuitous scratches. R.P.W. noted only faint scratches which included no letters which could be read with confidence. The published photograph suggests a numeral LX . . . (?).

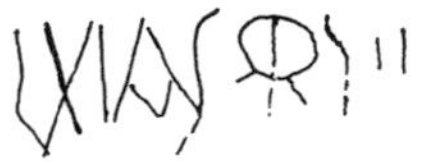

2503.621*

RIB 2503 A. STAMP ON COARSE POTTERY

1. Kingscote, Gloucestershire. Fragments from a jar in grey ware, lightly burnished on the shoulder, found in 1974–75 in a pit with second-century material. A stamp has been impressed vertically three times. Corinium Museum, Cirencester. Not illustrated.

Britannia viii (1977), 441 No. 80.

stamp: DIGL̩N͡PT

RIB 2504. ADDENDA TO *RIB* II, FASCICULES 1–8

Addendum to *RIB* 2402: Silver Ingots
FALSVM

2504.1.* Pulborough, Sussex. Sheet of silver, 110 by 85 mm, found in 1907–10 during excavations at the Roman villa. Present whereabouts unknown. Reprinted from *EE*.

EE ix 1368. Haverfield, *PSA*² xxiii (1910), 129. *Southern Weekly News*, 1 January and 9 April 1910.

in raised letters: EXOFF.C•|HONORE leaf-stop.

'An inferior copy of' *RIB* 2402.4, Haverfield, *PSA*.

Addenda to *RIB* 2404: Lead Pigs
FALSA

2504.2–3.* Cromford, Derbyshire. Two lead pigs, (a) 609.6 by 196.8 by 76 mm, (b) 482.6 by 127 by 101.6 mm, together weighing 'over two hundredweight' (= over 101.6 kg), found in or shortly before 1919 in digging a grave in the churchyard. Present whereabouts unknown. Reprinted from *JBAA*.

Anon., *JBAA*² xxv (1919), 268. Cockerton, *J. Derbys. AS* lxxxii (1962), 106.

inscribed or stamped: (a) XXX
(b) XV

'The ingots are roughly cast in rectangular moulds', but it is uncertain whether they were of Roman or medieval date.

For a Hadrianic pig found on Cromford Nether Moor, see *RIB* 2404.39, and for Roman numerals XXXII and VX punched on medieval boat-shaped ingots see Raftery, *J. Royal Society of Antiquaries of Ireland* lxxxviii (1958), 135 fig. 8.

Addendum to *RIB* 2405: Tin Ingots
FALSVM

2504.4.* Trereife, Madron parish, Cornwall. Ingot of tin, 406 by 203 by 50.8 mm, weight 29½lb (Gowland) [= 13.38 kg], found in or before 1846. Penlee House Museum, Penzance. Reproduced from Way.

Huebner, *Inscr. Brit. Chr.* 10.* *EE* ix, note to No. 1262. Le Grice, *Trans. Royal Geological Society of Cornwall* vi (1846), 43. Way, *Arch. J.* xxiii (1866), 284 with fig. Gowland, *Arch.* lvi (1899), 301 fig. 18. Haverfield, *PSA*² xviii (1900), 121. Tylecote, *Cornish Arch.* v (1966), 33 No. 9. Warner, *Cornish Arch.* vi (1967), 31.

moulded in relief: EIC cruciform device.

'The device on it bears no resemblance to anything Roman; on the other hand, it is exactly like some of the known marks of medieval and modern merchants in the west country', Haverfield, loc. cit.

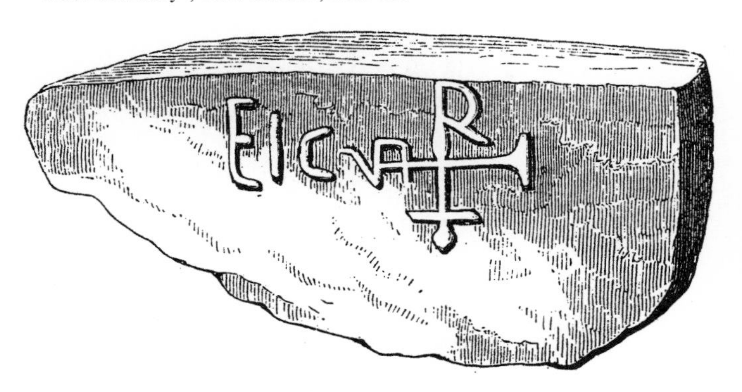

2504.4*

Addenda to *RIB* 2409: Dies

2504.5. Unknown provenance. Bronze die with ring handle (†), 22 × 17 mm, height 22 mm. From the collection of C. Faulkner of Deddington, Oxfordshire, and presented in 1936 to the Ashmolean Museum, Oxford. Drawn by S.S.F. from a cast by R.P.W., 1953.

engraved: PHIL | VIIC

The final letter of l.2 is probably C but G or O are not impossible, R.P.W. The surface is worn down with use.

2504.5

FALSVM(?)

2504.6.* Colchester, Essex. Bronze die (*c.* ½) wrongly described in *CIL* as a *patella*. Formerly in Colchester Museum. Now lost. Traced by S.S.F. from a sketch drawn from memory by M.R. Hull for R.P.W., 1954.

CIL vii 1336.154. *EE* iii 138; vii 1177. *Cat.* Colchester Museum (1863, 1869) No. 580.

in (?)raised letters: BIOKNO

BIOṚNO, R.P.W., archive, conject.

Haverfield after examination considered it not to be genuine (*EE* vii, loc. cit.) but doubt remains, since the object has the form of genuine stamps; compare *RIB* 2409.15, 16, 29, 30, 32, 33, 35 and 36.

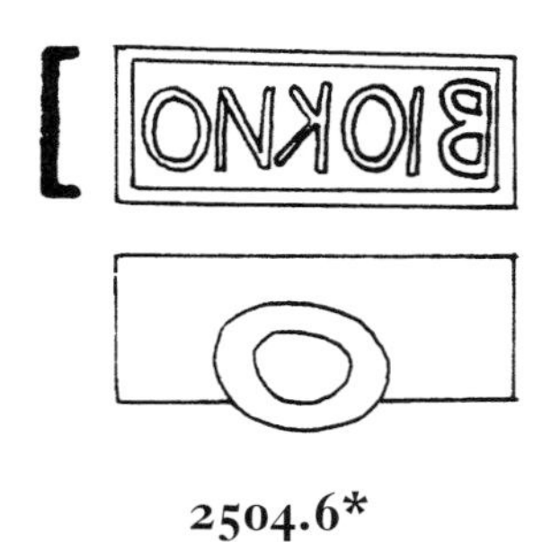

2504.6*

Addenda to *RIB* 2410: Labels

2504.7. Caerleon (*Isca*), Gwent [Monmouthshire]. Thin rectangular lead tag (1/1 and 2/1), 32 × 25 mm, with a small hole for attachment. Found in 1980–81 in the make-up of a mid fourth-century floor, during excavations at Roman Gates, Backhall Street (for which see *RIB* 2504.9) Caerleon Museum. Drawing: Glamorgan-Gwent Archaeological Trust.

Britannia xx (1989), 342 No. 60 with fig. 8. D.R. Evans and V.M. Metcalf, *Roman Gates, Caerleon* (1992), 85 No. 2 with fig.

Obverse: TR✳ III
  TR (denarii) iii
  '. . . three denarii'
Reverse: CALVINI | VARENỊAṆ | VIṚṂAE
  Calvini | . . .
  '(Property) of Calvinius . . .'

2504.8. Carlisle (*Luguvalium*), Cumbria [Cumberland]. Rectangular tag (1/1), 33 × 23 mm, cut from a sheet of lead, with a hole punched for attachment. Found in 1982 in a mid Antonine context during excavations in Castle Street. Tullie House Museum, Carlisle. Drawn by R.S.O.T., 1988.

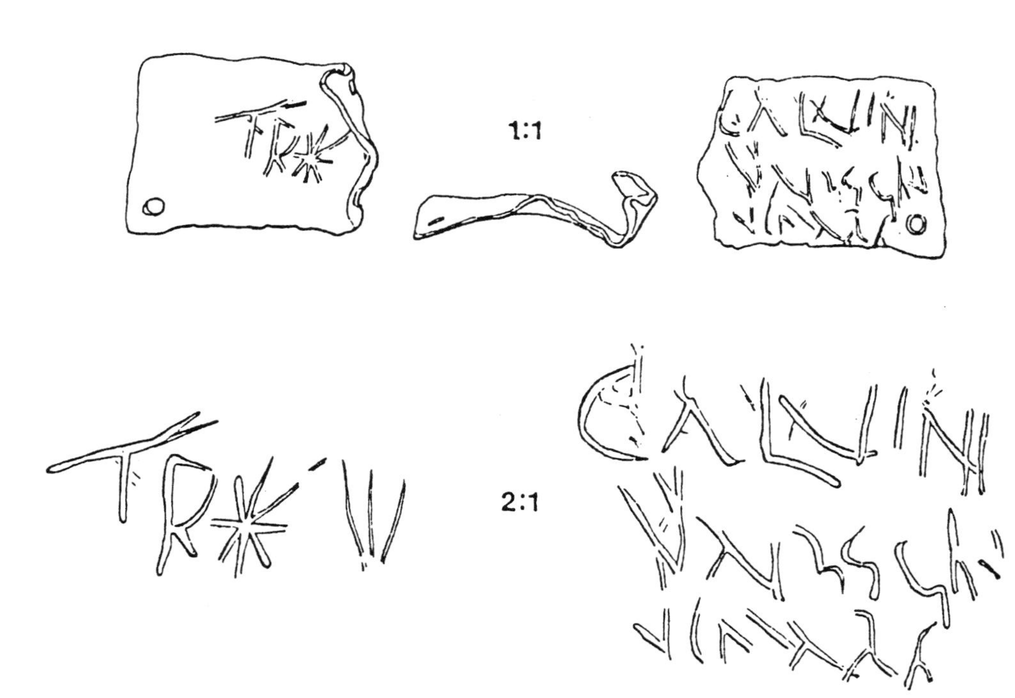

2504.7

Britannia xx (1989), 334 No. 14.

inscribed on each side, leaving the hole to the left.

Obverse: Ↄ[. .]GABIANA | IVLISVRITI | AR

(centuria) Gabiana | *Iuli Suriti* | *AR*

'(Property) of Iulius Suritus in the *Centuria Gabiana* AR'

Reverse: MARAS | LOTO ✕ IS | P

MARAS | *LOTO (denarii) (unus) s(emis)*

'. . . one and a half denarii'

The nomen *Gabius* is rare (e.g. *CIL* v 1225, 2631), and it is possible that *Gabiniana* was meant, Gabinius being much more common. In l.2 the final I of *Iulii* is crossed by a horizontal stroke suggesting T. But it seems to be casual damage, and the sequence -TS- is hard to accept. Initial *T-* is found in one or two unique cognomina, but it is easier to understand *Suriti* as the cognomen although *Suritus* seems to be unattested; compare however *Suricus* (*CIL* v 4856) and *Surica* (v 5618), one of several cognomina cognate with *Surus*.

The adjectival form of *Gabius* indicates the century's late commander, the command being temporarily vacant: see E. Birley, *Roman Britain and the Roman Army* (1953), 128–9.

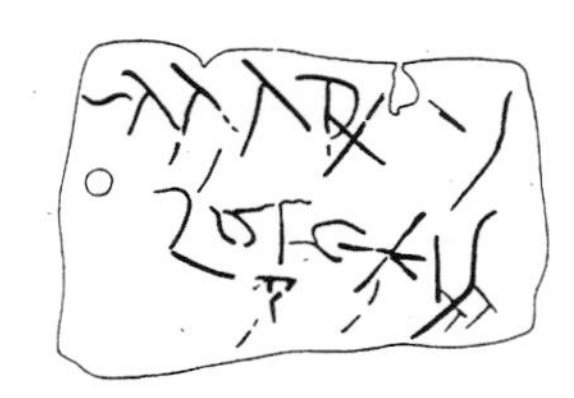

2504.8

2504.9. Caerleon (*Isca*), Gwent [Monmouthshire]. Rectangular lead tag (1/1), 60 by 40 mm, a parallelogram in form and with a hole for attachment in one of the short sides. When found, it was folded in half. Found in 1980 during excavation at Roman Gates, Backhall Street, in the *latera praetorii* of the fortress near the *porta principalis dextra*. Caerleon Museum. Drawing: Glamorgan-Gwent Archaeological Trust.

Britannia xix (1988), 506 No. 104. D.R. Evans and V.M.

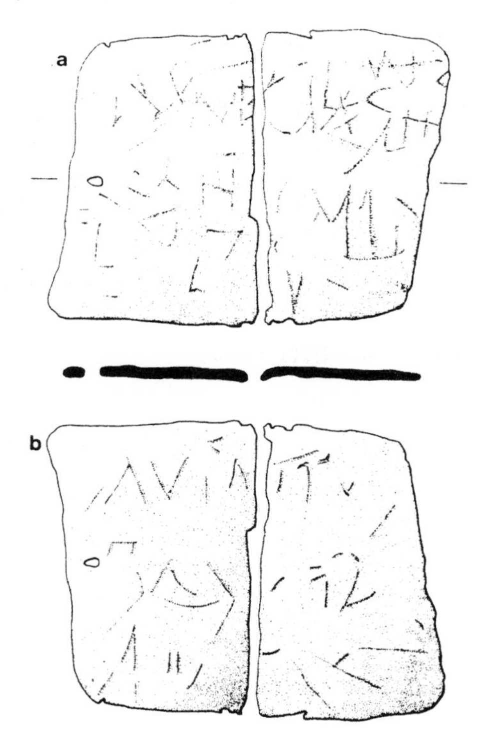

2504.9

Metcalf, *Roman Gates, Caerleon* (1992), 84 No. 1 with fig.

graffiti lightly incised on both sides:

(a) the outer face when folded:

A | SVMCIASIX | SA.TBC.V . . | VSA

(b) illegible, but probably inverted with respect to (a).

Side (a) was inscribed at least twice, and this may also be true of (b).

Addendum to *RIB* 2411.152–6: Lead Sealings

2504.10. Unknown provenance, probably Brough under Stainmore, Cumbria [Westmorland]. An additional example (156 A) of this type has been found in the Ashmolean Museum, Oxford (Inv. No. 1927–654a). Information from Michael Still.

Addendum to *RIB* 2414: Silver Vessels

2504.11. Unknown provenance, possibly Wales. Late Roman silver *trulla* ($\frac{1}{1}$), diameter 132 mm, height 66.5 mm, length of handle 114 mm, having a hemispherical bowl with flat base without a footstand; the handle, now rejoined to the bowl, carries two other breaks now repaired. Found 'a long time' before 1942 when it was purchased by the British Museum from the Red Cross shop, Edinburgh, to which it had been donated by Miss Fletcher of Saltoun; the vessel had come 'from her home in Wales, believed to be at Margam'. Traced by S.S.F. from a sketch by R.P.W., 1958 and from a photograph.

B.M. *Guide Rom. Brit.* (1951) 38 No. 7 with fig. 18.7. J.P.C. Kent and K.S. Painter, *Wealth of the Roman World* (1977), 54 No. 106 with fig.

inscription gilded on the handle: ΛH.IIIΛ ΛII

R.P.W. in 1958 read the third letter as a second H: only traces of its first stroke now survive.

Kent and Painter, loc. cit., and BM *Guide* erroneously state that the inscription is inlaid in gold. In fact it is simply gilded on the flat surface and has disappeared where the gold is worn away, in contrast to the surrounding decoration which is inlaid in niello set in deeply-stamped emplacements: information from Miss C.M. Johns, who writes that one of the repairs to the handle is done with an added plate of silver soldered to the underside, the same technique as used for repairs to the Capheaton silver vessels: 'I think that this is quite an old repair (18th–19th century) and that the vessel had been out of the ground a very long time before Miss Fletcher donated it . . . in 1942'. Miss Johns suggests that the inscription should be read inverted since almost all inscriptions on *trulla* handles (and spoon-handles) begin at the bowl end. We have not shown it thus because the first letter resembles Λ rather than V.

Addendum to *RIB* 2419: Glass

2504.12. York (*Eboracum*). Part of the base of a green glass bottle (scale uncertain), noted by D.B. Harden in 1948 in the Yorkshire Museum. Drawn by S.S.F. from a sketch by R.P.W.

stamped on the base: II
'Two'

2504.12

Addendum to *RIB* 2428: Iron Tools

2504.13. London (*Londinium*). Iron knife ($\frac{1}{2}$ and $\frac{1}{1}$), length 160 mm, with tanged handle and surviving rivets, found in 1981 on a spoil heap at Bethnal Green, the material of which came from a site in London either on the waterfront or the Walbrook. Museum of London. Drawn by Jenny Hall.

stamped: P·BΛSILI leaf stop
P(. . .) Basili (servus fecit)
'P. . ., (slave) of Basilius, (made this)'

The knife differs in style from the other knives of this manufacturer (*RIB* 2428.5–8) in having a riveted handle.

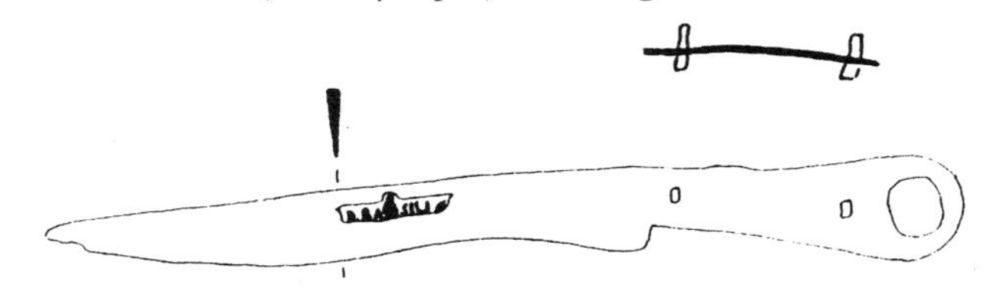

2504.13

2504.11

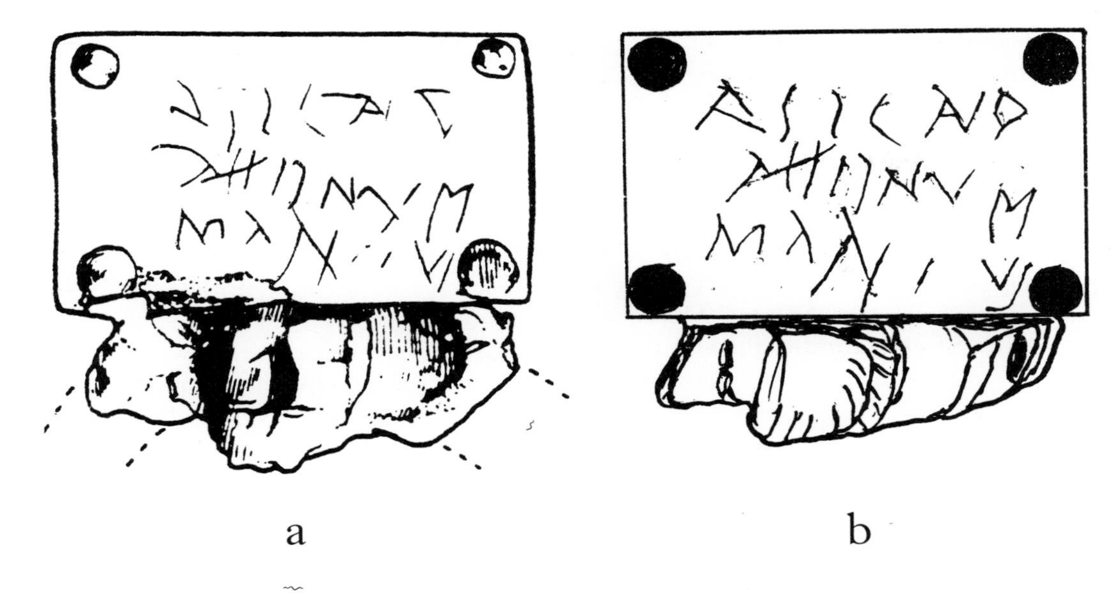

2504.14

Addenda to *RIB* 2429: Bronze Baldric- and Belt-fittings

2504.14. Bifrons, Kent. Bronze plate (2/1) from an iron buckle, found probably in 1867 during excavations at the Anglo-Saxon cemetery. Maidstone Museum. Drawing (a) by Marion Cox (by courtesy of Sonia Hawkes), (b) by R.P.W., 1955.

undeciphered cursive graffito

ASICA͡NO | AHIINVM | MANIVS, *Aesicano ahenum Manius*, 'Manius (has given) this bronze (object) to Aesicanus', R.P.W., archive.

l.3. perhaps more probably MARIṆVṢ, S.S.F.

AMBAṚAI | ḌVMNVAM, T.C. Skeat.

2504.15. Southwark, south London. Bronze ring and tag (1/1), found in 1981 in a foreshore deposit during excavations at the Winchester Palace site. Museum of London. Drawing by courtesy of Jenny Hall.

stamped: VD[. . .]

The object is not certainly of Roman date.

2504.15

Addendum to *RIB* 2432: Votives in Bronze

2504.16. Wood Eaton, Oxfordshire. Thin bronze votive label (1/2), 73 by 48 mm, with embossed border and hole for attachment, found before 1841 at the Romano-Celtic temple site. Ashmolean Museum, Oxford. Reproduced from Kirk.

EE iii 132. *JRS* xxviii (1938), 205 No. 18. R. Hussey, *Account of the Roman Road from Allchester to Dorchester* (1841), 38. Taylor, *JRS* vii (1917), 102. Kirk, *Oxoniensia* xiv (1949), 41 No. 2 with fig. 9.7.

incised inscription: [. . .]EDO

In the absence of the name of a deity in *-edus*, the inscription probably represents the end of a personal name in *-edo* such as *Macedo* or *Pedo*.

2504.16

Addenda to *RIB* 2433: Miscellaneous Objects in Bronze

ALIENA

2504.17.* (?) near Perugia, Italy. Bronze label (½), imported probably by a collector in the 19th century, height 120 mm, diameter 70 mm. National Museums of Scotland, Queen Street, Edinburgh. Drawn by R.G.C.

CIL xv 7141. *Arch. Inst.* York (1846), 8. *Cat. National Museum of Antiquities of Scotland* (Edinburgh 1892), 224 No. FT13.

incised inscription:
DE·STATIONE | C·CAESARIS | AVGVSTI
de statione C(ai) Caesaris Augusti
'From the post of the emperor Caius Caesar'

The tang is perforated by two holes probably for attachment to a wooden handle. The purpose is uncertain but perhaps to reserve a wagon of the *cursus publicus*, as suggested by Hirschfeld and Dressel. Compare *CIL* vi 8655a = xv 7142 from Frascati, illustrated by G.A. Ordericus, *Dissertationes* (1765), 231.

2504.18.* Winsford, Cheshire. Crescent-shaped stamp of bronze (½) with a small knob on the back for a handle, found before 1983 in the gardens of Vale Royal House. Reproduced from *Cheshire Arch. Bull.*

S.R.W. in *Cheshire Archaeological Bulletin* ix (1983), 107, 111.

engraved retrograde: PRIMIGENI | VOI·VIOḶ

The object is considered to represent an import from a 'grand tour' during the 18th or 19th century.

FALSVM

2504.19.* Horncastle, Lincs. Irregular triangle of sheet metal unspecified, perhaps bronze and apparently complete (½), 78 by 56 mm, thickness unknown, bought at Stansted (Essex) in 1887. The text is in capital letters cast in low relief on both faces. An annotated rubbing was found in the papers of G.F. Browne, Disney Professor of Archaeology at Cambridge (1887–92), by P. Hunter Blair. Present whereabouts unknown. Drawn from the rubbing by R.S.O.T., 1994.

in moulded capitals: (a) IMP·CAES·NERVA | TRAIAN·AVG· | GERM·PM
(b) [.]·SEPTIMVS | SEVERVSPER | TINAXAVG | IMP·

(a) *Imp(erator) Caes(ar) Nerva | Traian(us) Aug(ustus) | Germ(anicus) P(ontifex) m(aximus)*
(b) *[L(ucius)] Septim(i)us | Severus Per | tinax Aug(ustus) | imp(erator)*

SEPTIMVS is a mistake for *Septimius*. The object was condemned as spurius by I.A. Richmond and R.P.W. in 1953.

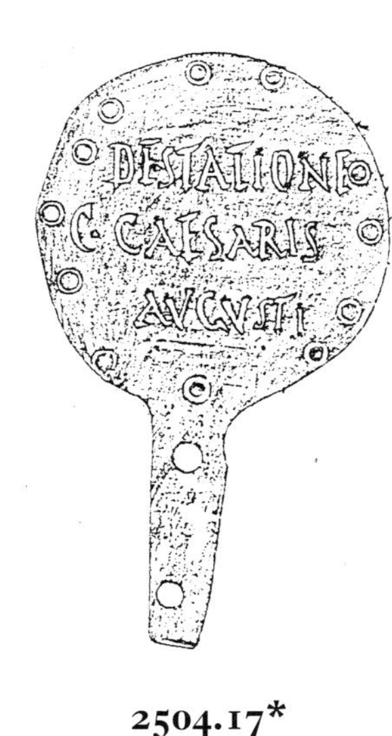

2504.17*

2504.18*

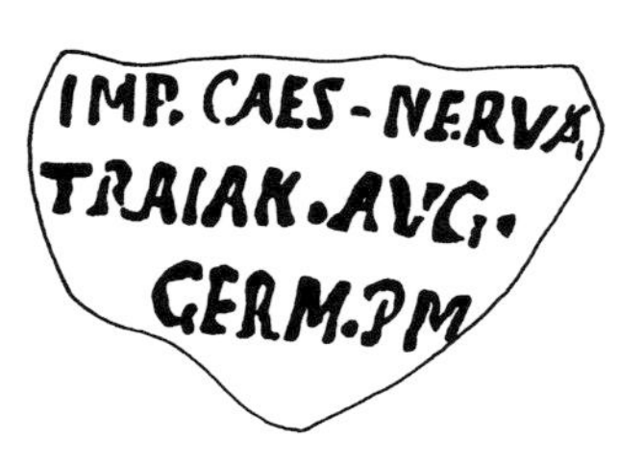

a

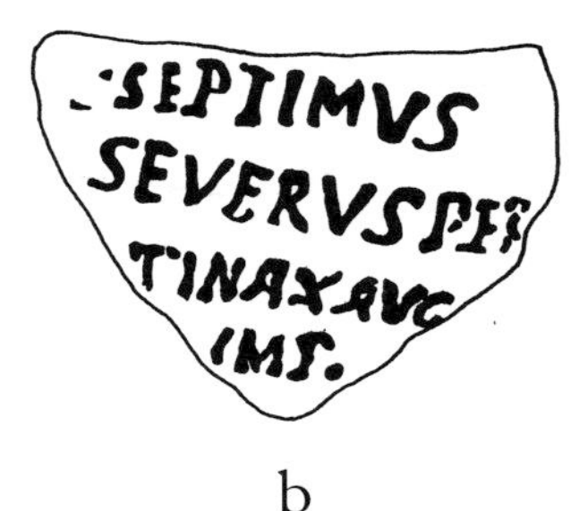

b

2504.19*

Addenda to *RIB* 2436: Lead Sheets

2504.20 and 21. Leintwardine (*Bravonium*), Hereford and Worcester [Herefordshire]. Two sheets of lead (†), found in 1964 in the top filling of a fourth-century drain in the bath-house lying immediately south of the fort. Shropshire County Council Leisure Services, on loan to Hereford and Worcester Museum Service. Reproduced from *JRS*.

JRS lix (1969) 241 No. 31 with fig. 45. Stanford, *T. Woolhope Nat. FC* xxxix (1968), 297 with fig. 33.

20. graffito: CARINVS | SIMILIS | CONSORTIVS | COMES MASLORIV[S] | SENORIX CVNITTVS | CVNITTVS CVNEDECAN | ES CEANATIS TIBERIN[VS]

Carinus, Similis, Consortius, Comes, Maslorius, Senoris, Cunittus, Cunittus, Cunedecanes, Ceanatis, Tiberinus

A list of names. Cunittus, Cunedecanes and Maslorius appear to be unmatched.

21. graffito: ENESTINVS | MOTIVS | COMITINVS

Enestinus, Motius, Comitinus

The names appear to be unmatched, but compare *Motus* (*CIL* iii 6490), and Comitius and Comitianus (Kajanto, *Cognomina*, 306).

It is possible that these two objects are parts of curse-tablets. They are included as Nos. 26 and 27 in R.S.O.T.'s list of curse-tablets, *Tabellae Sulis* (1988), 61.

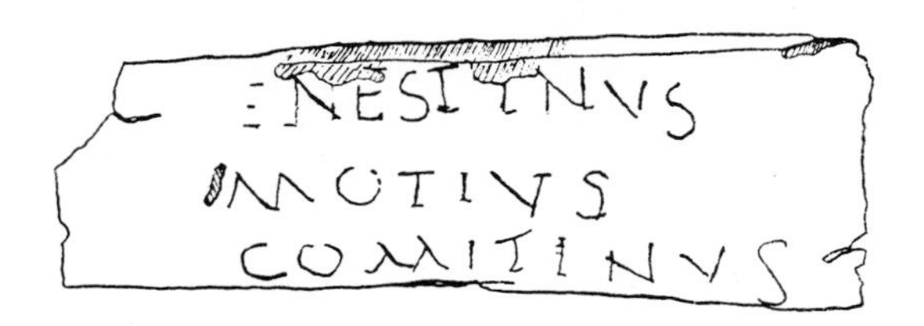

2504.21

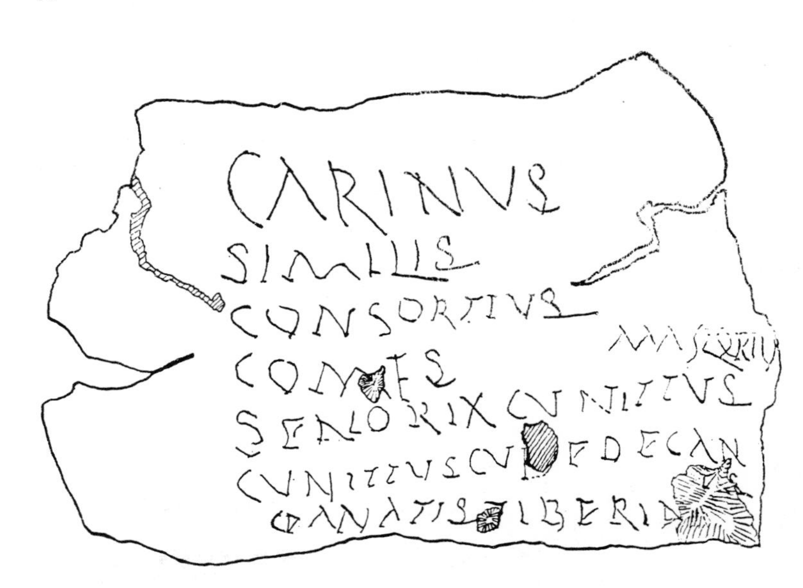

2504.20

2504.22. Chesterton-on-Fosse, Warwickshire. Fragment of lead sheet (†), carrying two successive texts, (a) in Old Roman cursive script, (b) in capitals (*RIB* 243), and with a longitudinal crease indicating that it had formerly been folded. Found in 1921 during excavations within the walled enclosure. Warwickshire Museum. Drawn by R.S.O.T., 1988.

RIB 243. *JRS* xi (1921), 239 No. 16. Anon., *T. Birm. AS* xlix (1923), 60 with pl. XXII.1. Tomlin, *Britannia* xx (1989), corrigendum (a) with fig. 9.

(a) Cursive text
[ ] traces [ ]
[ ]*is.i* traces [ ]
[ ] vacat *.ios* traces [ ]
[ ]*iogen.s* vacat *dalmatic* traces [?*D*]*iogen*[*i*]*s* *dalmatic*[*um*?]
[ ] traces [ ]
[ ] traces *os* traces [ ]
[ ] traces *ius* traces [ ]
[ ] traces [ ]

(b) Capital text (cf. *RIB* 243)
[ ]*seithaus* vacat
[ ]*dalmatiucm* [ ]
[ ] traces [ ]

(a) '. . . tunic of Diogenes . . .'
(b) '. . . tunic . . .'

(b) l.1. *Sethaus* or *Sethrus*, R.G.C., *JRS*.
[. . .]SEITHAVS remains unexplained: perhaps a personal name, R.S.O.T.

The fragment, of which text (b) was published as *RIB* 243, was re-examined in 1988 by R.S.O.T. for traces of underlying cursive script, text (a). Whether the object is part of a *defixio* is uncertain.

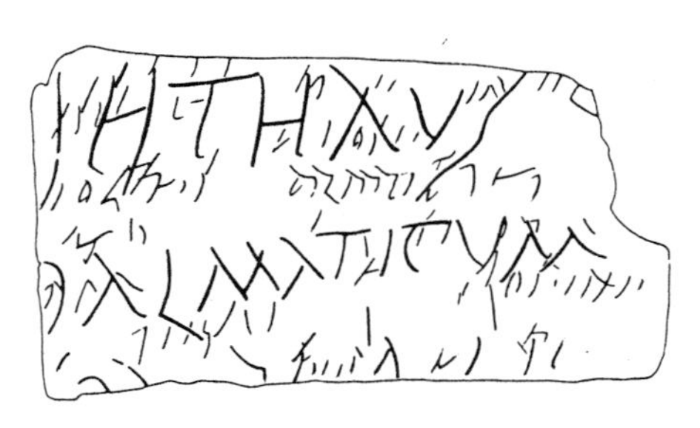

2504.22

Addenda to *RIB* 2437: Miscellaneous Lead Objects

2504.23. Southwark, south London. Pierced semi-circular lead tag (†), 36 by 22 mm, thickness 1 mm, found in 1983 in a waterfront deposit dated *c.* A.D. 120–160, during excavations at the Winchester Palace site. Museum of London. Drawing by courtesy of Jenny Hall. See also PL. VII B.

stamped: ΛḶΛ̣IΛ
Perhaps *ala i A(sturum)*

M·ΛIΛ for *M(arcus) Aia(. . .)*, F. Grew. ΛḶ·IΛ or ṂḶ·IΛ, M.Ẇ.C.H. As text, S.S.F. and R.S.O.T.

The second Λ shows faintly, perhaps because that part of the die was choked. To its left is an oval protuberance resembling a stop, which perhaps indicates the position of a tack fixing the stamp to its handle.

Ala i Hispanorum Asturum is attested in Britain in A.D. 98 and in the second century on diplomas (*CIL* xvi 43, 69, *RIB* 2401.6, 8, 10) but its stations are unknown before it reached Benwell probably late in that century. Compare *RIB* 2464 for the omission of *Hispanorum*.

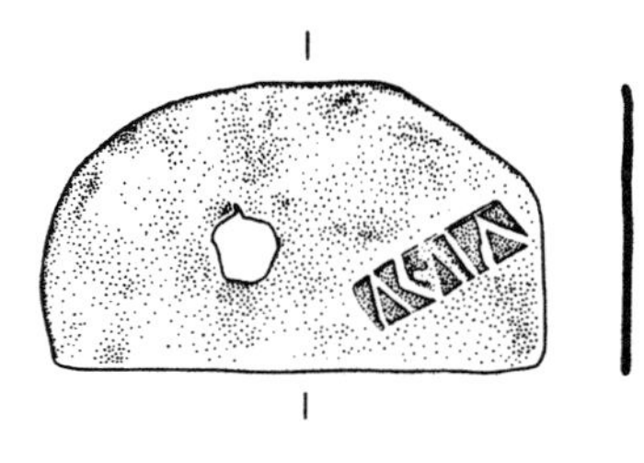

2504.23

FALSVM

2504.24.* Okehampton, Devon. Lead tablet (†), 40 by 15 by 5 mm, provenance unknown but bought at Okehampton *c.* 1962. In private possession. Drawn by S.S.F., 1993, from rubbings by L.P. Wenham, 1967. See also *RIB* 2408.5.*

Britannia ix (1978), 484 No. 91.

inscribed, side A: TI·CL·CAE | ·AVG
side B: DE temple VS | BRITANNIΛE
Ti(berius) Cl(audius) Cae(sar) | *Aug(ustus) deus Britanniae*
'Tiberius Claudius Caesar Augustus, god of Britain'

In line 1 of side B the crude representation of a temple façade containing a figure divides the two syllables of *deus*.

A modern forgery: the Es are of un-Roman form, and the omission of the S in *Caes(ar)* and the division of *deus* are epigraphically implausible. See *Britannia*, loc. cit., note 96. The forger probably had in mind Seneca, *Apocolocyntosis* 8, *deus fieri vult: parum est quod templum in Britannia habet . . . .*

2504.24*

Addendum to *RIB* 2439: Pottery Roundels

2504.25. Colchester (*Camulodunum*), Essex. Coarse pottery roundel (½), found in 1981–85 during excavations at Culver Street. Colchester Museum. Reproduced from Crummy.

Nina Crummy in P. Crummy, *Excavations at Culver Street, the Gilberd School, and other sites in Colchester 1971–85* (1992), 166 No. 683 with fig. 5.24.

two lightly-cut graffiti separated by a deeply-cut groove: IIM. | . . .

l.1: SHAV(?), Crummy.

l.2: AV . . ., Crummy.

2504.25

Addenda to *RIB* 2440: Bone Roundels

2504.26. An illustration (½) of *RIB* 2440.75, a bone roundel from Bishop's Stortford, Essex, drawn by S.S.F. from rubbings by R.P.W., is now provided.

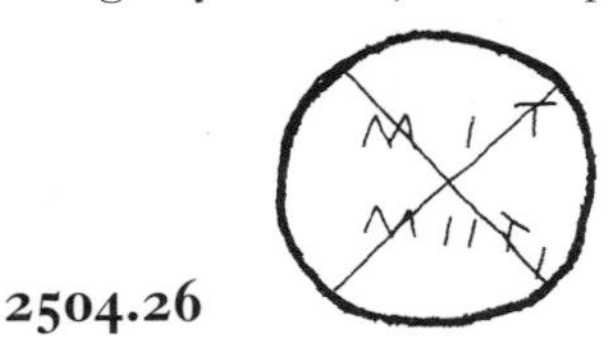

2504.26

2504.27. An illustration (½) of *RIB* 2440.140, a bone roundel from Chesterholm (*Vindolanda*), Northumberland, drawn by S.S.F. from rubbings by R.P.W., 1983, is now provided.

2504.27

Addendum to *RIB* 2441: Miscellaneous Bone Objects

2504.28. Colchester (*Camulodunum*), Essex. This bone handle (*RIB* 2441.8) has now been published by Nina Crummy in P. Crummy, *Excavations at Culver Street, the Gilberd School and other sites in Colchester 1971–85* (1992) (Colchester Archaeological Report No. 6), 177 No. 1319 with fig. 5.36, with a revised reading by M.W.C.H. Drawing: Colchester Archaeological Trust

'The text originally read FLAMMA SENOVARVS, but the last two letters of the name were erased and the letter I substituted to give a genitive', M.W.C.H.

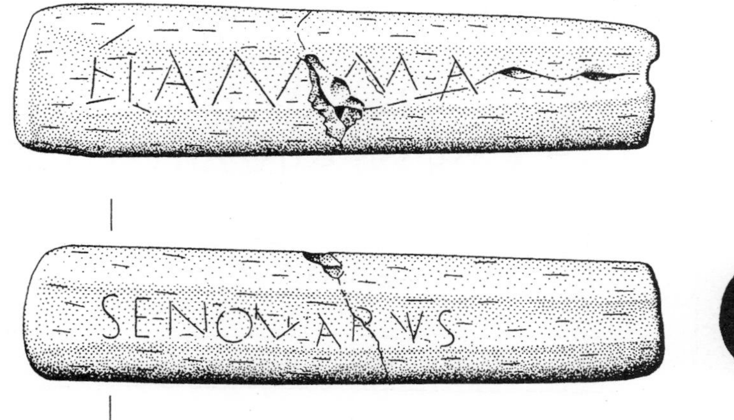

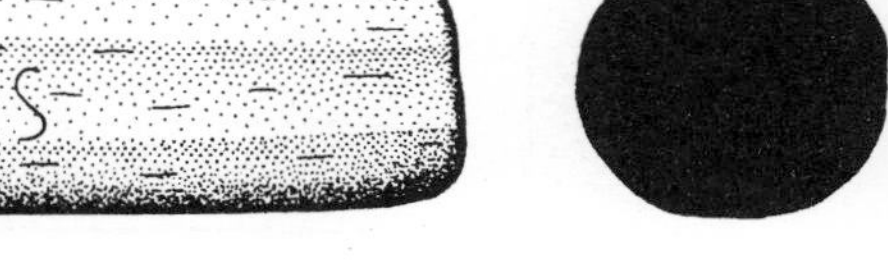

2504.28

Addendum to *RIB* 2443.19: Wooden Stilus-Tablets

2504.29. London. The full text of this stilus-tablet (2443.19) has been published by R.S.O.T. in *Britannia* xxv (1994), 302 No. 34 with pl. XX. Museum of London. Drawn by R.S.O.T. (†).

Imp(eratore) Traiaṇọ [Had]ri[ano] Caesare
Aug(usto) (iterum), Ç̣ṇ(aeo)
Fusco Saliṇatọre co(n)s(ulibus) pr(idie)
idus Martias.
Cum ventum esset in rem praesentem,
silvam Vẹrlucionium, arepennia de-
5 cem quinque, plus minus, quod est in ci-
vitạṭe Cạntiacorum pago DIBVSSV . . .
. . . . ṚABI . . . . Ạ. . Ṣ ạdf̣ịnibus heredi'bus'
7a *interlineated, traces of half a line*
et heredibus Caesenni Vitalis et via
vicinale, quod se emisse diceret L(ucius)
10 Iulius Beḷlicus de Ṭ(ito) Valerio Silvino
(denariis) quadraginta sicut emptione con|tinetur.
L(ucius) Iulius Bellicus testatus est se [. . .]

'In the consulship of the Emperor Trajan Hadrian Caesar Augustus for the second time, and Gnaeus Fuscus Salinator, on the day before the Ides of March [14 March 118]. Whereas, on arriving at the property in question, the wood *Verlucionium*, fifteen *arepennia*, more or less, which is in the canton of the Cantiaci in *Dibussu*[ ] parish, [ ], neighboured by the heirs [of . . .] and the heirs of Caesennius Vitalis and the vicinal road, Lucius Julius Bellicus said that he had bought it from Titus Valerius Silvinus for forty denarii, as is contained in the deed of purchase. Lucius Julius Bellicus attested that he [. . .]

For commentary see ibid., notes 37–9 and Tomlin in J. Bird et al.(eds.), *Interpreting Roman London: A Collection of Essays in Memory of Hugh Chapman* (forthcoming).

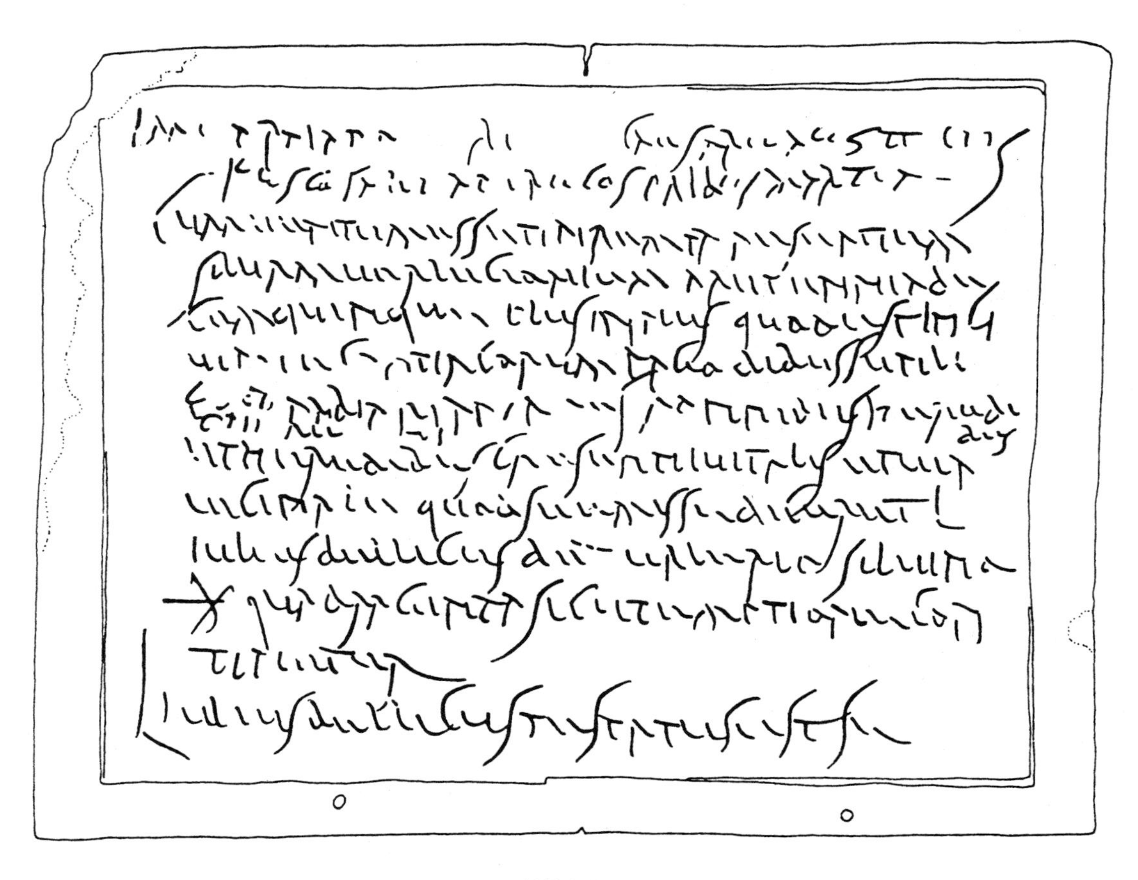

2504.29

Addendum to *RIB* 2449: Handmills

2504.30. Chesterholm (*Vindolanda*), Northumberland. Upper stone of a handmill ($\frac{1}{8}$) of local stone, diameter 415 mm, thickness 90 mm, weight 17 kg, found before 1974 during excavations in the *vicus*. Vindolanda Museum. Drawn by Adam Welfare.

incised on the upper surface: IΛII

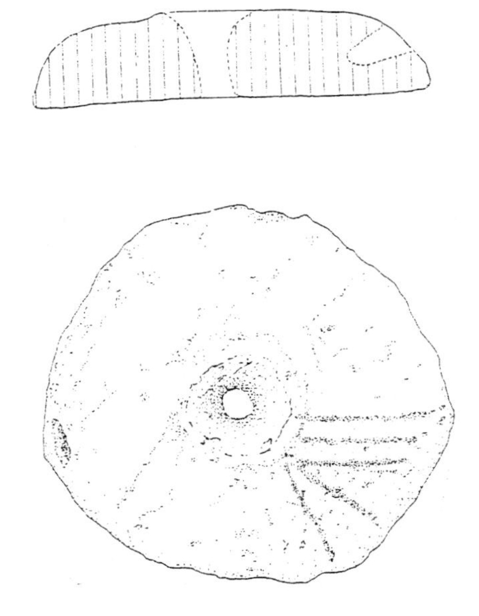

2504.30

Addendum to *RIB* 2453: Small Stone Votives

2504.31. Chedworth, Gloucestershire. Small stone 'candlestick' or altar ($\frac{1}{6}$), 152 by 114 mm, height 152 mm, with a shallow *focus* on top and inscribed on three sides, found during the 19th-century excavation of the villa. Chedworth Museum. Reproduced from Goodburn.

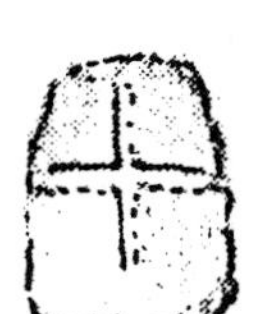
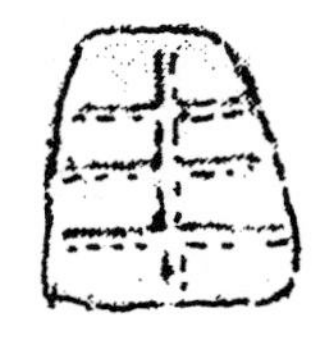

2504.31

Grover, *JBAA*[1] xxiv (1868) 132 with pl. XII.1–2. R. Goodburn, *The Roman Villa, Chedworth* (1972), pl. 12.8. D. Watts, *Christians and Pagans in Roman Britain* (1991), 174–5.

incised on three sides, (a): +
(b): possible Christian monogram I͡H
(c): X

For monogram (b), for IH(ΣΟΥΣ), to be viewed from the side, see Sulzberger, *Byzantion* ii (1925), 382–3 with fig. 22. We are indebted to George Boon for this reference.

Addenda to *RIB* 2454: Miscellaneous Objects of Stone

FALSA

2504.32* Filey, North Yorkshire. Fragment of shale ($\frac{1}{3}$), found in 1857 during excavations at a late Roman coastal tower. Sought in vain by R.P.W. at the Scarborough Museum. Now lost. Drawn by S.S.F. from an enlargement of the fig. in *JRS*.

EE iii 125; ix p. 562. Cortis, *Trans Scarborough Phil. Soc.* 1858, 18–26 with fig. Whellan, *North Riding* ii (1859), 895–6. Haverfield, *JRS* ii (1912), 212–13 with fig. Sheppard, *The Naturalist* (September 1914), 269–73. M. Kitson Clark, *Gazeteer* (1935), 82.

two graffiti (a): [. . .] | CAESAR SE | QVAM SPE
(b) (on the other side of the fragment): A

'a meaningless fragment; I fancy it may be even a forgery, the work of "Flint Jack" who forged one or two similar inscriptions and other alleged Roman antiquities in Yorkshire about the time of these excavations', F.H., *JRS*.

2504.32*

2504.33.* Cliffe, Kent. Oval plaque of shale (½), 85 by 100 mm, thickness 15 mm, perforated for suspension above the graffito. Found in or shortly before 1978 unstratified in mud on the foreshore at a site which has yielded pottery, coins and a brooch. Maidstone Museum. Drawn by D.B. Kelly.

incised graffito: X͡P
'Chi-Rho'

Romano-British material has been found on the foreshore here (*JRS* lvi (1966), 217 and *RIB* 2502.18), but this object of unknown purpose can be dismissed as a modern forgery. (Compare *Britannia* xxii (1991), 307 No. 57, for a more ambitious 'salting' of a foreshore site with 'Christian' graffiti). The Chi-Rho with its exaggerated loop and disproportionate letters is unconvincing.

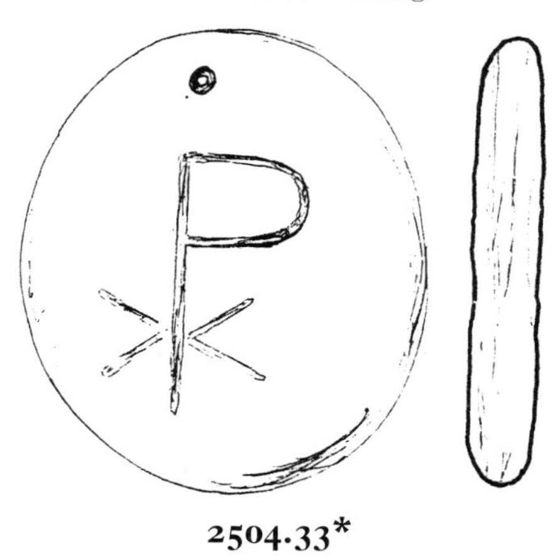

2504.33*

Addendum to *RIB* 2456: Figurines in Baked Clay

2504.34. Gestingthorpe, Essex. Part of the hollow dome-shaped base of a white pipe-clay statuette of Venus (½ and ¼), found in 1953–68 during excavations on the area of Building I and its yard and gullies.

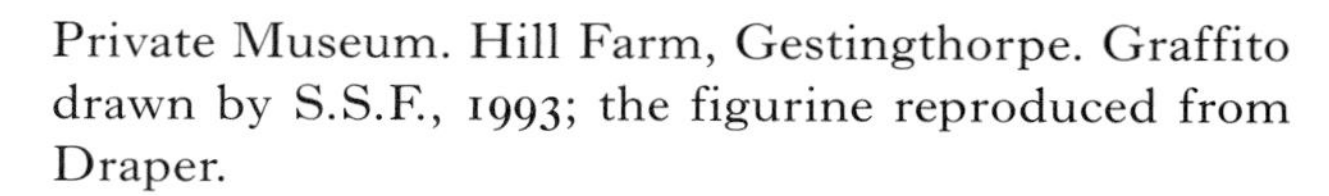

Private Museum. Hill Farm, Gestingthorpe. Graffito drawn by S.S.F., 1993; the figurine reproduced from Draper.

Jenkins in J. Draper, *Excavations by Mr H.P. Cooper on the Roman Site at Hill Farm, Gestingthorpe, Essex* (East Anglian Archaeology No. 25, 1985), 9, 86 No. 485 with fig. 42.485 (which omits the graffito).

graffito on the top of the inside of the hollow base: L͡V.

L͡VB, R.P.W., *RIB* archive. LVBRI, Jenkins, loc. cit.

The reading of L͡V is highly doubtful and the following B scarcely discernible.

Addenda to *RIB* 2491: Graffiti on Tiles

2504.35. Gloucester (*Glevum*). Fragment of tile (¼), found in 1975–76 during excavations at the second-century extramural tilery at St Oswald's Priory. Gloucester Museum. Reproduced from Heighway and Parker (drawn by C.J. Guy).

Heighway and Parker, *Britannia* xiii (1982), 34 fig. 6.3.

graffito: [. . .]AIIDC.[. . .]

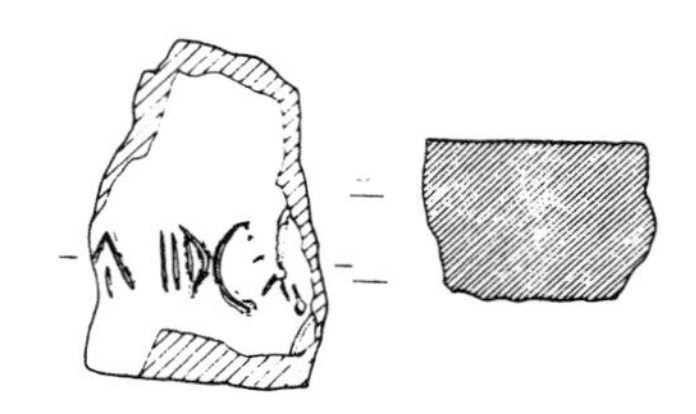

2504.35

2504.36. Ibid. Fragment of tile (¼), found in 1975–76 during excavations at the second-century extramural tilery at St Oswald's Priory. Gloucester Museum. Reproduced from Heighway and Parker (drawn by C.J. Guy).

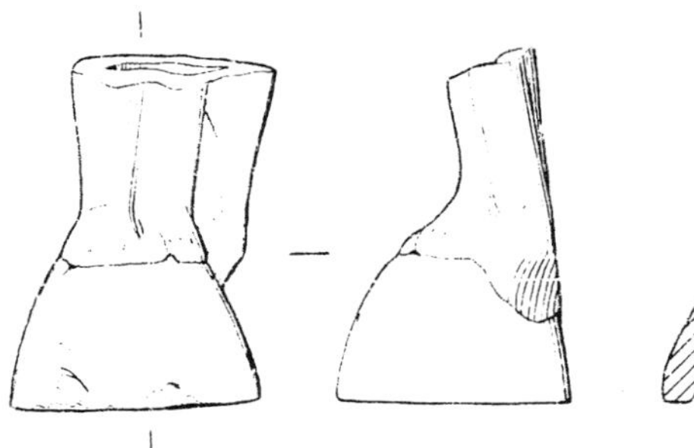
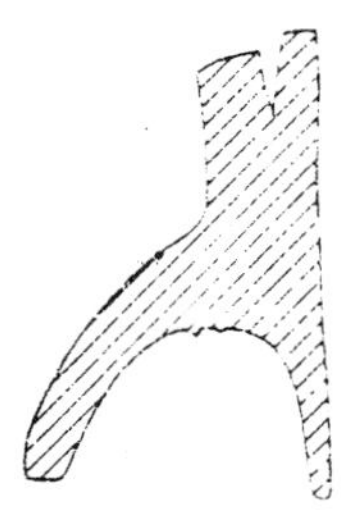

2504.34

Heighway and Parker, *Britannia* xiii (1982), 34 fig. 6.1.

graffito: [.]C.ÇẠL | .N.TOÇṾ[. . .] | [. . .].[. . .]

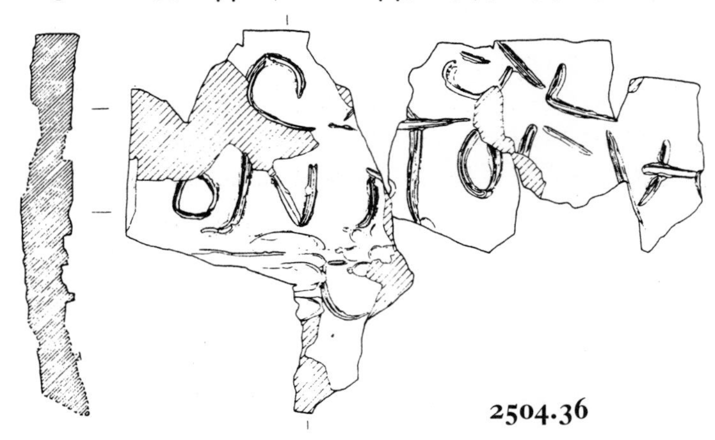

2504.36

2504.37. Ibid. Fragment of tile (¼), found in 1975–76 during excavations at the second-century extramural tilery at St Oswald's Priory. Gloucester Museum. Reproduced from Heighway and Parker (drawn by C.J. Guy).

Heighway and Parker, *Britannia* xiii (1982), 34 fig. 6.2 (shown inverted).

graffito: [. . .]IX K[. . .]

Probably part of a date.

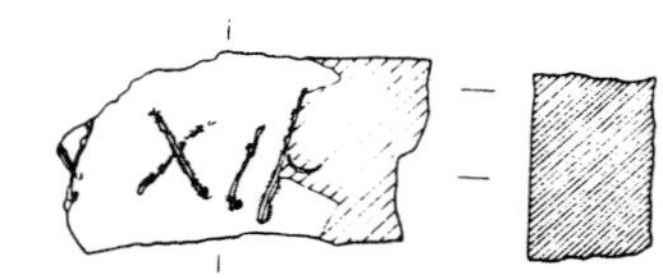

2504.37

Addenda to *RIB* 2492: Dipinti on Amphorae

2504.38. London. Addendum to the bibliography of *RIB* 2492.9: G. Milne, *The Port of Roman London* (1985), fig. 63.1 (photograph).

2504.39. Richborough, Kent. For dipinto *RIB* 2492.25 (f) compare S. Martin-Kilcher, *Die römischen Amphoren aus Augst und Kaiseraugst* (Forsch. Augst 7.2) (1994), which shows that Semponius's cognomen was Fuscus.

Addenda to *RIB* 2493: Amphorae, Graffiti cut before firing

2504.40. Wroxeter (*Viroconium*), Shropshire. Fragment (½) of a globular amphora in buff fabric, found in the early 1980s, probably in a dump of fourth-century material. Wroxeter Museum. Drawn by M.W.C.H.

Britannia xxiii (1992), 321 No. 40.

cursive graffito cut before firing:
[. . .]MAṬVRI | FVSCI
Maturi Fusci
'(Product) of Maturius Fuscus'

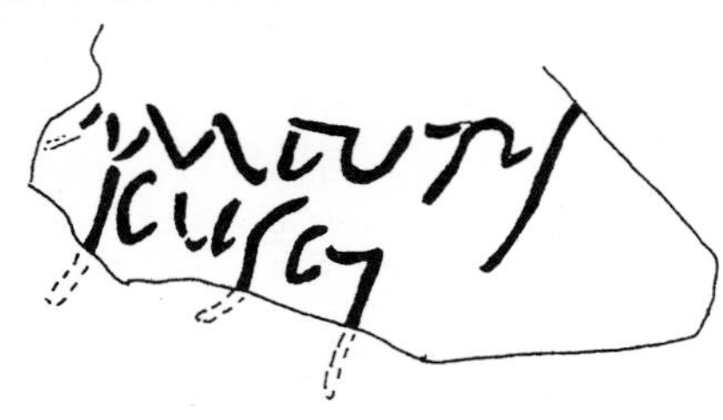

2504.40

2504.41. Carlisle (*Luguvalium*), Cumbria [Cumberland]. Part of a Dressel 20 amphora (½), found in 1981 during excavations in Old Grapes Lane. Tullie House Museum. Reproduced from Tomlin.

Tomlin in M.R. McCarthy et al., *Excavations at the Lanes, Carlisle* i (1994), 41 No. 2, with fig. 221.2.

graffito cut before firing on the wall:
POṢIN[. . .] | CO | FIIÇ[. . .]
Posin[. . .] co fec[it]
'Posin . . . made (this)'

A potter's signature. The only possibility for the name in Mócsy, *Nomenclator*, is *Posineius*, of which he notes a single instance from Spain (but not in *CIL* ii). If *Posin . . .* is a nomen, CO may be the end of the cognomen if the nominative enden in *-co*; alternatively it is the place of manufacture, the ablative *[. . . ?a]co* being used in a locative sense. R.S.O.T.

2504.41

2504.42. Caerleon (*Isca*), Gwent [Monmouthshire]. Sherd from a globular Spanish amphora (½), found in 1986 with dumped material dated *c.* A.D. 160–190 during excavations at the Cambria House site. Caerleon Museum. Drawn by M.W.C.H.

Britannia xxiii (1992), 323 No. 46.

graffito cut before firing:
[. . .]ṾSM. | [. . .]IΛS | [. . .]SΛ

2504.42

2504.44. Strageath, Tayside [Perthshire]. Two conjoining fragments of a buff amphora (½), found in 1985 in a Flavian demolition layer below the Antonine I *via sagularis*. National Museums of Scotland, Queen Street, Edinburgh. Drawn by M.G. Wilson.

Britannia xvii (1986), 450 No. 83. S.S. Frere and J.J. Wilkes, *Strageath* (1989), 267 No. 6 with fig. 133.6.

graffito: [. . .]TPV[. . .]

2504.44

Addenda to *RIB* 2494: Amphorae, Graffiti cut after firing

2504.43. Wroxeter (*Viroconium*), Shropshire. Sherd (½) from the tubular neck of an amphora in red fabric and buff slip, found in 1972 in the filling of a robber trench of the wall of the basilica of the baths. Wroxeter Museum. Drawn by M.W.C.H.

Britannia xxiii (1992), 322 No. 41.

graffito cut after firing: [. . .]XTV[. . .]
Perhaps *[(vinum) mi]xtu[m]*
'mixed wine'

Compare *CIL* iv 6914, *mixst. Mixtum*, presumably wine mixed with water, contrasts with *merum*, unmixed wine (compare *RIB* 2498.4)

2504.43

FALSVM

2504.45.* Manchester (*Mamucium*). Buff amphora-handle (scale uncertain), carrying a copy of *RIB* 578 (*EE* iv 674), a lost stone inscription from the fort. The copy was made by Thomas Barritt in or after 1796. Red Park Museum, Salford. Traced by S.S.F. from a sketch by R.P.W., 1952.

CIL vii 17.* EE iv 674. Holme, *Proc. Chetham Society* lxviii (1866), 47. W.T. Walkin, *Lancs.* (1883), 101.

graffito:
COHR I· |FRISIAVỌ | ⟩Ọ̣VIANVM | .PXXIIII
Coh(o)r(tis) i Frisiavo(num) (centuria) Quinṭịạṇị . p(edes) xxiiii

The inscription is on an ansate panel left in relief on a genuine amphora-handle, the recessed areas being stippled in the drawing.

2504.45*

Addendum to *RIB* 2499: Painted Inscriptions on Coarse Ware

2504.46. Chesterholm (*Vindolanda*), Northumberland. Part of a jug ($\frac{1}{2}$) in pinkish ware, found before 1986 in a deposit of Period III, dated *c.* A.D. 97–103. Vindolanda Museum. Drawing: the Vindolanda Trust.

E., R., and A. Birley, *Vindolanda* ii (1993), 99 No. 9 with fig. 12.8.

dipinto on the shoulder: MẠṚTIAḶIS
'(Property) of Martialis'

M.OTIALAS, Birley, loc. cit. As text, R.S.O.T. by conjecture from the drawing.

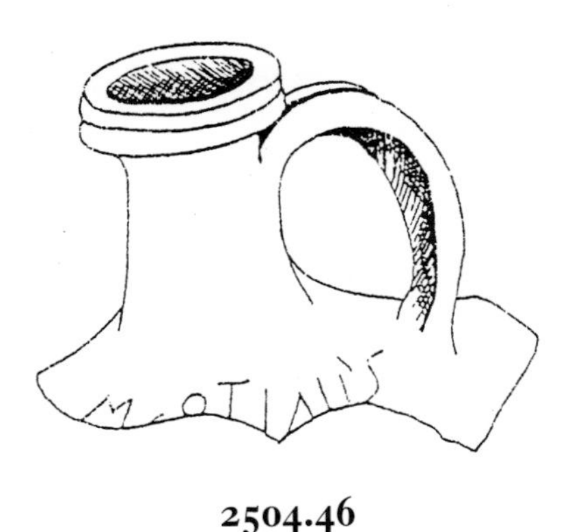

2504.46

Addendum to *RIB* 2501: Graffiti on Samian Ware

2504.47. Skeleton Green, Hertfordshire. Base of an Arretine plate (Loeschcke 1) ($\frac{1}{2}$), stamped RASN, found in 1972 in a deposit of Period I Phase ii, dated *c.* 10 B.C.–A.D. 20, during excavations at the pre-Roman settlement site. British Museum. Reproduced from Partridge.

Partridge, *Britannia* xiii (1982), 325–6 with fig. 12.3.

graffito beneath the base: TE

Compare *RIB* 2504.49.

2504.47

Addenda to *RIB* 2503: Graffiti on Coarse Pottery

2504.48. Skeleton Green, Hertfordshire. Base of a small coarse-ware jar ($\frac{1}{2}$), found in 1972 in a deposit of Period I Phase iii dated *c.* A.D. 15–25 during excavations at the pre-Roman settlement site. Hertford Museum. Reproduced from Partridge.

Partridge, *Britannia* xiii (1982), 325–6 with fig. 12.4.

graffito beneath the base: SE.

2504.48

2504.49. Ibid. Part of the base ($\frac{1}{2}$) of a terra nigra plate found in 1972 in a post-conquest deposit during excavations at the pre-Roman settlement site. Hertford Museum. Reproduced from Partridge.

Partridge, *Britannia* xiii (1982), 325–6 with fig. 12.5.

graffito beneath the base: TE

Compare *RIB* 2504.47.

2504.49

RIB 2505. CORRIGENDA TO *RIB* II, FASCICULES 1–8

Corringendum to *RIB* 2411: Lead Sealings, No. 98

2505.1. Kirkby Thore. *RIB* 2411.98 is now in Tullie House Museum, Carlisle. The corrected reading is:
obverse: [L]EG̣ | [VI] | V
reverse: OPTA | ṬID>̣

See *Britannia* xxii (1991), 311 corrigendum (f).

Corrigendum to *RIB* 2414: Silver Vessels, No. 40.

2505.2. Risley Park, Derbyshire, silver *lanx* ($\frac{2}{3}$).

Additional bibliography: Johns, *Antiq. J.* lxi (1981), 53–72. Johns and Painter, *Minerva* ii.6 (1991), 6–13. Keys, *Minerva* iii.1 (1992), 10–15. *Britannia* xxv (1994), 313 Addendum (a).

A copy of the lost silver *lanx*, 497 by 384 mm, height 25 mm, weight 4764.1 gm, came to light in 1991 when it was submitted to Messrs. Seaby. Examination in the laboratories of the British Museum and the London Institute of Archaeology showed that the object consisted of 26 fragments soldered together; they are evidently casts taken from moulds of the original broken pieces and, as the composition of the silver is typically Roman, they would appear to have been made by melting down and re-using the actual metal of the *lanx* itself. Examination of these second-generation fragments indicates that the decoration of the original *lanx* was cast, not chased as is normally the case in late Roman picture-plates. The fact that the original *lanx* had been cast, and the resemblance of the cast rim-beading to cast beading on pewter vessels, suggested to Johns and Painter that it had been made in Britain, and that accordingly the inscription referred to a church in Britain. British Museum. Drawing reproduced from Johns and Painter.

cast of original chased inscription on the footstand:
EXVPERIVS·EPISCỌ.VS·ECL·ESIΛE·BOC̣IE·
NSI DEDIT Chi-Rho.

Exuperius episco[p]us ec(c)lesia Bogiensi dedit. Chi-Rho
'Bishop Exuperius gave (this) to the church of Bogius (?). Chi-Rho'

Bogiensis is the adjectival form either of a place-name *Bogium* or of a personal name *Bogius*, perhaps an estate-owner.

Corrigendum to *RIB* 2419: Glass Vessel, No. 160

2505.3. Glass fragment from Catterick with Chi-Rho.

Dr. Jennifer Price, *Antiq. J.* lxx (1990), 454–6 with figs., has shown this to be a *Falsum*.

Corringendum to *RIB* 2457; Objects of Fired Clay No. 1.

2505.4. Shakenoak Farm, Oxfordshire. The name on *RIB* 2457.1 should read SΛTΛVΛCVS: see *Britannia* vi (1975), 294, corrigendum (d).

2505.2

Corrigendum to *RIB* 2487: *RPG* tile stamps with Duoviri, No. 10

2505.5. Gloucester (*Glevum*). The tile-stamp RPG | ATTO is complete. Three additional fragments were found in 1975–76 during excavations at the second-century extramural tilery at St. Oswald's Priory, Gloucester, one of which retains the right-hand edge of the stamp. Information from Dr. A.J. Parker.

Corrigenda to *RIB* 2492: Dipinti on Amphorae, Nos. 24 and 28

2505.6. Southwark, south London. The form of this amphora (*RIB* 2492.24) is Dressel 16, not 2–4: compare B. Liou, *Archaeonautica* 13 (1993). Information from Dr. Stephanie Martin-Kilcher (1994).

2505.7. London. Dr. Stephanie Martin-Kilcher informs us that from a study of photographs of the horizontal dipinto *RIB* 2492.28(a) at the British Museum, and from parallel examples, it should read ỌLIVAẸ.

Corrigendum to *RIB* 2493: Amphorae, graffiti cut before firing, No. 77.

2505.8. South Shields (*Arbeia*), Tyne and Wear. *RIB* 2493.77 should be deleted. It is replaced by *RIB* 2502.25.

Typographical and other minor Corrigenda

2404.58. reference should read *JRS* xlviii (1958), 152 No. 12.
2404.71. reference should read *Britannia* xv (1984), 348 No. 65.
2407.1. reference should read *Britannia* ii (1971).
2409.4. delete *EE* vii 1146.
2411.26, 27. obverse should read: type as *RIB* 2411.25.
2411.29. is now in the Museum of London.
2411.86 note. delete erroneous reference to a tile-stamp from South Shields of the *ala Sabiniana*.
2411.93. reference should read *Britannia* xix (1988).
2411.95. reference should read *Britannia* x (1979), 318.
2411.101. refernce should read Cat. 328 No. 8.29.
2411.103. reference should read 'Bruce compares rev. of *RIB* 2411.100.'
2411.139. now in Tullie House Museum, Carlisle.
2411.249a. should be deleted: it is identical with 2411.255.
2411.310. should be deleted: it is medieval or later. See *Britannia* xxiii (1992), 323 corrigendum (c).
2414.39. reference should read *CIL* vii 1350a.
2415.12. reference should read *EE* iii 131.
2417.37. for 'below two peacocks' read 'above . . .'.
2417.39. in 1949 on loan to the Fitzwilliam Museum. Present whereabouts unknown.
2417.41. add reference: Peal, *P. Camb. Antiq. Soc.* lx (1967), 28, 35, pl. V d.
2419.31. reference should read *JRS* xxi (1931), 236.
2419.160. location, British (not Yorkshire) Museum.
2419.172. add reference Lemmon and Hill, *Suss. AC* civ (1966), 95 with pl. II A.
2420.1. probably silver. Found in 1847. For illustration see *Arch Inst.* 1851, pl. facing p. xxvii.
2420.36. for illustration see *Antiq. J.* lxv (1985), pl. LIII B.
2420.47. reference should read . . . *Thetford Treasure* (1983), 117 No. 60. Dimensions should read: length 98 mm, bowl 70 by 45 mm, weight 37.5 gm.
2420.53, 55. references to BM *Guide to Rom. Brit.* should be transposed.
2420.59. for scale ($\frac{1}{2}$) read scale ($\frac{2}{3}$).
2422.2. add reference: O.M. Dalton, *Cat. of Early Christian Antiquities* (1901), No. 64.

2422.16. scale should read ($\frac{2}{1}$). Add references: Johns, *Antiq. J.* lxv (1985), 461 with fig.; *VCH* Essex iii (1963), 19, 57, pl. VIII c 7.
2422.25. reference should read *VCH* . . . 284.
2422.26. reference should read *Britannia* xiv (1983).
2422.32. add reference: Henig in J. Hinchliffe and C.S. Green, *Excavations at Brancaster, 1974 and 1977* (1985), 197.
2422.42. add references: G.C. Boon, *Roman Silchester* (1957), 131; *Silchester; the Roman Town of Calleva* (1974), 338 with note 28. C. Thomas, *Christianity in Roman Britain to A.D. 500* (1981), 131.
2422.44. for 'concrete floor' read 'cement floor'.
2422.46. add reference: C. Thomas, *Christianity in Roman Britain to A.D. 500* (1981), 131.
2422.62. reference should read *Britannia* xvi (1985), 328 No. 29.
2423.4. reference should read *Britannia* ii (1971), 301 No. 72.
2423.18. add reference: Neville, *Arch. J.* xi (1854), 212–213. For MISCE VIVAS, Neville read MISE VIVAS, Neville.
2427.17. reference should read *JRS* xxi (1931).
2429.1. reference should read *EE* 1316a.
2429.17. add reference: Haverfield, *Arch J.* xlix (1892), 199 No. 115.
2431.1. add reference: C. Thomas, *Christianity in Roman Britain to A.D. 500* (1981), 116 with figs. 7.2, 11.1.
2432.2. reference should read *Britannia* xix (1988).
2432.9. is a duplicate of *RIB* 82.
2433.12. reference should read *JRS* xiv (1924).
2437.2. reference should read D.E. Farwell . . . .
2437.5. add reference: *JRS* xliv (1954), 106 No. 23 with fig. 21.
2440.310. for L.F. Wenham read L.P. Wenham.
2441.7. reference should read *EE* iii 127. Add reference: G. Home, *Roman York* (1924), 190 with fig.
2441.11. add references: Anon., *Reliquary* xii (1906), 207–8; Toynbee, *JBAA*[3] xvi (1953), 17 with pl. IV.4; C. Thomas, *Christianity in Roman Britain to A.D. 500* (1981), 126.
2441.18. add references: Toynbee, *JBAA*[3] xvi (1953), 17. C. Thomas, *Christianity in Roman Britain to A.D. 500* (1981), 126.
2446. p. 44 Table I. delete Q. Iulius Martialis, No. 15.
Table I. reference should read Q(. . .) Lucillianus, No. 14.
Table II. delete Q. Iulius from entry for Martialis.
Table II. reference should read Polychronius, Aurelius, No. 21.
2446.14. add reference to Jackson, *Britannia* xxi (1990), 280 No. 28.
2446.29. reference should read *CIL* vii 1321a.
2447.33. reference should read *Britannia* viii (1977).
2449.18. reference should read *JRS* xxxv (1945).
2454.6. reference should read *Britannia* xi (1980), 410 No. 26.
2456.5. reference should read *The Archaeology of Canterbury* v (1995?).
2459.3 (xvi–xxvi). delete reference to *JRS* xxxi.
2459.12 (x) reference should read *JRS* xxxi (1941), 147 No. 1.
2460.7. delete reference to *JRS*.
2462.12 (xiv). reference should read *Britannia* ix (1978), 382.
2463.4 (xx). reference should read *JRS* xxvi (1936), 266.
2463.29 (xii). reference should read 2491.88.
2463.54 (vi). reference should read *JRS* xxvi (1936).
2463.55 (ix). reference should read *EE* iv.
2485.1. reference should read *CIL* vii 1235a.

2489.30.	reference should read *EE* vii 1135.
2489.40A (xxi).	reference should read *Britannia* xvii (1986), 442 No. 47b.
2489.40C (ii).	reference should read No. 47a.
2489.70J.*	reference should read *EE* iv 702.
2491.6.	reference should read *Britannia* iv (1973).
2491.7.	reference should read *EE* vii 1144b.
2491.11.	reference should read *Britannia* xii (1981), 396 No. 111.
2491.35.	reference should read *Britannia* xviii (1987).
2491.125.	reference should read *Britannia* xvii (1986).
2491.137.	reference should read *Britannia* vii (1976), 383 No. 20.
2491.149.	reference should read *Britannia* vi (1975), 286.
2492.37.	reference should read *Britannia* xiii (1982).
2497.29.	reference should read *Britannia* xviii (1987), 377 No. 57.
2501.802.	should be deleted, being identical with 2501.549.

INDEX OF SITES

PLATES

A. *RIB* 2502.23. Graffito cut before firing, from Dorchester, Dorset (†).

(Photograph: R.L. Wilkins)

B. *RIB* 2502.51. Graffito cut before firing, from St. Albans, Hertfordshire (†).

(Photograph: R.L. Wilkins)

PLATE II

A. *RIB* 2502.29. Graffito cut before firing, from Chichester, West Sussex ($\frac{2}{1}$).

(Photograph: Chichester Archaeological Unit)

B. *RIB* 2503.619. Graffito cut after firing, from Harlton, Cambridgeshire ($\frac{1}{1}$).

(Photograph: RIB *Archive)*

A, B. *RIB* 2503.119. Graffito cut after firing. The 'Colchester Vase' (height 216 mm).

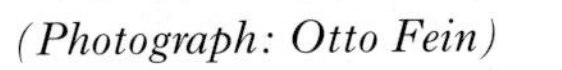

(*Photograph: Otto Fein*)

A. *RIB* 2503.362. Graffito cut after firing, from Dorchester, Dorset (†).
(Photograph: R.L. Wilkins)

B. *RIB* 2503.244. Graffito cut after firing, from Chelmsford, Essex (†).
(Photograph: Warwick Rodwell)

A. *RIB* 2503.177. Graffito cut after firing, from Newport, Isle of Wight ($\frac{1}{1}$).
(Photograph: Isle of Wight County Archaeological Centre)

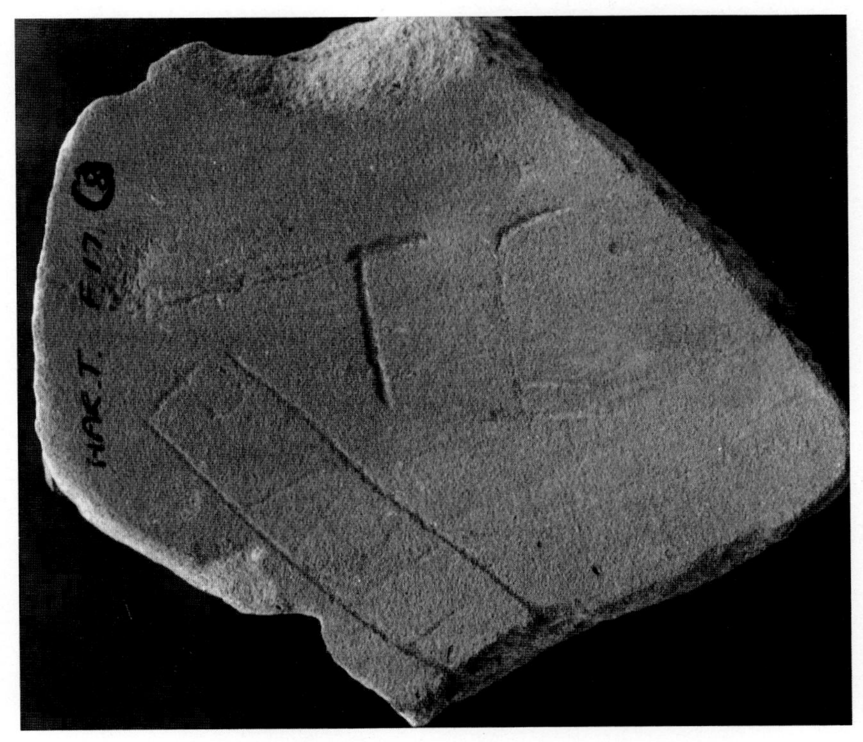

B. *RIB* 2503.107, b and c. Graffiti cut after firing, from Harlow, Essex ($\frac{2}{1}$).
(Photograph: G.W.C. Taylor)

PLATE VI

A. *RIB* 2503.439. Graffito cut after firing, from Colchester, Essex (1:1.4).

(Photograph: Colchester Museum)

B. *RIB* 2503.416. Graffito cut after firing, from Colchester, Essex ($\frac{3}{4}$).

(Photograph: Colchester Museum)

A. *RIB* 2503.134. Graffito cut after firing, from Exeter, Devon ($\frac{2}{1}$).
(Photograph: Exeter Museum)

B. *RIB* 2504.23. Lead tag from Southwark, south London ($\frac{4}{1}$).
(Photograph: Andy Chopping, Museum of London)

A. *RIB* 2503.620*. Anglo-Saxon urn from Spong Hill, Norfolk (scale uncertain).
(Photograph: Liverpool Public Museums)

B. *RIB* 2503.620*. Detail of the graffito (scale uncertain).
(Photograph: Liverpool Public Museums)